"This new edition of *Pilgrim Church* is a welcome contribution to the history of the Christian Church. Father Bausch and his collaborators have produced a readable account of the Church's history from its beginnings until the present. And they have done it well. Above all, it is a pastorally oriented study, courageous in pointing out the relevance of historical trends and movements to present-day church life. Only God is absolute, Karl Rahner was fond of reminding us. *Pilgrim Church* makes that point with regard to the Church. It is an excellent account of the changing life, thought, and worship of the Christian Community making its pilgrim way down the centuries."

James Hennesey, S.J.
Canisius College, Buffalo, NY

"The author's openness to the faults and failings of the people of God who constitute the Church from top to bottom is admirable, honest and forthright and that is a capital point that can never be made too often."

John Tracy Ellis
The Catholic University of America
Washington, D.C.

"...not just another Church history but rather one of the first to take into account ... the results of Vatican II and its ensuing uncertainties and searchings for new directions."

Cross and Crown

"Essential to the writing of a popular religious history is a command of the scholarly literature, an understanding of theology, a sensitivity to spirituality and devotionalism and a grasp of the factors that characterize a particular historical period. William J. Bausch's new edition of *Pilgrim Church* is popular religious history at its best. It is a well written narrative that reveals the author's commitment to clarity, candor, and historical truth."

Christopher J. Kauffman
Editor, *U.S. Catholic Historian*

"Bausch's popular history provides an ideal text for adult learners preparing for lay ministry. Bausch lays open for them an interesting and manageable narrative of how things came to be. More importantly, Bausch introduces them to the art of breaking open history in order to discover the lessons for today's church. I welcome this new revised edition with its up-dated ending which captures the key events of the 1980s."

Aaron Milavec
Athenaeum of Ohio

"Father William Bausch's book is well written, competent, and refreshing for its ecumenical perspective on church history, all of which make it suitable for classroom use as well as for the average reader. I also found refreshing its rather frank treatment of Catholic foibles and misdeeds over the centuries, particularly with regard to the theological polemics against Judaism and social oppression of the Jewish people, including the massive tragedy that was the Shoah."

Dr. Eugene K. Fisher
Catholic-Jewish Relations
National Council of Catholic Bishops

William J. Bausch

A Popular History of Catholic Christianity

PILGRIM CHURCH

━━━━━Revised & Expanded━━━━

Carol Ann Cannon, M.A.
Robert Obach, Ph.D.

⩚
XXIII
TWENTY-THIRD PUBLICATIONS
Mystic, Connecticut

For Ann
who also serves

Twelfth printing 1997

Twenty-Third Publications
P.O. Box 180
185 Willow Street
Mystic, CT 06355
(860) 536-2611
(800) 321-0411

ISBN 0-89622-395-7
Library of Congress Catalog Card No. 89-50938

Author's Preface

This is a generalized popular history of the Roman Catholic church written for the average educated Catholic, whether adult or student. Although this work has the flaws of popularization, I wish to justify the book on the grounds of the real need for ordinary Catholics to have a better understanding of their religious roots. The more I listen to people and the more I teach, the more I realize how wide is the gap between the average Catholic's understanding of our church, and our church's historical realities. Some of us seem to view our church as a massive entity moving unchanged and unalterable down the corridors of time. These persons are really only aware of their own small and brief experience of the church, which happens to be the Tridentine church (1563–1962), hammered out by the forces of the Reformation, the French Revolution, and by the conservative reactions of church leaders of the last two centuries.

Little do these Catholics know that our church has had many lifestyles, many variations in liturgy, ministry, and structure. Little do these believers know what is behind the legitimate (and illegitimate) happenings in our church today that so confuse and infuriate them. Many Catholic people have very little context, background, perspective, or prophetic stance from which to view both the chaos and the consolidations of our post-Vatican II church. Yet there are many things Catholics should know that only history can supply.

Here are some samplings, all covered in this book, that should help today's ordinary Catholic to understand our church: the origins of church structures within a loose collection of small local churches, and their evolution into a strongly centralized universal church; the rich variety of lay ministries in the early church, why they died out, and what circumstances are leading to their restoration today; why the church in the East and the church in the West split apart; why Martin Luther's agenda moved from reform of the church to the rejection of Catholicism; where "Modernism" came from, and why it was condemned by Pope Pius X; why the church's intolerance of Judaism gave rise to an anti-Semitism that helped prepare the way for Hitler's "final solution"; what brought about the Second Vatican Council and why the "role" of women in the church is a matter of great debate.

These, of course, are teasers. They are indications of the sweep of this book. I have made a sincere effort to be objective; I have made the effort to be selective on the basis of adult and student education.

This accounts for the omission of several large events, such as the conversion of Moscow (the "third" Rome), the contributions of Spain, the glories of the Muslim empire, and others. It also accounts for the format used, almost an outline, in order to keep the book within reasonable limits. I have interspersed some interpretive reflections as a summary of trends and ideas that molded our church in its long history. It is understood, however, that adult leaders or teachers, who have access to more scholarly books, will have to use their own larger knowledge and talent to flesh out what is written here.

But there is yet another reason for this popular history. It is no secret that we are currently witnessing a revival of a deeper spirituality. As we near the year 2000, we are finding ourselves with a gnawing disillusionment with science, secularism, and an almost pathological individualism, which are often the driving forces in our society. Talk of prayer, meditation, and small faith-sharing groups are replacing many a crusade in the churches as people search for the sacred amid the rubble of pervasive drug use, broken marriages, a plundered and revengeful environment, and a fearful AIDS epidemic. In an attempt to find answers, there is a noted effort to retrieve our ancient Western spiritual traditions, as well as an openness to those of the East. Some public schools are even adding the hitherto prohibited study of religion to their courses. People have gone back to asking questions about the transcendent and the meaning of life.

Although of necessity we could not develop a theme of Catholic spirituality throughout the ages (see *Christian Spirituality: Origins to the Twelfth Century*, edited by Bernard McGinn, *et al.*, New York: Crossroad, 1987, or Louis Bouyer's trilogy, *A History of Christian Spirituality*, Crossroad, 1963), nevertheless in this book we have given a framework for it, a sense of continuity, however fractured that might be, and an instinct that through the ups and down of movements and the lives of the high and the mighty for two millennia, there remains a thread of wholeness and holiness that has not and cannot be broken. To be a Catholic is to know this history, to know that "in the worst of times, in the best of times" the Spirit is at work. As we stand on the brink of a new century it is worth rediscovering our heritage—tradition, if you will—from which we can draw "new things and old."

I wish to thank all those people who attended my lectures and who gave me the hints and questions that have aided in the shaping of this book. In a special way I want to thank Msgr. John Tracy Ellis for his many criticisms given in the most kindly way. I also wish to thank Ann DeVizia who worked so hard and so long in preparing the manuscript. Finally, I wish to thank all those scholars and authors on whom I have relied and who helped us to know history better so that we shall not be condemned to repeat it.

William J. Bausch

Preface to the Revised Edition

It is customary for others to be invited to create a revised edition when the original author of a popular book has died. This is not the case with *Pilgrim Church*. Fr. Bausch is alive and well and ministering to his parish in New Jersey. But he is very busy with parish interests and the books he is writing. For our part, we have used *Pilgrim Church* in courses we have taught in the parishes of the Archdiocese of Cincinnati and elsewhere. When we heard that the book would go out of print because it had gone through so many printings that the original plates were literally worn out, and that Fr. Bausch was too busy to do the revision, we volunteered for the project. It has taken us nearly a year to complete the revision of Fr. Bausch's original material and to write another chapter to take the story beyond Vatican II to the late 1980s. Everything was first sent to Fr. Bausch for his approval before being sent on the publisher.

The revisions we made range from minor to major. For example, some names and dates needed correction; inclusive language was used throughout, as is fast becoming the norm in most educational settings; and the word "church" was used in reference to the "whole people of God" with a separate designation of church "leadership" when the hierarchy was intended. Some sections received a more extensive revision. These include celibacy, monasticism, women deacons, pseudo-religious orders of the pre-Reformation period, and several other topics.

Our thanks go to Fr. James Hennesey, S.J., and Dr. Aaron Milavec, who wrote to Fr. Bausch with suggestions for changes needed in specific areas. Special thanks are also in order for Mark Cannon, who read the entire revised text for continuity and cohesiveness, and for Stephen Scharper at Twenty-Third Publications for his patience and persistence throughout this process. We are particularly grateful to Fr. Bausch for his encouragement in allowing us to revise his work.

Carol Ann Cannon, M.A.
Robert Obach, Ph.D.

Contents

Pilgrim Church

CHAPTER 1

Background and Beginnings

TRIUMPH AND CHALLENGE

The great world religions are, as it were, great rivers of sacred tradition which flow down through the ages and through changing historical landscapes which they irrigate and fertilize. But as a rule we cannot trace them to their source, which is lost in unexplored tracks of the remote past. It is rare indeed to find a culture in which the whole course of this religious development can be traced from beginning to end in the full light of history. But the history of Christendom is an outstanding exception to this tendency. We know the historical environment in which Christianity first arose: we possess the letters of the founders of the churches to the first Christian communities in Europe, and we can trace in detail the successive stages by which the new religion penetrated the West.[1]

So wrote the historian of religion and culture, Christopher Dawson, some thirty years ago. He was only pointing up what Christianity has always boasted about: it is a historical religion open to the full light of investigation. Being a historical religion, however, is not only Christianity's boast but also its challenge. "Boast" because records and documents are accessible and do provide the foundation for Christian claims; "challenge" because each year, it is no exaggeration to say, something new turns up in Christianity: some new document or manuscript, some new artifact, some new monument, building, or wall painting that goes back to the very beginnings. The result of all this modern scholarship and discovery is the challenge to broaden and even revise our understanding of the nature of the church. The challenge is to harmonize the new insights with Christianity as it has historically developed over the last two thousand years.

Naturally, in the process of harmonization many sacred and vested traditions are going to be questioned. As theory and controversy trickle down from the scholar to the average person, there will be open distress over any tampering with what is perceived as the Christian faith. This distress has been most evident for Catholics living after Vatican Council II. Having very little historical background, such persons have no defense or explanation as to what is happening in their church. The believer only knows that change appears to be the church's modern hallmark, and that change seems to be based on the whim or the crass insensitivity of those seemingly out to destroy the Catholic church. Yet we maintain that history holds the key for such a person. For example, average Catholics will never understand the changes in the liturgy unless they appreciate the discovery of the liturgical forms of the ancient church. They will never understand the current controversies over the structures of the church, the revival of the diaconate, and many other things, unless they have really read Luke's (idealized) history book of the church, the Acts of the Apostles. They will not understand why Pope Paul VI created the synod of bishops, or why he made the gesture (not yet very effective), of saying that lay persons may be consulted in the nomination of bishops, unless they have some appreciation of the centralizing process of the Middle Ages. They will not understand the impact of the pastoral pope, John XXIII, unless they know the histories of Pius IX, Pius X, and Pius XII. They can never understand the rationale behind ecumenism unless they know something of the issues that led up to the sixteenth-century Reformation. They cannot understand the long road from the totally religious society of the Middle Ages to the almost totally secular society of today unless they know their history—our history.

Franklin Roosevelt uttered his famous phrase that there is nothing to fear except fear itself. St. Pius X (with an irony that will be evident as one reads his times) proclaimed the same sentiment when he said that the only real enemy of the church is ignorance. He was right and is right. It is necessary that educated post-Vatican II Catholics dispel some of that ignorance and acquire a new confidence in the historicity of their religion. "It is rare indeed to find a culture in which the whole course of this religious development can be traced from beginning to end in the full light of history." Rare indeed, but true for Christianity. As average people looking for direction and identity in our modern church, let us begin our investigation. Let us start at the beginning, with Judaism.

JEWISH HISTORY

Most Catholics have some vague memories about Jewish history before the time of Jesus. At best they can recall only a few things they have learned in school or read. But more than a vague memory is needed if they are to understand the beginnings of Christianity, for Christianity is a mid-Eastern religion imported to the West. It takes its roots from Judaism. Its early theology and liturgy are grounded in Jewish terms and ways and in the cultural context of Israel, an Eastern country, not a European one. Therefore, we must refresh our memories about ancient times, at least in broad terms and in simple outlines, for there are many gaps in Jewish history, and the Bible is not meant to be a historical record.

The Hebrews—or Jews as they were later called after Judah, the fourth son of Jacob, whose tribe, along with that of Benjamin, made up the kingdom of Judea—began as a grouping of small tribes. They were consistently overawed, overshadowed, and overcome by their more powerful neighboring states. It was only when these great and ancient empires were rising and falling—in the interludes as it were—that the Jews were able to gain political independence.

We recall that it all began with Abraham: his call and God's promise to him and his son Isaac that they would father a great nation. Isaac's son Jacob, later called Israel, had twelve sons who were to head the twelve tribes of Israel. (The twelve apostles as leaders of the New Israel were fashioned after these twelve tribes.) Of Jacob's twelve sons, Joseph, he of the multicolored coat, having been sold by his brothers into slavery, became in time the Prime Minister of Egypt. During a period of famine the Hebrews were forced to seek food from their southern neighbor and it was at this time that Joseph, now older and fully Egyptianized, revealed himself to his eleven brothers, exclaiming with tears, "I am Joseph, your brother!" (Genesis 45:4). These famous words were used by Pope John XXIII in warmly receiving a visitation of rabbis to the Second Vatican Council, and the warmth and ecumenical significance of the words were not lost on them. Through Joseph the Hebrews settled in Egypt. There they went from years of prosperity and peace to years of slavery, when the Hittites gained control of Egypt. From such slavery they were delivered by Moses and wandered in the Sinai desert wilderness for some forty years.

It was a period of trial and discipline, during which the Hebrews entered into a covenant, or agreement, with Yahweh, the God who led them out of Egyptian bondage (Exodus 19:3-25). The covenant came to be expressed in the Law (Torah), that is, the first five books of the Hebrew Scriptures. That covenant, a bargain of mutual love and mutual obligation between them and Yahweh, plus their religious ritual, constituted them as the "assembly" (*ecclesia*, in Greek) or the People of God. We shall see that this identity as God's chosen people was adopted by the early church, who thought of themselves as the "new" People of God. The Vatican II Dogmatic Constitution on the Church returned to that biblical concept by referring to the church as the People of God (L.G. 2).

PERIOD OF THE KINGDOM

There were people living in the Promised Land already, of course. These included the Canaanites and later, around the time of Jewish kings, the Philistines who gave the name Palestine to the area. From the Canaanites the nomadic Hebrews learned the ways of agriculture and urban life. They meshed their Aramaic tongue with the Canaanite language to produce the classical Hebrew in which most of the Hebrew Scriptures are written. (Later the Jews were to return to the original Aramaic, and this was the tongue that Jesus spoke.) In fact, their Hebrew language and their writings, the Scriptures, were to be among their great contributions to history. Their writings of religious genius were to shape the world for ages to come.

A serious threat from the invading Philistines made the Hebrew tribes clamor for a united front under a king, and the prophet Samuel reluctantly conceded to their wishes by anointing Saul as king. (It must be mentioned, however, that the new unity was more apparent than real as the northern and southern parts of the kingdom continued to be rivals. When the Philistine threat was allayed, the tribal alliance lost no time in separating.) The kings from Solomon onward worked hard to make Israel and Judea a part of the larger international life among the great powers in Asia Minor and Egypt. In this, they were acting contrary to the teachings of the Hebrew prophets who, fearing the contamination of foreign ideas and religious customs, vigorously preached a fidelity to the covenant and an avoidance of foreign alliances (isolationism). If the Hebrews copied much from their Canaanite neighbors, religion was the one thing that they refused to assimilate, and the prophets wanted to keep it that way. Yet, with Solomon, who built the first great Temple, Jerusalem was internationalized. The prophets' fears were realized as foreign religions and cults permeated the lifestyles of the Jews, as we may now call them.

Under Solomon's son civil war split the always uneasy north and south. In 721 B.C.E. the fierce Assyrians overcame the northern kingdom of Israel (with its ten tribes). The Assyrians deported the Jewish elite, leaving the peasants and the non-Jewish inhabitants to mix with each other. However, by the time of Jesus, a group called the Samaritans who lived in the North claimed to be the descendants of those original ten tribes. As a matter of fact, the Samaritans regarded the Jews of the two tribes in the South (Judea) as heretical because they accepted all the books of the Hebrew Scriptures whereas they (the Samaritans) only accepted the Pentateuch (the first five books). In addition, the Samaritans held that God's chosen place for sacrifice was on Mt. Gerizim in their territory; therefore, they regarded the Jewish Temple in Jerusalem as an apostate Temple. Naturally the Jews of the South, in turn, looked on the Samaritans as half-breeds and heretics, and so the hatred was mutual. Hence, we see the force of Jesus' reference to the Good Samaritan (Luke 10:25-37), and his conversation with the Samaritan woman at Jacob's well with her references to worshiping at Mt. Gerizim rather than Jerusalem (John 4: 3-42).

THE EXILE

The southern part of the Jewish kingdom, the kingdom of Judea,

survived as a political entity until 587 B.C.E., when the new world
power of Babylon conquered it, razed the famous Temple of Solomon and carried the Jews off into captivity. Here was a major crisis.
The great symbol of their religion, the Temple, was destroyed and
the Jews were exiled to foreign lands. This catastrophe was to have
fundamental results in many ways both for Judaism and Christianity. First of all, the tragedy caused the defeated and exiled Jews to re-
think their basic assumptions concerning their covenant with God
and the problem of evil. A principal emphasis on political liberation
gave way to aspirations for spiritual deliverance, restoration of the
Davidic monarchy, and a Messiah who would lead them in achiev-
ing all this. Secondly, the "Babylonian Captivity," as it is called,
changed the quality of the Jewish religion. Since the Temple was
now destroyed, the city of Jerusalem inaccessible, and the priesthood scattered, Jewish piety and religious life began to shift. The
Torah, that is, the Law as found in the Pentateuch, became all important. It was studied, explained, and commented on. All this commentary eventually became the great Jewish Talmud or the body of
civil and canonical law for the Jews.[2] It was also probably around
this time that, since the Temple was no more, the synagogue arose
as the place to meet, to pray, and to receive instruction in the Law.
We might recall that when, as a visiting rabbi, Jesus went into the
synagogue at Nazareth, he was allowed to comment on the Scripture reading for that day and to give instruction (Luke 4: 16ff).

Finally, the Babylonian captivity was to have great effects for
Christianity. Jewish people were now spread all over the world. In
time they would acclimate themselves in their respective countries
and form great Jewish centers. It would be to these communities
that the first Jewish Christians (such as Paul) would go on their missionary rounds and proclaim the gospel.

In 538 B.C.E., after 50 years of exile, Persia defeated Babylon and
allowed the descendants of the exiled Jews to return to their homeland. While some Jews chose to remain in their adopted lands, some
returned, and under men like Nehemiah and Ezra, the Law was restored. In 516 B.C.E. the Temple was rebuilt, and those who returned
remained in a kind of semi-isolation for nearly two centuries.

This is virtually all the information available regarding the lot
of the Jewish people between the time of Nehemiah and the invasion of Alexander the Great. On the other hand, it is certain
that this was a period of intense religious consolidation and, as

it seems, of remarkable intellectual activity. It was then that the forms of postbiblical Judaism evolved and acquired their profound hold on Jewish life in its every aspect. It was in that period that what was to be rabbinic Judaism struck its roots, that the synagogue emerged as an established institution, that the liturgy began to assume its definitive shape and that the works comprising the Old Testament assumed, as it seems, their present form and were assembled in an authoritative fashion. It was thus one of the great formative ages in Judaism, and therefore in the history of the Jewish people, which emerges from this period equipped with the literature, the outlook and the institutions thereafter to be so characteristic of it and the main secret of its endurance.[3]

CONTACT WITH THE GREEK-ROMAN WORLD

When in 331 B.C.E. Alexander the Great defeated the Persians, Palestine was annexed to Egypt where Greek ideas were able to penetrate the Jewish religion. This Greek-infiltrating process or "Hellenization" process via Egypt was especially successful among the Jews who remained and flourished in exile, the Jews of the Diaspora, or Dispersion, as they are called in contrast to those who lived in Palestine. For example, the Jews in Alexandria perhaps numbering a million or so, made that city the center of Jewish intellectual thought. Later, people like the famous Jewish philosopher Philo would make great efforts to reconcile Greek and Jewish thought. In fact, so thoroughly Hellenized did the Jews of the Diaspora become that at the beginning of the third century B.C.E. a translation of the Bible was rendered in Greek (the Septuagint) for those Greek-speaking Jews who no longer could speak or read Hebrew.

After Alexander's death his kingdom passed to the Ptolemies of Egypt who were tolerant of their Jewish subjects as regards customs and religion. However, when the rival Seleucid family of Antioch, Syria, overcame the Ptolemies, they proved less tolerant. In fact, they were bent on making the empire uniform in both culture and religion. Accordingly, they introduced into Jerusalem Greek gymnasiums whose naked athletes scandalized the conservative as it enticed the more liberal Jew. The injury to Jewish sensibilities did not stop there. A pig was sacrificed on the very altar of the Temple and a statue of Zeus was set up on the high altar becoming truly the "abomination of desolation" for the Jews of which the prophet Daniel spoke (Daniel 11:31). Such insults could only produce revolt, and eventually the Hasmonaean or Maccabee family drove the conquerors from the Holy City. The Temple was purified of the abominations perpetrated there and in 165 B.C.E. it was rededicated, an event which to this day is celebrated among the Jews as the feast of Hanukkah.

Still, the Jews were not at all united over this Hellenizing process. They divided into two camps. There were those who were quite conservative, the Sadducees, and consequently heavily nationalistic and isolationist. Their lives revolved around the Temple and its ritual. The other party, the Pharisees, was more willing to flirt with the cultural mainstream. They centered their lives on the Law (Torah). The tension between the two fostered a civil war over rival claims to the Hasmonaean throne. This broke out in 63 B.C.E. causing the new world power, the Romans, to intervene. General Pompey placed Jerusalem under Roman imperial power and sold thousands of Jews as slaves to Rome. The Jews, however, proved to be poor slaves since they would not work on the Sabbath and would not eat certain foods, but they were excellent companions and rose to positions of influence in Rome as time went by. (It was this influence that led the Pharisees to force Pilate to condemn Jesus, else they would put pressure on in Rome.) Although Jerusalem became a Roman protectorate, it was allowed some autonomy and a unique exercise of religion under its own high priest and local religious council of the Sanhedrin. Some thirty years later Mark Antony gave the wily Herod the Great the throne of Palestine. Herod built many palaces and, above all, he rebuilt the Temple on a grander scale. When he died, Rome partitioned Judea into several protectorates and finally in 6 C.E. placed it under a procurator or governor (v.g. Pilate, 26-36 C.E.).

To carry this history past our time of interest: in 70 C.E. the Jews revolted against Rome. The soon-to-be emperor Titus came and destroyed Jerusalem and, for the last time, the great Temple (and we might mention also the infant Christian church there). He left only the foundation standing,[4] and on his triumphal arch in Rome may be seen portrayed the Menorah or the holy seven-branch candelabrum that he took from Jerusalem. Also, at the time of this second destruction of the Temple a Jewish hero, Rabbi Johanan ben Zakkar, fled, taking with him his disciples and the sacred texts and commentaries. Since the Temple was no more, these texts provided the rationale for the permanent synagogue that had emerged the first time the Temple was destroyed, and rabbinic Judaism became the source and center of Jewish life.

Within the snyagogue the rabbi became the teacher and mentor rather than the Jewish priest. There was no more Temple in which to offer sacrifice, only a synagogue in which to expound the Law. The rabbi became *the* scholar and the charismatic rabbi became the new traditional Jewish folk-hero. The emphasis was placed on knowledge and the doing of the Law. The Jewish prayer became one of gratitude for having been delivered from three things: from being a Gentile, from being a woman, and from being ignorant. The Jews became the "people of the Book" and started their tradition of earnest study and academic excellence.

A second insurrection in 132-135 C.E. during the reign of the emperor Hadrian brought in the Roman army once more, sealing the fate of the Jewish state altogether.[5] Jerusalem became a Roman colony or, more accurately, little more than a Roman military campsite. Gradually, however, legal disabilities were removed and the Jews were allowed to resume normal life. But the Jewish state had disappeared and was not to be restored until modern times with the creation of the State of Israel on May 14, 1948. Significantly, the new state's Declaration of Independence reads, "The State of Israel will be open for the immigration of Jews from all the countries of their dispersion...." But from 135 to 1948 the "Wandering Jew" and the people without a country would be a painful reality for God's Chosen People.[6]

At the time of our immediate interest, however, it is about 4 B.C.E. Herod the Great is ruling, the Romans are in power. The Jews are in Palestine and dispersed throughout the world. They are looking for deliverance, both national and spiritual. Many Jews embodied this hope in the expectation of the Messiah who would achieve both. This sentiment was reflected at the ascension of Jesus when his disciples asked him, "Lord, are you going to restore the rule to Israel now?" (Acts 1:6). The Jews of Jesus' time divided along conservative (Sadducee) and liberal (Pharisee) lines. There were also other subgroups such as the Zealots who wanted nothing less than to drive out the Romans and restore the Jewish Kingdom, and the Essenes who lived strictly ascetical lives in small communes. These Essenes seem to be the forerunners of Christian monasticism and to have had an influence on the gospel according to Luke.

PAGAN CULTURE

Meanwhile, what about the non-Jewish world? This world abounded in religions, cults, and cultures that had crossed and recrossed during many centuries of warfare and conquest. To simplify the situation, we might say that in the Roman Empire as it existed at the time of Jesus there were, outside of the official Roman gods and emperor worship, three main categories of religious expression. At one end, there were the intellectual philosophical pantheisms of the aristocracy; at the other end, there were the many various local cults of the masses. In between these two there stood the so-called mystery religions. They were "mysterious" in the sense that they were secret, their teachings and rituals being revealed only to the initiated. These mystery religions gave great emphasis to the after-life and many of them had their types of deliveries, saviors, and heroes who died and brought life by that death.

All three types fed the anxious minds and hearts of a restless people at a restless time, causing a rather intense period of religious interest. In particular the mystery religions were appealing because their main motif was deliverance after death:

> Despairing of true happiness for themselves in this life or the triumph of peace, justice and prosperity on earth, men turned their thoughts to a future life beyond the grave or to a spiritual life detached from the material world. In the mystery religions...the dominant motif was to seek assurance for a life after death. As Attis was slain and rose again, so those who gained mystic communion with him and learned his secrets would live in blessedness after their earthly death. As Osiris was torn in pieces and brought to life, so those who were instructed in the ancient lore of Egypt would know the password to the world beyond. Souls purified by his mysteries Mithras would escort through the seven planetary spheres to the highest heaven, where they would live for ever in eternal light....[7]

JESUS, THE CHRIST

Into this mainstream of Eastern mysticism, Hellenistic culture, Roman rule, and deep Judaic longing for deliverance plus their fierce devotion to monotheism, came the Jew, Jesus of Nazareth.

Ironically, this most influential life that was ever lived comes to us exclusively from the four gospels written by anonymous authors within 40 to 70 years after Jesus' death. These gospels, more numerous and far older than any other ancient body of literature, are seen as creative faith expressions of the first Christians' belief in Jesus. They pose, therefore, the challenge of "getting behind" the texts to discover the real, historical Jesus. For a while, many scholars despaired of finding such a real person. However, recent studies of Jewish first-century culture and the findings of archaeology such as the Dead Sea Scrolls in 1947 have brought new credence to Scripture. As Oxford University Professor E.P. Sanders wrote in his 1985 book, *Jesus and Judaism*, "The dominant view today seems to be that we can know pretty well what Jesus was out to accomplish, that we can know a lot about what he said, and that those two things make sense within the world of first-century Judaism." The Jesus of history is especially accessible when the gospels, written in Greek, are translated back into Hebrew and some scholars believe that Jesus' sayings and deeds were recorded first in Hebrew—now lost to us—within a few years of his death on the cross and not put down by his followers until later.

The argument over "getting at the facts" is crucial to Christianity because its fundamental claim is that, in fact, all the things "concerning Jesus of Nazareth" happened in history, that Jesus was divine as well as human, that his suffering was not just a story but something that actually happened in a given time and place and that he rose from the dead and conquered death. This is a matter of record. The significance of Christianity claiming to be an historical religion becomes apparent when we realize that Buddhism has not claimed anything like this for Buddha nor Hinduism for Krishna, and nothing in these religions depend on such things happening. But everything in Christianity depends on the claim that the gospels are not simply a retelling of the exploits of countless other heroes and mythologial figures but a revealing of God's movement toward us, a conviction that these things did happen and that we can know about them.

What we do know, then, is that Jesus was born in Bethlehem in Judea, then a puppet state of Rome but with some independence, within certain limits, granted to the high priest and the local council, the Sanhedrin. Jesus would grow up in this conquered state, come into contact and conflict with the conservative party of the Sadducees and the liberal party of the Pharisees, and live among the constant undercurrents and aspirations for political freedom. He preached a life after death (resurrection) in opposition to the former (Luke 20:27 ff) and inclusiveness in opposition to the latter. His moral code was not nationalistic but universal, commenting that God would look more kindly on the repentant Samaritan than on the selfish Jew. Jesus did not deal with the specific issues of his time, but rather gave a law that goes beyond all law: the love of God and love of neighbor. In fact, all that was essential in his teachings was summed up in his own person, for he personified "the way and the truth and the life" of the believer. He was received by his contemporaries as a prophet heralding the forthcoming Kingdom of God on earth and was regarded as a teacher and mentor who trained his followers to live the Law in anticipation of that Kingdom.

During his public ministry, Jesus ran into more and more conflict with the leaders. He was brought before Pilate (an inscription unearthed in 1961 at Caesarea confirmed for the first time that Pilate was a first-century Roman governor), charged with the ever-sensitive political crime of treason, and was crucified as an enemy of Rome. But on the third day he arose from the dead, was seen by the apostles he had chosen and by many others, and on this one overwhelming root experience the early church was built. The one indisputable conviction for the apostles and other disciples was that Jesus rose from the dead:

> The theme of the kerygma was the resurrection of Jesus. This event was an act of God: "God raised him up." This unheard-of statement the apostles justified in three ways. First, by their own evidence; they took full responsibility for it. In essence, their evidence was that they had seen the risen Christ. The appearances of the risen Christ between Easter and the Ascension here take on their full meaning: their purpose was to establish the apostles' faith. St. Paul was later to show that they were one of the essential points in the tradition he received from the apostles. To have witnessed the risen Christ was the condition for being an apostle and as the last to whom the risen Christ appeared, Paul belonged with the Twelve. It is this evidence of the apostles which the church will transmit: the tradition is "apostolic tradition."[8]

This unshaken belief would be the source of the unflagging motivation urging the followers of Christ toward a new attachment, a new way of life, and eventually to a new church apart from the synagogue. All that Jesus said, all that he did, all that he was would be a radical inspiration of the new church. "Jesus proclaimed the message, the church proclaimed *him.*"[9]

But here we enter uncertain territory. In the history of the church the vaguest decades are the period between the death of Jesus in 30 C.E. and the writing of the last gospel about 90 C.E. After this latter time we know considerably more about the church; the six decades mentioned are less revealing. What we do know comes from a close source, not from outside contemporary sources. For instance, the Jewish historian Josephus, who lived during this time (from 37 to about 93 C.E.), has a distinct reference to Jesus. In fact, it was reported in February 1972 that two Israeli scholars had found an authentic text of Josephus (whose former reference to Jesus in Greek was always suspect as the work of Christian forgers), giving evidence from a non-Christian source of the existence and life of Jesus. The newly authenticated text from a tenth-century Arabic manuscript goes like this:

At this time there was a wise man who was called Jesus. And his conduct was good, and he was know to be virtuous. And many people from among the Jews and other nations became his disciples. Pilate condemned him to be crucified and to die. And those who had become his disciples did not abandon his discipleship. They reported that he had appeared to them three days after his crucifixion and that he was alive; accordingly, he was perhaps the messiah concerning whom the prophets have recounted wonders.[10]

Pliny, who died in 112, had but one indirect reference to Jesus. Tacitus, around the year 115, mentions that Jesus was killed in the reign of the emperor Tiberius. And that is it. But we said that we do know some things from sources close to Jesus. St. Paul was a contemporary to the events. He was converted around the year 35 C.E. and he wrote his first epistle to the church-community at Thessalonia in 49 or 51, some twenty years after Jesus' death. By the beginning of the second century we have all of the Christian Scriptures. We must remember, however, that at least the first three gospels are a setting down in writing of the word-of-mouth traditions that were necessarily very active from the beginning. Such oral traditions became systematized enough in due time to appear as little sayings, stories, and narratives until many (though not all; see John 21:25) surfaced in the gospel texts. But there was more in these early decades. There were specific outlines of a baptismal rite, a common eucharistic meal, the beginning of some organizational structure, and the common Christian slogan proclaiming that Jesus was Lord and Master (see 1 Corinthians 12:13). The final content that defined the church in these vague early decades was the common expectation that Jesus would return to earth again very soon in judgment and redemption. Thus, basically the early church (as the church of today) was an "eschatological" community; that is, it was a community always looking ahead toward ultimate fulfillment in Christ. The church of the first decades, as the church of today, is a community united by baptism, rooted in the Scriptures, nourished by the eucharist and awaiting Jesus' second glorious visit to earth. The only difference between then and now is the time element. The early church thought Jesus the Christ was coming immediately. When Jesus did not come, the church had to make adjustments, and in the process it had to meet three immediate and very severe crises. Two of these crises were external: they concerned Judaism and the Roman Empire. One was internal: it concerned heresy. Let us take a look at the first external crisis, reserving the others for the next chapter.

JUDAIZERS—THE FIRST CRISIS

We can get some appreciation of the serious problem that Judaism presented for the early church if we recall that the first Christians all were Jews: Jesus, his mother, his friends, and disciples. The Jesus movement began in Galilee and later was centered in Jerusalem, the Holy City where Jesus did much of his preaching, where he celebrated the Last Supper, where he died, and where Pentecost took place. With the new religion being born in so much "Jewishness" how would it, how could it, differ? If the new religion did differ, could it separate itself from the mother religion without pain and conflict? The inevitable answer to this last question had to be in the negative, especially if we recall that the Jews themselves ran the gamut from the conservative, Aramaic-speaking, kind to the Greek-speaking, liberal kind. The very presence of chronic tension between them would have to produce not only the antagonism of the old religion against the new, but also conflicts with the newly-born

Christian church itself.

In the very first days, although the followers of Jesus did not have a strong identity, they were aware that they were a special community. Even though they still continued to attend the Temple worship, certain new practices were added. For one thing, new converts were taken into the group by the initiation rite of baptism. There were private eucharistic meals in homes in addition to the Temple obligations. Right here was something to make many other Jewish groups suspicious of this new sect: the Jesus movement. The suspicions broke into open hostility when more of the Greek-speaking Jews took up the new way. The traditional tensions between conservative and liberal Jews were thereby heightened. In any case, the upshot was that the conservative Jews drove the Greek-speaking Jewish followers of Jesus out of Jerusalem. Naturally, as Greek-speaking Jews, these followers of Jesus gravitated to the Hellenized Jewish communities scattered throughout the East. In particular, they fled to Antioch in Syria, which served as a base for the missionary movement into the Diaspora. It was from here that Paul and Barnabas and others were sent, as the Acts of the Apostles tell us (13: 1-3). In fact, it was Paul, the most dynamic Hellenized Jew of them all, who became the main target of the anger of the conservative Jews. But they were hostile to Paul more for political reasons. A revolt against the Romans was brewing and the Jews needed all the loyalty and solidarity they could get. Paul, by his de-Judaizing, was threatening that unity. Thus, they followed him constantly and stirred up opposition to him and local persecutions.

It was at Antioch that the first "Christian" community was founded. Here, for the first time, the name "Christian" was used to describe the followers of the Christ (Acts 11:26). Other communities were quickly founded at Cyprus, Athens, and Corinth. From such centers as these, Christianity spread and, thanks to the Hellenized Jewish communities of the Diaspora, the gospel carried by the Jesus followers had a natural place to go. The clear result of such activity was that no longer would the emerging religion be Eastern, taught in Aramaic. Now it would be Mediterranean and taught in the cultured, world-wide languages of Greek and Latin. Spearheading much of the missionary activity, of course, was Paul, who, next to Jesus himself, was to shape Christianity for all time. He above all others was responsible for allowing the Gentiles to become followers of the Christ without also becoming Jews—thereby making Christianity truly catholic or universal.

Besides external persecution from the staunch conservative Jews who remained in Judaism, the question of "Jewish features" was a most acute personal problem for the early Jewish followers of Jesus. After all, for these people, just where did their new religion stand in reference to Judaism? Was it a continuation or a replacement? What *should* be the lifestyle of the new Jewish converts? Should they continue as they had been doing to observe the Mosaic Laws and the kosher food and dietary precepts? Should they continue with circumcision? The ancient Scriptures? Temple worship? Answers to all such questions among the Jewish Christians were by no means unanimous. There was a marked division in response. One faction centered around James the apostle, the head of the local Jerusalem church-community, which favored the retention of Jewish customs and traditions (Acts 2:26; 21:10). Opposed to them within the church were the Greek-speaking or Hellenized missionary party that came to be identified with Paul and, to a lesser degree, with Stephen and Philip. The struggle between the two different types of Jesus-followers became aggravated when Gentile converts were accepted into the church-community. Should Jewish customs and traditions (especially circumcision) be imposed on *them?* After all, such Gentile converts could hardly be expected to have the same emotional allegiance to the Covenant and Jewish practices such as circumcision. It came down to this: "For the Jewish Christians, the question of continuity as the question of their relation to their mother; for Gentile Christians it was the question of their relation to their mother-in-law."[11]

This question not unexpectedly arose in Antioch, which sent the problem to the community leaders and apostles who gathered in what has been called the Council of Jerusalem (Acts 15). It seems, moreover, that it was not just a question of Jewish customs such as circumcision, but also of nationalism. Once more Judaism was coming into political conflict with Rome. Therefore, it was especially important that non-Jews be circumcised, not for religious reasons, but for the sake of being identified with the Jewish national state. In any case, the answer that came from the council was in favor of freedom for the Gentile from Jewish customs, but certain compromises were made. Gentile converts were only to observe the prescription of not eating meat containing blood, or any food sacrificed to idols, and to refrain from marriage within certain degrees of kinship. This decision did not please the strict Jewish Christians, and it marks the first break between Christianity and the Jewish community. These strict

Jewish Christians, or Judaizers as they came to be called, opposed the decision vehemently and caused considerable dissension at Antioch, Galatia, Corinth, Colossae, and Rome—in fact, wherever the liberal Paul went. He and his kind thus continued to be harassed, not only by the traditional Jews who never left Judaism but also by those conservative Jews who had accepted Jesus as the Messiah.

Understandably the conflict grew worse when Jerusalem was destroyed and the Temple was razed to the ground during the Jewish-Roman war (67-70 C.E.). Another consequence of this war was that the Romans destroyed the Essene communities and killed most of the Zealots and Sadducees, leaving a leadership vacuum that was filled by the Pharisees. Judaism from this time on was basically Pharisaical Judaism. In the struggle to keep Judaism alive, the Pharisees allowed only their interpretation of the Law. At the same time, increasing numbers of Gentiles entered the church-communities. Once Christianity discarded the kosher food laws, Jewish religious ritual, and circumcision, it moved apace among the non-Jews. Paul, for his part, quickened that pace by his emphasis on justification as a pure gift of God and obtained by faith, rather than by external observances of the Jewish Law. Thus, the fall of Jerusalem put an end to the pressure that Judaism exerted on Christianity. Still, the early church had been too deeply engaged in the Jewish world to be able to separate itself from Judaism in one stroke. That is why the years between 70 and 140 constitute a period of search. The Jewish forms of thought will persist until they will later be recast in a Greek framework.

SYNAGOGUE AND CHURCH

We have now examined the first tension in the early church. Before we close this chapter we must make some pertinent observations about this initial conflict with Judaism, for to this very day there exists the ambiguity of the relationship of the church to the synagogue. It will be interesting to see, in fact, how the early church tried to resolve this problem in the first five centuries, and how its efforts have bequeathed to us today the very uneasy solutions they reached. One trend of thought that soon developed among the early Christian writers was to try to demonstrate that the Christian church was indeed connected with Judaism, but only in the sense that it had now taken over, not—unfortunately—that it had organically arisen from it. The church was seen as the new and the true Israel replacing the old. Other writers (such as Philo and Origen, whom we shall meet later) saw in the Hebrew Scripture types a preview of Christ and the church. We can see the trend to this sort of allegorizing even in the gospels, where Matthew goes out of his way to show that Jesus is a fulfillment of all that Moses and the prophets spoke of.

So, taking this clue, the early Christian writers made the psalms apply to the resurrection of Jesus. The Red Sea crossing under Moses became a symbol of the passage of Christians through the waters of baptism (thus explaining the many allusions in the Holy Saturday night's blessing of the baptismal water and in the rite of baptism itself). Jesus was seen as the suffering servant of Isaiah (Chapter 53), whose book became a kind of "fifth gospel." This sort of interpretation took the steam out of Judaism and came to represent a complete victory of Christian over Jewish thought. It must be admitted, however, that this victory was won to some degree by default since the Jewish community had become weak, out of touch with contemporary trends, and thus unable to meet Christian interpretations effectively.

The Hebrew Scriptures were seen as being fulfilled in the Christian Scriptures, and so the early Christian church filled its worship, songs and liturgy with allusions and references to the Hebrew Scriptures. In short, the church simply out and out appropriated the Jewish Scriptures, and Irenaeus in the second century would claim, "the writings of Moses are the words of Christ." Even if all this were legitimate, it did not solve the problem of Judaism itself. Judaism did not and has not phased out, and still has its Scriptures. The question remained that asked what should be the relation of the church to the synagogues, besides one of tolerant isolation and estrangement?

Not only the Jewish Scriptures and the Levitical priesthood, but other prerogatives and claims of the chosen people were consistently transferred to the church—a practice which was both an index to and a cause of the isolation of Gentile Christian thought from the Judaism contemporary with itself as well as from the Jewish Christianity out of which it had originally come.[12]

In later times, most unfortunately, the intellectual conquest of the

Christians over the Jews moved them to a position of indifference. The Christians tended to forget the holy history that had organically preceded them in Judaism. Ever so gradually, Christians began to falsely equate Judaism and paganism as if they were on the same level. Christian writers would go even further and claim that the Jews did not understand their own Bible anyway, else they could see that it clearly pointed to Christ. If they could not see, they were blind. If they were blind, then obviously they were deliberately blind—hard-hearted and stiff-necked as always. From this intolerant attitude and from the desire to show their difference rather than harmony, a distinct anti-Jewish bias sprang up that remains to this day. A whole theology grew up centering on exclusiveness and irreconcilability, rather than upon the common patrimony of the two religions.

One of these excluding tendencies can be seen in Constantine's declaration at the Council of Nicaea in 325. The new emperor stood up and declared that the Christian date of Easter should be changed from the Jewish Passover date, for "it is unbecoming beyond measure that on the holiest of festivals we should follow the customs of the Jews. Henceforth let us have nothing in common with this odious people; our Savior has shown us another path...." Constantine's anti-Jewish legislation was restated in the Theodosian Code of 438 and woven into the legal framework of the later Roman Empire and medieval Europe. The cry of "God-killer" would haunt the Jews through the centuries. Other church councils would condone anti-Jewish legislation. Christian crusaders in the Middle Ages would slay tens of thousands of Jews on their way to the Holy Land, and in 1099 would burn Jews alive in their synagogues. Twenty centuries of such bias would culminate in the terror of Auschwitz and Dachau. The non-Jewish world would be mute as six million Jews were exterminated in a massive holocaust.

When the chips were down, very few non-Jews came to the aid of the Jews during the holocaust—which for us was an eye opener with sad—not angry but sad—connotations...the sincere Christian knows that what died in Auschwitz was not the Jewish people but Christianity.... They were shooting thousands and thousands of Jews—entire communities, with machine guns, directly. There was a direct contact. And they had Ph.D.'s and some of them were theologians, and some of them, many of them, went to the priest, to confession and so forth. So

John the XXIII understood it...and therefore he opened the doors. And therefore he liberalized the church. That explains Vatican II, the ecumenical movement.[13]

In recent years the Catholic church has begun to repudiate any anti-Jewish bias. During the 1959 Good Friday liturgy, Pope John XXIII paused to take out his pen and publicly strike out all references to the "unfaithful" Jews contained in the lectionary he was using. He had been greatly influenced by Jules Isaac's book, *Jesus and Israel*, which led him to denounce anti-Semitism.

The Second Vatican Council declared, "What happened in His passion cannot be blamed upon all the Jews then living, without distinction, nor upon the Jews of today. Although the church is the new people of God, the Jews should not be presented as repudiated or cursed by God..." (Declaration on the Relationship of the Church to Non-Christian Religions, 4). That council might have said more, but fear of Arab reprisals against Catholics was a consideration. Still, theological questions remain:

The partnership between Judaism and the God of Israel is not questioned in the decree of the Council. The Catholic Church, it may be thought, admits that the ancient covenants of God with the ancestors and tribes of Israel, with various individuals of the Old Testament and with the primary heir, Judaism, have not been revoked.... But the question remains as to whether this type of ecumenical thinking can bring about a just verdict on Judaism, in view of its long and independent development, externally so far from Christ, and in view of its actual concrete type of existence today and its diverse interests.[14]

SUMMARY

We have seen Jewish background and Christian beginnings. We recalled the promises made to Abraham and his descendants. We saw the long history of the Chosen People, their setting up a kingdom, civil war and foreign conquest which sent the Jews all over the world. We saw that the Persians allowed them to return and how Alexander brought Greek culture to bear on them. We took note of the Seleucids who profaned the Temple and the Romans who took

Jerusalem under their protection. Jesus was born into all of this Jewish-Greek-Roman history. He died in 30 C.E. and left his disciples with the feeling that he would soon come again. When he did not return, his nascent church had to deal with the problem of its parent, Judaism, and its worship, rituals, and traditions. Inevitable and immediate conflicts between the new strict Jewish Christians and the liberal Greek-orientated Jewish Christians (plus the additional Gentile converts) led to a breaking away under leaders like Paul from Judaism and gave the church its catholic thrust. Predictably the axis of activity shifted from Jerusalem to Antioch, especially after the Jewish Temple was destroyed in 70 C.E. Shortly thereafter, the Gentile Christian converts would predominate. Judaism would recede more and more into the background and indeed become an enemy to be treated with polemic, and finally indifference. Meanwhile, Christianity began to spread with remarkable rapidity and increasing persecution from the imperial power of Rome.

CHAPTER 2

Expansion and Its Problems

EXPANSION

Christianity spread with amazing rapidity in the first decades after Jesus' death. First, as we have seen, Christianity spread during apostolic times to Asia—to cities like Antioch in Syria, Ephesus, Lystra, Derbe, Cyprus, Miletus, Smyrna, Philippi, Thessalonia, Athens, and Corinth, and in Europe to cities such as Pozzuoli and Rome, and all those other exotic towns mentioned in the Acts of the Apostles. In the second century, it spread to cities in France such as Vienne and Lyons (the home of Irenaeus), and Spain. There are sections in old Persia and Edessa that boast of second century Christian foundations. In all, the network of Christian church-communities in the first two centuries spanned from Spain to Germany and from the Yugoslavia of today to the Black Sea. Many cities would pride themselves on their early foundations. In an age of theological competition it was important for the larger and prominent cities to lay claim to being founded by one of the original twelve apostles themselves or by persons who lived in Jesus' time. Thus, Alexandria lays claim to being founded by St. Mark himself. There are more fanciful claims. Lazarus whom Jesus raised from the dead was supposed to be the first bishop of Marseilles, France. The boy who had the loaves and fishes in the gospel story turns up as another first bishop in that century. Such legends reflect the desire of the cities to lay claim to a title of dignity. We should take special note that the church spread to Africa in the first century and that its chief city, Alexandria (Alexander the Great's city), had a major role in the early church. It had become the main center of the Graeco-Roman or Hellenistic culture. It was at the crossroads of civilization. It was at Alexandria in the second and third centuries that Christianity, which came from a semitic people, got its Hellenistic coloring. "...At the level of ordinary Christian life it is in Alexandria that we find Christian morals, inherited from the Christian church, breaking free from their Jewish forms and putting on what was best in Hellenistic humanism.... The important point about the Alexandrian movement is the alliance of the gospel and Greek culture."[1] Later, this great Christian center and the whole African church were completely destroyed by the Muslim invaders but not before they gave to the church (and civilization) Tertullian, Cyprian, and the great St. Augustine.

Beyond the necessary missionary activity there were many reasons for this amazing spread. For one thing, adversaries were impressed with the courage of the Christian martyrs and grudgingly showed their admiration. Tertullian was right: the blood of martyrs *is* the seed of the church. The work of the missionaries was made easier by the *Pax Romana* (Peace of Rome), which provided the whole Mediterranean area with a unity of government, language and culture. As Origen noted in 185 C.E., the existence of many separate kingdoms would have been a major obstacle to the expansion of the religion of Jesus to the whole civilized world.

Finally, we might mention a third cause of the victory of Christianity in the hearts of all. Let us listen to the professedly agnostic scholar, E. R. Dodds:

But lastly, the benefits of becoming a Christian were not confined to the next world. A Christian congregation was from the first a community in a much fuller sense than any other corresponding group.... Its members were bound together not only by common rites but by a common way of life and, as Celsius shrewdly perceived, by their common danger. Their promptitude in bringing material help to brethren in captivity or other distress is attested not only by Christian writers but by Lucian, a far from sympathetic witness. Love of one's neighbor is not an exclusively Christian virtue, but in our period the Christians appear to have practiced it much more effectively than any other group. The church provided the essentials of social security: it cared for widows and orphans, the old, the unemployed, and the disabled; it provided a burial fund for the poor and a nursing service in time of plague. But even more important, I suspect, than these material benefits was the sense of belonging which the Christian community could give.... Within the community there was human warmth: some one was interested in them, both here and hereafter. It is therefore not surprising that the earliest and the most striking advances of Christianity were made in the great cities—in Antioch, in Rome, in Alexandria. Christians were in a more than formal sense "members one of another": I think that was a major cause, perhaps the strongest single cause, of the spread of Christianity. [2]

Fraternal love, it seems, was the most powerful force.

PERSECUTION—THE SECOND CRISIS

As we have seen, the first crisis was an attempt by strict Jewish Christians to require all Gentile converts to become fully Jewish in order to be followers of the Christ. The second crisis involved the reaction of the Roman government to the growth of this new movement. It was inevitable that this sudden worldwide (at the time) spread would attract the notice of the imperial powers. It is customary to speak of the Ten Persecutions of that imperial power; actually it was all the ebb and flow of one escalating persecution. Moments of peace, during which the church grew considerably, alternated with moments of hostility.

There were many reasons for the persecutions. For one thing, the Roman authorities were always quick to check the formation of a political or religious club that did not have their official sanction. They felt that not only did such new cults tend to undermine Roman morals but they feared that rebellion could get an easy toehold in the secrecy of any group that met under the pretext of divine worship. Secondly, as the contemporaries Suetonius and Dio Cassius tell us, there was the most natural error in identifying the (Jewish) Christians with the Jews, whom Romans did not highly esteem. Of course, as long as the confusion existed, the Christians could also reap a benefit: they could get in on the official protection that the empire gave to the Jewish religion (and contrariwise they would receive the brunt of persecution when the Jews rebelled against Rome). It was only when they separated from the Jews that the Christians were open to all sorts of accusations which may sound strange to our ears. They were accused of "atheism." This is understandable if we remember that to the Christians the old state gods were nothing but idols. This denial of them, therefore, led to the charge of atheism. This atheism charge also included the subversion of the state, since the state looked upon its official religion (no matter what people and leaders thought unofficially) as a strong cohesive force in the empire. To attack this force was to attack the strength of the state.

Another source of irritation was that the Christians kept aloof from many aspects of public life. People could not help but notice their absence from some public activities. At the public market they would not buy meats which had been offered to idols. A Christian jeweler would not decorate a pagan statue. Christian patients rejected the hospitals where pagan priests wandered through with their incantations. They would not attend the gladiatorial combats nor serve in the army since they were pacifists (although this would change in a few centuries). They shunned luxuries, not as the stoics of old, but for deeper reasons: They wanted to follow Jesus more fully.

The Christians, then, were "different" and, as Justin tells us, the very name "Christian" became associated with suspicions of every kind. Because of their eucharistic meal in which they ate the body and blood of the Christ, they were even accused of cannibalism. Then, there were those just waiting around for the second coming and so did not work, conveying to their neighbors a picture of indolence under the guise of religion. Even Paul felt the necessity of getting after such Christians by issuing his famous statement, "If anyone will not work, let him not eat" (1 Thessalonians 3:10). Others responded to the expected second coming by indifference. In their lifetimes phrases like "strangers and pilgrims" were common enough. Their attitude was expressed well in a line about Christians from the Epistles to Diognetus. "They live in their own countries, but as aliens; they share all duties like citizens and suffer all disabilities like foreigners; every foreign land is their country, and every country is foreign to them." Such a description of alienation prepared some for martyrdom.

Finally, some Christians did not help matters. They often failed to communicate their beliefs properly. Some, in their desire for martyrdom, went out of their way to be antagonistic. For all these reasons, the Christians were hated; they themselves were the cause of many public uprisings and left the civil officials no choice but to persecute them.

We mentioned in passing above that the early Christians were pacifists and would not serve in the army. In the light of modern thoughts about warfare, conscientious objection as a result of the Vietnam war, and more recently the United States bishops' pastoral, *The Challenge of Peace*, it is worth looking at the development of Christianity from such pacifism to militarism. There is no clear evidence of Christians serving in the army during the first century and a half; or, if they were in the army, they left after their baptism. A partial reason for this abstinence was that the Christians might be forced to engage in idol or emperor worship, but the fear of spilling blood was predominant. Tertullian noted that a Christian would rather be killed than to kill. Minucius Felix said it was not right to even see or hear about a person being killed, and commented that, in fact, the Christians "did not even eat meat rare," such was their horror of blood. Cyprian, Arnobius, the canons of Hippolytus all said that a soldier must refuse to kill. Later, concerning killing in war, St. Basil the Great said those who did so should abstain from holy communion for a three year period. Origen added his thoughts, "Christians should beware lest for warfare...we should take out the sword, for no such occasion is allowed by this evangelical teaching." Lactantius said that killing is forbidden in such a way that no exception is to be made.

Pacifism was such a characteristic of the early church that a pagan adversary, the Roman Celsus, warned that if everyone became Christian it would spell disaster for Rome because the Eternal City would be without military defense. It must be noted, however, that with the barbarians pressing near and spilling over the boarders, some Christians began to fight. But it was really from the time of Constantine on (early fourth century) that a whole change was made in the Christian's attitude toward war and peace.

Constantine, as we shall see, was willing to try out any god who would grant him victory. He tried Christ who, he felt, came through. Christians, of course, were elated to have the persecution over and become a preferred class. Suddenly, in the logic of things, the sword had become a friend, and theology lost no time underpinning Constantine's victory by the sword and from there, the spread of the faith by the same means. Jesus, in short, became a kind of god of war. The irony went full circle when by the year 416 one *had* to be a Christian to serve in the Roman army! Before long, several theories (notably Augustine's) appeared about the "just war." When the barbarians came into the church they brought with them a taste for violence, indicated by their choice of warriors for saints: St. Michael, St. Peter, St. Gerald the soldier, etc. Christians and their leaders—clerics, bishops and archbishops—freely went into battle to the extent that the church found it could not control Christian violence, even with "Peace of God" truces. The church wound up diverting this violence into the Crusades of the twelfth century. The Kingdom of the Prince of Peace was to be established over the Muslims by the sword. It is no wonder that, centuries later, perplexed Buddhists would remark that wherever Christianity has spread, blood has flowed—a remark far removed from that of Celsus!

This development was yet in the future. Meanwhile, getting back to the first persecutions of the Christians, we observe that in July 64 C.E. a terrible fire destroyed more than half of Rome. The Christians were blamed although it is said that Nero really caused the fire. This was the first persecution and it gave to the church its first martyrs whose names and deeds would fill the devotional books of the early Christian communities. Sts. Peter and Paul lost their lives during this time. Afterwards, there was a relative period of calm that the network of churches used to grow and organize. During this time converts were made even at high levels. Evidence of this can be found in one of the oldest Christian cemeteries, located on the Via Salaria, the property of a Roman aristocrat.

Other persecutions broke out under the emperors Domitian and Trajan (claiming the great Ignatius of Antioch), Hadrian, Antoninus Pius (claiming Polycarp of Smyrna) and around 162 Marcus Aurelius (claiming Felicitas, Perpetua, and Cecelia). Under the emperor Commodus the first known African Christians were martyred. Ironically, the better emperors unleashed the fiercest persecutions. The more seriously they took the state religion and its cohesion as good for the empire, the more seriously they persecuted dissent. Decius was the first emperor to expand the persecution of Christians worldwide (c. 250). He deliberately sought to kill off the leaders in the hope of killing off the movement. In the year 303, the emperor Diocletian issued a severe decree against the Christians calling for the destruction of all Christian places and instruments of worship, loss of rank for all Christians among the nobility, and a general loss of legal rights for all Christians.

The emperor Galerius in 311 issued an edict of toleration toward Christians. This toleration may have come through the emperor's Christian mistress, or it may have been the result of the influence of the Neoplatonist school under Plotinus, whose teachings of tolerance may have had an effect. In any case, the ebb and flow of the persecutions was at an end. Under Constantine, Christianity would be given freedom of worship and, in 381, under one of his successors, Theodosius, it would become the state religion. There were to be no more persecutions except for a brief revival of paganism under Julian, whom Christian history has dubbed revengefully "the Apostate" (361-363).

EARLY HERESIES

The third immediate and severe crisis facing the early church was internal: heresy. This internal disunity of doctrine proved to be more threatening than the external persecutions. There was, to begin with, some similarity between Christianity and the mystery religions that helped to blur the difference for some people. In addition, there were, of course, different traditions among the church-communities themselves. The Aramaean churches, the Asiatic churches, the Syrian and Roman churches, each had their own traditions that further confused the doctrinal issues. Thus, clashes took place not only between heretical and orthodox Christians, but also between the various local church-communities. Because the truth was important to the church, doctrinal orthodoxy was a constant concern in the struggles of the first centuries.

Contrary to the monotonously recurrent opinion that orthodoxy was not a factor in primitive Christianity, the church from the start, through the time of Paul to that of John and beyond, had an acute sense of the confessional or dogmatic principle. Concretely, this was a matter of thanksgiving for the boon of salvation. It found a first expression in the hymns and confessional formulas conserved by the New Testament writers, notably Paul. These were followed in the second century by hymns and creeds.... The concern for orthodoxy under the new conditions of the antagnostic struggle and of persecution in diverse provinces of the Empire, lay at the root not only of the creeds but of the accent on the allegiance to the bishop. Indeed, all developments from the late first century to the age of Constantine seem to have taken contour and direction from the commitment to orthodoxy as a positive and indispensable religious value.[3]

It would seem that some degree of doctrinal distortion was to be expected, because Christianity could only be explained in the terms and language then current. In those days each section of the empire had its infinite variety of religious sects and interpretations of life. In the process of attracting converts, the early church tried to present its case in the only language they understood, that is, an adaptation of the terminology of their own present beliefs. Obviously there was much room for misunderstanding, and at this early stage the church had no precedents, no ready-made definitions, to guide it. No one put the problem better than the perceptive nineteenth-century Cardinal Newman:

Language then requires to be refashioned even for sciences which are based on the senses and the reason; but much more will this be the case, when we are concerned with subject-matters, of which, in our present state, we cannot possibly form any complete or consistent conception, such as the Catholic doctrines of the Trinity and Incarnation. Since they are from the nature of the case above our intellectual reach, and were unknown till the preaching of Christianity, they required on their first promulgation new words, or words used in new senses, for their due enunciation; and, since these were not definitely supplied by Scripture or by tradition, nor the centuries by ecclesiastical authority, variety in the use, and confusion in the apprehension of them, were unavoidable in the interval.... Not only had the words to be adjusted and explained which were peculiar to different schools or traditional in different places, but there was the formidable necessity of creating a common measure between two, or rather three languages— Latin, Greek, and Syriac.[4]

We need to remember that at the beginning there were no special doctrinal requirements beyond the simple affirmation that "Jesus is Lord" (1 Corinthians 12:3). The Christians, of course, believed in the resurrection and such, but there was no formal doctrine accepted by all the church-communities. Rather the creeds and special formulas became a necessity as heretical opinions arose and struck at the heart of the Christian faith. From these conflicts came the early creeds and the formulated dogmas of church history. But it is important to remember that they arose out of the need to keep the faith intact and that they would run into the difficulties as described above by Cardinal Newman.

There would be other great heresies later, as we shall see. But during the times we are considering—the first two centuries—three main ones were prevalent: Gnosticism, Marcionism, and Montanism.

Gnosticism, the most pervasive and troublesome, had a great reactive effect even as it appeared in apostolic times. An amalgam of popular Near Eastern beliefs and philosophies, Gnosticism was really an attempt to reorientalize the faith.[5] Gnosticism claimed to be the private knowledge of a select few. Its basic teaching was the antagonism between the world of matter which was evil, and the world of spirit which was good. If this is so, the world and its creation were evil things and obviously the work of a lesser evil "god." Necessarily God would not take a body and become human, so Jesus' body was but a phantom and his death merely a piece of playacting. Having appropriated just enough of the language and symbols of the Christian faith, Gnosticism managed to deceive many and was a special distress to the early church. In Acts 8:9-24, we find Peter clashing with the Gnostic spokesman, Simon Magus. From a library of the Gnostics uncovered in 1945 in Egypt we know now that much of the early church's theology was in reaction to Gnosticism. In Paul's letters there are many examples of his refuting Gnostic ideas, as exemplified by the following: "Have nothing to do with the pointless philosophical discussions and antagonistic beliefs of the 'knowledge,' which is not knowledge at all" (1 Timothy 6:20).

This refutation went further. As we have indicated, it triggered the definite formulations of what actually was believed and held to be "orthodox" (that is, sound teaching). Reaction as a matter of fact produced the three stable Christian sources of orthodoxy: (1) the canon of Scripture; (2) early creedal statements; and (3) the episcopacy, as the authentication of the early oral traditions. Early creedal formulas like those used at baptism, the earliest creeds, the epistles, and the Fourth Gospel all show definite signs of reactions to Gnostic teachings.

Appearing about 120, Marcionism tried to go further than Paul in setting aside the Law. It held that there were two gods, one the creator of the material (evil) world (the God of the Hebrew Scriptures), and the other master of the spiritual realm (the God of the Christian Scriptures).

About forty years later the third heresy, Montanism, appeared. It held that Montanus was the incarnation of the Holy Spirit and that the second coming of Christ was imminent. Thus it undertook to form a group of elites and prophets who, while living an extremely ascetical life, placed themselves solely under the guidance of the Holy Spirit. The founders of these other heresies were individuals with highly personal views, who tended to lead their adherents away from the main body of the church. There is a noticeable difference between them and the Christian bishops. Irenaeus described the difference:

> The heretics are all later than the bishops, to whom the apostles have transmitted the churches, and the manifestations of their doctrine are different and produce a veritable cacophony. But the path of those who belong to the church, dwelling throughout the world and holding firm to the tradition of the apostles, shows that all have one faith and one kind of organization.

EARLY WRITERS

There were not lacking those Christians who, in the face of constant persecution, tried to uphold the faith and encourage the faithful. Such would be those who replaced the apostles after their death. These were the "apostolic fathers" who were quite conscious of their inferior position and in no way presumed to fill in for the apostles. They wrote to pass on the apostolic teachings, thereby forming an important link to the age that immediately followed them. Such apostolic fathers would include the famous names of Clement of Rome, who wrote a letter around the year 90 that was an attempt to settle the schism that arose in Corinth; Ignatius of Antioch, who was the first to use the term "catholic" of the church while writing seven letters as he was on his way to be martyred in Rome under the emperor Trajan; and Polycarp, who died a martyr in 155. There were the unknown authors of the *Epistle of Barnabas*, *The Shepherd of Hermes*, and the *Didache*, or Teaching of the Twelve Apostles, whose writings have given us valuable information about early liturgy and practice in the church. These last two documents go back to the end of the first century or the beginning of the second. They were largely inter-community writings that presumed familiarity with Christian life and teachings and were written to instruct and encourage the faithful.

But more was needed. The force of the early heresies and persecutions based on misunderstanding and prejudice called for an out-and-out defense of the Christian teachings, and so the church produced its defenders or "apologists" as they are known. These are the writers who went out to meet the intellectual enemy. They sought to answer the objections of the pagan philosophers and the defenders of Judaism. They strove to "prove" the doctrines of Christianity in the systematized manner of the various philosophical schools. In fact, they went even further. They sought to demonstrate that the present Christians were the authentic heirs to the Graeco-Roman civilization. Therefore, Christians do not reject the world in which they are living, but accept it wholeheartedly. Christians, in fact, are the empire's best citizens and have made the empire greater. In Christianity, Hellenism had found its true meaning.

So ran the apologists' defense of the church. Names among the apologists would include Tatian, Athenagoras, and particularly the better known Justin Martyr, and Irenaeus. The latter was active around the year 177 and was the first in a long line of theologians and biblical scholars that would include Hippolytus, Origen, the Gregorys, and Basil in the East, and Ambrose, Jerome, and the towering Augustine in the West. It was Irenaeus who began the theology of the atonement and redemption and who offered the first theory on how Jesus' death and resurrection saved humanity.

Tertullian (150-230) was the first to transfer the Greek intellectual terminology to Jewish Christianity. He coined words like "Trinity" and "consubstantial." Clement of Alexandria openly wanted to recast Greek philosophy into Christian terms. These scholars were trying to meet the critics on their own ground. But, once the early heresies like Gnosticism were subdued, and there was no doubt that Jesus the Christ had "come in the flesh," then other speculations began. If Jesus was human and divine—how could such two opposites be reconciled? These apologists and church fathers and, later the famous church councils, would try to come to terms with such questions about Jesus, his nature, and the correlative questions of the Trinity.

It is interesting to note that all this defensive and speculative activity was taking place in the East, the birthplace of Christianity. In the Latin West there were fewer theological conflicts. Gnosticism was relatively impotent there and dogmatic speculation was not strong. In fact, the Latin church (which largely meant, Rome) had a reputation for being conservative, as is evident in its much more subdued liturgy and hymns. It tended to be more legalistic and pragmatic. Significantly, Westerners like Tertullian, Minucius Felix, and Cyprian of Carthage were all lawyers who represented a more legal approach to Christianity. They and their Latin church tended to retain a greater respect for the traditional poets and Roman writers and were more influenced by the Stoic foundations of a Western Cicero than by the theological foundations of an Eastern Paul.

CHURCH AND PAGANISM

It is equally significant that the early apologists and church fathers tried to come to terms with paganism, because it soon became obvious that paganism also could boast of the good, the true and the beautiful. How did one explain this? How did one make a case for the difference of Christianity, if there was a difference? Various explanations were given. Tertullian used the idea of natural law; others maintained that good paganism came from the Hebrew Scriptures, which meant in effect that the pagans plagiarized the Scriptures. In time Christianity would claim that anything good in paganism was inspired by the pre-existing Son of God, the "Word" of the gospel according to John. But when this "Word became flesh," he naturally superseded not only Moses (Judaism) but Socrates (classical paganism and philosophy). In fact, whether they knew it or not, the pagans should have realized the "Christian" influence in their own writings. Just as in the Jewish Scriptures the "suffering servant" of Isaiah 53 was seen as the Christ, so in the ancient pagan writings "evidence" could be found of Christian revelation. Virgil above all came to be considered as a forerunner of Christianity. Later, in medieval times, legends would abound about Virgil's supernatural knowledge of Christianity. It is no accident that the greatest medieval poet, Dante, called Virgil "my master and my author." It is Virgil who leads the poet through the Inferno. Sybil, the famous Greek prophetess, was pressed into Christian service the same way. Catholics may still remember in the lovely hymn *Dies Irae* (which used to be sung at funerals) that the first verse tells of the coming day of wrath on the dual testimony and authority of King David and the Sybil.

> That day of wrath, that dreadful day,
> Shall heaven and earth in ashes lay,
> As David and the Sybil say.

Actually, the Christians were doing what the Jews had done when confronted with paganism: adapting and synthesizing. As we mentioned before, it was in this process that the Christian religion was modifying its Jewish forms and appropriating the thought patterns of the pagan Hellenistic world. It was Clement of Alexandria (150-214) who set the pace by declaring that the revelation of Christ takes many forms appropriate to various cultures. If the eternal "Word" were manifest in the ancient philosophies and then in the Jewish Scriptures, so it must make a new manifestation to the current Greek world. Clement argued that Christianity must now drop its semitic form and put on the Hellenist form. Christianity must now speak the language of Plato and Homer. It must transfer to the Greek culture. Gradually, however, classical paganism became to the Christians what Judaism had become: irrelevant. Philosophy teachers were considered harmless, and theology (it was felt, wrongly) had effectively replaced philosophy. Philosophy would become simply a tool to "prove" doctrine, and to that extent philosophy died.

From such an attitude toward philosophy, major results would arise to plague the church in later centuries. In the late Middle Ages, when the political and cultural underpinnings of Christianity began to erode, the church would not have the philosophical tools with which to work out a new image. Neglecting and despising philosophy, the church would be unprepared for the fifteenth-century Renaissance and its heir, the eighteenth-century Enlightenment. The lay leaders of the East discarded philosophical principles which supposedly were hostile to the church. Thus, the church would be ridiculed for holding on to a theological system no longer viable in the "modern" world. The secular and profane would take over with a vengeance and the church would have to wear the mantle of being anti-intellectual and anti-scientific, the price of her earlier putdown of philosophy. The historian Edward Gibbon would indignantly proclaim that Christian theologies have superseded the exercise of reason, resolved every question by an article of faith, and condemned the infidel or sceptic to eternal flames. In many a volume of laborious controversy they exposed the weakness of the understanding and the corruption of the heart, insulted human nature in the sages of antiquity, and proscribed the spirit of philosophical inquiry, so repugnant to doctrine, or at least to the temper, of a humble believer.[6]

THE MESSAGE: JEWISH OR GREEK?

It was at this period—the period of Christian apologists and the church fathers—that the basis was laid for a charge that would find expression in the twentieth century. The charge was that the original, "pure" Christianity was so penetrated and so overlayed with Greek philosophy and language, so "Hellenized," that much of Christianity's pristine Judaic richness had been lost; initial truths were frozen into Greek-thinking categories, and the spirit of Christ was stratified into rigid Greek formulas. In other words, the charge would be made that the truth of divine revelation had been subordinated to the philosophy of the Greeks, that Alexandria was too successful. Tertullian and Origen were thought to be especially guilty. Later, the medieval Catholic theologians would be accused of the same crime: Hellenizing Christ. The point (to groups like the Protestant Reformers of the sixteenth century, for example) would be that we have inherited a perverted form of Christianity. It was said that the church must eschew all dogmatic formulas as useless, especially those of the first four church councils, in order to find the truth. This criticism, which still persists, is now being put to rest. Scholars like Jaroslav Pelikan have shown that this is not true. In fact, the technical words used by the medieval theologians predated the thirteenth-century rediscovery of the Greek philosophers like Aristotle, and the terminology used by early church councils (such as Nicaea in 325 and Chalcedon in 451) "did not canonize Aristotelian philosophy as indispensable to Christian doctrine...." Pelikan says:

Taken as it stands, "hellenization" is too simplistic and unqualified a term for the process that issued in orthodox Christian doctrine.... Although theologians quoted Scripture in support of ideas originally derived from philosophy, they often modified these ideas on the basis of Scripture....Indeed, in some ways it is more accurate to speak of dogma as the "dehellenization" of the theology that had preceded it and to argue that "by its dogma the church threw up a wall against an alien metaphysic."[7]

Or, as another modern writer, Ben Meyer, puts it:

Indeed, like the councils that followed, Nicaea attacked autonomous wisdom in the name of tradition. Far from being a triumph of the hellenization of Christianity, it repudiated the substance of hellenic and specifically neo-Platonic thought about God. It did not, however, repudiate hellenic techniques of thought....[8]

MONASTICISM

Another kind of third-century expansion was monasticism, a movement whose name in Greek means "to live alone or apart." Before we proceed to the development of monasticism, we should note that there were precursors of this movement in the early church. From the earliest times, there were "wandering evangelists," men and women who moved from place to place preaching the message of Jesus. As one might expect, there were sometimes conflicts between them and the resident church-community leaders; yet these "apostles" were held in high esteem for their work on behalf of the Kingdom of God. At the same time, there were other men and women who devoted their whole lives to the service of their own church-communities. Usually they remained unmarried and lived at home, supported by their families while doing whatever ministry was needed by members of the community. Their way of life was referred to as the *vita apostolica* (the apostolic way of life). For these people to withdraw from the community for any reason would have been viewed as deserting the Body of Christ, which was the community. Yet, by the third century the churches were facing increasing persecution by the Roman government, and some people did flee—to the hills or the deserts—seeking refuge until the danger had passed, or wanting solitude to prepare themselves for martyrdom. Others came seeking a more perfect Christian life, away from the "laxity" of some church leaders who were readmitting to the church not only repentant sinners, but even those who had lapsed. People came to the monasteries in even greater numbers after Christianity became the state religion and multitudes entered the church with little preparation and commitment. They were seeking the way to live the Christian life to the fullest.

Two forms of monasticism developed in the deserts above the Nile Valley during the early fourth century. The first grew up around the figure of Anthony (251-356) who lived alone in the desert and was perceived by many as a most holy man. (Keep in mind that in the Hebrew Scriptures, the desert was the place where God chose his people and where people found God.) Soon others came to learn from Anthony and by the time of his death there were thousands of "hermits" (from the Greek word meaning "desert") living in the area. They lived a solitary life of prayer, meditation and Scripture reading, occasionally coming together for eucharist whenever a priest was present. Usually they were able to see to their own physical needs by foraging off the land. Athanasius's *Life of Anthony* helped to spread to the West the news of this way of living the Christian life. Soon there were groups of hermits in Italy, Gaul, England, and Ireland. It is important to note that these hermits were laymen, taking no vows, living under no rule, and staying only as long as they determined necessary (only a few remained as hermits for their whole lives). There were some among these hermits, especially in Syria, who took the ascetic ideal to extremes. They had themselves walled up in caves for extended periods or lived atop pillars for years at a time. For example, Simeon the Elder, also known as "Stylites," spent 30 years atop a pillar praying and preaching to pilgrims who sought his advice.

The second form of monasticism was developed by Pachomius (290-346), a hermit who felt a divine call to form a community from those men who came to learn from him. (At one point there were 7,000 men in his community at Tabennesis.) He insisted on regular meals and times for worship and meditation on Scripture. Members were required to put their wealth into a common fund, and each community supported itself, usually through weaving or farming. (This constituted the first "rule.") Eventually Pachomius helped women to establish similar communities. This communal type of monasticism spread throughout the East through the efforts of Basil the Great and Gregory of Nyssa. Others, like Martin of Tours, Augustine of Hippo and John Cassian developed the first monasteries in the West. But it was Benedict of Nursia who was called the founder of Western monasticism, because the rule he developed was used by nearly all the monasteries opened between the sixth and the eleventh centuries.

The monastic movement would have enormous contributions to make in the future of the church. The monasteries would serve as the "Nation's Innkeeper" for pilgrims and travelers during the Middle Ages. Some monasteries took care of the orphaned, the infirm, and the dying. The monks would preserve learning and culture after the collapse of the Roman Empire in the fifth century. They were sent forth to convert the pagan masses throughout the world. They would frequently set the pace for holiness, piety, and reform in the church. They would figure most prominently in the church councils and the fight against heresy. On the minus side, the rise of monasticism inadvertently fogged the question of the Christian vocation. Monasticism helped create the image of the "evil" world as the scene of ambition, war, pride, greed, and lust, thus leaving the distinct impression that salvation in such a world was nigh impossible. Those who did not opt to go into the monastery were compromised. If one were not a monk or nun, would salvation be possible? If one had to withdraw from the "world" in order to be saved, what hope was there for the vast majority of ordinary people? The net result— as can be seen in the long, long litany of the church's saints, most of whom were from religious orders—was that there never developed an invigorating lay spirituality until some beginnings were made in the thirteenth century with the foundation of the basically bourgeois religious orders of Dominicans and Franciscans and their Third Orders. Later in the seventeenth century, Francis de Sales would write especially on behalf of the spiritual life of the laity. Finally, and most important, the division between the lay and clerical state became unduly pronounced and all charisms became clerical property.[9]

Thus, we have seen the struggles of the early church. The terrible persecutions whose martyrs' blood, as Tertullian said, became the seed of faith and did much to win the admiration and applause of the church's enemies. During the first three centuries there was the fantastic spread of Christianity. At the same time, however, heresies active from the time of Peter and Paul brought confusion and disorder to the church-communities. To offset this, apologists and patristic writers came to the church's defense. They would meet the charges, hand on orthodox teaching, and bring to the fore the canon of Scripture and the early creeds. Finally, the monastic life would catch on and spread. The monks would become the great bearers of reform throughout the centuries. There now remains only one more point which we shall take up in the next chapter before we move to the church in its period of new-found freedom: the structural organization of the early church.

CHAPTER 3

The Structure of the Early Church

THE PEOPLE OF GOD

To the average Catholic the structure of the early church seems to pose no problem; it has always been the same as it is today. That understanding in diagram form might look something like this:

From the beginning

1. Jesus	directly appointed his
2. Twelve Apostles	including Peter who was
3. The Pope	Peter and the other eleven Apostles personally ordained their successors, namely,
4. The Bishops	who ordained as their successors the
5. Other Bishops	and so on until the present time. Thus is seen a series of links in the continuous chain of
6. Apostolic Succession	

Somewhere within this "diagram" the apostles passed on the priesthood as well, and somewhere in the course of time the cardinals came to replace the bishops as the rulers of the church under the leadership of the pope (the "president and his cabinet"). Yet the evidence in the Christian Scriptures points out quite clearly that we have to radically modify this diagram. The biblical testimony indicates that in the early church there were many forms of ministries and structures that defy any rigid diagramming. It is true that we do not have much detailed information about them. The years, from 30 to 90 C.E., for instance, are hazy; but for the years after the first century we possess a fairly accurate picture. In any case, realizing that we cannot arrive at a full answer concerning the organization of the primitive church, we can at least correct our former knowledge and give some reasonable probabilities which are more in keeping with the biblical evidence.

First of all, we must remember that the church began in Jerusalem, the scene of Jesus' passion, death, resurrection, and the great drama of Pentecost. Church-communities were formed which, as we have seen, did not separate themselves immediately from the synagogues and Judaism in general; they remained a sect within Judaism.

The organization must have been loose as the followers of Jesus struggled with their identity. In the late 30s, when persecution broke out, the Greek-speaking Jews who joined the community of Peter and the apostles had to flee (Acts 6:1-8). We saw that they fled to the scattered Jewish communities throughout the world, including such Greek-speaking cities as Antioch, Ephesus, Corinth, and others in Africa and Asia. They even fled to Rome itself, the imperial city of the still reigning emperors, around the year 40, so that when Peter finally did go to Rome, he found there an already existing church-community; he did not start it. Thus, in each city these church-communities appeared. Not all of them had the same kind of structure.

Nowhere in the Christian Scriptures is there mention of priests as we know them. Scripture scholar Raymond Brown suggests that because the infant church did not at first disassociate itself from Judaism, priests were simply taken for granted (for Judaism had them). No special mention needed to appear. As a matter of fact, the special and specific mention of priests in the early church is not evident until the church *does* separate itself from Judaism. This is because the notion of the eucharist as a sacrifice only gradually becomes apparent to the church. Side by side with this new self-understanding of sacrifice, the correlative notion of priests to offer this sacrifice comes to the forefront. Thus Brown, in an observation that may startle some Catholics, writes:

Such a picture of the development of the Christian priesthood must of necessity modify our understanding of the claim that historically Jesus instituted the priesthood at the Last Supper. This statement is true to the same real but nuanced extent as the statement that the historical Jesus instituted the church. By selecting followers to take part in the proclamation of God's kingdom, Jesus formed the nucleus of what would develop into a community and ultimately into the church. By giving special significance to the elements of the (Passover) meal that he ate with his disciples on the night before he died, Jesus supplied his followers with a community rite that would ultimately be seen as a sacrifice and whose celebrants would hence be understood as priests.[1]

Note that such a comment points up the fact that our notions of the ministries and structures of the early church are uneven because the church itself developed unevenly at that time. It would have to reflect on itself for a long time before the implications of everything that Jesus said and did became apparent. It would be the work of the early church fathers and councils to formulate many of the realizations. Again, the slow dawning of the Last Supper as both meal and sacrifice, and the need for a priest to preside over the ritual, are cases in point.

THE TWELVE

In our search for answers about the structures of the early church we need first to consider the twelve apostles and their unique function. They were the link with the leaders of the twelve tribes. (See Genesis 49:1-28; Matthew 19:28.) They were the foundations of the New Israel. We modern Catholics like to think of them as traveling all over the world and founding churches. Actually, according to the Christian Scriptures, this was not so. Most of them stayed put. They were not primarily missionary apostles. Rather, they were like "founding fathers." They were the resource of the faith *par excellence*. They were the pillars of the church with all of the stability and permanence that the phrase implies. They were the collective witness to the event and to the message of Jesus. They were the living depository of what he said, did, and taught. To this extent they did not have to travel.

On the contrary, there were apostles besides the twelve who did travel. They were not among the unique twelve but they were nevertheless regarded as apostles. They had seen the risen Lord (Paul in 1 Corinthians 15:16 speaks of Jesus appearing to some five hundred brethren after his resurrection) and, most determining of all, they were sent to preach the gospel, the sign of a genuine apostle. The twelve or the church-community appointed these apostles in order to ease their own job of preaching the good news. Thus they became the traveling apostles, the missionaries and founders of various church-communities. The most famous among these was, of course, Paul, a true apostle even though not numbered among the twelve. These "secondary" apostles (if you will) did not stay at one particular church-community (see Acts 13:1-5). They moved on, keeping in touch by letters and delegates (for example, the epistles of Paul; his delegates, Timothy and Titus).

PRESBYTER-BISHOPS

We can see several more elements of structure during the very lifetime of Paul and the twelve in addition to the "secondary" apostles. For example, there are the deacons about whom we shall speak in the next chapter, and there are the presbyters (from *presbyteros,* Greek for "elder"). There is evidence that these presbyters actually ruled some of the church-communities.

As founding fathers, the twelve themselves were free of administration and rule (see Acts 6:2-3). The itinerant apostles were just that: they founded church-communities and then moved on. The stable ruling power they left behind were the presbyters. We do not know exactly when they came on the scene, but it was during the lifetime of some of the twelve. We are not certain of the exact nature of the office of presbyter, although most scholars hold that it was identical with that of the bishop (from *episkopos,* Greek for "overseer"). In any case, we find in the Acts of the Apostles many references to the presbyter-bishops (the terms were interchangeable at this time). In chapter fifteen, for example, we find that the Christians at Antioch charge Paul and Barnabas to go to Jerusalem "to the apostles and presbyters." When they arrive, they are received "by the church, and by the apostles and presbyters." After their report "the apostles and presbyters assembled to consider the matter." Then "it pleased the apostles and presbyters, with the whole church, to send to Antioch" two messengers who took a letter that read: "The apostles and presbyters to the brethren at Jerusalem." In addition to this and other such explicit reference to the existence of presbyters, Paul and Barnabas themselves appointed presbyters in their own church-community foundations.

The interesting thing is that the presbyters usually functioned as a committee with one of their number serving as chairman (or "overseer"). This group, the presbyterate, ruled over some church-communities. But there was a significant further development:

> Very soon, however, the word "bishop" appears in the singular, implying that in a community there would be one bishop among many elders. Paul, for example, outlines the duties of various offices and writes about "a bishop...the office of a bishop" in the singular, then about "deacons" and "elders" in the plural. We can only suppose that the title of bishop was gradually given to the senior elder (or perhaps to the elder celebrating the eucharist at the time), who then became the chairman of the elders.[2]

In any case, recent scholarship has shown that toward the end of the second century the single presbyter-bishop was becoming the general rule. In short, the single bishop was replacing the presbyterate committee. The point to remember here is that this development was uneven. Ignatius of Antioch is witness to a single bishop by the end of the first century, while there is no evidence of a single bishop at Rome before 250.

FUNCTION VERSUS OFFICE

The deaths of the early church leaders and the deaths of those who knew them caused a crisis of leadership towards the end of the first century. In the Christian Scriptures we can find at least seven responses to this crisis of leadership.[3] Rule by presbyter-bishops who guarded the teaching of sound doctrine gradually became the norm. As the presbyter-bishops became the ordinary leaders of church-communities, they did so not by being appointed by the twelve or by the "secondary apostles" themselves (though this could be in some cases), but by being appointed *by the church-community*. There were two reasons for this. First of all, the church as a whole succeeded the twelve. The witness of the twelve was passed on to the living church. It was the living church that was to give evidence to the event of Christ and to ordain. The whole church-community called a person to an office. Notice the reference in Acts just quoted above: Paul and Barnabas were received *"by the church,* and by the apostles, etc...."; then "it pleased the apostles, presbyters, *with the whole church...."* Secondly, what was therefore important to the church was not that there be some kind of lineal descent, some physical connection, from one of the twelve. What was important was that the person in question—the new presbyter-bishops—faithfully reflect the apostolic witness and tradition. The pastoral epistle to Titus says, "The bishop as God's steward must be blameless. In his teaching he must hold fast to the authentic message..." (Titus 1:7ff). In short, the *function* was more important than the office. In and with the church the bishops were to preserve the church in its apostolic foundation. The bishops were to be the permanent resident authorities in the local church-community. (After 325 their authority was extended to include the whole "diocese," which was a division within the Roman empire.) The bishop's role was to represent and reinterpret the living good news of the gospel. They were to be authentic purveyors, with and for the church, of the Christ-event and the Christ message. If there was to be any idea of "apostolic succession" at all from the original twelve, it was to be a succession of message as obtained from them; it was to be a totally faithful witness to what was handed down by and through them. Perhaps Presbyterian theologian John Macquarrie puts it best when he says (and his words, very rewarding, bear careful reading):

...Let me simply draw attention to the parallel between the episcopate and other "embodiments" (the canon of Scripture, the sacraments, the creeds) which we met when considering the first three notes of the church. The episcopate, like the others, protects by an outward institution the inner life of the church. In all the threats of heresy and perversion to which it has been exposed, not only in the early centuries but later, the church has held to its apostolic heritage....The episcopate cannot be treated as if it were on a different footing with the other embodied forms associated with the fundamental notes of the church.

[Professor John Knox] shows how the various features of the early Catholic church were intended to establish its unity and integrity, and...developments of the New Testament understanding of the church. In particular, he draws an analogy among the canon, the creeds, and the episcopate. All came to be regarded as "apostolic," which means that the early Catholic church which in reality established these forms (or in whose experience they were first established), thought of itself as doing no more than recognizing what had been established by the apostles themselves. It is not a question of whether, as a matter of historical fact, the apostles wrote the books ascribed to them in the New Testament; or whether the Apostles' Creed was actually composed by the apostles; or whether the apostolic ministry in the form of the historic episcopate was plainly and universally present from the beginning. We are to think of these rather in the context of the church as "a visible, historical community," possessing an identity and yet developing in response to new demands and opportunities. The point about the various forms is that although they required time before they developed to the point where they clearly emerge in history, they express the mind and character of the church as it had been since the apostles.[4]

Again, a bishop was authentic, not by necessarily being "ordained" by one of the apostles, but by being appointed by the church (which afterwards imposed hands on him) to lead it in witnessing to the apostolic tradition. Any bishop has "apostolic succession" who can trace his lineage to this function.

There is every indication that the church-community appointed the bishops or, in the words of Macquarrie, "established these forms." The authority to ordain was given to the church as a whole. The church could confer the powers on those whom it chose to be ministers in the church-communities. This whole idea will be new and perhaps startling to average Catholics, yet they should recall a parallel. It is constant Catholic tradition that, even though the commission to baptize was given in the gospels *only* to the eleven apostles, *any* person, even an unbeliever, can baptize. How to explain this unless the authority of the twelve to baptize was passed on *to the church*, rather than to individuals? It appears not too far-fetched to suggest that the power of ordination was handed down the same way. It is the church as a whole that is the recipient of the apostolic power and tradition. It seems evident that it was the church that called people to the office of bishop. As we shall see in the next chapter, this also explains the long tradition of the people electing their own bishops. It is of further interest to note that this very point was brought up at the bishops' synod in October 1971. The official report on priestly ministry contains these excerpts:

> As scholars reflect on the data of Scripture and the earliest tradition of the church, they realize that the older popular understanding of apostolic succession has been too mechanical and oversimplified. It has perhaps been too quickly assumed that the twelve apostles appointed immediate successors, from whom in turn further successors were commissioned in an unbroken historical chain down to the present day.
>
> Actually Scripture and early church life point rather to the view that bishops succeed to the mission of the apostles, and then only by way of partial assumption of their function, namely caring for the churches founded by earlier missionary apostles.
>
> Theological reflection suggests that in a sense it is the entire church which succeeds the apostolic college, a succession realized in a dramatic but by no means exclusive way by the episcopal college of the Catholic church. For this reason the episcopate must be more clearly linked to the Christian community, precisely to manifest its apostolic credentials.[5]

Thus, as Raymond Brown reminds us, the episcopacy, like the priesthood, was established by Jesus himself only in the same nuanced sense that it emerged, under the guidance of the Holy Spirit, from an implicit principle demanded by the nature of the church that Jesus founded. "The fundamental 'apostolic succession' is therefore that of the church itself and of each individual Christian...What is required is the perduring agreement with the apostolic testimony.... Apostolic succession is thus primarily succession in the apostolic faith and personal confession, as well as in the apostolic ministry and life...."[6]

THE COLLEGE

Another important aspect of early church structure in regard to the episcopacy must be mentioned. A person was appointed bishop, not merely as the ruler and head of this or that particular church-community, but also as a member of the larger church. He was brought into the "college," which had the whole church as a concern, even though he was rooted in one local church (or diocese). Therefore, to show a bishop's essential unity with all other bishops in forming this college, there arose the custom (and later the law from the Council of Nicaea) that at least three bishops must co-consecrate another bishop. This explains that even to this day in the various eucharistic prayers of our liturgy we find phrases such as:

We offer them for N. our pope,
for N. our bishop,
and for all who hold and teach the catholic faith
that comes to us from the apostles. (Eucharistic Prayer I)

Lord, remember your church throughout the world;
make us grow in love,
together with N. our pope,
N. our bishop, and all the clergy. (Eucharistic Prayer II)

Strengthen in faith and love your pilgrim Church on earth;
your servant, Pope N. our bishop N.
and all the bishops,
with the clergy and the entire people your Son has gained for you. (Eucharistic Prayer III)

These prayers reflect an ancient realization, gradually developed into a fuller understanding in medieval times, that a bishop must be sensitive to the needs of the entire church and is in relationship to the whole church as well as to the members of his particular church-community.

THE PETRINE MINISTRY

We must hasten to mention here briefly that there would be one person who would be the outward sign of this unity among bishops. There would be one person who would be the visible expression of the college, an external sign of the whole church: This would be Peter and his successors. It is not that the unity of the whole college proceeds from Peter; "rather, he amalgamates it into an effective unity."[7] The Catholic church is a network of local churches, every local church being united with every other by virtue of the fact that each bishop is "in communion" with the others through their common union with the bishop of Rome.

That the bishop of Rome, "the pope" as we name this particular bishop, would hold such a position seems to have deep roots in early Christian experience. The texts of the Christian Scriptures concerning Peter do not prove any kind of continuing office of supreme church authority, but on the other hand they do not rule out such a gradual development. It is clear in the Christian Scriptures that the images associated with Peter—fisher of men, shepherd, pastor feeding the sheep, the receiver of special revelation, the rock on which the church was to be built—eventually outdistanced the images used of other apostles in a significant way. And so, as one writer put it:

> For the Roman Catholic church that later development of the Petrine trajectory represents the Spirit-guided development of a direction already given in the New Testament. In part that development was determined by the accidents of history. And in part it was due to the eventual joining of the Petrine trajectory to a related but separate tradition which was also developing, that of the primacy of the Roman church.[8]

As a matter of fact, there are already several examples of the Roman church instructing other churches by the end of the New Testament period: for example, 1 Peter, 1 Clement (written about 96), Ignatius of Antioch (d. 107). So strong is the tradition of Roman preeminence that the 1974 Catholic-Lutheran statement *Papal Primacy and the Universal Church* acknowledges "a growing awareness among Lutherans of the necessity of a specific Ministry to serve the church's unity and universal mission while Catholics increasingly see the need for a more nuanced understanding of the role of the papacy within the universal church" (intro.). They ask their churches "if they are prepared to affirm with us that papal primacy, renewed in the light of the gospel, need not be a barrier to reconciliation" (n. 32). The 1976 Anglican-Roman dialogue notes that "the only see which makes any claim to universal primacy and which has exercised and still exercises such *episkope* is the see of Rome, the city where Peter and Paul died....it seems appropriate that, in any future union, a universal primacy such as has been described should be held by that see " (22-23).

The word "trajectory" is key here: a seedling that was to flower later. Even though Irenaeus (d. 180) stated that the Roman church possesed a fuller primacy and that special importance was attached to the apostolicity of that church, nevertheless for the first centuries no thesis was elaborated about this primacy until the time of Pope Siricius who left us the first extant decretal letter (385) dispatched to Spain, and Leo the Great (440–461). The latter made the claim that he had the fullness of power as successor of Peter "who," he said, "gave power to the other apostles." This claim was rejected by the Council of Chalcedon (451) and also by Leo's later successor, Gregory the Great (d. 604), who said that Leo's claims infringed on the rightful autonomy of local bishops.

In the history of this trajectory, which included Gregory's nod to "the autonomy of the local bishops," Jerusalem, of course, had a primacy of honor. After its destruction in 68–70, this honor shifted to Rome, the seat of the empire. Eventually, to counter the heresies and divisions that grew up, every local bishop claimed to have apostolic succession and his local church was considered as having its own internal norm. However, due to divisions within the local churches themselves, appeals were made to the larger, prestigious metropolitan churches, which were founded by the apostles, and its bishop who became the "first" or "arch"-bishop. Thus the Latin-speaking churches appealed to Rome, enabling the archbishop of Rome to grow in prestige. But, on the other hand, a similar prestige was also developing around the metropolitan churches of Antioch, Alexandria, and Carthage.

Interestingly, because none of these great metropolitan churches claimed to be the final court of appeal, it was the emperors who, in the light of "global" divisions and strife, convened the first ecumenical councils. Furthermore, neither Rome nor any Western church was invited to the first Council of Nicea. By the fifth century, five metropolitan churches had their spheres of influence and their bishops were called patriarchs: Rome, Antioch, Alexandria, Jerusalem, and Constantinople. When the Western empire collapsed in the early Middle Ages the growing friction and isolation between Rome and Constantinople finally allowed Rome to emerge as uncontested center of the church.

OTHER MINISTRIES

We are not finished yet. We have spoken about the twelve, apostolic succession, and the presbyter-bishops and their functions. To add to our confusion and uncertainty as to exactly what the organizational set up was for the primitive church, we have indications of other jobs. Strange ministries are mentioned in the Christian Scriptures and we simply do not know what they all mean. Here, for example, is Paul's first epistle to the church-community at Corinth (12:28): "You, then are the body of Christ. Every one of you is a member of it. Furthermore, God has set-up in the church first apostles, second prophets, third teachers, then miracle workers, healers, assistants, administrators, and those who speak in tongues." Elsewhere the Christian Scriptures mention other ministries such as deacons and widows. Who they were, and exactly what they did, we can only make intelligent guesses. Again, the obvious point is that there were a variety of ministries, that the church was not obviously confined to one particular structure, and that it need not be so now.

We are not confined to what is written in the Christian Scriptures. Not everything was written down there, as John reminds us (21:21-24). Paul himself quotes from the sayings of Jesus not found in the gospels. But the point is not what is *not* written down in the Christian Scriptures, but what is. And what is written down tells of a variety of church structure and ministry, that other variations besides the episcopal system are possible. As John McKenzie states:

> First of all, it is obvious that pluriform structure is general in the New Testament. Nothing suggests a uniform structure imposed from above. This does not imply that development beyond the New Testament is impossible or undesirable; it does imply that such a development, when it occurred, was based on other than biblical reasons. To the degree to which these reasons were historical other structures can be suggested by other historical reasons. Pluriformity is not contrary to the New Testament, whatever else it may be contrary to.[9]

CONCLUSIONS

From all that we have seen, it is evident that our original diagram at the beginning of this chapter will have to be altered. Probably it should go something like this:

1. Jesus	gathered the unique
2. Twelve Apostles	as the foundation of his community of disciples. These twelve appointed to service
3. The Deacons	and also what we might call
4. The "Secondary Apostles"	mainly itinerant preachers who founded church-communities and then moved on. They left the ruling of such places to
5. The Presbyterate	which was a committee appointed by the local church-community. In this presbyterate there were contained, or there emerged the
6. Single Monarchial Bishop	who, with all other bishops, formed a "college." This college both guided and reflected the community and presupposed a close rapport with it. The visible image of the total or universal church and hallmark of episcopal unity was the one who held
7. The Petrine Office[10]	which evolved from Peter's leadership wherever he was, since Peter exercised leadership when he resided in Jerusalem and in Antioch. When he went to Rome, the local church of Rome and the Petrine Office were joined. In addition, there were
8. Other Ministries	such as healers, teachers, prophets, widows, elders, etc.

Again, we must remember that in the first decades of the church the scheme of this diagram developed unevenly in the various local church-communities. Rome and Corinth, for example, seemed to have held on longer to the presbyterate. Yet, as remarked earlier, by the end of the second century the monarchial bishop was the general rule and has remained so to this day. It is interesting to compare the two diagrams. In the second diagram given here, the "apostolic succession" is implied in the way explained previously. The succession is a succession of the function to bear witness to the apostolic tradition. This function of bearing witness belongs to the church as a whole and to the collegial aspect of the episcopacy. But there are some practical conclusions for the modern Catholic looking back at this development of the church.

The point that comes across is that from the beginning of the new church the controlling ideal of ministry seems to be the communities' needs arising from their grounding in Christ and the apostolic tradition. Any structure that serves this ideal is legitimate. The church did not consider itself bound only to forms that Jesus used. Rather it took from him that perfect freedom to build up his body, the church, and to proclaim the good news in those forms and structures that best seem to do the job. This being so, we should not be surprised to discover in the Christian Scriptures and contemporary Christian writings a great deal of fluidity in ministry and leadership, and no absolutely fixed forms of either. That would come later after the church settled down; until then the catchword is development.[11]

In addition, since the church is a community with a formal structure, any free-floating ministries and any "underground" churches so popular in recent history must not only have some structure; they must have some contact with the larger church-community in order to maintain themselves in the authentic tradition. Also, wholly "spiritual" churches contradict Christian origins:

> ...The idea of a pneumatic church is an attractive one and always has been. A handful of dedicated Christians working in a community in almost invisible fashion, exuding good will and love, and unconcerned about mundane things such as finance, administration, and communication, sounds terribly appealing. But even if it were possible for a community of humans to exist without a formal structure (and it is quite impossible), those who would object to a structured church and would prefer a pneumatic one should take the matter up with the Founder who wanted His church to be a thoroughly human organization and seemed prepared to accept the fact that in this human organization there would be all kinds of human imperfections....[12]

ECUMENICAL DIMENSIONS

Finally, the fact that the episcopate was a structure that gradually developed in the early church-communities, rather than having been a firm blueprint handed down by Jesus himself (at least as determined from a critical reading of the Christian Scriptures), raises some interesting ecumenical speculations. The first and most obvious speculation is the question, "Is the episcopate *essential* to the church?" The episcopate, as we have seen, developed in history and it authentically points to apostolic foundations and tradition. Still, there were some community-churches in Paul's lifetime that had no bishops nor presbyters but lived in close harmony with neighboring community-churches that did. It was not even necessary that bishops be present to ordain. The average Catholic may be surprised to learn that priests may indeed ordain, and that there is a constant tradition which holds that there is no absolute distinction between bishop and priest. Gratian's Decree sums up centuries of theological opinion: "A priest is the same as a bishop and it is only by custom that bishops preside over priests." Theologian Harry McSorley writes:

> Is it any wonder, in the face of strong doctrinal, canonical, and historical tradition, that the Council of Trent refused to accept the proposal that the difference between presbyter and bishop was of divine institution? Such a definition would not only have condemned the continental reformers, but a great number of Catholic theologians and canonists as well, including at least two fathers of the church....Even after the Second Vatican Council a Catholic theologian is free to hold that, under certain circumstances, an ordinary priest may ordain another priest.[13]

The point is that even within the church there is a wide latitude concerning a variety of functions, offices, and ministries. If the Catholic church would permit valid ordinations without a bishop (under certain circumstances), why not allow the same for the non-Catholic denominations? In fact, the Catholic church declares them to be more than "denominations" but recognizes them as having membership in the church of Christ. The Decree on Ecumenism says, "Nevertheless, all those justified by faith through baptism are incorporated into Christ. They therefore have a right to be honored by the title of Christian, and are properly regarded as brothers in the Lord by the sons of the Catholic Church" (3). If basic membership in the church requires faith and baptism, is there any cause (provided that there is agreement on doctrine) why other ministries cannot be valid?

The ecumenical question is that, with such variations, might it not be possible for the church of today to also recognize and even legitimatize other forms of church-community rule other than that of a bishop? Could not the church, which made the original clergy, appoint others? Could not the presbyterate be revived? Not that it should be, but in theory it could be. More to the point, might not the Roman Catholic church recognize another church's clergy? This would presume, of course, that this other church would agree on the basic doctrinal essentials with the Roman Catholic church. If, for the sake of argument, it did, could not the Catholic church simply recognize the other church's clergy, and by this simple recognition and appointment "ordain" them? Raymond Brown, who raises these questions, adds these wise words:

It may be objected that entry into union with a non-episcopal church without insisting on episcopal ordination is tanta- mount to admitting that one form of church government is as good as another. This is not necessarily true: such a union does not deny our belief that episcopacy evolved in the church un- der the guidance of the Holy Spirit, but recognizes that through unfortunate historical circumstances some Christians have not been able to appreciate how the episcopacy serves as an effective sign of unity and apostolicity. In particular, we may think of the medieval period when bishops became lords or princes and when the absentee bishop was not exceptional. The lack of pastoral concern in this reaction led some of the re- formed churches to consider the episcopacy as a corruption of the gospel rather than as an effective means of perpetuating it. We cannot expect such churches, which in the meantime have developed an alternative structure suddenly to regain an ap- preciation of the episcopate, especially if our insistence on it prolongs the divisions of Christianity or if they are asked to ac- cept a ceremony of episcopal ordination in which they have no real faith. [14]

In the light of these words, then, a further flexibility in church- community structure is possible, and Catholic Christians may ex- pect some developments along these lines in the future.

That the history of the structures of the early church is quite com- plicated has been evident throughout this chapter. Catholic Chris- tians once thought that their present knowledge of the pyramid structure of pope down to parish priest was the only true structure. It turns out that there is much more variety than formerly thought. Theologians are investigating these points, and ecumenists are working hard to reconcile Catholic-Protestant structures.[15] The point is that the reader should at least be aware of the basis for the discussion. Members of the Catholic church should realize that a very open alive issue of the contemporary Catholic church is once again rooted in the history of early Christianity.

CHAPTER 4

Ministries, Worship and Practices

DEACONS

The deacon is given a prominent place in the variety of ministries and structures of the early church. The diaconate, or office of deacon, developed gradually in the primitive church, and may have had its inspiration from the office of the Jewish levite. Such levites were connected especially with Temple religious ritual and service and aid to the needy. The Jewish levites served as doorkeepers to the Temple, administrators, chanters, and keepers of the sacred vessels. They worked full time and were supported by the people. The Christian deacon simply appropriated all these functions for the new church-communities.

At the start, the office of deacon was loosely structured. Only gradually were precise guidelines established for them. A step toward this was taken in the famous episode in the Acts of the Apostles (6:1-6). Here is the story of the apostles appointing the seven deacons in response to the complaint that only the Hebrew-speaking widows were being taken care of, while the Greek-speaking widows were being neglected (the old rivalry again). To serve these, seven deacons were chosen and they were chosen as full-time leaders and administrators in the church. They were not part-time or minor officers.

The deacons' task generally fell into three main categories. First and foremost, they assisted in the liturgy. In the second century, Justin Martyr describes this diaconate function:

> At the end of these prayers and thanksgiving, all present express their approval by saying "Amen." This Hebrew word "Amen" means "so be it." And when he who presides has celebrated the eucharist they whom we call deacons permit each one present to partake of the eucharistic bread, and wine and water; and they convey it also to the absentees.

Tertullian informs us that deacons also assisted at the marriage ritual and that they baptized. During persecution, the deacons were sometimes the ordinary ministers of confession and reconciliation, as we learn from the African bishop Cyprian:

> They who have received certificates from the martyrs, and may be assisted by their privilege with God, if they should be seized with any misfortune and peril of sickness, should without waiting for my presence, before any presbyter who might be present, or if a presbyter should not be found and death becomes imminent, before even a deacon, be able to make confession of their sins, that, with the imposition of hands upon them for repentance, they should come to the Lord with the peace which the martyrs have desired, by their letter to us, be granted to them.

In this connection it is interesting to observe that as late as the time of Ignatius of Loyola, the founder of the Jesuits (sixteenth century), he and others, following the teaching of thirteenth-century Thomas Aquinas, believed that in an emergency one could confess to a layperson. This may have some origin in Cyprian's third-century deacons who could hear confessions.

Second, the deacons took care of the sick and needy. There is also some evidence in the church-communities of Egypt that the deacons were permitted to anoint the sick. Service to the community was their watchword. They dispensed the charity and distributed the community funds. For this reason, a most frequent admonition to the deacons was that they be honest people.

Third, the deacons helped to administer the church. In this they were very closely associated with the bishop. They often traveled with him and became his eyes and ears. Bishop Ignatius of Antioch could write, "I send you greetings in the Blood of Jesus Christ, wherein is joy eternal and unfailing; all the more so when men are at one with their bishop—and with their clergy and deacons too." Many deacons followed their bishops to death. When Cyprian himself was finally martyred at Carthage in 258, his deacons stayed beside him and were killed. When in that same year Sixtus II, bishop of Rome, was arrested, four of his deacons stayed with him and died with him. One of these was the famous St. Lawrence, the deacon with the gallows humor; he told the torturers who were burning him to death to turn him over as he was done on one side.

As bishop of Rome from 236-250, Fabian divided the city into seven administrative areas, each under the authority of a deacon and their assistants, the subdeacons. Deacons had the function of bringing the sacred gifts to the altar at episcopal consecrations. Thus, the deacons, from the beginning, assisted at the liturgy, aided the sick and needy, and administered in the church-communities. Yet, even in early times tensions were beginning to show themselves that would eventually undermine the whole diaconate office.

DECLINE OF THE DEACONS

Signs of tension were slight but real between deacons, bishops, and priests. Basically, the problem was one of power. The bishops and priests felt on occasion that the deacons were becoming too powerful. After all, they handled the money and ran much of the church's administration. It is quite clear, for example, in the church's first General Council of Nicaea that the permanent diaconate is taken for granted, but it is also clear that the deacons are being put in their place.

It has come to the attention of the synod that in some regions deacons give the eucharist to presbyters. This is in accord neither with canon nor custom, that those who do not have the power of offering give the body of Christ to those who offer. Moreover, it is known that some deacons attain the eucharist before the bishop. Let those things cease and let deacons remain within their proper place, knowing that they are ministers of the bishop and less than presbyters.... Nor may a deacon sit in the midst of the presbyters. This is done contrary to canon and order. If anyone does not wish to obey after these constitutions, let him desist from the diaconate (Canon 18).

What added to further friction was the growing power of the priests. As priests were given more and more functions, their roles became confused with that of the deacons, and the two suffered what we call an identity crisis. The deacons lost out. Ironically, in our times the problem has reasserted itself as laypeople take over more and more of the priests' former functions.

During the long and eventful centuries from Nicaea to the reformation the permanent diaconate at first flourished and then declined. The seeds of diaconal decline were already planted with the rise of sacerdotalism (growing power and office-functioning of the priests) in the third century and the restrictive legislation of the early fourth century. A confusion of roles between deacons and "priests" and a struggle for identity continued into the Middle Ages. Gradually the diaconate receded in importance until the diaconal order became merely a preliminary and ceremonial step to the sacralized priesthood. [1]

Although the trend of diaconate decline had begun, deacons remained very much on the scene through the ages. For example, the Irish are reminded that St. Patrick was the son of a married deacon and the grandson of a priest. Ambrose, Jerome, Augustine, and Athanasius (a former deacon) all mention deacons as being quite active. As a matter of fact, crotchety Jerome complained of them being too powerful, especially those at Rome. In fact, such deacons became so proficient in assisting Bishop Leo the Great (d. 461) in the management of Rome that they were known as the "bishop's deacons." The Middle Ages would continue to look upon the deacon as the bishop's vicar general. But friction was growing and the diaconate was being less a full-time permanent job and more a temporary office, perhaps for a maximum of five to seven years.

In time a new theme began to emerge ever more strongly; namely, that the diaconate was but a preliminary step to the priesthood. By the eighth century, a favorite comparison was that the deacon was like Jesus washing his disciples' feet, the priest like Jesus consecrating the bread and wine at the Last Supper, and the bishop like

Jesus solemnly blessing the apostles. By the tenth century, the diaconate had become almost totally a temporary and ceremonial order, although deacons still functioned in the capacity of assistants and aides to the bishops. Yet some still had great administrative powers. In the thirteenth century, Thomas Aquinas stated that deacons were clearly inferior to the bishops and priests. They could not baptize by power of their office but only as necessity demanded, and they could not administer the sacrament of the sick even in necessity. (In earlier times deacons did both jobs as part of their function.) By the time of the Reformation in the sixteenth century the temporary diaconate had been reduced to merely liturgical functions. With the coming of the city life even the deacons' traditional role of charity was taken over by new urban secular organizations.

RESTORATION

During the Council of Trent (1545-1563), there was a realization that the primitive diaconate should be restored in view of the great needs of the church. However, lurking in the back of many council fathers' minds was a fear of a too powerful diaconate (this had distressed Jerome in the fourth century). In addition, there was the worry that the role of the priesthood, already attacked by the reformers, would be further confused or lessened by a restored diaconate. Nevertheless, Trent did restore it, although it did not function. Trent saw the diaconate as a part of the order to the priesthood and, though its service aspect was stressed, this did not become implemented until after Vatican II.

Impetus for implementation came later from Germany. There the restoration of the diaconate was underway, especially as a result of the experience of World War II and the horrors of the prison camps of Hitler. A group who would serve was clearly needed. In 1951 the diaconate was reestablished. In 1957, Pius XII was sympathetic to a universal restoration, but felt the time was not yet ripe. Actually, what was worrying many prelates was another related issue: celibacy. If the church once more admitted married deacons, would this not erode the discipline of a celibate clergy? Would not married deacons undermine the unmarried priesthood? Still, the need was urgent, especially in large cities where a sense of community was lacking. Full-time deacons could do wonders in comforting the sick, baptizing babies, and helping to administer parishes. Finally, on

September 29, 1965, the bishops at Vatican II voted overwhelmingly in favor of the restoration of the permanent diaconate to serve as ministers of the word (preaching, reading lessons), liturgy (baptisms, distributing communion, and such), and charity. Guidelines were issued: a deacon may be ordained if he is twenty-five or older, but the young man must remain celibate. Married men of thirty-five or over may also be ordained (with the consent of their wives). The deacons would be incorporated into a diocese just as the priest is and paid as full-time workers by the diocese. What would be his duties? The Vatican decree states that, with his bishop's approval, the deacon may administer baptism, give communion and benediction; he may witness marriages if no priest is available, preside at funerals, preach, administer charities, and assist the laity. In the United States many dioceses provide for the training of deacons.

The return of the full-time deacon will obviously have many benefits for the community. Nevertheless, as we have mentioned, his return may have an unsettling effect on the life of the priest:

Since the third century priests have often preempted functions appropriate to deacons and laity. In America the parish priest sometimes became all things to all men. When America urbanized, specialized, and went to college the priest found his functions siphoned off one at a time by a progressively better educated laity. No longer was he the best equipped social worker, teacher, counselor, administrator, coach, lector, or even preacher in an area. Yet his familiar role as an activist among activists was so deeply ingrained that the priest of the secular age eventually found himself in a confused and, until people got over the shock, disedifying identity crisis.[2]

The point is that with the return of deacons the identity crisis has intensified. By admitting and reestablishing the permanent diaconate, the question of marriage and the ministry comes to the fore once again, the very question which troubled the bishops of Trent and Vatican II. A married diaconate—will it be the step to a married clergy? During his pontificate, John Paul II has repeatedly reaffirmed the importance of priestly celibacy.

But there is another irony to consider. If the return of the deacons have unsettled the priest's identity, in the 1980s the rise of the laity's participation in formerly clerical jobs have unsettled the deacon's identity. With the severe shortage of priests that characterized the decades after Vatican II, lay people have been pressed into baptizing, giving Communion, lectoring, witnessing marriages, leading base communities, heading schools and diocesan departments, and pastoring parishes. As a result the specificity of deacon has been called into question and some dioceses have put the whole permanent deaconate program on hold.

WOMEN DEACONS

The exact status of women in the early church is hard to discern because of contradictory practices. In 1 Corinthians 11:5, Paul raises no objection to women who prophesy or pray aloud in church, so long as they have their heads covered. Yet in 1 Corinthians 14:34-35, he says that "women should keep silent in churches." Despite this, Paul makes several references to two groups of women who appear to have had some official status in the early church communities: namely, "widows" and women deacons. While both were active in the earliest church-communities, by the third century "widows" as an official group had disappeared, and only women deacons were mentioned.

In the third century, Tertullian listed the women deacons among the clergy, while "strongly opposing their exercising any ecclesiastical functions."[3] The bishops at the Council of Nicaea I in 325 taught that women deacons were not to be received by the imposition of hands, because they were considered as numbered "among the laity"; this is an indication that somewhere they were being "ordained." Yet, at the Council of Chalcedon in 451, the bishops described, in canon 15, that women deacons were received by the "laying on of hands."

In summary, we can say that women deacons did minister in the early church, probably more visibly in the East than the West, but that they disappeared from the scene between the sixth and eighth centuries, possibly being absorbed into monastic communities.

By the early sixth century, however, some of these monastic communities of women were headed by an abbess who was installed with mitre, crozier, gloves, and pectoral cross (all symbols of the bishop's office). These mitred abbesses exercised considerable feudal power during the Middle Ages and were even in charge, like any bishop, of the lesser clergy, assigning and appointing them without restraint.[4] (The last mitred abbess was made to relinquish her authority in the late nineteenth century.) These women were not, however, considered to be clergy. In fact, the scholastic theologians of the late Middle Ages declared that women were inferior to men and incapable of receiving orders. Thomas Aquinas was only reflecting the prevailing opinion when he wrote, "Since therefore in the feminine sex there cannot be signified some eminence of grade, because woman has the state of subjection, so she is unable to receive the sacrament of order."[5]

Vatican II, in resurrecting the office of the permanent diaconate, left unmentioned the role of women and, to date, no women have been ordained as deacons. It is also of interest to note that, while the Pontifical Biblical Commission, which was asked to study this question, concluded in 1976 that there is no clear scriptural basis for the exclusion of women from ordination,[6] Vatican documents continued to uphold the traditional position that women cannot be ordained.

THE ELECTION OF BISHOPS

We have seen in the last chapter that there is no evidence that indicates that the apostles themselves appointed individual men to succeed them with all of their prerogatives. Equally certain, however, is that there was leadership. There was ministry, order, and office.[7] By the second and third centuries, the bishop was the important man in the church-communities, but still one beholden to and dependent on the entire church-community and elected by the people. Cyprian made the famous statement, "I decided to do nothing of my own opinion privately without your advice and the consent of the people." [8]

After Nicaea, in 325, there was a measurable decline of this interdependency between community and bishop in the East, though the West still held to it. The Eastern metropolitan became more autocratic, more closely allied with the state, and a powerful church-civil figure, especially in the large cities. Only 150 years after Paul the great Origen could complain about the Eastern bishops of the large cities being absorbed in their own power, associating with the influential, and cutting themselves off from the poor and needy. Commenting on such a situation, Thomas O'Meara, in a powerful sentence, says, "He (the bishop) was the judge of a past tradition now extensively separated from its intrinsic note of promise about man's future. He became a powerful prince and a potent piece in political chess."[9] But this should not have been, for ideally the bishop was (and is) intimately related to the community as servant, leader, and presider. Interaction was the keynote. Yet, as time went on, instead of leading the community, he simply became an archivist: he preserved the past without relating that past to the present and future growth of the community. He was no longer the leader of the eschatological community; he became a distant figure, separated charismatically and physically from his flock.

In the West, the close interaction between community and bishop continued a while longer. The people still chose their bishops for almost a thousand years, and it was only in the late 900s that the pope became involved when called upon to settle disputes arising from the election of bishops. Thus Celestine I of Rome (d. 432) said, "No bishop is to be imposed on unwilling subjects, but the consent and wishes of clergy and people are to be consulted." Leo of Rome (d. 461) said, "On no account is anyone to be a bishop who has not been chosen by the clergy, desired by the people, and consecrated by the bishops of the province with the authority of the metropolitan." A sixth-century council repeated the same idea: "No one is to be consecrated as a bishop unless the clergy and people of the diocese have been called together and have given their consent."

The real threat to popular election came from the princes, and a great struggle ensued between the rights of the community to elect the bishop and the right of the prince or emperor to confirm or veto the choice. But in the terrible confusion and chaos of the times the bishopric became, as in the East, a political prize. In the West, by the ninth century, the election of a bishop was confined to the clergy. By the tenth century, the laity and local clergy had no real say. Their vote, as it were, was taken over by the nobles and the aristocracy. In the eleventh century, the papacy and the monks worked together to free the elections and wrest them away from the princes and nobility. With social conditions not permitting safe and orderly local elections, the papacy gave more and more guidance as more and more appeals to settle election contests went to the pope.

Gradually the bishop ceased to be elected at all, and was chosen by cathedral chapters. By the twelfth century, only the elite were involved in the bishop's election: chapters, kings, princes, or pope. The people no longer had any say. Later the field dwindled even more as king and pope chose the bishop in an arrangement whereby the king continued to nominate, and the pope confirmed his choice.

This arrangement, as we shall see, continued right up to the nineteenth century, when, in 1801, Napoleon and Rome made a concordat agreeing that bishops and priests must take an oath of allegiance to the government, that the state would nominate bishops to vacant sees, and had the power to veto any bishops appointed by the pope. For the past century or more, however, the appointment of a bishop has been the pope's exclusive prerogative, free of state interest (except where concordats with certain governments made it otherwise). Thus was the evolution of the choice of bishops from popular election to papal appointment.

With the great masses of people coming into the church and the turmoil of the barbarian invasions, the church as a community of mature people in constant intercommunication inevitably got lost. Accordingly, the role of the bishop diminished from charismatic leader to preserver of law and order, civil servant, and guardian of orthodoxy. It was also inevitable that both chaotic times and large numbers should have allowed the election of a bishop over a community to be decided thousands of miles away by someone outside that community (a centralized papacy).

In recent time, there has been a distinct movement to restore the popular election of bishops and so make the words of Cyprian, Celestine, and Leo real once again. Several dioceses in the United States, for example, permit their clergy to propose nominees for the bishopric. On May 12, 1972, Pope Paul VI issued a document assigning priests and laymen parts in the process leading to the nomination of candidates for bishop. The final choice would rest with the Holy See, but now each bishop must make private consultations with his clergy and certain qualified laymen about the choice of a new bishop. This is still far from a democratic kind of choosing, but it represents a trend toward a more open church, and a return to some of the practices of the early church.

Finally, there is growing insistence in today's Catholic church that the bishop, who unwittingly became a kind of "president of the corporation," must change his image. It is fitting that the bishop come from the community that he serves and be chosen from among them and dialogue with them. In recent years Rome has tended to choose more conservative bishops, those clergy who are "safe" regarding strict orthodoxy of thought, teaching, and practice.

EARLY WORSHIP

There were several distinctive features about early Christian worship that can be seen even before the split from Judaism. Its liturgy included a baptismal rite and primitive formulas. There were also early creedal affirmations that arose in connection with baptism. The sayings and deeds of Jesus were developing into routine patterns which would then emerge in written form as the Christian Scriptures. Over and above the Temple/synagogue associations, the disciples and followers met privately. Paul tells us, though, that not all such meetings were harmonious. He speaks of drunkenness, and of people shouting and competing to be heard at the house-church liturgies (1 Corinthians 1:20-22). Their worship continued to be held in private homes, as noted at the end of the second century by Minucius Felix who wrote, "We have no temples and no altars."[10] Indeed the "church" was the church-community of the faithful who gathered for worship at the homes of hospitable Christians. But this was the key. In addition to the catechesis, almsgiving, works of mercy, and prayer mentioned in the Acts of the Apostles, the central act of unity and worship was the eucharistic meal.

The eucharistic meal liturgy followed the general lines of the synagogue service. There was the chanting of the Scriptures, the recitation of psalms, prayers, instruction, and hymns. After this instruction service ("liturgy of the word," as we call it), there was the great prayer of "thanksgiving" *(eucharistica* in Greek). This great prayer was called the anaphora or canon. It was a narrative telling of the wonderful works of God and thanking God for them. (This narrative aspect is most evident in our modern fourth Eucharistic Prayer.) The earliest eucharistic prayers we possess are found in the *Didache* written about 70 C.E. Some eighty years later we have this description of the whole liturgy from the writings of Justin Martyr:

> On the day called after the sun (Sunday), all gather for a communal celebration. The memories of the apostles are read as long as time permits. Then the one presiding admonishes his hearers to practice these beautiful teachings. We say prayers in common for ourselves, for the newly baptized, and for all others throughout the world. Then bread and wine are brought to him who presides over the brethren. He gives praise and glory to the Father in the name of the Son and of the Holy Spirit, and gives thanks at length for the gifts we have received from Him. The whole crowd standing up cries out in agreement, "Amen." Amen is a Hebrew word and means "so be it." Then the bread and wine over which the thanks have been offered are distrib-

uted among all those present. This food is known among us as the eucharist. The deacon brings a portion to those who are absent.

The celebrant was free to make up his own eucharistic prayer. About the year 215, the priest Hippolytus gave this model, which is very similar to our second and third canons of today.

The Lord be with you...and with your spirit; Lift up your hearts...we have lifted them up to the Lord; Let us give thanks to the Lord our God.... it is right and just. We give you thanks, O God, through your beloved Servant, Jesus Christ, whom you did send us in recent times as Savior, Redeemer, and messenger of your will...who, in order to acquire for you a holy people, stretched forth his hands in suffering that he might release from suffering those who believe in you. And when he was delivered up that he might abolish death and show forth the resurrection, he took bread and giving thanks to you said, "This is my Body which is broken for you." And likewise taking the cup, he said, "This is my Blood which is shed for you. When you do this, make memory of me." Making memory therefore of his death and resurrection, we offer to you this bread and chalice, giving thanks unto you for finding us worthy to stand before you. We beseech you to send your Holy Spirit upon the oblation of the church, to gather into one all your holy ones who partake of it, that we may glorify you through your servant, Jesus Christ, now and forever.

This certainly was not *the* Roman Mass of the third century, for at that time there was still no fixed formula, but only a fixed framework. As a matter of fact, variations in the eucharistic liturgy were present from the beginning, even concerning what we call today the "words of consecration."

As all of us know, the accounts presented by the three evangelists Matthew, Mark, and Luke, and St. Paul differ widely in many particulars. Not even the words which our Lord pronounced over the bread and wine are reproduced in the same form. And, besides, the oldest extant texts of the Mass present the account in still different forms. What can be the reason for this diversity? It seems that this diversity can best be explained by supposing that the varying biblical texts represent, not so many hazy recollections of what our Lord said at the Last Supper, but the actual liturgical usages of the primitive Christian communities, each shaping and developing its own redaction of the tradition. If this is true, as we believe it is, then the New Testament accounts of the Last Supper disclose the first glimmerings of the liturgical life of the Christian communities of the first century.[11]

Thus, in 215, Hippolytus presented his example only as a model, a suggestion. Still, the formats presented here were kept substantially throughout the ages, because nothing else in the church is as unchangeable as the eucharistic rituals. That is why, right up to the present day, every Mass contains elements already present in the second-century formulas. We might note that because the biblical psalms and canticles were so pervasive, hymn singing did not develop very far in the first centuries. Only in the fourth century, men like Paulinus of Nola and the great Ambrose would give poems and hymns to the church.

There was, however, one change in the third and fourth centuries that proved very significant—that was a change in the language of the liturgy. The original language of nearly all the liturgies in the early church-communities was Greek, the "official" language of the Roman empire at that time and the language understood to some degree by nearly all of the people. By the third century, most people in the West spoke Latin as their everyday language and no longer understood the language of the liturgical celebrations. Therefore, at the instigations of several bishops of Rome over the next one hundred years, the liturgical language in the West was changed from Greek, which people no longer understood, to Latin, their daily language, so that they might better understand the liturgy. This is a most interesting bit of history, considering the controversy over the changing of the liturgical language to the vernacular after Vatican II for the very same reasons, that people might understand. Keep in mind that Jesus and his disciples spoke Aramaic at the Last Supper. The East retained their more ancient rites and their liturgical languages of Greek, Syriac, and Coptic. The West became latinized, less effusive, and more open to Western cultural influences.

As we know, many changes in style, ceremony, and dress have occurred throughout the centuries. The pallium and the stole, for example, were introduced in the 320s when bishops were given the status of civil judges by Constantine. Although priests of all ancient times before Jesus wore special vestments at ceremonial time (note, for example, the Jewish high priest's vestments), Christian clergy did not wear distinctive everyday clothes. During the fourth century, Augustine dressed like everyone else, and his contemporary, Ambrose, remarked that it was by his charity that people were to recognize a bishop, not by his clothes. Actually the change came in the fifth and sixth centuries. After the barbarian invasions, the laity abandoned the long traditional Roman and Eastern dress in favor of the invaders' short clothes, while members of the clergy continued to wear the long robes (cassock). Special vestments existed for liturgical ceremonies but our modern church vestments are modeled from the dress of polite Roman society of the fourth and fifth centuries.

There is a certain fascination in seeing how, throughout the ages in the West, many additions to the eucharistic liturgy have obscured its meaning and purpose. Court and medieval ceremony, especially from France, intruded, as is evidenced in the ermine wrap of the bishop, the princely throne, the ring, the kissing, etc. Gradually the priest began to turn his back to the people, as the altar was pushed against the wall. The language became unknown (Latin) and physical separations such as the altar rail were erected. Obviously the people's role was effectively reduced to that of spectator. Undoubtedly out of concern for the passive lay spectators, a man in the Middle Ages named Amalar of Metz worked out in elaborate detail how every movement in the Mass was an allegorical presentation of Jesus' passion and death. The washing of the fingers represented Pilate, the cord around the priest's waist stood for the cords that bound Jesus, the last blessing was Jesus blessing his disciples before his ascension into heaven, etc. All this was well meant but it was simply erroneous. Such "passion play" interpretations were a far cry from the intimate meal sharing of the Last Supper. It would be only a matter of time until the insufficiency of this sort of allegorizing would become apparent. The pristine meaning of the Mass would be restored when liturgical renewal became a reality. In our own day, such renewal has been accomplished, but by no means completed. Pope Paul VI, in his apostolic constitution of April 3, 1969, felt obliged to appeal to the past:

> No one should think, however, that this revision of the Roman missal has been suddenly accomplished. The progress of liturgical science in the last four centuries has prepared the way. After the Council of Trent, the study of ancient manuscripts in the Vatican library and elsewhere, as Saint Pius X indicated in

the apostolic constitution *Quo primum*, helped greatly in the correction of the Roman missal. Since then, however, other ancient sources have been discovered and published, and liturgical formulas of the Eastern Church have been studied...."

POPULAR DEVOTIONS

Besides the official liturgical worship, there were popular devotions as well among the Christians of the early centuries. It was during the fourth century that Sunday became an official holiday, Christmas began to be celebrated in Rome, and Lent came into being. Other private devotions took their cue from the monks; prayer, fasting, and almsgiving. Perhaps the most prevalent popular devotion was the cult of the martyrs, honoring those who paid the final price of commitment (our word "martyr" is from the Greek for "witness"). Mass was often celebrated near and finally on the tombs of Christian martyrs. A lives-of-the-saints type of literature grew up, and relics became more important. The pilgrimage became a fixture of the Christian life, continuing through the late medieval ages. The modern mind finds it difficult to appreciate the medieval pilgrimage to the gravesite or relic of a popular saint. We have difficulty understanding that the sincere pilgrim, in gazing at the relic, was doing so not as a tourist, but as a believer deeply convinced of the supernatural, the after-life, and the intercession of God's friends. There was a spiritual involvement. Since the home of Christianity was in Jerusalem, this explains the desire of the Christian to go there, to visit the very spots trod by Jesus himself. This will be a factor in the first crusades that had all the earmarks of a great pilgrimage.

THE FERVENT CHURCH

It was inevitable that in its fervor the early church would tend to strictness in a variety of ways. A balance always emerged, but not before some Christians went too far, fell into heresy, and split off from the main body of the church. (We shall see some of these people in the next chapter.) But a certain strictness was evident in many ways, even for those who did not separate themselves from the church. For example, we have seen how the monastic movement (the one purely Eastern contribution taken over by the West) was partly inspired by the desire to live a more deeply spiritual life, free from the cares and distractions of this world. There was a desire to take the gospels seriously, and the fear that this could not be done "in the world." There were the Donatists in Africa (whom we shall mention in the next chapter), who felt that any Christian cleric who lapsed in time of persecution should not be readmitted to his ministry. Tertullian, who became so rigorous that he fell into heresy, was angry with the bishop of Rome for being lenient with grave sinners. It would seem that some Christians were so scandalized by Jesus forgiving the woman caught in adultery (John 8:1-11) that they tried to delete it from the Scriptures. Yes, fervor to the point of rigorism was an element. There are two areas in particular where rigorism shows up in the church: penance and celibacy. Let us look at them.

PENANCE

The early church was ever conscious, not only of sin, but that Jesus came to redeem the sinner. Jesus had said, "I have come to call sinners not the just" and even his deathbed legacy was his body "given for you" and his blood "shed for the remission of sins." Paul said that Jesus' death reconciles us with God. Baptism, of course, was *the* place for repentance and forgiveness. Baptism for the early Christians signified their putting on of the "new self," a total and unflagging dedication to the kind of life enjoined by the gospel. But some of the baptized did commit grave sin. Such an instance is seen in Paul's instructions about the treatment of the sinful man in 2 Corinthians 5:1-13.

It was the persecutions that seem to have led to the formation of a reconciliation ritual. By the second century persecutions had become the occasion for some followers of Jesus to renounce their faith (to lapse). When the threat of suffering became remote, some of these Christians (known as the lapsi) sought to return to the church-community. Some leaders said "no," but the opinion of Hermas prevailed—God wanted repenting sinners taken back, "but not repeatedly, for there is only one repentance for the servants of God." Thus, the practice of forgiving grave sins only once became the norm.

During the fourth century, a ritual developed that required the serious sinner (guilty of committing murder, apostasy, or adultery) to come before the bishop and acknowledge the sin committed. The sinner was then enrolled in "the order of penitents." Such a person was separated from the rest of the community by his or her not being permitted to receive the eucharist, and by being bound to do severe penances which could last for years. For example, these "penitents" had to wear clothes made of goat hair to symbolize their estrangement from the flock of Christ, or perhaps they had to carry chains that signified their slavery to sin. Reconciliation took place after the penance was completed at the Easter vigil, when the "new" Christians were received into the church. When such figures as John Chrysostom (d. 407) and Bishop Innocent I of Rome (d. 417) sought to introduce more leniency for repenting believers, they were severely criticized. Thus, from the fourth through the sixth centuries, the norm of "forgiveness only once" prevailed in the church. It should be easy to understand then why many Christians put off being reconciled with the church until they were on their deathbeds.

It was the Irish monks who developed a new form of forgiving. As part of their Celtic asceticism, they frequently confessed even their minor sins to one another. Soon the practice was adopted by the laity in Ireland, for the monastery had greater influence there than the episcopal structures. It was these Irish monks who introduced private confession to the mainland in the seventh and eighth centuries.[12]

By the beginning of the ninth century, frequent confession was urged (for example, by the great St. Boniface), and by the end of the ninth century, the confession of devotion was added. Needless to say, with the introduction of private confession the strictures on those three sins were lifted, but the existence of such a discipline shows once more the fervor of the early church.

CELIBACY

Celibacy has been an issue in the church throughout the centuries, but perhaps never more so than in recent times. Yet most people do not realize that while the *ideal* of celibacy is to be found in the gospels, the *law requiring a celibate clergy*, which is another matter, developed over centuries.

Not much is said about celibacy in the Christian Scriptures. It was Jesus himself who pointed out that his followers, to whom the hidden treasure of the kingdom of God had been revealed, could not really do otherwise than to leave all things, including the choice of marriage, and follow him. Once the disciple had discovered the kingdom, there could be no going back to married life (Luke 14:26) or to concerns about mere possessions (Mark 10:21; Matthew 19:21).

The contemporary theologian Edward Schillebeeckx summarizes this ideal in this way:

> It can only be explained on the basis of the incalculable inner logic of a total surrender to the kingdom of God, next to which everything else pales by comparison. In the synoptic gospels "celibacy" is not presented as an abstract idea, not as a requirement imposed from without, not even as a desideratum. Jesus approvingly states a fact of religious psychology: in view of their joy on finding the "hidden pearl" (Mark 4:11) some people cannot do otherwise than live unmarried. This religious experience itself makes them unmarriageable, actually incapable of marriage; their heart is where their treasure is. Paul already thematizes this experience; he sees its inner logic as an ideal towards which all Christians are invited (1 Corinthians 7:7-8; 28-35).[13]

There are, Jesus said, eunuchs for the sake of the kingdom of God, but not everyone can accept this; it is only for those to whom it is given (Matthew 19:11-12). Thus, there is no suggestion that there is a legal necessity that all Christians be unmarried. Rather, a religious experience of great force becomes, for some people, a condition that makes marriage impossible, not because they despise marriage, but because they are so caught up with the kingdom of God that it demands their undivided allegiance. We have already seen an example of such dedication to the service of the kingdom in those men and women who were the precursors of monasticism. Thus, from the earliest times celibacy was practiced by some within the Christian communities and it served as a mark of holiness. Some married clergy lived continent lives. Yet, at that same time, there was the old Gnostic "matter-is-evil" theme that regarded celibacy as attractive and marriage as evil. The church fathers resisted this interpretation vigorously. Most of them said that marriage was indeed very good—but virginity was better. However, there were a few, like Clement of Alexandria, himself a celibate, who suggested that marriage was more commendable. "One is not really shown to be a man in the choice of single life; but he surpasses men, who disciplined by marriage, procreation of children, and care for the house...has been inseparable from God's love."[14]

With all this ambiguity it is understandable that requirements for celibacy were slow in coming to the early church. A study of the patristic period reveals that there were both married and unmarried clergy among both priests and bishops.

LEGISLATION

This ideal of celibacy as necessary for total commitment to the teachings of Jesus was gradually raised to the level of church law as various local synods restricted the marriages of those deacons and presbyters who were already ordained, as in Ancyra in 315, Neocaesarea in 320 and at Nicaea, the church's first ecumenical council, in 325. In the East this has remained the law: a man may get married before ordination, but not afterwards.

Regarding the churches in the West, the pronouncement of Nicaea in 325 was taken as an ideal; many local synods and councils repeated the dictum that priests cannot marry after ordination and, if they do, that marriage is considered invalid. Yet history does record the names of many priests, and even a few bishops, who married after ordination and continued to function in the church. This ambiguity, however, did lead to abuses: there were priests or monks who did not marry, but who "kept" a woman in a house nearby; there were married men who deserted their wives in order to become priests. (This last was eventually forbidden by civil law: however, if the man could persuade his wife to enter a convent, he could be ordained.) Such scandalous behavior on the part of the clergy was denounced by many reformers from the Middle Ages through the Reformation.

Primarily through the influence of monasticism, where celibacy had always been mandatory, enforcement of clerical celibacy was accomplished. Through the efforts of those monks who became bishops and popes, the clergy were reformed and celibacy was mandated. In particular, it was Gregory VII (1073-1085), formerly the Benedictine monk Hildebrand, who effectively enforced the ban on clerical marriages, even persuading secular powers to help bishops enforce church law. Thus, civil governments forcibly separated priests from their wives, and the children of priests were declared bastards with no right of inheritance. In 1139, the Second Lateran Council made it obligatory that in order to be ordained a man must be celibate. This law in the West has been repeatedly upheld from the Council of Trent in the sixteenth century to the popes of the twentieth century. Some have suggested that the medieval church wanted a celibate clergy so that clergymen's sons would not inherit church property. This was certainly one motive, given the feudal arrangement of medieval society (as we shall see) but only a minor one.

In modern times there have been two developments on the issue of celibacy. The first development is that the bishops of Vatican II have been cautious not to offend the dignity of the married laity. Thus, the phrasing concerning celibacy simply says that celibacy makes it "easier" to give oneself totally to God. In a word, celibacy is not essentially bound up with the priesthood but has a close connection with it. The second development concerns the real issue, which is *not* "Is there any connection between Jesus and celibacy?" for we have seen that there is. The real issue is one of law. Can the church, should the church, require clerical celibacy by law? Can a freely given charism be legislated? Some would contend that there has not been due emphasis given to the other words of Jesus, "Not everyone can accept this" (Matthew 19:12). What about those who cannot? Must they be denied the priesthood? This question will certainly be addressed again as we approach the turn of the century when, futurists have predicted, church membership will increase by 10 percent and the number of clergy will decrease by 50 percent.

THE IDEAL OF THE PRIMITIVE CHURCH

One of the most enduring examples of fervor in the early church is the splinter group. This is the group, whether it remains within the church or breaks off from it, which seeks a firmer, more basic Christianity. Some of these groups have remained within the church, such as the monks and religious orders; others have broken off, such as the early heretics, the Montanists, and Donatists. The noteworthy thing, however, is that there exists almost a tradition of "radical" groups (in the sense of "root" Christianity) up to the present day. This radicalism is usually some aspect of a rigorous fervor, an imitation of some of the demands of the early church. There is a loose term called the "Believers Church," which refers to those who claim that it was really the heretics who have maintained Christianity in its pristine purity throughout the centuries. These same Christians claim that, especially after Constantine (whom we shall meet in the next chapter), when the Roman empire and the Christian religion joined, Christianity went off course. These small groups, considered heretical by the larger (political-religious) body, claim that they have kept the candle of the primitive church lit. As we shall see in the chapter of the Reformation, the main thrust of such "heretics" was to look backward, in order to restore what they considered the virtues of the primitive church.

Especially in the centuries preceding the sixteenth-century Reformation, there was a plethora of sects with strange-sounding names: Albigenses, Waldenses, Manicheans, Cathars, Humiliati, the Poor Men of Lyons, Publicans, Henricians, Leonists, Varini, Brethren of the Free Spirit, Lollards, Picards, Fraticelli, Anabaptists, Quakers, Moravians, Hutterites, the Plymouth Brethren, Mennonites, Disciples of Christ, Methodists, etc. All would claim (along with the major Reform bodies) that Roman Catholicism and even early Protestantism had obscured the basic primitive church as "founded" by Jesus. These various sects held that their own particular denomination represented a return to that ideal or, at least, a survival of the original fervent church of apostolic times.

Actually there is a certain misconception held by the Reformers of the sixteenth century and the Believers Church groups that idealized the primitive church. For example, one has only to read Paul's first epistle to the Corinthians to find that the early Christian church communities contained factions, jealousies, hatred, backbiting, and lack of charity. Paul scolds the Corinthians for being divided into factions over him and a man named Apollos, for putting up with one of their congregation who entered an incestuous marriage, for relapsing into impurity, and so on. He gives many practical and disciplinary directives, all indicating that the pristine church-community was made up of human beings still in need of redemption.

A CHURCH OF CHARISMS

It is also worth noting that, in time of stress, one or other charismatic aspect of the primitive church would again be taken. As we shall see, for example, when certain Protestants got tired of all the sterile theological wrangling and fighting with the Catholics and other Protestants, they retreated into pietism, a movement centering on the emotions and feelings. The Quakers were one of those movements, with their emphasis on the "inner spirit" and prophesying. The Moravians represented a group which wanted to go back to the communal Christian living as described in the Acts of the Apostles. The Amish in our country are a group of Moravians who live in early Christian simplicity and represent a return to primitivism. Such groups longed for the simplicity, common living, sharing, and the charisms they found in the Christian Scriptures.

In the early 1970s one growing phenomenon of a return to some of the charisms of the early church was the pentecostal movement among Roman Catholics. In fact, it has come to be called a Charismatic Renewal and puts the emphasis on a deep experience of the Holy Spirit in the lives of its members. There is a tendency to emotionalism, the practice of prophesying and the speaking in tongues—charisma of the Christian Scriptures. Pentecostalism in the U.S. Catholic church started in the mid-1960s at Duquesne University in Pittsburgh and then moved to Notre Dame, Indiana. By 1968 there were about 150 participants at the convocation at Notre Dame. In 1969 the number had grown to 450; in 1971 there were 1,400 people, and by the 1972 meeting there were over 11,500 Catholic Pentecostals coming together. By the late 1980s, the U.S. Catholic bishops began presenting diocesan convocations on the Catholic Television Network of America on the Saturday before Pentecost.

The important point for us is to note how sensitive the leaders of the pentecostal movement have been to the dangers that lurked in similar movements in the early church. Three main problems that troubled the early groups are precisely the problems that the leadership warns against now: emotionalism, anti-intellectualism, and elitism (which implies splintering off). The affinity to the early church, and particularly to the gifts of prophesying and speaking in tongues among Pentecostals, is unmistakable. The simple point we wish to make here is that no one can appreciate and assess the various "Believers Churches" or religious movements within the church without knowing something of the early church and its experiences.

We now leave the early church, its structures, ministries, and practices. The apostles are dead, the church-communities are spread all over Asia and Europe, and the persecutions are reviving in full vigor. Still, organization has been improved and the church has gained in strength and numbers. In fact, very shortly a new age is approaching for the church: a day of liberty, freedom, and theological refinement. The age of Constantine is at hand, and to this we will turn in the next chapter.

CHAPTER 5

The Fight for Orthodoxy

CONSTANTINE

Politically, during the third and fourth centuries, the Roman Empire was going through severe crises. There were civil wars as Roman leaders vied for the imperial power. Eventually the army wound up making and breaking emperors. From 217 to 253, there were twelve emperors and not one of them died a natural death. After 253, it is difficult to count the emperors enthroned and deposed. This internal power problem was certainly a great source of weakness. There was, however, another source of weakness, an external problem that we shall talk about in the next chapter: the constant pressure on the empire's borders. Applying this pressure were the great Germanic barbarian hordes. We might also mention the chronic financial chaos of the empire and problems of inflation and famine.

Finally, in the year 303, the emperor Diocletian decided on a plan to help stabilize the empire. He divided the vast empire into two sections, the East and the West. Each section was to be administered by a senior emperor, the Augustus, assisted militarily by a junior emperor, the Caesar, who had the right of succession. This, Diocletian hoped, would prevent the frightful and destabilizing infighting over the throne. To further assist this plan, Diocletian voluntarily resigned and Galerius took his place: the senior emperor, Constantius Chlorus and his junior partner, Severus, in the West, and Galerius and his junior partner, Maximinus, in the East. Unfortunately, upon the death of Constantius Chlorus, the plan broke down. His son, Constantine, usurped the power when Severus, the rightful successor, was killed by another usurper, Maxentius.

In the midst of all this political maneuvering Constantine startled many by becoming a member of the minority sect of Christianity (though he remained unbaptized till his deathbed[1]). He reputedly saw a vision over the Milvian bridge where he was to meet his rival. The vision, according to Eusebius, who was writing some twenty-five years later, was a cross in the sky with the words around it saying, "In this sign you will conquer." It is said that Constantine had this sign painted on his shields. He defeated his rival, Maxentius, thus becoming sole emperor of the West. One of his first acts was to give Christianity freedom by putting it on an equal footing with all other religions as Galerius had done in the East. Finally, in 324, Constantine became the sole emperor of both East and West.

With a status equal to that enjoyed by members of the pagan cults, Christians could worship publicly and their priests were exempt from civic duties. Constantine could and would go no further than this, for the vast majority of his subjects were still pagan and he had no intention of alienating them. For Christians this was enough. Now they were free. The emperor himself was one of them. Persecution would be no more, except for a brief period under Julian. Soon, under the emperor Theodosius I, Christianity would become the state religion (381), and paganism would be outlawed (392).

CHURCH AND STATE

We must take time here to point out the implications of what it meant for Christianity to be free and later to become the state religion. It meant that from the beginning of its full freedom Christianity was allied with the empire. It meant that a tradition was started which held that Christianity best flourished under the protection of the empire; that, indeed, the empire and the emperor were really divinely appointed to rule and to render that protection. The thousand-year union of the Christian state and Christian church had its origin here. The beginnings of the church-state theory were laid at this time. The church needed the empire and the empire needed the church. It seemed that they were partners divinely ordered to run the world. But, like other partnerships, at times there were struggles for domination of one over the other. Sometimes the church had the upper hand and sometimes the state did, even though, in theory, they were cooperating "for the sake of the kingdom of God."

We cannot fault the early Christians who looked upon the church-state union this way. Having just emerged from some two hundred and fifty years of persecution and semi-terror, it would be quite understandable that they would look upon Constantine and the empire as their champions. It was a very easy step to feel, in the afterglow of release and freedom, that the empire and the church were made for each other. We can sympathize with one bishop who later attended the Council of Nicaea. As he walked down the long aisle between scores of Roman soldiers to take his place beside the emperor himself, he rightfully wondered if the millennium had arrived. The scars of persecution were still on his body. Could he be blamed for his thoughts? Later, could even the great Augustine be blamed if he said that the empire was divinely ordained for the church? Indeed, the alliance from the start seemed to be a "natural" one.[2] But it turned out not to be always the best alliance, as shall be seen.

In the years ahead another very logical result occurred from the empire's liberation of the church. The church assimilated the Roman organizational genius, and the "diocese," the unit into which a province was divided, became the area of jurisdiction for a bishop. The church also acquired various external trappings; such as large buildings, court ceremonies, and discipline.

Later, in 330, as the emperors abandoned the West for the new capital at Constantinople, a power vacuum was left at the ancient capital of Rome that was filled by the bishop of Rome. Thus it was that the West looked to Rome's bishop for leadership on matters of both church and state.

Bishops freely presided over their subjects, indeed, which the emperor allowed. The bishops thereby became a kind of privileged class. In fact, the bishops in the chief towns of the empire came to be known as archbishops. The bishops of Jerusalem, Antioch, Alexandria, Constantinople, and Rome were known as patriarchs. The Roman patriarch was considered to be preeminent by many, for he could claim descent from Peter who died in Rome. It was also during the fourth century that the church was granted the right to own property and to manage its own affairs.

We see here also the beginnings of two separate jurisdictions and systems of penalties. In the future, emperor and pope would clash over clerical immunities. Nevertheless, having its own laws, the church was truly becoming a separate power, co-equal in its spiritual realm to the empire in its political realm. The foundation theory of the two swords, that is, the spiritual and temporal powers, working closely together, was being laid down.

> Christianity thus became the official, and gradually also the normal, religion of the Roman Empire. The effect on the church was mainly bad. As converts came in no longer by conviction, but for interested motives or merely by inertia, the spiritual and moral fervor of the church inevitably waned. To the empire the official change of religion made little difference: the old corruption and oppression of the masses by officials and landlords went on unabated, and the last remnants of public spirit faded away. Nor is this surprising for the object of the church was not to reform the empire but to save souls. To contemporary Christian thought the things of this world were of little moment, and the best Christian minds preferred not to touch the pitch of public life lest they be defiled. Men of high conviction and character became bishops or hermits, and government was left in the main to careerists.
>
> Nevertheless, to the future of Christianity its official adoption by the empire was momentous, for Christianity thus acquired the prestige and glamor of the Roman name; it became synonymous with that ancient civilization whose grandiose buildings, stately ceremonial, luxurious life and ordered discipline fascinated the uncouth barbarians of the north....[3]

COUNCIL OF NICAEA

All that we have just said was to develop in the near future. For the time being we now return to Constantine. It has been said by some that in Christianity he perceived the cement of unity for his vast empire. But in this he was to be disappointed. Christianity, he discovered, was often divided within itself. The first infighting he experienced was the Donatist heresy. It arose this way. In previous persecutions some Christians had lapsed from the faith. Some even handed over the Scriptures to be burned. There were those who were willing to readmit the former to the faith but not the latter. The bishop of Carthage opposed such rigorists led by a certain Donatus. This controversy, plus the chronic political rivalries among the Africans, aggravated the situation. The matter was brought to Constantine and he in turn referred it to a synod of bishops from Rome, Arles, Autun, and Cologne. The synod sided against the Donatists, who refused to submit. Then Constantine called a local council at Arles which, in 314, also condemned the Donatists. They still rejected the condemnation. Violence broke out and the Donatists stayed on to plague the church in Africa until its fall to Islam in the eighth century.

Right after this the most disastrous heresy in the early church broke out: Arianism. It too began in Africa, in Alexandria. Arius held that "there was a time when the Son was not," thus reducing the Christ to a creature, like humans but exalted over them. His opponent, Athanasius (a deacon at the time), held that Christ was the Son of God and existed as such from all eternity. Constantine, fresh from the intrigues of the Donatist controversy, was horrified at the prospect of another schism within the Christianity he had hoped would bind the empire. At last, he took a step which would become a precedent for many ages: he decided to settle the matter by consensus. He would call a worldwide, or ecumenical, council. Thus he sent a circular letter to all of the bishops:

> That there is nothing more precious in my eyes than religion is, I think, clear to all. Whereas it was previously settled that the congress of bishops should be at Ancyra or Galatia, it has now been decided for many reasons that it should meet in the city of Nicaea in Bithynia...in order that I may be near to watch and take part in the proceedings. I therefore inform you, beloved brethren, that I wish you all to meet as soon as possible in the above-mentioned city of Nicaea....

There was not an overwhelming response to the emperor's letter. Sylvester, bishop of Rome, excused himself on the grounds of poor health and old age but sent two deacons to represent him. Bishops from both East and West did come, however, and so in 325 the first ecumenical council of the church, the Council of Nicaea, was held. Constantine took an active part in the proceedings and no doubt his royal presence stifled some freedom of discussion. Nevertheless, the Council of Nicaea pronounced against Arius and adopted the word "consubstantial" to denote the two Persons of Father and Son sharing the one divine nature of the Godhead. "Consubstantial," the word proposed by Constantine himself (prompted by Hosius, his Spanish bishop-advisor), and the formula of the Trinity were on their way to being fixed. But not everyone was satisfied with the word because, for the first time, doctrine was stated in philosophical rather than biblical terms. The creed of Nicaea containing the controversial word pleased neither the Orthodox party nor the Arian party, but no one dared to tamper with it until after the emperor's death. Arius was banished by Constantine from the empire. Here for the first time we have the state inflicting a civil punishment on someone the church judged to be a heretic. This was the foreshadowing of the various inquisitions of the Middle Ages.

Other pertinent matters were settled at Nicaea. For example, the council decreed that bishops must be consecrated by at least three bishops (as we saw in the last chapter). Bishops and clergy were not to wander from city to city but to reside in their own sees. The practice of kneeling at prayer on Sundays and during the time between Easter and Pentecost was condemned. Inasmuch as the Eastern position of prayer was standing, kneeling was condemned, then tolerated and then, in the West, became the normal praying position. Bishops, priests, and deacons were not to have female companions to keep house for them unless they were relatives. Another motion at the council provided that if a man were already a married priest he did not have to separate from his wife (a motion to the contrary was voted down). Instead, an old rule was kept; a man could marry before ordination but he could not marry after ordination. Also, at this council the bishops agreed that Easter should be celebrated by all Christians on the Lord's Day, Sunday, the day of the resurrection rather than on the 14th of Nisan (the Jewish Passover), as many in the East had done since earliest times. This had been a sore point between Christians in the East and the West for a very long time. Once more, Constantine set the tone for anti-Semitism by declaring, "It seems unworthy to calculate this most holy feast (Easter) according to the customs of the Jews who, having stained their hands with lawless crime, are naturally, in their foulness, blind in soul."

CHRISTIAN INTOLERANCE

In the year 330 Constantine made a momentous political decision. He transferred his capital from Rome to the old town of Byzantium in the East. He renamed it "New Rome" (later renamed Constantinople in his honor), and rebuilt it over the next five-and-a-half years, filling it with grand buildings, monasteries, and convents. Here art, music, and architecture flourished. In a word, a whole new civilization emerged from Constantinople, the Byzantine Empire, a combination of the West and the East. The vacancy at Rome was quickly filled by its bishop, to whom the people turned for leadership and assistance. Constantine died in 337, having been baptized on his deathbed by an Arian bishop. His empire was divided between his two sons, one of whom supported the Orthodox creed and the other the Arian creed. For the next fifty years the empire was divided over the issue of Arianism. It has been estimated that at the time of Nicaea only about 50 percent of Christians believed that Jesus was divine.

This religious division was settled in a way that startled both sides. In 361, the emperor Julian succeeded to the throne. He was a mystical type, favorable to religion but disenchanted with Christianity for its harassment of the pagans. He therefore restored paganism and persecuted the Christians. Only his death in 363 brought relief. He was succeeded by Theodosius I, the emperor who not only restored Christianity but made it the official religion of the empire. The church naturally began to grow stronger under such auspices. The clergy were given privileges, and monasticism was growing. Ancient philosophers were being bent to the service of the church and intolerance of the pagan was increasing.

We have already taken note how pagan temples were sacked and that being a pagan or denying the Trinity were punishable by death. Not all Christians were pleased with this, of course. Men like Hilary of Poitier (d. 367) preferred reason and refused to use force against the pagan. His approach to the pagan in his writings was to foreshadow the great medieval scholastic tomes. Hilary, however, was the exception. More common was the attitude of Augustine, who appealed to the political arm to suppress heresy. In fact, Augustine would refine the church-state relations by proclaiming in his famous *City of God* the superiority of the church over the state. (By stressing the church's spiritual foundation he did the church a great service: when the barbarian invasions that occurred in his lifetime shook the old Roman Empire to its foundations, the church did not topple with it.)

FOUR MORE COUNCILS

Since the Arian controversy was still raging, Theodosius called another council, the second ecumenical Council of Constantinople in 381. (We notice that the first eight ecumenical councils were called by the Byzantine emperors rather than the bishops of Rome.) Arianism was condemned again and Nicaea's creed was reaffirmed and expanded to include belief in the divinity of the Holy Spirit. (This creed of Nicaea-Constantinople is what we have come to know as the "Nicene creed.")

If this council settled the Arian question, it raised others. One issue concerning the see of Constantinople was to be a problem for centuries. The council gave to the bishop of that see a new prestige based on the fact that it was now also the imperial capital. After the bishop of Rome, the council said, the bishop of Constantinople was to rank next. This was a dangerous step in a growing web of ecclesiastical rivalries. Already, for example, there were hard feelings between the centers of Antioch and Alexandria, which represented different schools of theology. Arius was an Alexandrian who had studied at Antioch, and it was an embarrassment for Alexandria to have him condemned by two councils. When the see of Constantinople was vacant twice, an Alexandrian candidate was set aside in favor of the recent incumbent, John Chrysostom, who had been deposed by a series of intrigues. This sort of jealousy among the cities gives the clue to the future problem caused by the council's nomination of Constantinople as the second see of importance, putting it over all other Eastern patriarchs. It would not be long before there was a rivalry, and eventually a split, with Rome itself.

More major heresies and more councils were in the offing. The issues were as confusing as they were often symptomatic of factional rivalries mentioned above. Still, on the benefit side, there was a growing unfolding of the meaning of what Jesus said and did and who he was.

These great councils performed a great negative service. They did not exhaust all the meanings of the Christian religion, nor did they set Christian belief into one final, everlasting formula. They did not pretend that they said all there was to say about Jesus, the Christ.

They only said that whatever he is and whoever he is and whatever he did and whatever his life meant, it is *not* what the heretics claim. What Jesus did mean would have to be unfolded as the centuries passed, and every age would have its own particular insight. Thus, the council's definitions were negative guides to what Jesus did not mean, whatever else he meant. Some later churchmen would try to use the formulas of a council like that of Chalcedon as positive statements; that is, that the statements contained the final accurate word on revelation concerning Jesus, the Christ. These churchmen failed to understand the conciliar statements as negative guides to be used in the search for fuller truth. Scripture scholar John McKenzie expresses the idea:

> In these early heresies, the church acted as teacher rather than proclaimer.... Had heretics not introduced the language of Greek philosophy to define the content of their belief, the church would not have had to employ the same language to define Catholic belief....The church then became aware that, if this belief is to be safeguarded, other propositions not directly belonging to belief must also be safeguarded....Thus in the Christological and Trinitarian controversies of the fourth and fifth centuries, the simple statement of belief that Jesus is the Son of God was not enough; the church also arrived at fairly precise definitions of nature, substance, and person, which permitted it to formulate its Christological and Trinitarian beliefs as belief that God is three persons subsisting in one nature. Was it necessary that belief be formulated in these terms? Absolutely speaking, it would seem that it was not, but one can rarely speak absolutely in history and cover all the facts. So many erroneous ways of stating belief appeared that the church settled on a single formula which would remove the errors which it knew. The formula would not necessarily protect it against errors which it did not know.[4]

The issue which provoked the church's third ecumenical Council of Ephesus in 431 centered around Nestorius, the bishop of Constantinople. Nestorius had difficulty with Mary's title as "Mother of God": how could a human being be the mother of God? So he taught that Mary was the Mother of the Christ or the God-Man. To some this suggested that Jesus was two persons—God and a man. Bishop Cyril of Alexandria took up the fight, defending the Orthodox position that Jesus was one person with two natures.

We should notice that he was bishop of Alexandria, and as such a rival to the Antiochene school of thought represented at Constantinople. Cyril sent protests to Celestine, the bishop of Rome, who condemned Nestorius while asking Cyril to receive his submission. But Cyril went beyond these instructions. Instead, he drew up a series of twelve propositions that Nestorius was required to sign. This would hardly be likely since the propositions were written in distinct Alexandrian terminology which was in direct contradiction to Antiochene theology. It would be like General Motors signing a safety promise couched in the slogans of Ford. So Nestorius appealed to the emperor while the twelve propositions made the rounds, stirring up all kinds of controversy.

In 431, the Council of Ephesus was called, but unfortunately it turned into a network of intrigues and complications. Although the delegates of the bishop of Rome were late in coming and the members of the Antioch school were delayed, Cyril opened the council without them. Nevertheless, the council condemned and desposed Nestorius. When the people from Antioch arrived, they denounced the council. The emperor arrested both Cyril and Nestorius until a full council could convene and settle the issue—which it did, in favor of Cyril and against Nestorius. Thus, the hard feelings between Alexandria and Antioch were further aggravated.

COUNCIL OF CHALCEDON

Some of the followers of Nestorius claimed that Jesus would be two persons if he had two natures. Thus, another heresy appeared, that of Monophysitism, which taught that Jesus had but one divine nature (thereby denying his humanity). Again, the issues involved were argued from opposite sides by the two schools of Alexandria and Antioch. It was an involved situation with much conflict of personalities, intrigue, deposition, imprisonment, and the interference of the emperor. Finally, in 451, the fourth ecumenical Council of Chalcedon was called, and the heresy was condemned with a definition of faith gathered from previous teachings by Leo, bishop of Rome.

Our Lord Jesus Christ is one and the same Son, the same perfect in Godhead and the same perfect in manhood, truly God and truly man, the same of a rational soul and body, consubstantial with the Father in Godhead, and the same consubstantial with us in manhood...one and the same Christ, Son, Lord, only-begotten, made known in two natures without confusion, without change, without division, without separation, the difference of the natures being by no means removed because of the union.

This marks the first major Western contribution to church teaching.

At the Council of Chalcedon other matters were discussed. One was a protest of imperial interference in church affairs—a kind of first official sally in the general warfare between church and state that would fully erupt in the future. Another decision was the reaffirmation of the primacy of honor for the see of Constantinople after Rome. This brought protests from Leo at Rome,[5] as well as from Antioch and Alexandria. One of the more far-reaching results from Chalcedon was not any doctrinal pronouncement but an emotional reaction. Once more the school of Alexandria met defeat at the hands of a council. The clergy and the monks were so upset that they rallied to the side of their bishops and formally denounced the whole Council of Chalcedon. They elected heretical Monophysite bishops to their sees who were only expelled by imperial troops. Yet many of these anti-Chalcedon Christians gathered together to form the Coptic church (so called for the language of their liturgy). In time, some returned to orthodoxy and today our Catholic church includes Catholic Coptic Rite Christians.

The East was thus more divided than ever along religious lines. (The West, as we shall see in the next chapter, was too busy with the barbarian invasions.) As usual, every emperor was desirous of healing such politically debilitating divisions. As usual, that faction that had its own emperor dominated (and persecuted) all others, thereby adding to religious chaos.

The fifth ecumenical council of the church (the second Council of Constantinople) met in 553 as another attempt to heal the split caused by the Monophysite heresy. It was convoked by the emperor Justinian, the last of the Latin-speaking rulers. This was a strange council. It decided that, to clear the air once and for all, a solemn condemnation should be made against all those theologians who were friendly to Nestorius and his teachings. Of course, all such theologians and Nestorius himself were dead, so this was to be a posthumous condemnation. The only problem was that some theologians were involved who had also upheld the decisions of Chalcedon. It is not difficult to understand the uproar, street-fighting, and revolt caused by this approach. Even the dissenting Bishop of Rome, Vigilius (d. 555), at this point was kidnapped by Justinian (who kept him prisoner for ten years), and only later would this old man, past his eighties, yield to the plan of posthumous condemnations.

After Justinian's death the empire went into political decline. Some fifty years later a new emperor regained some of the prestige, but in striving for unity he ran once more into deep religious divisions—divisions more intolerable than ever in the light of the new Muslim power on the horizon. Once more a new plan was put forth to reconcile religious differences. Once more the plan involved another formula which not only contained the old Monophysite heresy but gave birth to a new one, Monothelism, which held that there was one will (a "unity of wills") in Jesus. The emperor Heraclius accepted the formula and so did the Monophysites. Unfortunately, when this formula was presented to Honorius I of Rome (d. 638), he missed the point and in essence agreed with the heretical statement. Naturally, his approval helped spread the new heresy of Monothelism. In 649, Martin of Rome held a synod that renounced monothelitism and taught that because of Jesus' two natures, he also has two wills working together in one person. This angered the Emperor Constans II who charged Martin with high treason and exiled him to the Crimea, where he died.

The issue was finally put to rest when the emperor Constantine IV called together the bishops for the sixth ecumenical council (Constantinople III) in 680 at the request of Agatho, the bishop of Rome. The council gave full affirmation of Chalcedon and condemned all those who had accepted monothelitism—that list included Honorius, bishop of Rome. Leo II of Rome, who approved the decrees of the council, softened the charge against his predecessor to that of "neglect" to suppress a heresy. Yet this incident of the condemnation of a bishop of Rome was raised by the Reformers in the sixteenth century, and again by the opponents of papal infallibility at Vatican I in 1870. Today's church historians tell us, "The reply of Honorius provided matter for controversy both then and thereafter, but now there is a measure of agreement that he failed to recognize the theological significance of the proposal...."[6]

EAST AND WEST

Before we close this chapter with its maze of councils, intrigues, and divisions we must take note of a few points mentioned briefly before. First of all, there was Justinian (d. 565). He would not be noteworthy for his ecclesiastical dealings. His fame would rest on his great restoration of the Roman Empire. Barbarians had overrun much of it in the West, and he pushed them back (for the time being) to their original boundaries. His representative ruled in the West at Ravenna in Italy, which to this day gives evidence of the great churches and Eastern style with which these Western representatives embellished it. He was also the one who authored the famous Justinian Code of laws, which both church and state would imitate for a long time. With Justinian, the East, already associated with the emperor, would become tied to him. Church and state were closely joined. The emperor controlled the election of the patriarch of Constantinople. He sanctioned church councils. It was characteristic both of Justinian's genius and his union with the church that he rebuilt the magnificent church of Santa Sophia in 538.[7] Justinian meted out penalties to heretics, fostered missionary activity, and nominated all the bishops, excepting Rome's. Still, he did not scruple, as we have seen, to use the pope for his own ends, even while he admitted the pope's primacy.

With such activities as Justinian's, plus the fact that the capital of the empire was now in the East, there grew up a natural anti-Roman feeling. Roman territory had been abandoned by the emperors and was being overrun by the barbarians. In a short time there was an obvious difference between the barbarized Rome and the splendid cosmopolitan city of Constantinople. It is no wonder that the East was showing signs of independence from the West and that the see of Constantinople was declared by several councils to come immediately after that of Rome. The Eastern church even used as the official tongue the Greek language rather than the Latin, which was as indicative as anything of its independence from Rome and the West.

We must also repeat that after Justinian the empire went into decay. The barbarians repossessed many of the territories wrested from them by Justinian. Then the greatest of all blows to Europe occurred: the rise of Muslim power and the Muslim invasions. The Muslims quickly overran Syria, Palestine, Egypt, Spain, and Armenia. Even southern Italy and Sicily would fall into their hands. In

718, they would unsuccessfully attack Constantinople itself and this city would withstand them for six centuries. Ironically, the reduced Eastern Byzantine empire would transfer its ancient Greek culture to the Muslims and they in turn some day would transmit it to the West by way of their conquests in Spain. That culture would be the basis for the rebirth of the West after centuries of isolation caused by the iron grip of the Muslims. Meanwhile, we must return to the end of Constantine's era, and the great invasion poised on the border of the empire.

CHAPTER 6

First Reflections

BIBLICAL REFLECTIONS

We have now reached a point where we must pause briefly for a backward look and assess all that we have seen so far. On reflection, it should be apparent that certain realities consistently stand out between the lines, realities which we cannot intellectually ignore, but which in practice we have emotionally denied. These realities are uncertainty, change, and diversity in Christianity from its very beginning. But, as we said, we have emotionally denied these facts because in our defense against the Protestant Reformers we insisted that the "true Church" was the institutional church that was "always and everywhere the same." Indeed, if average Catholics were to be asked to search the Scriptures for a suitable image to describe a scheme that best seems to depict the origins and development of Christianity, Jesus' parable of the mustard seed would probably be chosen. Jesus says that "the reign of God is like a mustard seed which someone took and sowed in his field. It is the smallest seed of all yet when full grown it is the largest of plants. It becomes so big a shrub that the birds of the sky come and build their nests in its branches" (Matthew 13:31).

One might easily conclude that Christianity is like this parable. After all, it could be reasoned that Jesus, who was God, came to earth. He preached, taught, lived, died, and rose again. After his resurrection, when he, like the mustard seed, had pushed through the earth, the new faith, under the infallible and sure guidance of the promised Spirit, sprang up. And it sprang up sure, single, strong, direct, and, in one unbroken thrust, grew into a mighty shrub for all to see. To this day, people the world over, like so many birds, nest in its protective branches. If we want to trace our origins, it is easy. Just start where we are right now, go down the trunk, as it were, in an unswerving line, right down to the roots. Landmarks are precise, certain, clear, simple, and neat.

As attractive as this parable is, the preceding chapters of this book clearly tell us that perhaps another of Jesus' parables might be a far more accurate description of the origins and development of Christianity. This is the parable of the sower and the seed he tossed onto varied terrain (Matthew 13:3ff). Some seed falls on rocky ground, some among the thorns, and some on good ground. Yet, even here—on the good ground—the results are quite uneven, ranging from thirty- to sixty- to a hundred-fold. This parable, rather than the other, is closer to the truth because it catches the notions of uncertainty, variety, change, and diversity. It implies that Christianity is not that solitary mustard seed growing straight, uninhibited, and singleminded into a mighty tree. Rather, Christianity is more like a wild garden where seed has been scattered willy nilly, where many varieties of beliefs about and responses to Jesus abound. At one time, one shrub predominates, at another time, another bush gains the ascendancy. And all the while, some growths survive and prosper while others decline, are choked off, and disappear. In the best of situations, the yield varies from thirty- to sixty- to a hundred-fold. This diversity, this change, this mosaic is more reflective of the truth about Christianity from the beginning to the present day. Let us now group together five themes from the past pages which support this view.

JUDAIZERS

About sixteen years after the death of Jesus, the apostles and elders (presbyters) of the Jerusalem church met in what has sometimes been called the first general council of the church. They came with various intentions in their hearts. Some had received the message from Jesus that led them to believe that his movement was but an expression of Judaism, basically a Jewish subcult, so it was obvious to them that converts were bound to Mosaic observances. This group intended to keep the Jesus movement within Judaism, and this process had already gone far in Palestine. Others, like Paul, were in a panic because they saw the larger issues. If Jewish observances were to be upheld, then Jesus would have done nothing for Gentiles outside Judaism, and the whole enterprise would turn out to be not a free, charismatic community of mixed believers, but a modern Jewish assembly still bound by the Mosaic law.

From the beginning, then, there were different interpretations of the life and message of Jesus, and Luke understates it when he speaks of a "disagreement between those who spoke Greek and those who spoke the language of the Jews" (Acts 6:1). Luke is guilty of further understatement. His account of the confrontation in the Acts of the Apostles is that the opposing parties met, agreeably ironed out their differences, and decided in Paul's favor, demanding only that a few minor dietary observances be imposed on converts (Acts 15:1-29). This was hardly the case according to Paul (Galatians 2:1-10), a biased and hot participant. In fact, the decision from Jerusalem was ill-received in some quarters. The Jerusalem community tended to recede more into Judaism, while others of their mind followed Paul and his camp around, raising havoc and hounding him from one town to another. Even Peter wavered, for he at first began to socialize with the Gentile converts but later, under pressure from the Jewish Christians, backed off, earning Paul's well-publicized rebuke (Galatians 2:11-14).

Matters, then, were by no means settled as to whose version of Christianity would triumph, and the possibility was very real that Palestinian Christianity, which saw Jesus' religion as a Jewish subcult, would have won the day. What most likely turned the tide was the simple political fact of the destruction of Jerusalem in the year 70. Not only was the Temple forever destroyed, but also the Jerusalem Christian community. Jerusalem would no more play a central part in the development of the church. Jerusalem was soon forgotten, as the center of the new faith shifted to Antioch in Syria, and later to Rome. Paul's Gentile Christianity, freed of the law, as he put it, would have the field to itself. For our purposes, however, it is worth noting that change, division, and diversity were the birth pangs of the new religion, and in the process some scattered seeds had been choked off.

THE SECOND COMING

Clearly, the first Christians understood that Jesus was coming again very soon on clouds of glory. Paul himself, in the earliest piece of Christian Scripture, the letter to the Thessalonians, believed this. As long as the hope of an immediate return held firm, then the Christians could live as formless, expectant groups. But the Lord did not return. Hope gave way to bewilderment, lethargy, and even despair. The second and third generations of Christians obviously had to come to terms with this profound change. They had to modify their expectations. We sense this change in the way they began explaining to themselves and to others what to do. We sense it in their growing sense of entering history. One of Luke's reasons for writing his account of the gospel was his desire to provide a link between the Jesus movement and history. Luke told his readers that it might be many generations before Jesus would come again: "Lord, are you going to restore the rule to Israel now?" His answer was, "The exact time is not yours to know. The Father has reserved that to himself." (Acts 1:6-7). Live on in hope and unity, Luke is saying, and then he hands them a story to live by and a memory to cherish: "I have carefully traced the whole sequence of events from the beginning." (Luke 1:3). He writes this to give his readers some kind of motif and rationale for their existence and their continuation as church. This shift from immediate expectation to hope was a critical change in the early church communities. Such expectations of an early return fell on rocky ground indeed.

SCRIPTURE

We have seen that the Christian Scriptures were written from twenty-five to sixty-five years after the death of Jesus. Mark's, the first gospel, was written around the year 70, Matthew's around 80, Luke's around 85, and John's around 90-100. There were some other nonscriptural Christian writings also circulating, such as the *Didache*, the *Shepherd of Hermes*, and the letters of Clement of Rome. Before this there were, of course, the oral traditions. An early witness named Papias speaks of the "sayings" of Jesus which eventually found their way into the written gospels, as did other pithy sayings, liturgical hymns, and doxologies. Here, once again, change and diversity are evident. Notice, for example how sometimes the identical parable spoken by Jesus will get not only different emphases by the evangelists, but even different conclusions and applications, depending on what the evangelist was trying to correct or underscore.

The gospel writers knew many different church-communities in dozens of towns, each with its own traditions. They knew of different kinds of leaders and missionaries preaching in the name of Jesus, and not all of them represented the same attitudes. An obvious attempt at such unity is Luke's Acts of the Apostles. Reading it, one would never get the impression that there was any other early Christian missionary except Paul. And while Luke gives a somewhat detailed account of the spread of Christianity eastward toward Syria, Greece, and Rome, he tells us nothing about the great spread southward into Africa and its huge centers at Alexandria and other Palestinian-influenced countries. Luke was not especially favorable to the Palestinian type of Christianity, and he was not going to advertise this form. But his very silence gives credence to the diversity that existed.[1]

THE NATURES OF JESUS, THE CHRIST

We have noted before that its monotheism was one of the attractions of Judaism for a pagan world jaded with multiple gods. As a result, for both Gentile and Jewish converts to Christianity, the nature and relationship of Jesus to God was an enormous problem. The Christian Scriptures just accepted the tension, gave their answers, but attempted no theoretical reconciliation. They proposed the divinity of Jesus, while at the same time maintaining his distinction from the Father. The Christian Scriptures simply demonstrate the operation of Father, Son, and Spirit as completely parallel (see 1 Corinthians 12:4-6). This approach found its expression in early liturgical formulas such as Paul's "The grace of the Lord Jesus Christ and the love of God and the fellowship of the Holy Spirit be with you all" (2 Corinthians 13: 13) and Matthew's trinitarian baptismal formula (28:2-9).

But later ages wanted to speculate, and here is where the nationalism, preconceptions, and divisions became acute. Gnostics gave one interpretation of Jesus. The Docetists gave another, claiming that Jesus' body was only a phantom. Arius, as we saw, said that Jesus was not divine, and a host of other thinkers offered a great variety of interpretations about Christ. In the year 390, a certain Bishop Filastrius, who made a hobby of such things, counted in his day at least 156 distinct heresies. The church councils, of course, mark a definite turning point in this overrun garden of speculation, and were designed basically to point out incorrect theology amid the great diversity of doctrine. Nor were differences expressed and offered with dispassion and courtesy in the process. The modern reader is positively appalled at the vicious name-calling and character assassination that opposing sides heaved at one another. It is not hard to appreciate, by the way, the keen interest of the empire and the meddling of the emperors. Doctrinal disunity brought social and political disunity, especially since heresies tended to be antiauthoritarian, and either tribally or nationalistically inspired. It is no accident, therefore, that all of the first councils were called by the emperors, not bishops or popes.

The councils, valuable and ultimately successful as they were in bringing about external doctrinal unity, did not solve all the problems of diversity of beliefs about Jesus. One Christian church that exists to this day, the Coptic church, has never accepted the formulas and explanations about Jesus given by the Council of Chalcedon. In any case, our reflections hold true: in those early centuries variety—even about Jesus—was the rule. No single doctrinal shrub here.

CHURCH STRUCTURE

It is also evident that our preceding chapters have shown a variety and diversification of church order and structure. Since, as we have seen, Jesus did not return immediately, Christianity had to move into history, and it had to move into history with some form and structure. It would appear that the general structure Catholics know today, at least in its basic forms, goes back a long time. There is ample indication that from the end of the first century there was some kind of hierarchical order and a variety of offices set off from the ordinary people. By the second century, we find the early emergence of the single bishop as head of the local community. Paul himself, or more likely whoever wrote the pastoral epistles, gives us for the first time the titles of bishop and deacon. But other structures existed. The church at Jerusalem was apparently administered by the apostles and presbyters. At Antioch, the church-community was ruled by prophets and teachers, and at Philippi by bishops and deacons, and at Rome by a committee. Some Protestant historians speak about "early Catholicism." By that they mean that after the end of the first century there does appear in the primitive church all those elements associated with the Catholic church of later ages: a hierarchical structure, a rule of faith, apostolic succession, and the sacraments. But before that, they speculate, church-communities, especially the early Pauline ones depicted in Romans and Galatians, were more free-floating, charismatic sorts of communities. The bearer of the Spirit was the entire community itself, not any individual office or officer. The transition to this (Catholic) position came later. Therefore, they say, Roman Catholics have been too selective. Roman Catholics have tended to select and develop the "early Catholic" tendencies, and have neglected the more informal church organization and more charismatic atmosphere of the primitive period.

The church must certainly reassess her usage in light of those biblical theologies that she has not followed in order to be certain that what God meant to teach her through such theological views will not be lost. For example, if the church has chosen to follow as normative the ecclesiastical structure attested in the pastorals (bishop/presbyters, deacons), she must ask herself does she continue to do proportionate justice to the charismatic and freer spirit of the earlier period. A choice between the two was necessary and this choice was guided by the Spirit of God; but the structure that was not chosen still has something to teach the church and can serve as a modifying corrective on the choice that was made. Only thus is the church faithful to the whole New Testament. In New Testament times the church was ecumenical enough to embrace those who, while sharing the one faith, held very different theological views. The church of today can be no less ecumenical.[2]

CONCLUSIONS

The developments we have examined so far are: the growth of the early communities from a Jewish subcult into a separate religion; the settling into a more historical posture after the delay of a second coming; the formation of the gospels; and the arguments over the nature of Jesus—all of which demonstrate that the early church was, in fact, quite pluralistic while maintaining an essential unity. Luke's simplified view that "the community of believers were of one heart and mind" (Acts 4:32) was not quite on target. Uncertainty, change, and diversity were the real characteristics.

To return to our opening metaphor, Christianity was not a simple mustard seed shooting uninhibited into solitary splendor. It truly was more like that garden of domestic and wildflowers where variety, more than conformity, ruled. To put it another way: there was never a Golden Age in apostolic times. That is a misconception. We shall see that future ages tried to make it so, but the facts tell a different story. The apostolic age was surely normative in the sense that there were people living who had known, heard, and learned from Jesus himself and they, especially the apostles, became the touchstone of tradition and truth. But, beyond that, there was no normative unity in all Christian things whatever until after the great councils. Even then, a certain amount of diversity continued to flourish, and responses to the message of Jesus continued to be as varied as the difference between thirty-, sixty-, and a hundred-fold.[3]

CHAPTER 7

Chaos and Consolidation

THE CHURCH IN THE WEST

The period of the early church is over. We now come to the interesting evolution of the church from its original, loosely-knit church-communities into a strong, centralized organization. We shall trace how this took place in the next three chapters. We shall see how the strands of church and state became so interwoven that it formed one cloth called Christendom. Since this process took place in the West, we must begin there.

We have seen that under the emperors from Constantine to Theodosius, Christianity moved from repression to toleration to privilege. Following the Council of Constantinople I in 381, Christianity was declared to be the official religion of the empire. No longer meeting in secret assembly, the faithful now took possession of the old pagan temple sites and built new churches of their own. During the reign of Sylvester I of Rome (314-335), the great basilicas of St. John Lateran, Santa Croce, and St. Peter's were begun. St. John Lateran church, really an enlargement of one of the huge halls of the palace of the Laterani family, was presented to the Roman bishop by Constantine in 311. It became Christianity's first church. To this day it carries these words inscribed on its front: "The Mother and Head of all churches in the city of Rome and in all the world." (It is, in fact, the cathedral church of the bishop of Rome.)

Privileges were now being given to the clergy. They were excused from certain civic duties, such as paying taxes and serving in the Roman legions. Church officials were now to be tried in church courts rather than civil courts. As we noted previously, the church was permitted to receive grants of money and land, and in time many noblemen and kings would give great grants of land, making the church Europe's greatest landowner. The bishops, already the established leaders in many towns, became, in effect, representatives of the emperor.

The bishop of Rome already claimed a primacy of honor and privilege as successor to the seat of Peter, but there were other bishops, the patriarchs, who also claimed prestige, though in second place to Rome. The emperor was in the East, with a subordinate emperor in the West residing at Ravenna. Several councils had been held. The worship of the church continued to center around the eucharistic liturgy. Further, we should notice that most church activity was taking place in the East. The reasons for this are obvious. First of all, the Christian religion started in the East. Second, the East held the capital city, the seat of the emperor. Third, Christianity was simply not that entrenched in the West. Gaul, Spain, Italy, and Africa could be considered as having Christian settlements in the big cities, but the rest of Europe and beyond was pagan.

Moreover, one of the two areas, Africa, was being racked by controversy. The Donatist heresy was taking place there. This was the heresy that said the validity of the sacraments depended on the goodness or state of the soul of the person who administered them. Some bishops and priests had concealed or even come close to denying their faith during some of the Roman persecutions. The Donatists believed that if such men administered the sacraments, these sacraments were invalid.[1] The orthodox Catholic view was (and is) that the sacraments are effective regardless of the sanctity or lack of sanctity of the minister who administers them. In any case, in every African city, rival Donatist bishops were causing confusion and inciting division in the Catholic church. The greatest opponent of this heresy was Augustine of Hippo. He was to be the greatest single influence in the church for a thousand years. By his defense of the

Catholic faith, he gave a decided Latin thrust to Christianity (as opposed to the previously predominant Greek thought and writings), thus putting Latin or Western Christianity on a footing of respectability.

We might mention that Augustine also defeated another troublesome heresy of the time, Pelagianism, which held that people could attain salvation by their own unaided efforts. It was Augustine's contemporary, Ambrose, bishop of Milan, Italy, who gave another tone to Western Christianity. He was the one who confronted the emperor Theodosius (at one time, the emperors resided in Milan), teaching that the emperors were not above the church. Theodosius I had killed seven thousand people in revenge for an uprising against new taxes. When he went to Ambrose's church for eucharist, Ambrose refused to celebrate in his presence. The emperor had to do penance, and Ambrose set the tone, as it were, for future defenses of the church in the West against the encroachments of the state. Another contemporary was Jerome (345-420), the irascible and learned man who translated the Bible into Latin for the West.

Such was the West. It was mostly pagan, yet honeycombed with Christian communities. It was harassed by heresies, yet it produced some leaders of genius who would give prestige and foundation to Christianity. What about the others? Besides the city-dwelling Christians in the populous and prestigious East or in the less significant West, there were the crude rustics (*paganus* in Latin) who lived in the rural areas and worshiped the "old gods." This title "pagan" was also applied to the tribes who had been kept out of the empire by much superior Roman legions. But it was precisely some of these foreign "rustics" who were about to overthrow the Roman Empire in the West, and almost the church itself.

BARBARIAN INVASIONS

The rustic barbarians had been hovering on the outskirts of the Roman Empire for centuries. As long as the empire remained strong, the Roman armies patrolled the borders, and great fortifications were erected, the barbarians were deterred from entering the empire. However, when the power of the empire waned, the Germanic barbarians increased their contacts. An emperor like Julian, in 358, had even allowed some of them to settle within the empire in return for military service. Some were employed as mercenaries by the Roman army. This helped to keep the others out, since in effect such troops were only one stage less barbarous than their opponents. The last two great imperial warriors of antiquity, the generals Stilicho and Aetius, were Germans.

But there were other contacts. For one thing, some of the barbarians had already been converted to Christianity. Justin Martyr speaks of Christianity among the barbarians as early as 165. The only trouble was that these barbarians were converted to the heretical Arian Christianity (Jesus was not divine, but a creature), and this was to prove an enormous difficulty to the church.

In the fifth century, new and strenuous pressures were being put on these border barbarians. The pressures took many forms. There was the need for land. There was no way that they could expand eastward, since they had been repulsed by strong Chinese emperors. Westward was their only avenue. The terrible Huns were also forcing this westward push. They swept all before them, leaving the other barbarian tribes nowhere to flee except into the Roman Empire. Thus, in the year 406, these tribes crossed the Rhine River and invaded the Roman provinces of Gaul (roughly, today's France). Wives, children, and livestock came in an unending stream. The barbarian invasions had begun and would last some 250 years until the sixth century. Europe would only catch its breath when the Muslims would bring their warring crusade. Finally, in the tenth century, the last series of invasions, that of the Vikings, would take place. It is easy to see why, with three major body blows in 500 years, these ages are called "dark" (although unjustifiably in many ways, as we shall see).

It was not only the pressure for land and the fear of the Huns that enabled the barbarians to pour into the Roman Empire. There was the simple fact that the empire was already in decline and internally weak. Military strength was low and, more significantly, the simple will to be great was gone among the Romans. The softness of life and the decay of morals were other factors. Then, too, the capital was now at Constantinople, leaving Rome in second place and, in fact, vacant. The emperor's representative resided in Ravenna, but the strength and the power were in the East. Furthermore, as it was later discovered, the Eastern emperor at Constantinople had made secret treaties with the barbarians, who were to spare the eastern section of the empire in exchange for non-interference by the imperial legions. The invaders would be allowed to enter the Italian peninsula.

So it was that, in 407, the Visigoth Alaric invaded Rome and, in 410, sacked the city. Actually, not much damage was done, because Alaric was seeking food more than plunder. Rather, it was the emotional blow that hurt so much. For the first time in seven hundred years Rome had been invaded! The Eternal City, the heartbeat of the empire, had been desecrated, although no emperor had lived there for 140 years. No wonder many thought that civilization itself had come to an end. Fifty years later, the "scourge of God," Attila the Hun, led his warriors into northern Italy, and it was Leo I, bishop of Rome, who went out with his clergy to talk with Attila and get him to spare the city for the payment of an annual tribute. The barbarians continued to overrun Gaul, Britain, and Africa. Mercifully, Augustine had died before the barbarians overran his town of Hippo in Africa. The Ostrogoths were the last of this wave of barbarians to invade. A certain Odoacer had made himself the king of Italy and deposed the last subordinate Western emperor in 476. This usually marks the date of the fall of the Western Roman empire. The Eastern emperor, of course, still ruled at Constantinople, and his authority was still respected, but he was far away and powerless in the West. By the time of Pope Gregory the Great (d. 604), the Eastern imperial rule over the West was restricted to Ravenna, Rome, Naples, and Sicily.

New patterns were developing. Little tribal kingdoms replaced the unity of the Roman empire. Still, there is one overriding historical reality that we must remember if we are to understand the church's role: the barbarians did not wish to destroy Roman civilization. They wanted desperately to adopt and imitate it. So powerful was the Roman empire, so prestigious its name, so regarded as the depository of a superior civilization, that the Germanic barbarians submitted eagerly to the Roman way and tried to follow Roman political institutions. They had no hatred for the Roman life. They wanted nothing more than to become Romanized as soon as possible. Each local barbarian king went out of his way to be recognized by the Eastern emperor. Each barbarian king (sometimes to the point of ridiculousness) sought to wear the clothes, hold the court, and affect the titles of imperial Rome.

We can imagine the upheaval Europe was in. The utter despair and confusion were apparent. The West was saturated with German barbarians. There was, however, one moment of recovery. The great emperor of the East, Justinian, having successfully rejuvenated his Eastern empire, turned to the West in 529. He wanted to restore the whole empire to its former glory and unity. He attacked the barbarians, and with great skill defeated them all, except the Franks. For a brief moment the empire once more was united, and Justinian celebrated his victories by building the famed Santa Sophia in Constantinople. However, before Justinian could return to conquer the Franks, he was diverted by the Persian and Lombard threats on his own eastern borders. The Lombards were finally rerouted to Italy and were the last barbarians into Europe. Justinian could have still dealt with both Franks and Lombards but for a new menace at his own doorstep: the Muslim holy wars.

MUSLIM INVASIONS

In the seventh century, the Muslims, bound together with a new religion, set out to conquer the world. Armed with fanaticism and the sword, they swept Asia before them and penetrated deep into Europe. The very lands of Syria, Palestine, and Egypt, which had witnessed the great events of Christianity and which had produced the church's greatest scholars and martyrs, were now lost to the infidel. (The ill-fated crusades of a later century would attempt to win these places back.) Christianity in these regions withered away, and from this point on the great patriarchates of Alexandria, Antioch, and Jerusalem would have no influence in the workings of the church. The church in the West would tend to forget these areas of its origins and former glory. Next the Muslims invaded Africa and crossed into Europe via Spain, until they were stopped at Poitiers by Charles Martel in 732. On the other end of the empire they assaulted Constantinople itself but were unable to take it. What really saved Christendom from complete conquest were the divisions within the Muslim world itself that caused the thrust of aggression to dry up. As a matter of fact, the Muslim world finally polarized into three distinct political centers—Baghdad, Cairo, and Cordova (in Spain). Divided, it was no longer a united danger, but it continued to harass Christianity in many ways and for a long time.

The important thing to remember is that from the seventh century on, the Muslims effectively separated Europe from the East. They locked in its economy, made the Mediterranean a Muslim sea, and prevented commercial expansion and development. It is no wonder that feudalism arose, no wonder that capitalism did not arise, no wonder that Europe was landlocked, and outside stimulation was absent. Only about five hundred years later would there be some headway against the Muslims. Then Europe would break out once again into the waterways; cities could begin to revive, commerce thrive, and the Renaissance become possible. But for the time being, Europe was continuously threatened by the Muslims, hedged in and thrown back on its own resources. The Eastern Empire spent the rest of its days trying to withstand the Muslim pressure, losing contact with the West—except for Venice—having its moments of glory and still maintaining its influence until its fall in 1453.

CHURCH AND BARBARIAN

Thus, from the fifth to the eighth centuries, Europe was racked with invasion and assault by German barbarians, Lombards, and Muslims. (One more assault remained: the Vikings.) The western Roman Empire fell. But our interest is the church. How did it fare? What was its relation to the barbarian? On the intellectual front, pagans and Christians had their explanations for the invasions. For the pagans, the invasions were seen as punishment from the gods for abandoning them. For the Christians, the invasions were a punishment from God for the immoral lives of the people. Augustine's *City of God* was an answer to those who blamed Christianity for the invasions, like the fifth century monk who wrote:

> Events prove what God judges about us and about the Goths and Vandals. They increase daily; we decrease daily. They prosper; we are humbled....You, O Roman people, be ashamed; be ashamed of your lives. Almost no cities are free of evil dens.... It is not the natural vigor of their bodies that enables them to conquer us, nor is it our natural weakness that has caused our conquest. Let nobody persuade himself otherwise. Let nobody think otherwise. The vices of our bad lives have alone conquered us.[2]

Be that as it may, the church provided the one point of stability in the general upheaval of the times. Although some clergy were killed and church property ravaged, the devastation was really not that widespread, since the barbarian was not engaged in a war of conquest but was searching for land, food, and markets. The church was thereby enabled not only to survive but to eventually overcome the invaders. One by one the pagan as well as the Arian barbarians embraced the church. Why was this? There were a number of reasons. First, we must remember that there was a power vacuum left by the emperor's moving his capital to Constantinople. The subordinate emperor left by him in the West was weak, and eventually he departed. The church found itself in a leadership position by default. Constantinople was far away and embroiled in its own problems. "The continuity and the authority of the church of Rome stood out in marked contrast against not only the turbulent heresies and imperial control of the church in the East, but also against the short-lived kingdoms which rose and fell in the West."[3]

Second, the church of Rome had a sophisticated episcopacy. The bishops were men of rank in society with many privileges and quasi civil status conferred on them by Constantine and his successors. They were almost always drawn from the old leading Roman families, and so, in effect, they were the Roman ruling system perpetuated in the church rather than in the government. They therefore had power, prestige, and a natural tradition of leadership and decision making. As transformed civil servants they were able and ready to meet the challenge of the barbarian. As sophisticated aristocrats they were able and ready to bring system and organization to the task.

Third, the Roman church was the custodian of the heritage of law, always a magnificently strong point of Roman genius. Making, collecting, and codifying laws was a tradition in Rome. Very early Roman bishops like Gelasius I (d. 496) began to classify the various laws and decrees of the many Western synods. Rome also kept a system of dating the calendar, an authoritative list of saints, and a basic reference system of all ecclesiastical matters. When anyone had a question or there was a dispute, where else would they turn but to Rome? As obviously important as is this one factor alone in assessing the rise of Rome's primacy in the church, our interest here is the relationship to the barbarians. They, very simply, had no law, at least not written down. It was the Christian missionaries, sent from Rome, who effectively demonstrated the superiority of having things down in writing. As a natural effort in stabilizing an erratic society, the missionaries put the Germanic tribal laws into written form and records—and in the process they Christianized them. The Roman legal genius in making and codifying laws aided the rapid penetration of the Christian religion among the barbarians. Finally, the church was conscious of its mission to convert the world. The church felt compelled to take the lead and so, "it brought the West under the great civilizing influence of Christian doctrine."[4]

We should not fail to observe that at the same time an essential relationship was also forming. The barbarians needed the Roman church, its organization, and its personnel. Gradually, the church, severed from the East, would need the protection of the tribal kings. A mutual but uneasy alliance was beginning to form.

The new barbarian kingdoms had taken over the military and political functions of the empire—they held the sword, they levied the taxes, they administered justice—of a sort—but everything else belonged to the church—moral authority, learning and culture, the prestige of the Roman name and the care of the people. A man's real citizenship was not to be found in his subjection to the barbarian state, but in his membership in the Christian church, and it was to the bishop rather than to the king that he looked as the leader of Christian society.[5]

What we are seeing here, then, is a slow but total penetration of Christianity into the Western societies from the fifth to the ninth centuries. And, what we are also witnessing is the process of Roman ecclesiastical centralization, as the barbarian tribes were becoming linked to Rome by law and by the episcopacy. In a word, for any barbarian tribe to be civilized meant in effect to be Romanized and to be Romanized was also to be Catholicized.

This is not to say that the church itself remained unaffected by the encounter with the barbarian. During those hectic times—called the dark ages by some—the church could not help becoming somewhat barbarized. We see this in the dramatic rise of the biggest single popular Christian devotion, which lasted some 800 years: the use of relics. No Christians, be they peasant or noble, would be without their store of relics. Nor would any decent Christian pass up the opportunity to visit a shrine which housed a famous relic. The demand was enormous, the traffic huge. Frauds were not infrequent, and shrines rose and fell because of the popularity of their relic contents. Between towns, as between the individual rich, one-upmanship was not unknown.

Another factor to note was the decline of literature. There were no new or original productions. There were no more Augustines or Ambroses or Jeromes. Latin literature simply stopped, and the classical age was over. Whatever literary energy existed was used in rescuing the past and transmitting the past to the future. The monks dedicated themselves to copying precious masterpieces of antiquity so that they might not be lost forever. With no time to be creative, there was only the immediate desire to preserve Roman culture. "In short, it was not because it was Christian, but because it was Roman that the church acquired and maintained for centuries its control over society; or, if you will, it exercised a preponderant influence over modern society for so long merely because it was a depository of a more ancient and more advanced civilization."[6]

THE MONKS

There were other factors which made the church the preserver of Western civilization when the civil government faded away. One of the most vital factors was the beginning of the monastic tradition in the West. As we saw earlier, monasticism had its beginning in the East during the third century. These Eastern monks were in pursuit of perfection. They subsisted on charity alone and lived on the bare edge of survival. Such a lifestyle could, in fact, be supported in the imperial East, but not in the impoverished West. In the West, therefore, from the beginning, the monks tended to be self-sufficient and active, thus playing a larger role in their society.

During the fifth century, monasticism took an early hold in Ireland. In fact, it became the predominant expression of church. There were Irish bishops, but they served in the more ceremonial functions. The real leadership and power lay with the abbots. It is evident that such a system as existed in the Emerald Isle was a threat not only to the institution of the episcopacy, but also to any centralizing movement from Rome. And the threat grew as the indefatigable Irish monks made successful and consistent journeys of evangelization to the mainland of Europe.

Rome's answer to this came through Gregory I (bishop of Rome from 590-604), and the Benedictine monastic tradition from which he came. The Benedictines were founded by Benedict of Nursia, who began his monastic life as a hermit and later gathered others around himself to found a monastery atop Monte Cassino—on the site of a former temple to Apollo. For the next seven hundred years, Benedictine monasticism was predominant in Europe. The reason for this predominance is easy to see. Benedict's rule was the soul of sensibility. In sharp contrast to some other foundations, it was sane, strong, flexible, and without eccentricity. Moreover, it was distinctly an upper-class movement. The men it drew were literate, could keep accounts, and were apt at organization. They appreciated stability and order. This was precisely the kind of monasticism that Rome, unable to tame the free-spirited Irish monks, could harness for its use. Rome was also not unaware that monks sent as missionaries under papal aegis would be so many ambassadors of the Roman way.

The Benedictines soon numbered hundreds of houses throughout Europe. They did not start out with the intention of preserving and passing on culture, but that is what they did. In establishing their houses, these upper-class men began to clear forests, reclaim land, and give some system to agriculture. In so doing, they were laying the foundations for economic recovery and stability. In addition, the monks began the process of copying manuscripts so that nothing of the glorious past was lost. The copying of manuscripts grew into a large monastic industry. Much knowledge of the ancient world has survived only through the efforts of these monk copyists. In the natural course of events, the Benedictine monasteries eventually became the inns and hospitals of the time, because they were often the only havens of peace and security in a world of upheaval and war. Furthermore, because these monasteries were often freed from control of the local bishop by papal privilege, the monasteries were more flexible and far less likely to become the pawn of local kings who controlled and appointed the bishops. This is worth noting, because in the future, when reform was needed, it would come from the monasteries, not from the politically beholden bishops. Significantly, where there were reforming bishops, they often as not came from the monasteries. The Benedictines eventually would give to the church literally thousands of bishops and twenty-four of its popes. For the moment, however, it was this new monastic movement favored by Gregory which, in its conversion efforts among the barbarians, would spread the Latin language and Rome's way of doing things.

ARIANISM

There was one major problem, however, in the conversion of the barbarians. Many of them had already been converted to a faith that professed that Jesus was only a creature and not divine (Arianism). These Arian Christians continuously persecuted the Roman Catholic majority and gave the church many of its martyrs. The Arian king, Theodoric, much to the scandal of the faithful, even went so far as to imprison the bishop of Rome for appealing to the Eastern emperor for aid against the Arian Germans.

In any case, the church needed an ally among the barbarians themselves. They found one among the relatively small tribe of the Franks. Their king, Clovis, in 493 married Clotilda, a Burgundean princess who was Catholic, not Arian. In 496, Clovis and his whole tribe were baptized by the Catholic bishop Remi of Rheims. Now the church had a champion and the bishops threw their weight and prestige behind Clovis. In the name of the new faith, Clovis broke the Arian Visigoth power and forced all Arians to accept Catholic baptism. Even after Clovis's death, as the Frankish kingdom spread, so did the power of the Catholic church. Since the Franks alone ultimately survived among all of the various tribes, they and the church would therefore have a permanent influence on Europe. In any case, Arianism would soon disappear. The conversion of Clovis, the fact that the Roman clergy was better educated than the isolated ignorant Arian clergy, intermarriage between conquerors and conquered—all these factors bridged the religious gap. Added to this, of course, was the need on the part of kings to consolidate their newly seized lands; conforming to the faith they found in the empire helped them keep their lands. Considering that the barbarians were so anxious to adopt Roman civilization, whose religion was Catholic Christianity, what would be more natural than for the Arians to switch sides? Thus Arianism gave way to Catholicism.

But the conversion of the Franks was a two-way street. Their kings felt the obligation not only to protect the church but to interfere with it as well. By a local council, for example, the king of the Franks got permission to nominate bishops. It was easy to see what would happen. The king would nominate only those whom he could trust and who would be more civil servants than ecclesiastics. It was the beginning of that deadly combination, the prince-bishop who would plague the church for centuries, and who frequently enough would be more ambitious prince than servant bishop—to the great scandal in the church. It is no wonder that monks, rather than bishops, would figure in the great reform movements of the church: The bishops were often the *objects* of reform.

GREGORY THE GREAT

All of the activity of the church on behalf of the barbarians during the centuries can be summed up in one person, Gregory the Great. Gregory had been a monk, and this is significant. This meant that when he was elected bishop of Rome in 590, he brought a monk's discipline, missionary instinct, and sense of order and rule to the church. He is often called the founder of the modern papacy, in that he began in earnest the centralization process towards Rome. He was also the first "pope" to use the title still used today, "Servant of the servants of God."

From early on, Rome was accorded a preeminence as the church of Peter and Paul. Once Christianity was tolerated, however, the bishops of Rome began to claim powers of jurisdiction and supremacy that went far beyond the primacy of honor usually accorded to Rome. In addition, we need to remember that although the term pope (from the Greek *papas*) was originally a title of respect used for all bishops, "...by the end of the fifth century 'pope' usually meant the bishop of Rome and no one else. It was not until the eleventh century, however, that a pope could insist that the title applied to him alone."[7]

Yet a change of circumstances forced the Roman bishops to exercise more than a primacy of honor. When the emperors moved to the East, the vacancy of leadership in the West was filled by the bishop of Rome. He became the chief magistrate in Rome. He fed the populace when the Emperor's representative at Ravenna could no longer do so. It was Leo I (440-461) who went out on behalf of the city to placate Attila the Hun. Later by donations of land made to him by the Franks, the pope became a political power as well.

If the pope's power of jurisdiction and supremacy had been vaguely defined previously, it was Gregory who sharpened the definition. He was an able leader and one of only three popes to earn the title "great" after his name. [Nicholas I (858-867) and Leo I (440-461) were the other two.] He was fifty years old when he became pope, frail but energetic. Before he became a Benedictine monk, he had been the highest civil official in the government of Rome. But he had other things going for him as well as filling the void left by the emperor. He had his own personal prestige. He had literary skills, and began to write about and interpret religious thought. His homilies and commentaries are still read today, and his book, *The Pastoral Care of Souls*, along with Boethius's *The Consolation of Philos-*

ophy, were the two most widely read books in the Middle Ages. He also had organizational ability. He reorganized and consolidated church finances so that he made the church at Rome financially independent and thus able to experiment.

Finally, he had a sense of priority and knew what the pressing problems were. The most immediate was the invading Lombards whom he temporarily placated by an annual tribute. His other problem was one of support. He was shrewd enough to know that he could no longer count on the Eastern emperor for help. He would therefore have to strengthen his own position. To do this he must have the backing of the barbarians. To have the backing of the barbarians, he must convert them all (not just the Franks). Thus Gregory took every interest in all the Germanic tribes. More than any other individual, he was responsible for ending Arianism in Spain and Italy and for gathering the Irish church to Rome. But above all, he was interested enough to send forth missionaries. In this endeavor he was the first pope to bring monasticism into active service on behalf of the church. The combination of papacy and monasticism was to bring Europe into the church. For this he has also been called the "Father of Europe."

EVANGELIZING THE BARBARIANS

Gregory's masterful achievement was to send the Benedictine monk, Augustine (d. 604, and not to be confused with Augustine of Hippo who died in 430), to evangelize the English. Actually, Christianity was already in England, having been brought there by some Roman soldiers in the fourth century, but it was not active. (And Britain, of course, probably produced St. Patrick, the apostle of Ireland. No one really knows how Christianity got to Ireland; the faith was there before Patrick, but there is no doubt that he completed Ireland's conversion by the middle of the fifth century.) Augustine converted the king of Britain, established his see at Canterbury, and became the first Catholic bishop of England.

There were other monks in the north of Britain. These were the Irish monks (such as Aiden and Columba) who had brought with them the Celtic form of Christianity. Soon the island was divided—Celtic Christianity in the north and Roman Christianity in the south. A council meeting at Whitby in 664 settled the matter in favor of Augustine's party. The significant effect of this act was to bind England to Rome and the pope. English Christianity adopted the forms, administration, and policies of Rome, and Rome's influence would be felt until the sixteenth century when the Catholic king, Henry VIII, would provide the occasion for a break that had been seething some time before him.

After the Whitby meeting, England was to return the compliment to Gregory by sending its missionaries back to the continent to evangelize the barbarians. Their contribution was the greatest apostle of his time, St. Boniface, who is known as the "Apostle of the Germans" (680-794). Again, the significance in this conversion of Germany and England was that they were directly beholden to the pope. Their bishops were subject not to the king, but to Rome. These countries would look to Rome for leadership despite the fact that the popes were still technically under the Eastern emperor who ratified their election either directly or through their representatives at Ravenna. The new Christians knew only the pope as their leader and they revered him as the Vicar of St. Peter. (The title, Vicar of Christ, was not used by the pope until the mid-twelfth century.) Thus, the pope had an independent base of wealth and the allegiance of whole nations who looked directly to him. No longer would the papacy have to be in a subordinate position to the emperor, especially those Eastern emperors who had abandoned the West to face the barbarians alone, and who on different occasions antagonized the papacy.

When Boniface embarked on his mission, religion and culture in the Frankish kingdom were at a low ebb, and the victorious tide of Muslim invasions was sweeping over the Christian lands of the western Mediterranean and northern Africa. By 720 the Saracens had penetrated as far as Narbonne; and in the following years all the old centers of monastic culture in southern Gaul, such as Lerins, were sacked.... But the creation by St. Boniface and his Anglo-Saxon companions of a new province of Christian culture on the northern flank of Christendom had an importance that far exceeded its material results.... It involved a triple alliance between the Anglo-Saxon missionaries, the Papacy, and the family of Charles Martel, the de facto rulers of the Frankish kingdom, out of which the Carolingian Empire and the Carolingian culture ultimately emerged.[8]

And antagonism there was. Fifty years after Gregory (d. 604), this antagonism from the Eastern emperor flared up again. The Eastern emperor Constans II had sent Martin of Rome into exile. In 692 the emperor Justinian almost did the same to Pope Sergius over a theological quarrel. But there were signs that this sort of subordination would not last long. In 725, when the emperor Leo II tried to force the iconoclast heresy on the West, Gregory II hedged. The emperor had expected to find him as docile as the other patriarchs. Although Gregory II distinctly showed his defiance, he was not yet ready for an open break, because the emperor, even far away, was still too powerful. The papacy would have to wait for a more opportune time. More precisely, the bishops of Rome would have to be assured of a powerful protector to defend the papacy against the emperor if need be. As a matter of fact, there was such an ally in the background. He belonged to the church-related Frankish tribe. He was a local mayor in the palace of the Frankish Merovingian kings and he was fast supplanting that decadent line. His name was Pepin, and under his great grandson, Charlemagne, the great marriage between the church and the Western empire would take place and the Eastern emperor would become a mere figurehead to the West.

CHAPTER 8

The Carolingian Era

THE CAROLINGIAN DYNASTY

Clovis, the founder of the Merovingian dynasty, was king of the barbarian tribe of the Franks. We noted in the last chapter that he had become a Roman Christian and that his whole tribe followed him. In enlarging his kingdom he also spread the faith. What happened to him and his descendants afterwards? His kingdom under his descendants became weaker. There was no real central government, and in time the many local princes grew in strength and wealth at the expense of the Merovingian rulers. Under the feudal arrangement, local princes took over the protection, land, and care of the peasants and became more wealthy and powerful than the king himself. Moreover, in order to purchase the loyalty of such princes, the king would give them some of his land, and in due time reduced his own power. As a result, the one united Frankish kingdom under Clovis was replaced by many minor municipalities that were practically independent of the king. It only remained a matter of time before some strong figure, some local prince, would arise and substitute his clan for the old Merovingian clan of Clovis.

The man who was destined to make this replacement was Pepin. By gathering land through intrigue and warfare, his Carolingian clan became quite prestigious. This prestige was considerably enhanced by Pepin's son, Charles Martel (the Hammer). He was the one who defeated the Muslims in 732 at Poitiers (in France), thereby confining the Muslims to Spain and saving the rest of Europe from their invasion. People almost forgot that Charles despoiled church property and buildings to finance his army and the newly invented institution of knights-on-horseback. In any case, the church had more reason to remember Charles's son, Pepin the Short. He was the man who felt that the only way to soften and eventually annex his troublesome pagan neighbors was to convert them to Roman Christianity. Accordingly, Pepin lost no time in giving every cooperation to the great St. Boniface. We must remember, however, that Boniface was an English Benedictine and loyal to Rome. To this degree, Boniface unconsciously became an intermediary between Pepin and the pope. It was a quickly growing mutual relationship. Pepin decided to take advantage of it.

But Pepin had a legal problem. He was the actual ruler of the Franks, while technically the old Merovingian line was the royal family. He asked Pope Zachary (742-752) whether it was right that the old impotent family should rule when, in effect, he was doing all the work. The pope, wisely following Gregory the Great's assessment that the West could no longer look to the Eastern emperor for assistance, gave the answer that Pepin wanted: the ruler in practice should be the ruler in theory. Accordingly, Pepin was crowned king, and the Carolingian line replaced the Merovingian line. The significance of this event lay in the fact that Pepin was now, in effect, king by the approval of the pope, thus making Pepin beholden to the papacy. The papacy, in turn, henceforth associated itself with the Frankish empire and turned its back forever on the Eastern emperor. The papacy had its protector now and did not need the East.

In 750, while arrangements were being made to make Pepin king, the Lombards in northern Italy again went on a rampage and began invading further south. In fact, they captured Ravenna, where the Eastern emperor's representative resided, and from which he fled. Rome itself was now in peril. Since arrangements with Pepin were not complete, the pope appealed to the Eastern emperor for assistance. Help did not come, and Pope Stephen III arranged a forty-year truce with the Lombards, which they promptly violated. Then the pope decided to make the long, hard journey over the Alps to entreat Pepin's aid. Pepin agreed, took his army over the Alps, and defeated the Lombards.

It was at this time that another significant event took place. Pepin gave some of the lands taken from the Lombards to the pope. This land became known as the "Donation of Pepin" and later formed the basis for the papal states. This was the property that in centuries to come would make the pope not only a spiritual leader, but a sovereign power as well. This was the property that would in time be a source of conflict with kings and governments. This was the nucleus of the property that stood in the way of Italian unification in the nineteenth century and that Victor Emmanuel II would then seize, causing Pius IX to remain in the Vatican as its voluntary prisoner. Finally, a concordat between Pius XI and Mussolini in 1929 would cede the papal states to the Italian government, leaving only the 108 acres forming today's Vatican City (but all this is another drama we shall investigate later).

We must pause for a moment to note that Pepin's action in giving lands to the pope was based on *The Donation of Constantine*. This was supposedly a document written by Constantine to Pope Sylvester in 315, but it was really written in the eighth century. It tells how Constantine gave to the pope and his successors the supreme temporal power in the West, the universal rule in both spiritual and temporal realms, and the lands of the Western Roman empire. Pepin believed in that document, as many others did, and so he felt that he was only restoring to the pope lands taken by the Lombards, lands rightfully belonging to the pope. Pepin's *Donation*, in other words, was based on Constantine's; Pepin was only giving the pope back his property. It was also in virtue of the *Donation* document that the pope felt he had the power to transfer to the Franks the Western imperial lands which belonged to the emperor now residing in the East. Discoveries in the fifteenth century, however, would prove that this document, *The Donation of Constantine*, was a forgery, not in the sense of a fraud, but rather as a substantiation of what most people at that time believed to be true.

There was yet another novelty in these events. For the first time, the pope formally became a prince, a sovereign king in charge of lands. He and his clerics would run these states, but obviously they would be subject to the jealousies and intrigues of the old time Roman nobles and military leaders who formerly (before the Lombards) ran these lands, and who would ever aspire to seize these lands once more. The implication of this would someday bode ill for the papacy. It would mean that, since such states were protected militarily by papal troops, the only way such Roman barons and nobles would ever again be able to control the papal states would be to manage somehow to control the papacy. Unfortunately, this came about. In other words, since the pope was now an earthly ruler, what would be more natural than that unscrupulous men should covet the papacy? To be pope was not to be spiritual leader alone. To be pope was also to be a temporal power.

For the present, however, the picture seemed ideal. Empire and church were interrelated. Rome, the capital of the old Roman empire, became the capital of Christendom. Now there existed a true religious empire with a king of the Franks who was so "by the grace of God." The groundwork laid by Gregory the Great in the sixth century was fulfilled in the eighth. This supposed church-state ideal would reach its height under Charlemagne. The origins of the *Holy Roman Empire* were at hand.

CHARLEMAGNE

Charlemagne (literally "Charles the Great": 768-814) was the son of Pepin the Short. He is one of those figures in history who completely captured the popular imagination. His name was to remain the most honored for the rest of the Middle Ages, and deservedly so, for his achievements were many. He was a first-class warrior (and lusty barbarian, with five wives and many mistresses). He waged war against the pagan Saxons, those who had not migrated to England. This was the first religious war on the part of the Christian state, because Charlemagne said that the Saxons had to accept baptism or die. He next defeated the Avars, the Slavs, and fought well against the Muslims. One of his battles against the Muslims occasioned the first epic poem, *The Song of Roland* (c. 1080). Finally, at the pope's request, he defeated the ever-troublesome Lombards, thereby annexing Italy to his kingdom as well. All in all, Charlemagne's empire included most of Europe.

By the very fact of his conquest of Italy, he became its ruler and was given the title "Patrician of Rome." He had no choice but to have an intense interest in the church, and indeed he came to consider the church as a kind of partner. But there were dangers in this paternalism (for example, the overlordship such as the Eastern emperors had over the Eastern church). Yet the leadership of the church was not unhappy. In fact, when Charlemagne was attending Christmas Mass in the year 800, Pope Leo III craftily surprised him by placing a crown on his head and bowing before him as one only does to the emperor. Charlemagne, according to his biographer, was annoyed. Not that he minded being dubbed as emperor, but he minded being beholden to the pope. In any case, the result was clear for his times and ever after. Charlemagne was not merely king as his great grandfather Pepin had become when he replaced the old Merovingian line. No, he was a genuine emperor of the West in the old Roman tradition. The sole and real emperor of the East was hardly pleased with this usurpation, but what could he do? He did the only thing left. Since the Roman Empire had always tolerated kings along with the emperor (remember that in Jesus' time Herod was king while the emperor Tiberius was reigning), he pretended to recognize Charlemagne as such. Grudgingly, some fourteen years, later the Eastern emperor finally bowed to reality and accepted Charlemagne as a "brother" emperor.

Thus far, under the impulse of *The Donation of Constantine* (supposedly giving the pope full spiritual and temporal power), the pope had transferred the Western part of the Roman empire to the Franks, and given the imperial crown to an outsider (Charlemagne). Indeed, the pope was now a kind of super emperor himself. He lost no time in taking on the trappings of such a title. For example, the papal residence, the Lateran Palace, which had been given to the Roman bishops by Constantine, was renamed the Sacred Palace in 813. For the first time, the pope put on the imperial scarlet, and officious imperial titles were conferred on papal officials. Once more, there were those who felt that this was a far cry from the fraternity of the little church-communities of the Acts of the Apostles. It is not surprising, then, that groups in succeeding ages would claim that the *Donation* had seduced the church, or that the reformers would see a vast difference between apostolic Rome and imperial Christian Rome.

In any case, Charlemagne's coronation was one of the most significant events of the Middle Ages. It signified not only the rebirth of the old Roman empire, but also the birth of a Christian one (the Holy Roman Empire as it would be termed by the twelfth century). As a matter of fact, Charlemagne wanted to restore the old Roman empire, and except for England and Muslim Spain, he did. There was another significant consequence—the beginning of a power struggle between the emperor and pope. That is why Charlemagne was annoyed at being crowned by the pope. If the pope could give the crown, he could take it away. In a showdown, it would be the pope who would have the final say. For this reason, Charlemagne refused to return to the pope many of the lands seized anew by the Lombards. He was ever wary of papal ascendancy. But the die was cast, and ever afterward (until the title did not really matter anymore), every emperor would feel the compulsion to be crowned as "Holy Roman Emperor" by the pope. The two powers were now officially united, and the scene depicted in the mosaic in St. John Lateran's would hold true for centuries. In it, both Pope Leo III and Charlemagne are kneeling in front of St. Peter, one receiving from him the keys of heaven, and the other the pallium, the symbol of civil power. Both are thus equals in the running of people's lives, but significantly both receive their mandate from the church (Peter). Historian R.W. Southern has this shrewd observation:

It seems very likely that the papal coronation of Charlemagne as emperor was intended to show that the pope could delegate imperial authority in the West to whom he would, in accordance with the terms of Constantine's gift. But it is certain that Charlemagne did not acquiesce in this view of his position. Indeed it is evident that the idea of a Western empire as a means of extending papal authority was a mistake from beginning to end. It was a mistake primarily because in creating an emperor the pope created not a deputy, but a rival or even a master. The theoretical supremacy implied in the act of creation could never be translated into practical obedience to orders given and received. Hence the pope's practical supremacy over his emperor came to an end at the moment of coronation. It is not surprising that the popes of the later Middle Ages sought to exercise their supreme temporal lordship through other channels than the empire, which Pope Leo III had rashly created for this purpose on Christmas Day 800. This action was the greatest mistake the medieval popes ever made in their efforts to translate theory into practice.[1]

The mistake was not so evident at first, because Charlemagne was a genuinely religious man, and desired to see realized the ideal of empire and church united as one entity. In fact, according to strict measurement, Charlemagne did have the upper hand in arrangement. From the beginning, he and his successors looked upon the clergy as their functionaries (as indeed they were) and the pope as simply their (the emperors') chief bishop. But there was no open conflict, and no need to challenge the relationship, because both church and empire saw themselves as working hand in hand. Both, in Charlemagne's eyes, were engaged in a cooperative effort to foster a truly Christian state. This accounts for Charlemagne's intimate interest in the Church's activities. It was he who instituted reforms and really directed church affairs. In fact, to be accurate, Charlemagne represents the medieval version of the old pontifex. He was an imperial ecclesiastic, a royal priest. He was the real head of the church. It is not without reason, therefore, that paintings and mosaics and statues portray the emperors of this era in actual clerical dress looking like benign bishops.

DECLINE OF THE EMPIRE

There were many reasons why Charlemagne's empire began to decline. For one thing, it was too big. Second, there was always tension between the king and his princes, many of whom were more powerful than Charlemagne. They were rich in land, had absorbed many people into their feudal domains, and were powerful enough to be almost independent of the royal will. In short, they were very effective in undermining the kingship as a central power. Finally, under Charlemagne's sons and grandsons, who took to warring against one another, the empire dissolved into fragments. The once proud empire broke up into some fifty smaller municipalities and some five major divisions. With the Treaty of Verdun in 843, two large sections remained, the future France and the future Germany. Between these two was a vague buffer area: the future Netherlands, Belgium, Luxembourg, Switzerland, and northern Italy. There were several other external forces that hastened the disintegration of the empire. New invaders were harrying Europe: the Magyars and the Slavs. The Muslims penetrated as far as Italy, and sacked Rome in 844. Last of all came the Vikings!

The Vikings descended from the Scandinavian north in the ninth century. They included the Swedes, the Norwegians, and the Danes. They had been active before. For some two hundred years, the Norwegians had been assaulting Ireland and other places. Hatefully anti-Christian, the Vikings destroyed Christian foundations wherever they went. They usually made straight for a monastery knowing they would find portable wealth there. They besieged the towns all along the Mediterranean, sailed up the rivers in Italy and France (attacking Paris in 886). Some places were spared only by the age-old practice of buying off the marauders. It was at this time that medieval Europe became dotted with castles for protection against the Vikings.

Charles the Simple, one of the last of the Carolingian line in France (before the Capets took over), decided to allay the Viking terror by offering one of their leaders, Rollo, some land in France. Charles hoped that the Vikings would thus settle down and also defend their land (and the rest of the country) from fellow Vikings. Rollo accepted the offer, and in time his Viking descendants accepted Christianity and intermingled with the native population. They became known as the Normans (a shortening of Norseman or North-men), and their territory is still known as Normandy, an area made famous in World War II by the Normandy invasions of the Allied Forces. Five generations after Rollo, one of his descendants, the famous William the Conqueror, would leave his Norman France, cross the channel, and conquer England in 1066. As we shall see by this event, he laid the foundation for the perennial rivalry between France and England.

The Viking raids left Europe in a state of almost total chaos. Civilization suffered a great setback. Learning declined and disorder reigned everywhere. The effect was immense, both on society and on the church. A contemporary lamented:

> The Northmen cease not to slay and carry into captivity the Christian people, to destroy the churches and to burn the towns. Everywhere there is nothing but dead bodies—clergy, laymen, nobles and common people, women and children. There is no road or place where the ground is not covered with corpses. We live in distress and anguish before this spectacle of the destruction of the Christian people.

FEUDALISM

The breakup of the Carolingian empire left the field open to the local lords and nobles. Power soon became localized in these nobles, who were the real rulers. Thus, feudalism was born. Feudalism rests on the fact of a decentralized government. Small counties or areas became self-contained islands. Such feudal areas were created primarily for war: war against another's feudal domains, protection from the terrible Vikings, robbers, and outlaws. Since the feudal enclave was primarily military, obviously the relationship of the master or lord of the area to his subjects or vassals was that of allegiance. The lord swore to protect his subjects, they swore to give him soldiers, service, and loyalty in return. Many of these little feudal domains became quite powerful (ruled over by the famous counts and lords of history and literature), and they did provide a stabilizing influence. They became, in effect, like the Greek city-states of old. Feudalism certainly answered a need in troubled and fitful times, but it eventually worked havoc with the church in several ways.

With the feudal system, the building of monasteries and churches was done by the local lord. He even staffed them, so that the priest or abbot could be hired or fired at will. By the eighth century, churches created in this manner, beholden to their lay masters, far outnumbered those churches under the authority of the local bishop. In short, the parish churches had fallen into the hands of the laity as disposable property. We can see the consequences of this. A priest or abbot or bishop who was a hireling and vassal of the local lords must have a double allegiance: to the spiritual needs of the people and to the master. As vassals, they had to supply soldiers, give military service, do homage to their lord, and attend the feudal courts. It is not difficult to see how the lord would naturally tend to appoint his own men as priests or abbots or bishops within his little "city-state." It is easy to see how such clergymen would often be more warriors than clerics, their priestly functions subordinated to their military functions. The clergy became closely allied with the secular order of the day. We shall see how in another hundred years, under the German emperor, Otto I (936-973), the bishops became, in effect, national servants in a German state-church. The German bishops would gain a reputation as mighty warriors, and it became a common saying that a German bishop could not be pious. They had become, in effect, soldiers with miters.

There was one other problem connected with feudalism. The local lord (or emperor) began not only to appoint bishops and priests, but also to "invest" the bishop. That is, he gave his appointee the symbols of the episcopal office: the crozier and the bishop's ring.

The lord might permit the traditional election of the bishop by the people or the abbot by the monks, but if he did not like the candidate, he simply withheld the land on which the monastery or diocese lay. Obviously, this whole system undermined the authority of the church. This problem of "lay investiture," that is, a layman investing a bishop with the signs of his office, would have to stop. Equally obvious is the fact that this system could not be stopped without a great struggle between church and state.

Other scandals followed from the general chaos of the times. Lay investiture produced its counterpart evil: simony, the buying or selling of church offices. An unscrupulous lord might sell a diocese or abbey. An unscrupulous churchman might buy it for his cousin or nephew or bastard son. Naturally, if the new bishop or abbot had to pay a high price for his office, he in turn would tax his peasants and clergy to regain his money. Such cynical practices were certainly demoralizing in many ways.

In the ninth century, some monasteries had resident prostitutes; priests and deacons openly took wives and mistresses. Unworthy men were putting themselves into church offices, and church offices were being filled by unworthy men. It is no wonder that some bishops were little more than barbaric and coarse warriors wearing the miter. Some bishops never saw their dioceses. During this time, the practice of charging fees to dispense the sacraments arose. The one salvation for all of the mess was a strong papacy. Unfortunately, the general deterioration of the times had reached the highest office as well.

THE PAPACY

The basic problem for the papacy was certainly hidden when Leo of Rome crowned Charlemagne as emperor in 800. The Holy Roman Empire had been effected, but there were some unanswered questions. How, for example, would either side prevent the other from encroaching? The emperor still appointed the bishops. But if the emperor appointed the bishops and the pope conferred the imperial title, could not one blackmail the other if the need arose? With Charlemagne, in general, there was no problem, but this was not to be the case with his successors. True, Pope Gregory IV came out on the side of Lothair, Charlemagne's grandson, in the contest for power with his father, Louis. The very fact of the pope's intervention, and his bestowal of the crown on Lothair, was significant. In fact, the papal power ascended as the fortunes of the empire descended. Several strong popes took advantage of this. Nicholas I (858-867) was a forceful pope who not only preached the equality of papal and imperial power but preached the superiority of papal power. Nicholas stated flatly—and acted accordingly—that the pope could intervene in imperial affairs.

Papal power continued to grow in part because of the "Pseudo-Isidorian" decretals, a mid-ninth-century collection of legislation and disciplinary decisions supposedly going back to the second century. Some of them were genuine, while others were definitely forged. These documents were aimed at protecting the rights of bishops from the interference of lay nobles by declaring that all ecclesiastical authority rested in the papacy. Thus, bishops were independent from all local jurisdictions, and they had the right of direct appeal to Rome. This also made the pope the prime ruler over all his fellow bishops. It is doubtful that a pope as strong as Nicholas would need or use those forged documents to prove his position, but they did exist and were used by some to bolster papal power. Nicholas did, however, go so far as to try to compel the Eastern church to reconfirm his primacy and, as we shall see later, felt free to excommunicate its patriarch, Photius. Nicholas's successor, Pope John VIII (872-882), felt sure enough of his position to crown as emperor, not Carloman, personally chosen by the previous emperor, but Charles the Bald. The point to note is that, as the Carolingian empire declined, the popes were able to become strong enough to make and break emperors. Ironically, they could do this only as long as they had the protection of the very emperors they were domineering, since the pope and his small papal states would never have enough power to resist aggression.

This logic, however, worked both ways. If the pope could make or break the imperial crown, would it not be possible, if the emperor's protection were withdrawn or enfeebled, to obtain the crown from the pope by force, violence, or intrigue? The answer was a shameful affirmative. When Charles the Bald died, and the feudal lords assumed power at the break-up of the empire, the papacy was left exposed. For the next years, the papacy was at the mercy of the current strong man. Charles the Fat, for example, forced Pope John VIII to crown him emperor in 881. A certain Gui, a local feudal strongman from Spoleto, forced Pope Stephen VI to crown him as emperor. Gui forced Pope Formosus to crown his son, Lambert, the same way. Later, when Formosus intrigued to oust Lambert, whom he had unwillingly crowned, Lambert stormed into Rome, had the newly dead pope's body exhumed, conducted a trial over the cadaver, and handed the dead body over to the populace, who threw it into the Tiber River. This sordid incident, as much as any, reveals the distress of the times and the low level of civil and ecclesiastical life.

With no strong central power since the decline of the Carolingian empire, unscrupulous men and their wicked families used the papacy for their own ends. Nor did they and others hesitate, in the barbarity of the times, to use every treachery to get their own men on the papal throne. Family rivalries revolved around the papal prize, as can be seen from the fact that, between the 870s and 990s, there were thirty-seven popes, many of whom were good men who were murdered by their opponents.

Roman families like the Theophylact, Crescenti, and Tusculoni got their hands on the papacy and for seventy years rotated their proteges on the papal throne, even while local reform councils were being held to rescue the papacy. These men were the personifications of the "bad popes" of history. Pope Adrian II (d. 872) was married, and his wife and daughter lived within the Lateran palace. Pope Stephen VI was imprisoned and strangled in 896. John VIII was hammered to death. John X was murdered. The Theophylact family had two daughters, the notorious Theodora and Marouzia. Pope Sergius III had a son by one of them, and this son later became John XI. This was the pope who would witness the marriage of his mother to her brother-in-law. Pope John XII was not yet twenty years old when he became pope. Having lived the life of a layman and giving great scandal, he died while visiting his mistress. Benedict VI was strangled in 974. John XIX was a layman who in one day received all of the ecclesiastical orders in order to ascend the papal throne. He was assassinated in 984. Pope Gregory V was poisoned in 999. Sylvester III sold his papal title to Gregory VI.

In all, the average reign of the popes in those disastrous times was about three years. In between the intrigues of the Italian families, the emperor Otto I (the greatest emperor since Charlemagne), and his successors, Otto II and Otto III, were trying to force their choices on the papal throne. These were generally good men, but every time the emperors returned to their native Germany, one of the local Roman families would depose the new pope and insert one of its own. It was during this period, by the way, that the legend of a woman pope, Pope Joan, came into being. Her sex was discovered, the story goes, when the "pope" supposedly gave birth during a solemn procession. The origin of this legend must likely is based on a misreading of the common abbreviation of *Joan.*, for *Joannes* (John), in early medieval manuscripts. Whatever the origin of this legend, it must have received some reinforcement from the times, when the shady ladies mentioned above ran the papacy and provided some of its mistresses.

To appreciate how such a sad state of affairs could exist at the very highest level of the church, we must recall once more the general chaos of the times. The Vikings had just left Europe exhausted. The East and West were then fighting over the Photian schism. The Muslims were renewing their attacks on Europe and Italy. They sacked the great monastery of Monte Cassino (Benedict's first foundation) in Italy, and Rome itself was threatened. There was no strong emperor around to protect Rome or the papacy. All kinds of rivals were seeking to be emperor, and therefore seeking to control the papacy, which crowned the emperor. Italy was in a state of siege, and the local Italian families were vying for both political and spiritual control. Without any real central political strength (such as Otto would provide) and strong popes, the disgraces listed above were inevitable.

But there was hope. Underneath all this evil, all this deterioration of the church, a spirit of reform was inexorably moving. The papacy simply had to be rescued from outside manipulation. The monasteries needed reform. The secular clergy needed rescue from the lay investiture problem. Celibacy was honored more in the breach than in the reality and simony was rampant. For example, the count of Toulouse went into "partnership" with another noble in 1016 to charge 100,000 shillings as the price for the privilege of nominating the archbishop of Narbonne. The emperor Conrad II in 1025 appointed bishops to Liege and Basel for a high price. There is the oft-quoted comment of an archbishop of Rheims, who said in 1069 that his office would have been more enjoyable if he did not have to say Mass now and then. In brief, the needs were so great that an answer had to come, and it did. It came, not unexpectedly, from the monasteries, rather than from the bishops (who were, in reality, princes beholden to their feudal lords). As objects of reform themselves, and with their vested interests in their feudal lord's service, the bishops could hardly be expected to initiate reform. No, it must come and did come from the monks.

CLUNIAC REFORM

We must keep in mind that the essential structure of the church remained intact in spite of the corruption at high places and the manipulation of bishops and popes by unscrupulous kings or noblemen. Indeed, no other structure was available for, as we have said so often, the church was the ghost of the old Roman empire.[2] There was the papacy, the bishops, their see cities, and surrounding dioceses. There were the parish churches that in the tenth century had multiplied all over the countryside, and there were the monasteries. In spite of princely patronage and interference, these monasteries remained the centers of piety, the idealized refuge in troubled and turbulent times, where a person could flee from the world and find peace and holiness. In fact, the monasteries increasingly drew men and women into their walls, particularly if a monastery could boast of a holy person, a saint. Even some of the knights repented of their ways and became monks. As such, the monasteries continued to draw those sincerely interested in holiness and, as time went on, the demand grew for a better and stricter discipline. Such were the beginnings, here and there, of what would erupt into the great monastic reform of the eleventh century, the Cluniac reform—a reform movement that would last for the next three centuries.

The monastery at Cluny had one big advantage since its founding in the tenth century. Each monastery was not autonomous, but under the great abbot of Cluny. Therefore, each monastery was not subject to its local abbot, who might be a nobleman's kin or protege, but subject to the one overall abbot at Cluny. He, in fact, ruled over some 3,000 priories and was in turn loyal to the pope. Moreover, the Cluniac order was egalitarian. The smallest peasant could advance as far as his talents would lead him. The Cluniacs were for the most part men of talent, ability, and high moral standards. Many a bishop came from the Cluniac monasteries, and from this sort of infiltration gradual reform was brought about. Not only were the monasteries working for reform, but also, outside their walls, there were many outstanding bishops seeking reform.

Another approach to the problem lay in the many attempts which were made by individual reforming bishops. In Italy there were outstanding bishops like Atto of Vercilli (d. 964) and Rathier (d. 968) at Verona; in Germany we may mention Wolfgang at Ratisbon (d. 994), and his two successors in the same see, Bernard (d. 1022) and Gothard (d. 1039); while in France and most notable were Gerard at Toul (d. 994) and Fulbert at Chartes (d. 1029). These men were indefatigable in visiting their dioceses, in checking abuse, in raising the very low standard of clerical literacy and in fighting to secure an incorrupt and chaste clergy. Yet a good bishop might be followed by a bad one—some rich man's son or a relation of the prince—and all the good work might be undone....[3]

Such men were convinced that the dependency of the church on the imperial and princely power was immoral. The church could never flourish and fulfill its mission until it became absolutely independent of all temporal powers and interests. Bishops belonged to the church, not to the prince. Priests belonged to the church and not to the world, their wives, and families (for the marriage of priests was tolerated in practice). The reformers, therefore, had a program. No ecclesiastical appointments should ever be made by a layman. Priestly celibacy must be restored in all its vigor (this would also prevent the sons of the clergy from inheriting church property). The church must be wholly spiritual and canon law must be completely observed. Since the church must be free of temporal interests, and free of king and emperor, it must of necessity gather round its spiritual head, the pope. Such was the essence of the Cluniac reform.

The reform began to take hold in the tenth century and had spread everywhere by the eleventh. A whole new spirit, a whole new piety was the result. Monasteries were founded in vast numbers. Religious enthusiasm ran high. Piety, processions, and ceremonies were everywhere. There was now no monastery that did not boast of its saints. The laity sometimes protested the marriage of priests. The "peace of God," which interrupted wars on feast days, was introduced. It is no wonder that the eleventh century became the age of great church building, and great donations to the monasteries and to the church. There was regeneration abroad. The big question was: Would it reach up to the high places? Would and could the Cluniac reform rescue the papacy? It could and it did. As we shall see in the following chapter, two great forces were joined: monasticism and the papacy. Together they would lead the church to a renewal and a period of fruitful reform.

CHAPTER 9

The Rise of Papal Power

THE GERMAN EMPERORS

It was not only the whole spirit of Cluny that eventually led to a reform in the papacy but also, with no little irony, the efforts of the German emperors. The irony, as we shall see, was that the emperors' success in placing good men on the papal throne was the very cause of the future conflict between emperor and pope. Let us backtrack a minute. In 919, Otto I became king of Germany. This was not the Germany we know today. Rather, this was what was left after Charlemagne's grandsons divided his empire into three parts with one Carolingian king over each, one of them being designated as emperor. The middle section (northern Italy, central Germany, Holland, Belgium, and Switzerland today) soon fell into disarray, with the result that the remaining two sections divided the middle between themselves. The upshot was that there were now two kingdoms, comprising what we may roughly call the future France and Germany (parts of the middle section would remain bones of contention for centuries, as they swung from one kingdom to the other until, very late in history, they gained independence). As we shall see, the last Carolingian in "France" died and was replaced by a new line, the Capet line. In "Germany," with the death of the last Carolingian, Louis the Child, the local princes and magnates, in 911, elected the new Saxon line of Henry the Fowler. Henry was a hard-working king and bequeathed a rather strong kingdom to his son, Otto I. Otto is rightfully called the "Great" and may be regarded as the first German monarch. When he became emperor, the Holy Roman Empire of Charlemagne was revived—minus France—and the seat of political power shifted from France to Germany. It is Otto's kingdom that is considered by the Germans to be the first kingdom or "reich." (Later, Hitler would call his infamous "kingdom," or rule, the Third Reich, the second being the Hohenzollern rule under Chancellor Bismarck.)

Otto was quite conscious of the power of the princes, for there was really no such thing as a centralized government in the Middle Ages. Princes and lords were often more powerful than the king, who might be merely a desired figurehead. Local lords were the real rulers of their terrain and frequently had policies at variance with those of the kings. Otto, therefore, decided to offset the power of the princes by wooing the Catholic bishops. He made them his secular princes and rulers, which meant that they were his vassals. He gave them lands and made *them* lords on a par with the princes; or, in effect, Otto secularized the church in Germany. The possession of the diocese or see became the possession of the empire. It was inevitable that such bishops would be beholden to the king. We have already seen, in the last chapter, how the German bishops were more noted for their military service to the king than their piety. Of course, the investiture problem was most pronounced in such a situation.

This alliance of church and king became the cornerstone of the new political order established by Otto the Great—an order which was consummated by Otto's coronation at Rome in 963 and the restoration of the Western empire. The new empire was thoroughly Carolingian in tradition and ideals. Indeed, Otto I went even further than Charlemagne in his reliance on the church in the practical administration of the empire, so that the bishops acquired the functions of government. This conversion of the episcopate into a territorial and political power was to some extent common to all the lands that had formed part of the Carolingian empire....But nowhere did the process go so far, or have such serious political and religious consequences, as in the lands of the empire in Germany and Lorraine, where it was destined to condition the relation of church and state for six hundred years. Even the Reformation did not exhaust the consequences of his anomalous situation, and the German episcopate remained inextricably entangled with the political order until the ecclesiastical principalities were finally liquidated in the age of Napoleon.[1]

The whole situation can be compared to the President of the United States (if he had the power to do so) making the Catholic bishops governors of the fifty states and members of his cabinet. In due time, it would not be difficult to see that a strong president would not only pick such governors, but see to it that the proper men became bishops in the first place. He might even go so far as to give the bishop his insignia of episcopal office as well as swear him in as governor of his state. It would also not be difficult to see that such a bishop would soon be more politician than cleric, more loyal to state than church. This is roughly analogous to the situation that prevailed under Otto the Great. The pope could hardly be happy about this state of affairs, but at this particular time he was being besieged and Italy was being threatened. The pope not only could not protest against Otto, but actually had to beg him for aid. The price of this aid was that the pope crowned Otto as emperor. Otto was now Holy Roman Emperor, although his empire was restricted to Germany and northern Italy (not France). This would have momentous effects on both church and state.

Italy, for one thing, as part of the empire, was now tied to Germany. This naturally meant that the church was also similarly tied to the Germanic empire. Indeed, the emperor felt quite responsible for the church and for the papacy. (As an aside, we might mention that this over-concern with Italy and the papacy distracted Otto and his successors from Germany proper. The result was that, while France and England would soon emerge as great nations, Germany would not do so for many centuries—all because its emperors were constantly being wooed by the largely unrealistic concept of a Holy Roman Emperor in charge of Italy and the church.) In any case, Otto continued his dominance of the church. He appointed bishops and the popes. Otto I, Otto II, and Otto III all had their choices on the papal throne at one time or another. In fact, Otto III had even considered moving to Rome so that he would sit at the pope's side as the two of them jointly ruled Christendom.

It must be admitted that the German emperors were also bent on reforming the papacy by picking good popes and deposing bad ones, though for their own ultimate designs. They had to be dissatisfied to see the papacy the plaything of the local Italian families. Thus, when a new German emperor, Henry III, went to Rome for his coronation as emperor, he went full of zeal, determined to rescue the papacy from the contending families. He deposed the current rival popes (there were three put forth by different families at this time), and put in his choice, Clement II (1046). Clement II was a good pope as were his successors, Damasus II, Leo IX, and Victor III. (We shall see more of Leo IX later.) They were Germans who were filled with the spirit of Cluny and free of Italian connections. But precisely as such they were bound to have conflict with the emperor, because now the scattered reform movement became centralized in the papacy. We must remember that one of Cluny's programs was that the church must be free in order to function. The emperor's interference was clearly contrary to that freedom. What place, these reforming popes argued, could the temporal power of the emperor have in such a total spiritual reality as the church? It was not right that the popes should be beholden to the emperor— even a well-meaning emperor—who appointed them. Besides, in the last analysis, the popes knew that it was they who must make the Cluniac reform workable. If the key figures were the bishops (and they were), then the bishops must be controlled by the popes, not the laity—be they local princes, kings, or emperors. The latter should not be the ones investing the bishops with their office. No, the bishops must be free men, not beholden to emperor, king, or local lord. In other words, lay investiture must cease.

The first really able and spiritual pope in two centuries was Leo IX. He was filled with the spirit of reform and was able to influence the power of the papacy for centuries to come. He begins the real growth of papal power. He made alliances with the Normans, dealt with the Eastern church, sent delegates, and began the vast amount of centralizing correspondence. We shall see Leo IX later in connection with the East-West schism.

However, the man who was to bring the crisis to a head was Pope Nicholas II (1058-1061). Even his choice of name was significant, for the first Nicholas (858-867) had been an ardent opponent of imperial power. This Nicholas would no longer openly tolerate the protection and the appointment by the emperor. He threw down the challenge when he decreed in 1059 that hereafter the pope was to be chosen only by the college of cardinal bishops. He also decreed that the papal election did not even have to take place in Rome if conditions were unsettled (as they often were), but in any safe place. Nicholas, in true Cluniac spirit, went further and condemned simony and forbade a married clergy.

GREGORY VII

Nicholas's policies were successful, as was apparent in the choice of his successor, for the College of Cardinals in their first election elected an avowed anti-imperial, Alexander II (1061-1073), as next pope. Finally, open warfare broke out with the election of Alexander's successor, the long-time mentor to previous popes, the Benedictine monk, Hildebrand, who became Gregory VII in 1073. Gregory is often called the founder of the papal monarchy. He was a Cluniac reformer. As such he did not and could not believe that reform should come from the civil power, however well-meaning. No layman, Gregory was convinced, not even an emperor, should run the church. What this meant, of course, was that Gregory decided that the old concept of the divine right of kings had to go. It was different with a Charlemagne who was truly a universal ruler, but now the empire had shrunk into the several feudal municipalities. Christianity and a single empire were no longer coextensive, and Christendom was "larger" now than the territory of the empire. In other words, it seemed that the pope who represented a religion that transcended the boundaries of the empire should now assume universal power and full political and spiritual supremacy. That is why Gregory encouraged remote territories such as Spain, Denmark, and Hungary to accept the protection of the Holy See, implying that he, the pope, rather than any emperor, was the real universal center of things.

To achieve this end, Gregory lost no time in aligning the proper roles of civil and ecclesiastical power. A whole series of propaganda tracts on each side of the question began to flood the countryside. Gregory drew up the famous *Dictatus papae* ("rescripts of the pope"), and by his letters left no doubt of the position of church and state. Among the many things he insisted on were: the pope could be judged by no one; the pope alone could depose and restore bishops; he alone could make new laws, move bishops, depose emperors, and absolve subjects from their allegiance to their rulers. Certainly this was a large and bold extension of papal power. Gregory would soon have the opportunity to put his notions to the test.

Two years after his election, Gregory acted by forbidding clergymen to marry. At the same time, he cautioned the people not to receive the sacraments from married clergy (a position that could be interpreted in the old Donatist heretical sense). He condemned and forbade lay investiture to any ecclesiastical office under the pain of excommunication. No emperor, king, or local lord was to henceforth bestow the ring and crozier on any man and make him bishop. We can see the urgent crisis this provided for the emperor if we recall that the German kings and emperors had made the bishops their feudal princes. If the emperor could not continue to control such bishops, the very ground of his control system was cut out from under him. His own men, as it were, were suddenly removed from his employ. The emperor, Henry IV, could not but respond with resistance.

His first tactic was the usual one of trying to get Gregory declared unworthy of the papacy and thus deposed. Henry miscalculated badly. He failed to take into account the effects of the Cluniac reform, nor could he get enough support from his own followers. Gregory, for his part, had powerful allies, such as the other non-German bishops, Henry's own Saxon political enemies, the Normans, and the powerful Countess Matilda of Tuscany. Gregory responded to Henry's maneuvers by excommunicating him, thus freeing his subjects from allegiance. Henry, seeing his weak position, had no choice but to submit, for the time being. We have the famous and often romanticized scene at Canossa on January 28, 1077. Gregory was on his way to a council meeting and stopped at the castle of Canossa (one of Matilda's). Henry sought him out there in the snow and piercing winds, and for three days waited outside for an audience. Gregory had no illusions about Henry's sincerity, but what could he do, especially for one seeking spiritual forgiveness? Gregory absolved him.

Henry quickly regrouped his forces, attacked the name of Gregory, and set up an anti-pope. Gregory again excommunicated Henry, who in turn marched on Rome to enforce his will. But Gregory shut himself up in the impregnable Castel Sant' Angelo. Henry was then forced to flee Rome before an advancing Norman army that freed Gregory, who soon died in their company outside Rome. The sequel to this story was that Henry's anti-pope was simply not received, even though he took up his residence in the Lateran palace. Gregory was acknowledged as the true pope and even venerated for his courage. Later, Henry was forced to abdicate before his enemies. Finally, the whole struggle between emperor and pope ended in a compromise which, under the circumstances, was a victory for the papacy. In 1122, a concordat was signed at Würms that allowed the bishops to be appointed solely by the church, but, after their installation, they must swear loyalty to the emperor, who had the right of veto. Actually, the power struggle between pope and emperor would seesaw back and forth for centuries. In reality, the only thing that solved the problem, as we shall see, was no solution at all. The whole struggle simply became meaningless as both the notions of king and pope fell into disrepute, and Europe found out that it could do without both.

However, more far-reaching results were to occur beyond the vision of the antagonists. One interesting side effect was that, with the imperial power in church affairs definitely and officially broken, the princes filled the vacuum and were greatly influential in the appointment of the bishops since, we recall, the bishops were still secular princes holding fiefs from the prince landowner. Pope Pascal II (1099-1118), interestingly enough, wanted the bishops to solve this problem by abandoning their fiefs; the emperor, however, would not give his consent to this, for he knew that should this happen, the vast territorial wealth of the bishops, conceded to them by successive German kings, would fall into the hands of the lay princes. It is worth remarking that in this instance, the kings insisted that the bishops keep their territorial wealth—so that the kings could use it as a tool for their own political purposes.

CONSEQUENCES

Much would be made of Gregory's outlandish pretensions in later centuries. The pretensions of Innocent III and Boniface VIII, for example, went even further. Outrageous as such claims may seem to modern eyes (and we shall examine them in another chapter), we must not read modern concepts into medieval situations. Gregory was basically trying to reestablish the church's right to rule itself and to free the church of state control.

At first Gregory seems to have hoped for imperial cooperation in implementing further reforms. But Henry IV's resistance to his decree banning lay investiture prompted the pope to excommunicate the emperor in 1075 and again in 1080 and to justify his action on the basis of the superior character before God of the ecclesiastical power. It must be emphasized, however, that although a profoundly significant and potentially revolutionary confrontation with lay authorities did in fact take place throughout Europe, this was not the purpose of the papal action. To Gregory and his successors this confrontation seemed necessary to the achievement of their aims. Its ultimate consequence, a papal interference in lay affairs rather than the opposite, was scarcely foreseen at the time.[2]

Indeed, Gregory started the great centralizing trend that his successors would continue to the point of absurdity, and that would collapse by the middle of the seventeenth century. But this trend did not substantially compromise the essential Petrine office. Rather, the seventeenth-century collapse was an end of an era, a policy, a style—not the end of the papal office itself. We must remember that the legal concentration of all civil and church authority in the papacy was a product of human decisions and can be traced to specific dates in history, such as Gregory's time. This whole process did not touch the essential office of the pope as the principle of unity.

Another fact worth noting is that Gregory VII has been at different times accused of being a visionary who attempted to ruin the state, and a calculating cleric who wanted to subordinate the state to the church. Historian Henri Pierenne makes this comment:

For these reasons, Gregory has been regarded as a sort of mystical revolutionary, an Ultramontane endeavoring to ruin the state. But this is to introduce modern ideas into a conflict where they are entirely out of place. To begin with, in the case of Gregory there was no trace of Ultramontanism. Ecclesiastical discipline was still very far from being dependent on Rome. He made no claim whatever to nominate the bishops. What he wanted was to ensure that the church should no longer be defiled by secular meddling. As for his conflict with the state, what does the accusation mean? The Empire was not a state. It was actually governed not by the Emperor but by the princes. As we have seen, there was no administration; noth-

ing in the shape of what we must call, for the want of a better
term, a central power, giving it a hold over its inhabitants. If
the Emperor's power was diminished what injury was inflicted on society? None, since it regarded him with indifference;
since it was not he who defended and protected it. No catastrophe could follow from the victory of the Pope, and the
church was bound to benefit by it. If we are to understand the
situation we must regard it from this point of view. We must
not forget that this was the heart of the feudal period, and that
social and political evolution were on the side of these princes,
who, as we have seen, were the real organizers of society. And
they were on the side of the Pope. The feudality was working
for him, just as he, without intending to do so, was working
for it. A little while ago it was the rising bourgeoise that was
taking the part of Rome; now it was the feudal magnates. Here
what we call the State is not secular society, but the royal power, subjecting the church and diverting it from its mission in
order to support itself.[3]

Pirenne's description of the emperor as simply a royal person
without capital, court or power is accurate as we shall have occasion to show elsewhere. Thus, Gregory was not defying the (fiction-
al) state; he was fighting against a specific royal personage who
wanted the papacy for his own ends.
   A final unforeseen and unintended irony from the whole lay investiture victory was that Gregory was unconsciously but actually
inaugurating the complete secularization of the state. This would
come many centuries later, but the seeds had been planted. The
close cooperation of kingdom and church, the ideal of the Carolingian empire, gave way as that empire waned and disappeared.
From this point on, there existed the possibility that if the church
could do without royal interference, the state could do without the
church. Where national states would grow up in the future, this nascent novelty would become a reality.

VICAR OF ST. PETER

Having seen the inauguration of the centralized papacy under
Gregory VII, let us see how far this power went. The contrast between what the papacy was and what it would become will be more

apparent if we return to a very old title of the bishop of Rome as the "Vicar of St. Peter" ("vicar" means "the representative of"). This strikes modern Catholics as an awkward title, for we know another. Yet there is no doubt whatever that the most significant root of papal prestige in the centuries prior to Gregory VII was the fact that Peter lived and died in Rome.[4] Peter's tomb was, for centuries, the touchstone of Christianity—the observable, physical, material link to Jesus himself. Peter was in every sense the "rock" on which the church was built. Up until medieval times, people swore on the tomb of St. Peter; documents incessantly called on Peter as witness to this or that. Because of the centrality of Peter, the pope's position was unique. The pope was considered nothing more or less than Peter personified. St. Peter, as it were, was still active—but through the pope. More than once, there was the spontaneous acclamation that Peter had spoken through such and such a pope. Devoted Christians, missionary monks, bishops, all were conscious that Peter was involved, and that they were claiming converts, not for Pope so and so, but for Peter.

From the eighth to the eleventh centuries, the most active force in Rome was Peter, and his "presence" was the main source of Western unity during these centuries. It must be especially noted that this unity, centered on the presence of Peter, did not necessarily have anything to do with administration. As R.W. Southern puts it:

It was a unity compatible with the very slightest exercise of administrative authority. The affairs of the church received little direction from Rome. Monasteries and bishoprics were founded, and bishops and abbots were appointed by lay rulers without hindrance or objection; councils were summoned by kings; kings and bishops legislated for their local churches about tithes, ordeals, Sunday observance, penance; saints were raised to the altars—all without reference to Rome. Each bishop acted as an independent repository of faith and discipline. They sought whatever advice was available from scholars and neighboring bishops, but in the last resort they had to act on their own initiative.[5]

After the eleventh century, as we have seen with Gregory VII, the era of centralized administration began. This era has lasted down to modern times. Yet, such a trend in centralization ironically started out almost by accident, and for the highest motives:

In essence [the papal reform under Gregory] was to be a thorough overhauling of the body ecclesiastic, a purging of its major abuses, notably simony, clerical marriage, immorality, and over-much involvement with things secular. This was to be done by means of various improvements in the machinery of ecclesiastical government, in particular its more effective centralization in Rome. As a consequence, the papal office gradually assumed a new character. Under the influence of contemporary canonists, Rome came to be regarded as something more than the see of the Apostle Peter and the place of his tomb, a holy object of pilgrimage, and possessing a spiritual predominance over all other churches. It became in fact the center of an effective system of jurisdiction, sometimes referred to as the papal monarchy.[6]

VICAR OF CHRIST

From the eighth century on, we have already noted the beginnings of the growth of papal centralization. We saw *The Donation of Constantine* set the tone by claiming that the pope was to be an active and, above all, an independent ruler. The *Donation* document, we recall, was a forgery,[7] telling how Constantine gave the pope and his successors the supreme temporal power in the West, the universal rule in both the temporal and spiritual realms, as the only and genuine heir to the old Roman empire.

The Donation of Constantine was the work of someone else other than the pope. It was the work of some people who were filled with a romantic concept of the past, who wished to restore what they considered the power and grandeur of the pope before the German emperors took over. This forged document, therefore, had great appeal. Soon, under Gregory VII, whole sections of the *Donation* were included into new collections of church law. Still, the *Donation* fell short in some respects, because it depicted Constantine allegedly delegating authority to the bishop of Rome. This undermined papal claims to complete authority. Thus, another basis for papal power was sought in other texts such as the *Isidorian Decretals*. These texts were unrelenting in their affirmation that the pope, from God and by divine decree, was the supreme ruler in all Christendom in both spiritual and temporal matters. If, in the eighth century, the popes had turned from the Eastern emperor to tie their fate to the Carolingian empire, now in the eleventh century, under Gregory VII, they turned from the Carolingian successors to stand alone.

Perhaps as significant as anything is the noticeable shift in terminology in the old phrase we saw above, the "Vicar of St. Peter." Now the phrase the "Vicar of Christ" took its place. The prestige of the papacy now rested not only on Peter, but also on Christ. Thus, Innocent III (1198-1216) could claim, "We are the successor of the Prince of the Apostles, but we are not his vicar, nor the vicar of any man or Apostle, but the vicar of Jesus Christ himself."

EVIDENCES OF PAPAL CENTRALIZATION

In the hundred years after Gregory VII's death in 1085, the centralization process reached its peak. The vast amount of business, and the consequent administrative machinery needed to handle it, provide a perspective on this centralization process. From all over the Western world letters came to Rome. Even with the rapidly expanding society from the eleventh to the fourteenth centuries, the number of letters written by the popes at this time reveal the extent of centralization. For example, under Sylvester II (d. 1003), about ten papal letters a year were written. Under Leo IX (d. 1054), some thirty-five papal letters were written. Under John XXII (d. 1324), over 3,646 letters a year were written. The growth of a bureaucracy should be obvious, because the correspondence covered a multitude of matters, from the granting of benefices to the settling of major and minor jurisdictional quarrels. By the twelfth century, the papal court was handling thousands of litigation cases. It is no wonder that canon law received its greatest impetus during these centuries. By the thirteenth century, the complex papal bureaucracy set the stage for viewing the church as a pyramid with its ruling monarch, the pope, at the top, in control of the minds and spirits of all believers.

As indicative as anything else of the growing Roman activity are the church councils themselves. From the seventh to the twelfth centuries, there were only three councils, all held in Byzantine territory with no Westerners attending except the papal delegates. However, from the twelfth to the fourteenth centuries, there were seven ecumenical councils. All were held in the West, all were called and presided over by the pope, and all were almost exclusively Western in attendance.

Further testimony to the rapidly growing centralizing machinery at Rome is the fact that, from 1159 to 1303, every pope was what history has termed a "jurist pope"; every one of them was a lawyer. While such popes did bring stability to medieval society and laid the foundation for modern society, they achieved this at the expense of their primary pastoral tasks. Interested in keeping the wheels of papal government going, they could not give the time and energy to the spiritual leadership that was needed. In short, such popes were hardly distinguishable from any other able secular leader.

Because the papacy had become such a center for immense daily business, Europe was disturbed but not let down when the papacy moved from Rome to Avignon from 1306 to 1376. Since the papal set-up was where business was conducted, the location really made no difference. Indeed, the whole business machinery had moved into fantastic elaboration. It must always be remembered, however, that papal power grew largely because it satisfied the needs of the great mass of clerics and even, as it turned out, the needs of the secular princes. When these needs were rerouted in the fourteenth and fifteenth centuries, all of the seeds of disaster inherent in the papal system sprang up and choked it to death. Meanwhile, the system continued to grow and included three main categories: indulgences, arbitration, and appointments to church offices.

INDULGENCES

An indulgence (a forebearance or lenience) first arose in the early church-communities as a compassionate response to the severe penances of that time. Usually, a confessor or soon-to-be martyred Christian would intervene to shorten the time of penance for a sinner or lapsed Christian. The first really large-scale granting of indulgences began during the crusades, when the pope granted participants complete remission of the punishment due to their sins. Later, indulgences were granted to anyone who performed a service for the church; still later, indulgences were granted for anything, at the discretion of the pope. In time, the pope gave others the privilege of granting indulgences (confessors, priests, royalty, etc).

Indulgences were also granted for large donations, then for smaller donations, and then simply for a good work done, such as going on a pilgrimage. Thus, in 1300, Boniface VIII granted a plenary indulgence for those who visited Rome during the Jubilee year that was then celebrated once every hundred years. Gradually, the time was reduced until such jubilee years were every twenty-five years. It was Clement VI in 1343 who put the granting of indulgences on its theoretical basis. He said:

One drop of Christ's blood would have sufficed for the redemption of the whole human race. Out of the abundant superfluity of Christ's sacrifice there has come a treasure which is not to be hidden in a napkin or buried in a field but to be used. This treasure has been committed by God to his vicars on earth, to St. Peter and his successors, to be used for the full or partial remission of the temporal punishments of the sins of the faithful who have repented and confessed.

Catholic readers may recognize this teaching as substantially the same as they were taught in grammar school.

Finally, local churches outside Rome were given the same privileges. The whole indulgence business flourished from then on. By the fifteenth century, the ways and means of giving and granting indulgences were beyond counting. Since the "spiritual treasury" was inexhaustible, there could be no theoretical end to it. However, it was on this very issue of the selling of indulgences that Luther challenged the church in the sixteenth century.

INTERNATIONAL POLITICS

By the thirteenth century, it was assumed that the pope possessed all political power as well as supreme spiritual power. It was also assumed that the emperor was the pope's delegate *par excellence,* and depended on papal coronation for his existence. Since the emperor was the chief "delegate," it was thought necessary for the pope to dominate him in order to keep the lesser lords in line. The result was much in-fighting and rivalry between emperor and pope. Obviously, with this situation, the pope had to enter politics full time. Only direct papal jurisdiction over all civil and religious matters could assure the supremacy of the papacy. This accounts for the constant preoccupation of the popes with international politics; why a man like Innocent III had his hand in the politics of every country of Christendom. This situation also explains how the papacy became the seat of all arbitrations among the secular princes. In Italy, of course, where the pope was a fellow land-holding prince, he could not play the role of neutral Grand Arbiter; he had to enter into the military defense of his territories. Pope Julian II was not adverse to leading his soldiers in battle, and he was as much at home in soldier's armor as in papal robes.

GRANTING BENEFICES

As we have seen, the early church had a more democratic process of choosing its leaders. The community was involved by popular acclamation or through its representatives—and this included the election of the bishop of Rome. Because of the strength of tradition and habit, no rules were ever laid down for a papal election before the year 1059. Until that time, the emperor claimed to represent the people in the papal elections. Since he was a kind of spokesman for the Western church, he also felt deputized to speak for them in the choice of the pope. The only trouble, as we have seen in the cases of the German emperors, was that they were too far removed from the scene at Rome. Thus, any papal vacancy was left to be filled by the men on the spot. The "men on the spot" were the clergy and people of Rome or, more precisely, the ruling noble families. We have seen the disgraceful machinations of the Theophylact, Crescenti, and Tusculoni families. Other powerful families were also able to get their men on the papal throne. Innocent III, Gregory IX, and Alexander IV were from the Conti family, Honorius III and Honorius IV from the Savelli family. Later, there was rivalry not only among the local Italian families but also among the French families.

When Nicholas II (1059-1061), in order to be freed of outside control, made the election of the pope dependent on the cardinals, matters were not cured. In fact, the process was simplified because now all the nobles had to do was to influence the electing cardinals! Despite this apparent simplification, the fact remains that in the one hundred and twenty years after Nicholas's decree there were more anti-popes than in any other comparable period in the entire history of the papacy. The situation was not brought under control until the third Lateran Council in 1179, when the requirement was given that a two-thirds majority secured a valid election. In 1945, this was increased to a two-thirds majority plus one. More recently, Paul VI outlined a whole new procedure that would limit the number of companions who could accompany each cardinal, as well as allowing only cardinals under the age of 80 to enter the conclave and elect the next pope.[8]

EPISCOPAL ELECTIONS

We have already spoken in a previous chapter of the election of bishops. Here we will merely recall the general trend. From the eighth to the eleventh centuries, the theory that a bishop was chosen by the people was, in practice, translated through the local lay ruler. Kings, after all, were responsible for the temporal and religious well-being of their subjects, and so they claimed to represent both clergy and people. However, by the twelfth century, the clergy had, as canons of the local cathedral, begun to choose the bishops. Since it was inevitable that there would be factions, squabblings, and rivalries, an arbitrator was needed. This opened the way for more direct papal control over those chosen to be bishops, especially as the theory to support this new process was being formed at the same time. The operative phrase was "plentitude of power." The pope had it, and the other bishops shared in it. This was not a true "college" of equals but a board of junior partners under a senior partner. By the fourteenth century all episcopal confirmations (*not* elections) were in the hands of the pope. Benedict XII summed it all up in 1335:

> We reserve to our own ordination, disposition and provision all patriarchal, archepiscopal and episcopal churches, all monasteries, priories, parsonages, and offices, all canonries, prebends, churches, and other ecclesiastical benefices, with or without the cure of souls, whether secular or regular, of whatever kind, vacant or in the future to be vacant, even if they have been brought to be filled by election or in some other way....

But this teaching did not mean that the lay rulers were completely out of the picture. On the contrary, things were only made more simple. The lay ruler, instead of dealing with a network of clerics and canons, had to deal with only one man now, the pope. By force, bribery, or compromise the lay rulers secured the confirmation of their loyal friends to episcopal sees.

This process of lay rulers seeking papal confirmation of their episcopal candidates continued until the nineteenth century, when the papacy assumed full authority to appoint bishops, except where there were concordats or treaties giving specific rulers that right. In 1980, Juan Carlos of Spain became the last monarch to give up that right.

Finally, we must mention that centralized papal control extended beyond the bishops all the way down to the most humble ecclesiastical office. This naturally led to literally thousands of petitioners coming to Rome to seek the multitudinous clerical offices. Those with the greatest amount of secular support—which meant the kings and local nobles—got what they wanted. Thus, the new system merely simplified the access of the mighty to the affairs of the church and reinforced the very undue influences it was designed to suppress.

SIGNIFICANCE

There is one final overview in our look at the rise of papal power and centralization. We saw that, with all of the business flooding into Rome, it was necessary to have many laws. These laws, some old, others innovative, had to be codified if their sheer volume were not to collapse the whole system. Thus in the middle of the twelfth century, a monk named Gratian was asked to assemble all of the existing material and laws into one vast code. He has been regarded as the founder of canon law for this achievement. Under the lawyer popes (1059-1103), Gratian's codification was expanded. This is significant because it brought about a measurable change in church order and structure. This was evident in its internal life as well as in its external organization:

> ...The decretals rather than the gospel became the basis for moral judgments. Even the sacraments came to assume a legal complexion, and a sacramental jurisprudence developed. Baptism was now considered as a legal act through which in law the newly baptized became a member of the Christian body, itself a juristically constructed entity. Matrimony was considered as a legal contract whose validity depended on avoidance of canonical impediments drawn up by the Holy See. Ordination to the priesthood was determined by legal enactments which placed jurisdictional rights above holiness of life as qualifications. A knowledge of canon law became requisite for

ecclesiastical preferment. Throughout the remainder of the Middle Ages, canon lawyers rather than theologians dominated the papacy. The role of the papacy in medieval theological matters is incredibly unimpressive.[9]

Since all the laws were being centered in the person of the pope, the old structures disappeared or became empty forms. This meant that the old metropolitans, archbishops, and bishops lost control of their local areas or sections to the centralizing power of the pope. Significantly, the loss of power by the episcopacy meant that collegiality and collaboration of any sort were on their way out. If the "fullness of power" rested with the Holy Father, what need was there for consultation, local councils, and area synods? In short, the community was suppressed and corporative rights were re-routed into papal channels. The general ecumenical councils now took over, and they could only be summoned by popes. The rights of canonization passed from the bishops to the popes, who act freely on their own. The right of a cathedral chapter to elect its own bishop was undermined by papal restrictions and reservations. A huge and one-sided development was taking place. It produced the absolute papal monarch. There was only one culminating power not explicitly claimed by the pope: papal infallibility.

However, as the papacy successfully escaped the control of the emperor, it had to seek protection elsewhere. It consolidated the papal states, became a little empire in its own right, and then had to assume the role of military protector. But the pope and his little kingdom needed more protection than that. So the papacy began the dangerous course of allying itself politically with various nations and kingdoms. Usually it turned to France, then later to Spain, and later still to Austria. The price for this protection was, in fact, to reduce the church to the status of a department of the state. Worse than this, however, the net result was to ally and identify the papacy with royal absolutist power, so that when the first democratic stirrings were aroused, the papacy found itself emotionally wedded to the royal monarchist establishments. The papacy simply could not take kindly to democracy, and wound up inflaming severe anticlericalism by its "old regime" posture.

From all that we have said, we can see that it has been a long, complicated road from the original church-communities of the first centuries, to Byzantine and Frankish imperialism, and finally to Roman centralization. The church had changed its "look." Gone were the old varieties of ministries, and simple terms such as presbyter, deacon, and widow. They had been replaced with the terms of officialdom: chancellor, cardinal, and pope. Gone was the circle concept of community. It had been replaced with the pyramid concept of ascending hierarchical power and control. (We shall have occasion to mention later how the church of the Second Vatican Council sought to change some features of the pyramidal structure by means of the internationalization of the curia, the formation of a synod of bishops, the establishment of local parish councils, and so forth. These are all reactions of the modern church to a medieval pyramidal church that had grown too top-heavy.)

CHAPTER 10

A Time of Greatness

PAPACY AND REFORM

In the last chapter, we saw how the papacy reached the height of its power. At no other time in history were church and society so interconnected. Everything else seemed to reach its peak at this time, thus earning for the thirteenth century the epithet, "the greatest of centuries." This may indeed be an exaggeration, for there were many flaws, but there were enough significant events and developments to give some substance to the title. What had happened was that the reform movement had unleashed new spiritual forces. The creative elements that we associate with the achievements of the late Middle Ages came from the dynamic fusion of this reform movement with the papacy. A central unity had been created, and this joined most of the active elements in Christian society in a common program. There was a common cause, a supra-territorial spirit—a whole European brotherhood had brought out the best in everyone. Look at what happened: the first universities were founded; scholasticism hit its stride; chivalry flourished, and the new romantic notion of love was introduced. Towns were revived; a merchant class was starting; civic life was growing, and hospitals were being built. The Gothic cathedral came into being, and learning flourished, thus producing some of the greatest scholars of any age. New religious orders were founded. The list is impressive.

In this chapter, we will examine the greatness of the age before the shadows fell. We can do no better than to start with an event that reflected the whole spirit of papal reform. This event formed a constant background to the late Middle Ages for two centuries and was, in no small way, responsible for the revival of commerce and all that went with it. We refer to the crusades.

THE CRUSADES

The crusades lasted from the eleventh to the thirteenth centuries. Although they ended in dismal failure, they started out with genuine idealism and religious fervor. Let us begin with some background. The Muslims had surrounded Europe and penetrated into some areas. For centuries, they were to remain a chronic source of fear, conflict, and confinement. However, by the tenth century, they were beginning to lose some ground in Europe, and the Christians were having some military successes here and there. By the eleventh century, the Christians were taking the offensive against the Muslims. It was partly in the spirit of these local successes, and partly as a continuation of them, that the first official crusade was initiated.

We have already made reference to the pilgrimage as an act of popular piety in the Middle Ages. Even more than the two other great centers, Rome and Compostela, Jerusalem was the object of special veneration. Pilgrimages increased, and many references were made using the image of the Holy City, such as the "new Jerusalem" when referring to the church. Many a person wanted to see the land blessed by the sufferings and the death of the Savior. Particularly around the year 1000, the usual hopes or fears that the world would end gave special urgency to the desire to see Jerusalem before that happened. Many reasons underlay the first crusade, but there can be no doubt that the majority of people joined it in the spirit of a pilgrimage.

The thought of a crusade was not entirely unexpected. The Byzantine empire of the East, constantly besieged by the Muslims, often asked aid from the West. This petition was a mark of its desperation, since East and West had recently split over disciplinary and authority issues, as well as doctrinal differences. In addition, although the Muslims had been quite tolerant of Christians visiting the holy places in Palestine, a new group of Muslims, the Seljuk Turks, came to power in the East and began persecuting all Christians—visitors and residents alike. An appeal was made once more to the pope by the emperor of the East. It is worth noting that the appeal went to the pope, not to any emperor or king, a fact which was a commentary both on the weakness of the kings and the growing universal power of the pope. The pope who answered the appeal was Urban II. He was the successor of Gregory VII, who, we recall, had recently died in exile, at odds with the emperor. The emperor, Henry IV, despite his submission to the church at Canossa, still wanted to rule the papacy, and had installed an anti-pope, Clement III, at Rome. Thus it was that Urban was at the little French town of Clermont. There, in 1095, in a masterful speech to a large mob who had originally come to look into the investiture quarrel between the pope and Henry IV, Urban called for a crusade. The speech skillfully combined an appeal to the highest spiritual and practical motives. Urban claimed that the honor of God demanded that sacred Christian shrines should be in the hands of Christians, not infidels. Besides, a crusade might provide more land and food. This last appeal was not lost on the majority of the French there, who were suffering from famine at the time.

We must recall that the spirit of Cluny was still very much alive, which accounts in part for the instantaneous and almost fanatical response to Urban's appeal. Indeed, for the most part, the crusades were basically mobs of armed fanatics already keyed up by the never-too-far-beneath-the-surface millenarianism (the expectation of the end of the world and the introduction of a Golden Age). The crusades, in short, gave emotional and political vent to the large social group that was neither nobility nor clergy, but simply "nobodies." The crusades gave them an alternate route to that instant sanctity seemingly monopolized by the clergy and the wealthy. That was one reason why these vast crowds picked up Urban's impassioned "God Wills It!" as the crusading slogan. They painted red crosses on their shirts and shields so that no more red paint or cloth could be found in Clermont that day.

There was no doubt that genuine religious motives played a powerful part in this excited response. After all, there was a promise of a full indulgence for the sins of one's life for all crusaders. In addition, people were truly incensed at the thought of Christ's tomb in infidel hands. Of course, in such a large undertaking, there had to be other motives in the background. Perhaps, in the back of the pope's mind, he felt that the Western church could extend its influence at the expense of the East. For some feudal nobles, the prospect of a crusade gave a legitimate outlet for their warlike and landless sons. For others, the appeal may have been in the postponement of their financial debts, or the simple thrill of adventure and the enticement of new lands and new wealth.

There were the usual fanatics like the rabble-rousers, Peter the Hermit and Walter the Penniless, who prematurely led a group of some 50,000 naive enthusiasts to the East to their deaths. The first real crusade (which finally got started in 1097) included no kings or emperor (still a papal enemy), but was composed mostly of French knights and nobles with their armies. Unfortunately, the fervor to kill the infidel spilled over to the Jews, many of whom were murdered by the crusaders on their way to the Holy Land.

> ...When the crusaders cried out "God exalt Christianity," it seemed often to be a mandate to abuse Judaism. When Pope Urban II, the disciple of Gregory VII, addressed the crusaders as "the children of Israel," his words may well have carried for his excited listeners a reminder that the Jews were children of the devil, Jesus' murderers, and God's enemies. What point was there in redeeming the Holy Land, asked popular preachers of crusading like Peter the Hermit and Walter the Penniless, if they left behind them the worst offenders of all? Hence, as great masses of humanity began to tumble together preparatory to setting out for the Levant, they began to swoop down upon one Jewish community after another...In almost every instance local officials—ecclesiastical and feudal—sought to quell the rioters, with some successes in a few places.
>
> Thereafter, however, the inevitable accompaniment to every crusade was a preliminary bloodbath...St. Bernard of Clairvaux, the chief preacher of the crusade, vainly sought to persuade Christians "to leave the Jews in peace...."[1]

Finally the crusaders reached Constantinople. For their part they were literally overawed. There was no village in the West to compare with Constantinople. It had paved streets, night lights, shops, parks, theaters, a magnificent imperial palace, a hippodrome (whose doors later would be used as the doors of St. Mark's Cathedral in Venice), and the splendid basilica of Justinian, Holy Wisdom (Santa Sophia). The Easterners, for their part, were aghast at the crude "Franks" (which was the name they gave to all barbarians), who did not wash, fought among themselves, and whose clergy was actually in armor along with the common people. Enamored by the wealth of the city, the crusaders had to be prodded by the pope to get to the business at hand. Finally, they made it to the walls of Jerusalem. In 1099, the city fell in a massacre so severe that the blood literally flowed like a river through the streets. Even the crusaders themselves were later ashamed for the atrocities committed.

After this, the crusaders began to settle down and proceed to carve out for themselves kingdoms along the Mediterranean. But being so far away from home and in the middle of hostile people, it was impossible to maintain them. Still, these outposts lasted for some two hundred years. Meanwhile, to care for the sick and to protect their kingdoms in the Holy Land, unique military religious orders were founded, the Knights Hospitalers and the Knights Templars. Ironically, the crusaders got along much better with their infidel enemies, with whom they lived side by side for these two hundred years, than they did with their fellow Eastern Christians. In fact, the crusaders got to cherish luxuries they never knew about—such as Persian carpets, brocaded walls, inlaid furniture, wide windows, and running water. It was this romance with the East that would produce the revival of trade.

There were other crusades, more than eight in all, but none of them ever matched the fervor and piety of the first one. The great Bernard of Clairvaux preached the second crusade, but it failed to achieve anything. This was partly due to the lackadaisical response of the comfortable crusaders already in the East. Besides, in Europe, cynicism was setting in, as is shown by the fact that some took the cross of the crusades but paid someone else to go in their place. The third crusade was notable in that three of Europe's great kings took part: the emperor, Frederick Barbarossa (who drowned while on the crusade), King Philip of France (who deserted the venture for an emergency at home), and Richard Lionheart of England (who worked out a compromise with the Muslims). A fourth crusade, preached by Pope Innocent III (1198-1210), was shamefully turned by Venice toward commercial ends. Venice forced the crusaders to sack a rival Christian city and even Constantinople itself in 1204, thus deepening the breach between East and West.

As time went on, it was harder and harder to get anyone except adventurers and riffraff to go on the crusades. The holy places were lost, regained, and lost again to the Muslims. While the crusades had some glorious moments, they lost their appeal and their spirit as European society's interests turned to other matters. There were, however, long-range results, both good and bad. East and West were now more personally hostile to each other than ever before, but commerce was reopened. Luxuries, new foods, and materials were imported from the East, giving great stimulus to trade, navigation, and the rise of the Italian maritime cities. The crusades also brought an extreme intolerance. Back in the ninth century, Charlemagne had at least offered the Saxons baptism or death. Now it was simply death to the unbeliever. Extermination rather than conversion was the forerunner of punishment for the heretic. The Inquisition was just around the corner. For the moment, however, the crusaders represented an ironic ideal of a war for Christ. They would produce many a hero and saint alongside the scoundrel and self-seeking villain.

REVIVAL IN LEARNING

Literacy at this time was almost completely restricted to the church's clerics who wrote and spoke the official Latin. The clerical leadership ran such local and monastery schools as there were. By the twelfth century, however, in the newly expanding towns, several schools were emerging which would grow into the great universities. The first medieval universities, unlike those of today, had no fixed quarters: any place where the small corporation (*universitas*) of pupils and masters could meet would do. In time, rooms were rented, but the whole small university was still quite portable. As in modern times, there was often hostility between the university people and the town. Riots in which people were killed were not unknown. It was the pope who ruled that the university had the right to rule its own affairs. Since this self-rule meant that the university could leave a town, something which no town, anxious for prestige and wealth, wanted, the animosity between the two lessened.

What stimulated the development of the university was the introduction to the West of the ancient Latin and Greek authors in translations made by the Muslims and Jews. The Greek pagan, Aristotle, who was to have such a tremendous influence on the church, was the chief import for study. Furthermore, new types of schoolmasters arose, men who urged their pupils not just to memorize, but to think. Perhaps the most famous of the time was Abelard (d. 1142), known more today for his romance with a pupil than for his intellect. Yet he had the keenest mind of the day, and asked probing questions about faith and reason. He asked so many deep questions that he was condemned by various churchmen and evoked the fulminations of the great Bernard himself. Abelard was the real forerunner of the scholastic scholar, anticipating the work of Thomas Aquinas by a hundred years.

When Abelard was about forty years old, he became tutor of the eighteen-year-old Heloise. At first it was all study, but in time they fell in love. Heloise became pregnant, and they went off to her sister's home, where the baby was born. Abelard wanted to marry her but Heloise was, at first, unwilling to ruin his teaching career. They did get married, but the girl's uncle had Abelard castrated. Abelard became a monk, and Heloise a nun. Abelard continued to come under attack for his theological opinions, and in the end submitted to authority. It is not surprising that he has become the epitome of both the star-crossed lover and the liberal intellectual persecuted by the establishment.[2]

A contemporary of Abelard, and the man who really started the revival of theological speculation, was Anselm of Canterbury. His line of thinking was shaped by the views of the time that had revived a deep sense of sin and thoughts of the suffering and death of Jesus. (In the four accounts of the gospel, the stress is not on the suffering and pain of Jesus, but rather on his attitudes toward his Father and others, even during his passion.) Anselm wrote a book, *Why Did God Become Man?* in which he outlined a theory of redemption (the satisfaction theory in contrast to the earlier ransom theory). In Anselm's medieval society, where rank was important, it was easy for people to conclude that an insult was measured, not by the deed, but by the dignity of the person offended. Thus, Adam's insult to God was most grave because of the infinite dignity involved. Anselm reasoned that no mere human could repair the harm. Adequate apology demanded a person as infinite as God. Thus, only Jesus, the God-become-man, could offer satisfaction. Although some Catholics still hold this view, the satisfaction theory is much criticized today because of its feudal (hierarchical) world view and its underlying legalism.[3]

In any case, the universities received stimulus from thinkers like Abelard and Anselm. By the twelfth century the universities of Paris, Bologna, Padua, Oxford, Cambridge, Vienna, Prague, Heidelburg, Basel, and Salamanca had been founded. By the thirteenth century, the philosophy of Aristotle was really coming into its own. While pagan Aristotle's teaching was condemned by some, others refused to give it up. Theologians like Albert the Great, Bonaventure and, most of all, Thomas Aquinas, "baptized" Aristotle. They were condemned as heretics for this by the Archbishop of Paris. Thomas himself was also censured by the theological faculty at the University of Paris where he taught. His old teacher, Albert the Great, then eighty-four years old, came to his defense. Thomas became quite acceptable fifty years after his death in 1274. Late in the nineteenth century, Leo XIII declared Thomas's system of thought the basis of study in seminaries and colleges. It is to Thomas as poet that we owe the venerable Benediction hymns sung by many generations of Catholics: *O Salutaris* and *Tantum Ergo*.

From this general revival of learning came not only the wandering scholars, but also the first wandering troubadours who sang their love songs in the vernacular and poked fun at the fashions of the times and the foibles of the church. They were responsible for introducing the new concept of romantic love and the elevation of courtesy. Romantic love was a concept formed in reaction to the loveless marriages arranged strictly for purposes of property and power consolidation. The troubadours extolled the love between those not married to each other because "medieval marriages were entirely a matter of property, and, as everybody knows, marriage without love means love without marriage."[4] These songs and poetry of troubadours, in time, turned to other themes besides love. Noble and spiritual themes appeared later, as refinement and courtly culture critiqued a brutal and rough society. The great epic, the *Song of Roland*, was composed at this time. Other stories, such as the tales of the legendary King Arthur and his knights of the Round Table, became the forerunners of the modern novel. In the fourteenth century, English would come into its own with Chaucer's *Canterbury Tales*. When the troubadours went to Italy, the Italian dialects took over, and within a hundred years produced the language in which Dante's *Divine Comedy* was written. Courtly culture and romantic love would find its best expression in that wandering troubadour, Francis of Assisi.

Seeds were planted at this time, that would later cause a crisis to which the church would adapt with difficulty. New ideas and theories would arise to severely challenge the faith. By extolling reason as capable of reaching truth in its own right, Thomas Aquinas and his followers would provide ammunition for those theorists of a later time who would reason that political institutions could, therefore, rest on logic and reason. In effect, this was saying that the state did not have to validate itself in terms of religious or ecclesiastical foundations. The foundation was being laid for the state as a completely secular (this-worldly) reality.

There were other famous notions arising in the universities which were to have profound theoretical effects. One point worth mentioning was the controversy as to whether abstract universal concepts really represented reality, or were just convenient terms to describe essentially a collection of individual terms. This schoolman's argument was to have great practical results in the future. If abstract concepts were only nominal catch-all words, then there are no universal ideas such as truth or, more ominously, government or church. There are only individual citizens and individual Christians. In short, there is no such entity as "church," no need for a universal papacy. Esoteric thoughts like these would do much to underpin church dissenters and reformers of a later time.

CATHEDRALS

Medieval art had one purpose: to make the people feel inspired and awed. Back in the time of Constantine, emperors had encouraged church building. When the barbarians came, they brought their talent for metalworking, woodcarving, and ubiquitous animal motifs. The Irish book of Kells and other manuscripts demonstrate exquisite miniature drawings and paintings. Gregory the Great gave impetus to church music in the chant named after him. In the eleventh century, church and monastery building flourished as a result of the Cluniac reform. The Romanesque style, with its arches and splashes of interior color tapestries, developed and matured.

The first Gothic cathedral, built by the famous Abbot Suger, appeared in the twelfth century. Others soon followed Suger's example, and shortly magnificent cathedrals sprang up all over Europe. Notre Dame was begun in 1163 and completed in 1253; Chartres, the queen of all cathedrals, was started in 1194 and completed in 1260. Then came Rheims, Amiens, and others. They were feats of designs and architecture. Using the ribbed vault and flying buttresses, they gave a graceful, airy, and spacious effect, filled with soft light coming in from walls made of stained glass. Sometimes, a Gothic cathedral was the work of the people themselves. Chartres, for example, was built by men, women, children, even lifelong enemies, carrying stones on their backs. But beyond romantic examples like this, the singular fact is that the cathedrals were professional jobs done by paid labor and overseen by a master craftsman or carpenter. Such cathedrals started out as religious places to celebrate the sacraments, but were soon diverted to large and stupendous shrines to house the ever-popular relics. The bigger the name associated with the relics, the bigger the cathedral. Therefore, the cathedrals were generally not the result of any spontaneous impulse of the common people, but the result of the aspirations of the wealthy. The cathedrals were for highborn monks and noblemen, not for the ordinary person.

A visit to any European cathedral will readily show that they are spectacularly inefficient for public worship. The choir, for instance, is almost totally cut off from public view so that the monks might sing in private and be protected from the drafts. Rood screens cut off other portions. The people did not come there to worship as they did to a parish church. The cathedrals were, in effect, large private chapels for the aristocrats. This is seen in the growing custom after the eighth century of burying prominent archbishops within a cathedral. Little by little, anyone who could pay for the privilege was also allowed to be so enshrined.

The cost of these cathedrals, as might be imagined, was enormous. Money was frequently raised by the selling of spiritual favors, such as indulgences. Money ran short as often as not, which explains why some famous cathedrals took centuries to complete. In one sense, the glorious cathedral was the epitome of everything that was wrong with the late Middle Ages: signs of privilege and wealth, segregation of the masses, and vast centers of relic collecting, money-making shrines, and vast commercial enterprises inflicted on the common people by nobility and wealthy aristocrats.

Eventually, such cathedrals became the center of the town. Plays were often performed on their steps. Preachers preached there. Business was conducted inside. Town meetings literally meant that the townspeople were fitted into the cathedral. Finally, the cathedral was the place of worship and a catechism in stone. There were hundreds of statues and pictures portraying people beset by devils and aided by angels while on their journey to God. Later, the snobs of the Renaissance would look down on such masterpieces, calling them barbaric or "Gothic" (the name of one of the barbarian tribes). The generations since the Renaissance, however, have continued to look upon the great Gothic cathedrals as magnificent works of art. Kenneth Clark catches the spirit when he writes:

> ...Chartres is the epitome of the first great awakening in European civilization. It is also the bridge between Romanesque and Gothic, between the world of Abelard and the world of St. Thomas Aquinas, the world of restless curiosity and the world of system and order. Great things were to be done in the next centuries of high Gothic, great feats of construction, both in architecture and thought. That was the age which gave European civilization its impetus. Our intellectual energy, our contact with the great minds of Greece, our ability to move and change, our belief that God may be approached through beauty, our feeling of compassion, our sense of the unity of Christendom—all this, and much more, appeared in those hundred marvelous years between the consecration of Cluny and the rebuilding of Chartres.[5]

THE TOWNS

There had always been a few towns in Europe, but they were small fortress places or residences of the bishops. Perhaps they had a cathedral or a monastery. But these towns never grew. The barbarian invasions, the Slavic invasions, the Viking maraudings, and the whole landlocked economy imposed by the Muslims left no need or role for towns. However, as we have seen, it was the crusades that reopened trade between East and West. Maritime towns like Venice began to flourish. Eventually, as the Muslims lost more control, even the Baltic Sea became accessible. The great fairs of the Middle Ages began to grow into great enterprising centers where people from all over the world brought their goods. It was no accident that, with its extraordinary coastline and Venice's predominance, the Italian towns should be the first to grow into large centers. With commerce, the means of exchange would arise in Italy.

There arose the first banks (from the word *banc*, or bench, at which they transacted business), credit, and, above all, the revival of money. In due time, in the face of so much commercial pressure and the new stimulation of capital, the leadership of the church was forced to change its attitude on the taking of interest on loans. In the previous land economy, taking interest on loans was considered exploitation (usury). In the new money economy, this could not be the case anymore, and so the church modified its stand.

Along with this revival of trade, commerce, and money came a new merchant class of people. For the first time, large groups of people were not attached to the soil but were wanderers, carriers of new merchandise and new wealth. When commerce became more a way of life, trade made towns more practical. The town began to grow (it was crowded, wretched, and unsanitary—but *free*). For that reason, it drew serfs and artisans into a growing middle class dedicated to keeping their common liberties and prepared to obey their common officers. As these people took a hand in the running of their towns, civil, as opposed to clerical, administration began. In due time, a few prominent merchant families ruled the towns. Merchant guilds appeared to control competition among the artisans, and civic pride was born. The medieval town of the eleventh and twelfth centuries became a real conglomeration of free people engaged in trade, crafts, and industry with a free civil government. If at one time a person would travel in Europe from monastery to monastery, it was soon becoming the norm to travel from town to town. Like the monastery, the town became an oasis of security and peace in a world of insecurity and war.

From this condensed description of the rise of the town, one sees that drastic changes in church and society were in the offing. For example, the town, as its administration grew, began to employ secular personnel. The secular personnel began to use the vernacular language of the people in their transactions, not the traditional Latin of the church. This was another sign that the church was less at the center of the lives of the people. While the townspeople were religious (witness the many religious guilds founded at the time), the feeling grew that the official church should keep out of the commercial matters. The church's influence also lessened, because towns gave rulers an independent source of wealth and power. Towns also fostered independence and a variety of lifestyles. Towns created a class of business-minded people who one day would replace church legal procedures, remove clerical financial exemptions, and take away the church's educational monopoly. In short, the towns, although allied with the papacy against the empire, would be the pivotal point for a whole new secular (this-worldly) orientation of life.

NEW RELIGIOUS ORDERS

To demonstrate how rapidly and basically society was changing, we may note that for almost seven hundred years there was practically only one religious order in the church: the Benedictines.[6] Then, in the twelfth century, about eight major types of religious communities and their derivative branches appeared on the scene. No longer, as in the past, did kings and nobles seek the spiritual aid of monks in the unwavering belief that the spiritual weapons of the monasteries were as necessary to the safety of the kingdom as armed knights. No longer would monks be asked by all manner of people to do penance on their behalf. People feared that all who left repentance incomplete would end in hell. (This was before the medieval doctrine of purgatory was formulated.) No longer would the Benedictines be the only outlet for the landless children of the noble families, or for women who preferred not to marry.

This appearance of rival religious orders did not mean that the Benedictines ceased to perform great service to the church and state. Yet, by the twelfth century, religious life began to decline. Life was becoming more complex. Some monasteries had become rather socially exclusive, their sources of revenue were drying up, and they had fossilized into great symbols of stability from which no innovations could be expected. As society expanded, new ways to live and pray were sought, and they were found in the new orders. On the one hand, there were the Augustinians. An informal group compared to the structured Benedictines, the Augustinians dedicated themselves to practical service to others (in contrast to the self-perfection of the former monks), and to survival in a world of change. These Friar Hermits of St. Augustine were formed in 1256 by uniting several communities who were believed to have been started by the great Augustine of Hippo himself before the fifth century.

In contrast, on the other hand, a group of reforming Benedictines at Citeaux in 1098 wanted to flee change and the world, and return to pristine Benedictine rigor and purity. Thus, the Cistercians, as they came to be called, fled the world and pushed far into the uninhabited lands of Europe. They were so successful in clearing the land, improving agriculture and livestock breeding that, in spite of themselves, they became wealthy frontiersmen with the frontier virtues of work, aggressiveness, and organization.

FRANCISCANS AND DOMINICANS

As a sign of the changing times, it is significant that the new towns brought into existence the two most influential orders of the times, the Franciscans and the Dominicans. The older orders, like the Benedictines and Cistercians, were rooted in the soil, but these new orders represented a decided shift away from the country to the city. They were bourgeois middle-class orders founded by middle-class people (Francis was the son of a merchant). These orders, as Henri Pirenne reminds us, "lived on the alms of the bourgeoisie; and it was for the sake of the bourgeoisie that they exercised their apostolate, and the success of this was sufficiently proven by the multitude of brothers of the tertiary order, among both the merchants and the artisans who were associated with the Franciscans."[7] This was something new: an order of brothers (*fratello* in Italian), or friars. They were not, as of old, to withdraw from the world, but to penetrate it. They gave to the age the common spectacle of the traveling friar and itinerant preacher.

The Franciscans, of course, were founded by the universal saint, Giovanni Bernadoni, nicknamed the Frenchman, or Francis, for his preference for the French fashions. He made his decisive conversion to Christ the day he forced himself to kiss the sores of a leper. From then on, with his high taste for romance, he chose to live the simplicity of the gospel or, as he would say, to court Lady Poverty. Unlike others, Francis did not hate material things; his was not a stoical attitude embracing poverty for its own sake. Francis sought poverty as a means of liberation: the freedom to be, to grow, and to rejoice in the beauty of the world. It is not without reason that the modern age has chosen Francis as the patron saint of ecology. It was no sour-faced mystic who composed the *Canticle of the Sun* or who saw delight in all the creatures on earth. It was no spiritual Scrooge who invented the Christmas crib and sang happy songs. He loved the towns and dedicated himself to ministering to the townspeople.

Francis's followers soon grew in numbers. In spite of local jealousies from the monks and secular clergy, he obtained approval for his new order from Innocent III in 1208. Inevitably, dissension took place with rapid growth, and with heavy heart Francis resigned his leadership. Much of the difficulty was over style and order. Was it practical to beg one's food from day to day? For five men this was no problem, but for five hundred? How strict should the order be in following poverty? In due time, many interpretations of the Franciscan ideal arose that splintered off into the many Franciscan groups we know today. Francis died in 1226 and was canonized two years later.

...of course, St. Francis's cult of poverty could not survive him—it did not even last his lifetime. It was officially rejected by the church; for the church had already become part of the international banking system that originated in thirteenth-century Italy. Those of Francis's disciples, called Fraticelli, who clung to his doctrine of poverty were denounced as heretics and burnt at the stake. And for seven hundred years capitalism has continued to grow to its present monstrous proportions. It may seem that St. Francis has had no influence at all, because even those humane reformers of the nineteenth century who sometimes invoked him did not wish to exalt or sanctify poverty but to abolish it.

And yet his belief that in order to free the spirit we must shed all our earthly goods is the belief that all great religious teachers have had in common—eastern and western, without exception. It is an ideal to which, however impossible it may be to practice, the finest spirits always return. By enacting that truth with such simplicity and grace, St. Francis made it part of the European consciousness.... It was only because he possessed nothing that St. Francis could feel sincerely a brotherhood with all created things, not only living creatures, but brother fire and sister wind.[8]

In spite of severe internal problems, Francis's spirit continued in his friars, in the related women's order founded by his friend, Clare, and in the Third Order of associated laypeople that was the forerunner of the many lay confraternities that exist today.

Dominic Guzman (d. 1221) was a Spaniard. He had joined the Canons Regular of St. Augustine and, along with a papal delegation, had been sent on a mission to convert heretics. Dominic soon perceived that the official pomp and high living of the papal delegates would convert no one. Rather, poverty, simplicity, and learning were necessary. He, therefore, gathered like-minded men around himself to be an order of preachers who lived a life of poverty. From this emerged the Dominicans. They soon spread all over Europe, like their new contemporaries, the Franciscans, and drew into their ranks some of the West's greatest scholars. (Dominic is said to have received the rosary from Our Lady and given it to the world. Actually, this is a legend propagated by the Dominican Allen de Rupe in the fifteenth century. The rosary, at least in a primitive form, had been around as early as the ninth and tenth centuries.)

It was not long before both Dominicans and Franciscans entered fully into the academic life of the new universities, which so far had been little more than training grounds for civil administrators. But the friars wanted to convert the world, and for that they had to delve into every branch of learning. They brought a new dimension and excitement to study and expanded theology. It is not surprising, therefore, that the greatest names in medieval theology belong to the friars: Albert the Great, Aquinas, Eckhart, Bonaventure, Duns Scotus, and William of Ockham.

From the perspective of the people, both orders were a welcome reaction to the formalized attitudes of the regular clergy. The friars proved to be an effective antidote to the pervasive anti-clericalism of the times, which looked askance on the low morals, bad conduct, and ignorance of the regular clergy. Both Franciscans and Dominicans soon developed into a corps of professional clergy, preachers, university teachers, and confessors. Their work on behalf of the church at this period can hardly be over estimated. They became the personal agents and emissaries of the reformed papacy. Later, however, this prophetic and evangelizing vocation of the first friars was subordinated to the demands of ecclesiastical power politics. This produced a split in the reforming movement from which medieval Christendom never quite recovered.

ALBIGENSIAN HERESY

There were no significant heresies in the church for eight or nine hundred years. It seems strange that the problem of heresy (a teaching that goes contrary to the expressed faith of the church) should reappear in the church at the height of her power. Perhaps heresy did not have a chance to get a foothold before because of the sheer preoccupation of the church with other matters, such as the various invasions and consequent adjustments over the centuries. Now the church was consolidated. But with consolidation came a certain rigidity and intolerance. In any case, at the height of her glory, the rift of heresies appeared.

One such group, known as the Waldensians, was started in the twelfth century by a wealthy French merchant, Peter Waldes. He called for reform and a return to primitive Christianity. He had ample reason to call for reform. The crusades had fallen into disgrace and failure. Some of the crusaders had even been excommunicated for looting a Christian town. Clerical celibacy was still a dead issue, and the religious orders were ineffectual. His group started out, like the Franciscans, to live simply and to preach repentance. In time, when their teaching became heretical, they were forbidden to preach, and then excommunicated when they disobeyed. As a result, they became more extreme and incurred the hostility of the community. Eventually, they were forced to flee into the towns of northern Italy, where they lived quietly until obtaining religious and political freedom in 1848.

At this time, there was a more dangerous and more widespread heresy that the historian Edward Gibbon has called the fourth great crisis in the Catholic church. This was the Albigensian heresy, named for the town of Albi. This heretical sect revived the old Manichean dualism between matter and spirit that stems from their belief in two gods: one who is good (spirit) and one who is evil (matter). Therefore, they denied that Jesus had a human body, because matter was evil. They rejected the eucharist, the Mass, the visible church, and all authority. Sexual intercourse was evil, and extreme asceticism was thought to be the way of the "perfect."

Everything was done to root them out. Bernard of Clairvaux preached against them, but to no avail. They grew stronger, and drove Catholics from their churches. A crusade was launched against the Albigensians with great cruelty on both sides. The campaign went on for twenty years complicated by political overtones. Yet the crusade ended with the heresy still intact. One more tactic was left.

In 1233, Pope Gregory IX turned to the inquisition (not to be confused with the later Spanish Inquisition). Influenced by a new emphasis on Roman law, the death penalty and the use of torture were introduced to root out heresy. The Fourth Lateran Council gave the inquisition its final form and approval. It was a newly founded tribunal—a kind of ecclesiastical Interpol—to seek out and punish heresy. The Franciscans and Dominicans figured prominently in this new office. In the mentality of these times, heresy was to be punished not only for the good of the church and state, but for the good of the individual as well:

> Heresy was considered the greatest of all sins because it was an affront to the greatest of all persons, God; it was worse than treason against a king because it was directly against the heavenly sovereign. It was worse than counterfeiting money because it counterfeited the truth of salvation, worse than patricide and matricide, which destroy only the body. Whatever penalties were appropriate for these crimes were all the more fitting for the greatest crime. To burn the heretic was an act of love toward the community, deterring by fear others who were inclined to the same sin. It was an act of love towards the heretic, for he might be recalled by fear of the fire and save his soul.[9]

Unfortunately, people of every age have rationalized that torture and death are necessary for the preservation of the "truth." (Not only Catholic leaders were involved. During Reformation times, Luther would condone the killing of the peasant uprisers. Calvin would burn Servetus at the stake. Cromwell would kill in the name of the Lord. The Puritans would seek out and burn "witches." Queen Mary would kill Protestants and Queen Elizabeth would kill Catholics. Governments would have their purges of political purification.) The Inquisition and its use of torture to elicit confessions was a distinct backsliding. Fearful churchmen failed to see that the Inquisition not only violated the heretic, but also harried the innocent who would often confess to anything in order to find relief from the torture.

SUMMARY

The twelfth and thirteenth centuries in many ways could be said to represent something of a Golden Age. There were the rise of the new religious orders, the building of the churches, monasteries, and glorious cathedrals. This was the age when the great universities began. It was the age when theology reached a peak in the system of

Thomas Aquinas. It was the age of great saints: Robert, Anselm, Bruno, Bernard, Albert the Great, Louis, and Bonaventure. It was the age of great teachers: Abelard, Aquinas, Peter Lombard, and Ockham. It was the age of the Franciscans, the Dominicans, and Dante. It was the age of the town and the growing merchant class. It was the age of innovation in many ways. Commerce was being renewed, and the economy was undergoing rapid expansion. Capital, money, credit, and banking were started at this time. New notions of romantic love were being purveyed by the troubadours, and vernacular literature was beginning.

It was the age of full papal power firmly based on the two strong pillars of law and wealth. Pope Innocent III, who died in 1216, is considered to be the greatest of the medieval popes, a person genuinely dedicated to the cause of reform:

> Innocent III's pontificate is the brief summer of papal world-government. Before him the greatest of his predecessors were fighting to attain a position of control; after him, successors used the weapons of power with an increasing lack of spiritual wisdom and political insight. Innocent alone was able to make himself obeyed when acting in the interests of those whom he commanded. We may think, with the hindsight of centuries, that the conception of the papacy which he inherited and developed was fatal, in that it aimed at what was unattainable and undesirable, the subordination of secular policy to the control of a spiritual power, but this conception was as acceptable and desirable to his age as has been to our own the conception of an harmonious and peaceful direction of the world by a league or union of nations.
>
> ...It is impossible to dismiss the whole of Innocent's government of the church....The man who, in the midst of business, could recognize and bless the unknown and apparently resourceless, radical Francis was not only farsighted but spiritually clearsighted. He died when the world needed him, when he might have saved the papacy, as he saved the church, from imminent disaster. He died at Perugia; his court left him, and his robes and goods and very body were pillaged by his servants. Yet he did not die alone, for it is all but certain that Francis had been present at his side.[10]

Nothing was beyond Innocent's interests. He put all of France under interdict at one time. He intervened in England, fought for the rights of the clergy in Norway, interfered in the politics of Denmark, Hungary, and Poland, and protected the Jews from violence. There were six ecumenical councils between 1123 and 1274. Innocent called the great Fourth Lateran Council, the "first in the Middle Ages which really attempted to grapple with the problem of the parish priest and his people."[11]

This last point was important because, with the ministrations of the friars, the ordinary people could receive instruction and spiritual help more than ever before. Preaching to the people became so important that many cathedrals were specifically designed to center around the pulpit. Still, people did not frequently receive the sacraments, as is evidenced by one of the canons of the Fourth Lateran Council commanding the faithful to receive the eucharist at least once a year.

It was the age of great devotion to the Blessed Mother, to whom most cathedrals were dedicated. It was the age of increasing devotion to the passion of Jesus. At this time, the Latin hymns *Salve Regina, Jesu Dulcis Memoria,* and *Stabat Mater* were written. It was an age of the flowering of many arts. In Germany, the people were pioneering in mining and the use of the water mill. The Franciscan Roger Bacon was filled with a new scientific spirit. Medicine moved ahead, given impulse by what was learned by the crusaders in the East. In many ways, it was a time with many contradictions. Greatness was there, but it was not going to last. Already there were shadows cast over the "greatest of the centuries."

CHAPTER 11

East and West

THE MYSTERIOUS EAST

It is a major tribute to the effective tragedy of the split between East and West that few Europeans or Americans know anything about the East. For the average Westerner, for the average Western Catholic, the East is "mysterious." One may picture Persian carpets, exotic customs, and all the other images inherited by a movie-going public. A great deal of insensitivity and misunderstanding has brought this ignorance about. For the Christian, this ignorance is a double tragedy, because the East is the origin of the Christian religion. All the first great ecumenical councils were held in the East and some of the greatest saints and theologians were Eastern. This brief chapter surveys the causes and the events that have led to the schism within the Christian church—the first long shadow cast over Christendom.

We have noted earlier that elements of friction were present early between East and West (which usually means friction between the sees of Constantinople and Rome). Many early heretics were from the East, but that was only because Christianity was strong there and very weak in the West. More to the point, in the effort to settle heresies which were rending the empire asunder, emperors seriously tried to bring about reconciliation. Here we have one of the inherent problems contributing to the final split. The emperors, beginning with Constantine himself, felt obliged to have a kind of protectorate over the church. They felt the compulsion to establish religious unity and doctrinal purity. In short, they thought it a part of their imperial mandate to regulate the church in the interest of the state. Thus it was that the emperors, in their efforts to suppress heresy, were the authors of many formulas of doctrine. They called all the first councils. They would continue to be a constant third party disturbing Christian harmony between East and West.

When Constantine moved the capital of the empire from Rome to Constantinople, that city was raised to a special prominence. Obviously, its patriarch would be an important personage. Equally obvious, in the logic of the emperors, they must favor, choose, and control their patriarchs. This imperial interference might not have been so effective but for the fact of the Muslim invasions. By taking over much of the East, the Muslims suppressed the old patriarchates of Antioch, Jerusalem, and Alexandria, leaving only Rome and Constantinople to share the Christian world between them. Constantinople knew it was a latecomer on the Christian scene and easily gave the nod of respect and primacy to Rome. Yet, at the Council of Constantinople I in 381, the attending bishops, mostly from the East, declared Constantinople to be the *second* most important see after Rome. This brought protests from Leo of Rome, since the declaration implied that prominence came from being the imperial capital rather than for religious distinction. (Rome was known as the Church of Peter and Paul, while Constantinople could claim no such apostolic founding.) In general, however, there was harmony and interaction between Rome and Constantinople for the first seven hundred years. After the Muslim onslaught, many Eastern clerics took refuge in the West, and no one minded. Of the seventeen popes between the years 654 and 752, all but five were of Eastern origin. Emperor visited Rome and pope visited Constantinople in the seventh century.

Still, there were differences. East and West did things differently. The West, for example, reconciled penitents in front of the church community, while the Greeks did not. They each received communion differently. The Easterners used leavened bread at Mass. Eastern clergy could confirm and Western clergy could not. Such nonessential differences would eventually be exaggerated, when other more serious events would inflate them. Examples of these serious events include the insistence of some Eastern emperors to impose Eastern ideas on the West, and the emperor's imprisonment of Pope Martin I in 649 for disagreeing with him on doctrine and formula. These instances left bitter memories (and fear) in the West.

One of the most disastrous cases of imperial interference was over the issue of iconoclasm, the breaking of images. This dispute began when the Eastern emperor forbade the use of images and, in 729, tried to force this position on the West. The pope reacted to this, and many lost their lives in the resulting long and bitter quarrel. The emperor punished the pope for his resistance by transferring patriarchal jurisdiction of Greece, Sicily, and Illyricum from Rome to Constantinople. But perhaps more important to note was that the papacy began to shy away from the overbearing East, and began looking for a protector in the West.

POLITICAL SEPARATION

The idea of cutting loose politically from the Eastern emperor was not without some support. With the loss of much of the Eastern areas to the Muslims, the balance in numbers was tilted in Western favor. There were more Christians in the West than in the East. The efforts of the great Western missionaries were bringing whole countries and whole tribes under direct papal influence. This led to practical support for Western independence. Moreover, when the barbarians did come into the Western church, they added a certain discontent with the East, especially with the Greek-speaking popes and the Eastern-styled papal courts. In brief, the feeling grew that Rome ought to be the exclusive property of the West. Such was the feeling when the opportunity for a political break with the East presented itself. Recall that the Lombards were the last of the barbarian invaders to ravage northern Italy in the eighth century. They succeeded in breaking the hold of the Eastern power there. Zachary of Rome was not sorry, in the light of all that we have said, to see the imperial power broken; but he was not ready to be dominated by the Lombards, either. He needed an ally to fill the vacuum. This was the occasion when he turned to Pepin, who drove out the Lombards and donated their land to the pope. The net result was that

Italy was now divided between the papacy and the new Carolingian empire. With the crowning of Charlemagne by Leo III in the year 800, the political break from the East was complete. We have already seen that the pope crowned Charlemagne by surprise as an overt notice to the East that he now had his own man. Even though the Eastern emperor technically was still the universal ruler in both East and West, in practice there were now two co-emperors. Emotionally and spiritually there was still unity and Christendom was one; politically there was division.

CHARLEMAGNE

In the year 787, Adrian, bishop of Rome, sent his delegates to the Council of Nicaea II, the last general council of the church acknowledged by both East and West. The pope sent only delegates in the realistic appraisal that the West had no theologians to compare with the sophisticated East. Charlemagne disagreed. He felt slighted and ridiculed the whole council and the "stupid" Greek church. In effect he was telling the Greek world that it should not be so theologically high-hat; he was also indirectly warning the bishop of Rome that he should not be so influenced by the East. But the Greeks laughed at the fulminations of a man who could neither read nor write, and the pope had no intention of replacing the sophisticated Greek theologians with Western barbarians.

Charlemagne's interference and denigrating of the East did not stop there. He decided to play theologian himself. The background was this: the creed from the Council of Nicaea in 325 included the statement, "I believe in the Holy Spirit." This expression of belief was expanded at the next council, Constantinople I, in 381, by the declaration that "the Holy Spirit proceeds from the Father." However, some theologians in sixth-century Spain unofficially added the phrase "and the Son," which in Latin is *filioque*. Charlemagne adopted this addition and, true to all rulers of the times, he insisted that everyone else in his kingdom make the addition, too. Although the bishop of Rome refused to add the *filioque* to the creed, it was added nearly everywhere without Rome's approval. The popes were reluctant to tamper with a version of the creed that had been accepted by both East and West for many centuries. However, by the eleventh century, the subtle pressure on Rome caused it to quietly add the word. There, for the first time, was a clear-cut case of an actual theological difference between East and West. Naturally, the Easterners strenuously objected because, as they reminded all, any alteration to the creed was expressly forbidden by the councils of the church. This whole incident illustrates how far East and West had grown apart in two centuries. Rome had, in effect, adopted a Western point of view because it had lost theological contact with the East. To show how much distance was really traveled, we may remark here that from the middle of the eighth century until the fifteenth century, there is not another Greek pope. In any case, the whole issue of the creed opened the door to the disaster of the Photian schism.

PHOTIUS

The Photian affair started out in the usual maze of intrigue. A certain Ignatius was appointed patriarch of Constantinople. When the empress who appointed him was forced out of power, Ignatius was deposed, and, in 858, Photius took his place. For some, this led to the question of who was the legitimate patriarch. Pope Nicholas I declared in favor of Ignatius, but the pope's decision was ignored. What was not ignored was the deep resentment toward the Roman pope's interfering in the internal affairs of the East. A public schism developed.

To add to the tension, another event took place at this same time. A certain ruler in Bulgaria (an Eastern area) was baptized by the Byzantine missionaries but, for political reasons, he requested that the pope send him a Western hierarchy. Roman missionaries were quickly dispatched. The point was that certain areas of Bulgaria had never, at any time, belonged to the Western church. This was blatant poaching, and the East feared a total takeover by the West. As if this were not enough, the West insisted in adding the fateful *filioque* to the creed in that region.

Photius, no friend of Rome, quickly denounced the *filioque* addition as heresy, and had a local council depose and excommunicate Nicholas, who had used some strong language in making papal claims. A sudden change of government forced Photius to resign. Union with Rome was restored. Ignatius, too, was restored, only to be replaced by Photius when Ignatius died. This time both Photius and pope were more moderate in their approach, and full communion was restored. But the damage had been done. This was the first out-in-the-open clash between the East and West over the Roman primacy.

We may comment here that there was never any question that the bishop of Rome had a certain primacy. The real question was what was the extent of that primacy, and did it include jurisdiction? Was Nicholas justified in poking into Eastern ecclesiastical affairs? Did the pope have the final word? Actually, there was ground for discussion on such issues. We must recall that the Council of Constantinople III in 680 saw the condemnation of Pope Honorius. That was most significant. It meant that Rome concurred in the condemnation of one of its popes and therefore there really was common ground between the errors of the East and those of the West. The whole attitude in these matters can be summed up in the following words which could have been written today, but which were written in 1136 by an Eastern bishop to a bishop in the West:

My dearest brother...we do not deny to the Roman church the primacy amongst the sister (patriarchates); and we recognize her right to the most honorable seat at an ecumenical council. But she has separated herself from us through her pride when she usurped a monarch which does not belong to her office.... How shall we accept from her decrees that have been issued without consulting us and even without our knowledge? If the Roman pontiff, seated on the lofty throne of his glory, wishes to thunder at us, and, so to speak, hurl his mandates at us from on high, and if he wishes to judge us and even to rule us and our churches, not by taking counsel with us but at his own arbitrary pleasure, what kind of brotherhood, or even what kind of parenthood can this be?

...We should be the slaves, not the sons, of such a church, and the Roman see would be not the pious mother of sons but a hard and an imperious mistress of slaves...I ask your pardon when I say this about the Roman church, for I venerate her along with you. But I cannot follow her along with you through everything; nor do I think that she should necessarily be followed through everything.[1]

This quotation shows not only the Eastern complaint against the West, but also the source of dissatisfaction with the West itself. Interestingly, ideas similar to those of the Eastern bishop cited above were the foundation for much of the agitation about papal infallibility, the drive toward an internationalization of the Roman curia, and decentralization that took place in the decade following Vatican

II. The modern trend toward national hierarchical meetings is based on the belief that there is a fundamental equality of all bishops (collegiality), even the bishop of Rome. As far back as the second century, Ignatius of Antioch said that the church is fully manifested wherever the bishop who represents the eternal priesthood of Christ celebrated the eucharist in the presence of the faithful. Of course, part of the problem between East and West over the exact nature of papal primacy was that the East was not always consistent in its grounds for rejection. The East did not have a firm theoretical basis to refute papal claims. On the other hand, the West had by now a fully developed theory which was consistent and complete. This situation naturally aggravated the tension between the two.

MICHAEL CERULARIUS

As background to the case of Michael Cerularius, we must make mention of a growing "nationalism" in both East and West. The Greek, or Byzantine, empire had regained some of its lost territories, with the result that it achieved a new sense of solidarity and identity. The West was now wedded to the Frankish kingdom; it had its protector. The net effect was that the mentality of both sides changed considerably. The East felt itself now politically equal to the West and, as always, culturally superior. The West looked on the East as heretical and decadent. It was from this mind-set that the principal actors in the Cerularius affair would speak.

Ironically, at the beginning, the time was ripe for reunion, because both East and West were facing a common enemy in the eleventh century. The Normans had invaded southern Italy, an area that belonged politically to the East but ecclesiastically to the West, at least up to the eighth century, when an emperor had transferred the territory ecclesiastically to the East. (Remember the issue of iconoclasm.) The common interest was that the emperor wanted to regain political control from the Normans, but he needed the West's aid to do this; the West wanted to regain ecclesiastical control. Cooperation in this venture against the Normans would be a big step towards unity. Unfortunately, the bishops in southern Italy were quite unwilling to have Latin ways imposed on their Greek churches as part of the deal. Pope Leo IX stated the West's position in the letters that made very strong papal claims. He lavished praise on the emperor but only distain and chastisement on the patriarch. In turn, the patriarch of Constantinople, the ambitious and immoderate Michael Cerularius, imposed Greek customs on the Latin churches in the East. The pope's spokesman at Constantinople, Cardinal Humbert (who may have authored Leo's letters), retorted with equal incivility, and left the impression that reunion meant the East's total acceptance of the Roman claims and customs. The ultimate result was that on July 16, 1054, the Cardinal publicly delivered the bull of excommunication to Cerularius. In turn, an Eastern synod condemned the Western "heresy" and excommunicated the cardinal and his associates. This mutual excommunication of East and West was seen by many as a point of no return.

Still, all relationships were not completely broken, but at the very least the lines were definitely drawn up. Reunion would mean a package deal: The pope would politically support the Greek emperor in return for Greek ecclesiastical obedience. This package remained by far the most attractive consideration for many centuries. We close the Cerularius affair by noting two recent developments. First, Pope John XXIII (1958-1963), who had been nuncio to the East—Bulgaria, Turkey, and Venice (as the latter's patriarch)—and thus in sympathy with the East, had concluded that both sides were responsible for this schism. Second, the mutual excommunications rendered in 1054 were lifted on December 1, 1965, by Pope Paul VI and the Ecumenical Patriarch, Athenagoras I.

THE CRUSADES

We have observed in another place how, contrary to the directions of Innocent III, the crusaders rerouted themselves to Constantinople and, in 1203, captured that city. The following year they sacked and looted the city and even its churches. This was a terrible blow, and increased the East's hatred of the West. Moreover, in the political turmoil of the times, the pretender that the crusaders ostensibly helped to the throne was murdered. They then proceeded to put a Latin emperor on the Greek throne, thus inaugurating a Latin empire in the heart of the East. They divided the European sectors of the Eastern empire among the Franks and the Venetians. The Greek emperor and his Greek patriarch were forced to stay in exile at Nicaea. The pope accepted the already accomplished fact, and tried to bind the empire and its churches to the West by appointing a Latin Patriarch. (These appointments continued until 1555, which was one hundred years after the Byzantine empire ceased to exist.) In 1261, Byzantine armies recaptured Constantinople and restored the legitimate Eastern emperor and patriarch. This whole episode could hardly endear the Easterners to the Westerners, even though political urgency compelled the search for reunion to go on.

THE COUNCILS OF LYONS AND FLORENCE

There were two brief moments of possible reunion. The first took place at the Council of Lyons in 1274. Negotiations were opened for political motives. The Eastern emperor wanted the pope to put pressure on the king of Naples, who was threatening to invade the Byzantine empire. To achieve this, the emperor was willing to talk about reunion between the churches. Terms were agreed upon and the East substantially accepted Western demands; but the high level agreement came to nothing. The common people were the determining factor. So deep was the mutual antipathy that they simply refused to accept agreements made by their leaders.

There was a second try. During the fourteenth century, due to the writings of Thomas Aquinas, the Easterners began to see the West in a new light. To the Greeks, here was a Westerner who had "baptized" one of their ancient philosophers. Here was a cultured and worthy mind. Clearly, the West was emerging from its barbarian state and was now worth listening to. Unfortunately, the West never arrived at a similar respect for the East. The West had grown somewhat. A new spirit of self-criticism had emerged, and the West was ready to admit its responsibility in bringing about division. The stumbling block was still the papal claims.

However, by the fifteenth century, time was running out for the Easterners. The Muslims were at their doors. They needed Western aid. So the East came to the West at the Council of Florence in 1438. The emperor himself came with many of his Greek bishops. There were long and fruitful theological discussions. Being in a poor bargaining position because it needed Western military aid, the East submitted to the demands of the West. The Greeks agreed to the addition of the *filioque* to the Nicene Creed, the primacy of the pope, and all the rest. In one sense, it was moral blackmail, although in another sense, genuine theological advancement and agreement had been made. But it all made no difference. Once more centuries-old mutual distrust and hatred would not permit the common people to accept what was agreed to at the Council of Florence. People in the East were heard to say, "Better the turban than the tiara."

The bull of reunion which was drawn up at Florence on July 6, 1439, and proclaimed in 1452 at Constantinople, came to naught, except for some Eastern churches in the Ukraine that accepted union with Rome, to become known to this day as the Uniate churches. The Greek church, however, refused to accept the bull. There was no time for persuasion or anything else. In six months the Muslims captured Constantinople. The Greek empire fell in 1453, and the union of Florence fell with it. Rome now had the field to itself. A strong, unyielding, centralized papacy gave the West political stability during these tumultuous times. It is regrettable that the cost of this was division of Christendom itself.

RETROSPECT

It may be well to end this sad story of division with the summary of the historians Knowles and Obolensky:

> ...The Greeks could not but feel that Rome had chosen to be alien. These forces of division were aided by the conquests of Islam, which eliminated the balancing weight of the other eastern patriarchs...It is true that, regarding things solely on the level of history, the tradition of Christian unity was strong, and the tradition of the primacy of some kind of the apostolic see of Peter was primitive and widespread. Events, however, were to show that human weakness and unwisdom were too strong for higher considerations of the common good to prevail. On the closed world of the ninth or eleventh century— closed to the minds of the age, whatever might be the movements of Muslim, Hungarian, or Northman—when all thought was Christian and when intercourse between East and West was rare and very slow, legal distinctions, ritual differences, and alleged heretical opinions seemed far more dangerous and abominable than the bitterness and hostility aroused by acts of violence, mutual excommunications, and the extravagant manifestos. No doubt the errors and faults of individuals and groups were many and grave. The irresponsible and brutal acts of power on the part of emperors, with regard both to Rome and their own hierarchy, the accidental but serious

shock of the Iconoclast campaign, the weakness and debasement of the papacy, the factions of Rome and Italy, the intolerant, unspiritual jousting of Anastasius the Librarian or Humbert...the almost complete lack of wide and charitable vision on the part of both popes and patriarchs of Constantinople after the pontificate of Gregory I—all these had their share in making the calamity fatal....[2]

CHAPTER 12

Half-Way Reflections

WHAT HISTORY TEACHES

Although this brief chapter interrupts our narrative, it provides a pause to weigh the implications of what we have learned so far. It is a reflection on what has been happening in the post-Vatican II church. What the modern church is doing is ultimately based on some of the history we have seen so far.

We have learned, for example, that the pope need not be an Italian, for we have come across Greek and German popes. We now know that the pope does not necessarily have to reside in Rome, for we have seen that, in fact, Peter resided first in Jerusalem and then in Antioch. We have seen that the pope does not have to appoint the bishops to their dioceses, for the people or the rulers used to do this. We have seen that the clergy need not wear special clothes, since they did not do so for five hundred years. We have seen that even the term "pope" was applied to any bishop or cleric for several centuries. We have seen that the clergy have been married, and celibacy was the ideal held up "for those to whom it is given." Indeed, we have learned that women had offices and functions in the primitive church. We have learned that the liturgy need not be celebrated in the same way, in the same language, in every region of the globe. We have seen that there were many ministries in the early church, that not every church-community had a bishop, that committee rule is possible, and that other denominations may have valid ministries—the list supplies us with some foundation for many of the churches in the modern church.

WHO IS THE CHURCH?

But we must go deeper and raise some other issues that show distinct but subtle change throughout the ages. For example, Vatican II declared that the church is the whole people of God. This may not sound like much at first, but in the light of the past few chapters, this understanding is an attempt to correct a one-sided view of church. We have seen how the church in effect became identified with the pope and the hierarchy.

If asked what they mean by the church, it is likely that a majority of Catholics would respond in terms of the clergy. They would be unconsciously echoing the framework laid in the Middle Ages and (as we shall see) expanded in the Councils of Trent (1545-63) and Vatican I (1869-1870). They would be picking up a late tradition from the time of Gregory VII, when the real cleavage between clergy and laity became apparent.[1] Not long after Gregory, the First Lateran Council (1123) began to talk of "clergy, religious, and laity." This division was heightened when the church's leadership clung to Latin (which only the clergy understood), when the priest turned his back to the people, when the altar rail was introduced.

Vatican II (and many scholars and theologians before that) went back, as it were, to the first chapters of this book. They saw the church—not a division, not the old pyramid with the laity on the lowest strata and the pope on top. They saw, rather, a community, a whole people interacting with their various gifts and ministries, each having their own functions in the Christian family. Then the council looked at what the church had come to be, a kind of super corporation with the hierarchy as chairmen of the board, and the people left with the threefold duty of "praying, obeying, and paying." So the council said that the church, as a matter of gospel fact, is all the people, and that the whole church's mission applies "equally to the laity, religious and clergy" (Dogmatic Constitution on the Church, 30). The council said that by virtue of baptism the laity are called to proclaim the gospel and that "the lay apostolate is a participation in the saving mission of the church itself" (33), not merely a subordinate arm of the hierarchy.

After Vatican II, some of the practical applications of this historically renewed vision became obvious. Parish councils were established in many places, the synod of bishops was evoked to work with the pope, the laity began to participate in the liturgy as lectors, cantors, etc. The altar rails were removed, churches were being built "community-style," some of the laity were asked for their opinions in the selection of bishops, while others became members of papal and diocesan commissions.

THE POPE

From what we have said above, it is also obvious that the pope's role has to be seen in a different light today. When Vatican I defined papal infallibility, some saw in this the crowning and perfection of absolute, monarchial papal power started by Gregory VII (1073-1085). After Vatican I, some people felt that infallibility meant that, in practice, the pope alone was the entire church wrapped up in himself, that he would never need to consult anyone and that councils would be obsolete. Vatican II corrected some of that.

In the early church, every church-community was independent under its own leader (usually a bishop), and yet each church-community was also in communion with every other church-community. Bishops conferred with one another and consecrated each other to demonstrate their unity in diversity. Each bishop was bishop *in his own right*; no bishop was bishop in dependence on or through designation by the bishop of Rome. The episcopal college and the pope together form the hierarchical structure, neither one being able to do without the other, neither one being independent of the other, and both being the recipients of a commission from the risen Jesus (Matthew 28:18-19). The pope and the bishops are the symbols of unity, the practical representatives for the authentic tradition of the church.

To be sure, the pope is the head of the college of bishops, but he is nothing without the college, and vice versa. His primacy does not mean, as it seemed to develop after the time of Gregory VII until the definition of infallibility, that the pope has full jurisdiction all over the world himself, that he can act independently of his fellow bishops. On the contrary, it must be historically maintained "that the pope and the bishops *cannot* exercise their respective functions one *against* the other, and should not, whatever the circumstances, do so one *without* the other. Certainly the pope will fulfill his functions as necessary and irreplaceable *leader* of the college, and the bishops will fulfill their functions as necessary and irreplaceable directing *members* of the same college...."[2] This concept explains why, for example, Pope Paul VI acted differently from Innocent III or Pius IX. Unlike those two pontiffs, he knew he was not the whole show. He knew that he and the college of bishops were inseparable.

Since the election of John Paul II, tensions have developed between the universal church, as represented by the bishop of Rome, and some of the national and local churches, as represented by their bishops. For example, the Dutch bishops of the 1960s and 1970s seem to have been perceived as threats to the authority of the bishop of Rome. So we see that not all has been resolved, even though contemporary theology tends to portray the pope as

> the leading moral authority in the church, who, nevertheless, shares our human condition in all things, including sin and error. His authority, though supreme, is never divorced from that of the rest of the college of bishops, nor indeed can it be independent of the Spirit that has been given to the whole church.[3]

THE KINGDOM OF GOD

We shall meet Boniface VIII in the next chapter. He is the pope who, pressed by the developing nation-states and failing to read the "signs of the times," resorted to claiming the most extreme form of papal authority in order to bolster his position as the temporal and spiritual leader of the whole world. In his famous bull, *Unam Sanctam* (1302), he wrote:

> We are compelled by the true faith to believe and hold that there is one, holy, catholic and apostolic church. This we firmly believe and simply confess. And outside of this church there

is neither salvation nor remission of sins...We are taught by the evangelical works that there are two swords, the spiritual and the temporal, in the control of the church.

...Therefore both the spiritual and material swords are under the control of the church, but the latter is used for the church and the former by the church...Therefore if the temporal power errs, it will be judged by the spiritual power. But if the spiritual power errs, the minor will be judged by the superior—the supreme spiritual power can be judged by God alone, not by man.... We therefore declare, say, affirm, and announce that for every human creature to be submissive to the Roman pontiff is absolutely necessary for salvation.

Since that time, however, the leaders of the church have backed away from this extreme position. Vatican II officially recognized that others can and will be saved, even those who are not baptized. "The Catholic church rejects nothing which is true in these religions," says the council in its Declaration on the Relationship of the Church to Non-Christian Religions (2). Of those who *are* baptized the same council says, "...all those who have been justified by faith through baptism are incorporated into Christ. They therefore have a right to be honored by the title of Christian and are properly regarded as brothers in the Lord by the sons of the Catholic church" (Decree on Ecumenism, 3).

Such words recognize that the kingdom of God and the Roman Catholic church are not one and the same thing, as Boniface implied. Anyone who is united to God by charity is in the kingdom. The Catholic church is permeated by that kingdom but not identical with it. A good Muslim, for example, may well be a member of the kingdom of God, while an irreligious Catholic may not be. The church exists to proclaim the kingdom here on earth and hereafter (the church has always had an eschatological dimension.) A Christian church (of any denomination) is that body of baptized persons who believes in the lordship of Jesus and the mission of the community that professes his name. The Catholic Christian church does the same but it also professes the conviction that the college of bishops united with the pope at its center is an indispensable factor (given by Christ) in the formulation and the proclamation of the gospel of Christ.

Thus, Protestant and Catholic alike belong to the church (meaning the people of God). The Catholic, however, believes that the

Catholic church has the *fullness* of revelation, the fullness of Jesus' expression for his church. Thus, converts from Protestantism are not looked upon as ones who have left their sinful and erroneous ways, but as people continuing their Christian tradition and moving into a fuller degree of it. Vatican II has arrived at such conclusions only by seeing what the church was in history, what the church became, and what the church ought to be. With its emphasis on the church as the people of God, with its notions of the kingdom of God, the Catholic church is trying to correct a certain notion of church which had developed since the Middle Ages.

DOGMATIC TEACHING

Another rather complex subject indicates some directions in which the modern church seems to be going. It concerns dogma (the most solemn teaching of the church). Chapter 5 dealt with several formulas on the nature of Jesus Christ that were defined during the first four councils of the church. We saw that such formulas or doctrinal statements had more of a negative value. They provided the church with a touchstone to test theological statements regarding what was the truth and what was not; that is, Christological statements regarding the relationship between God and Jesus would be judged true or false when measured or brought next to these conciliar teachings.

Moreover, it is important to remember that such statements were made in the language and in the context of questions of those times. We know more today of the history surrounding them. Thus, theologians may legitimately challenge such statements as to their language, their style, their thinking-patterns, their conditioning, and even their content. For example, when theologians ask *how* Jesus is present in the eucharist, they may find that transubstantiation, the old term of Thomas Aquinas's time, is not adequate anymore, and perhaps a fuller term might be better.

In addition, dogmatic teachings are not so immutable that they cannot develop. How they do so is a most complex and subtle issue, beyond the scope of this discussion. All that we wish to point out is that dogmatic teaching is conditioned by history and that the church realizes that even dogmas are involved in the process of living history and can develop. Vatican II states, "There is a growth in the understanding of realities and the words which have been handed down.... For as the centuries succeed one another, the church constantly moves forward towards the fullness of divine truth until the words of God reach their fulfillment in her" (Constitution on Divine Revelation, 8). The point is that what God communicates is not so much information as it is self-communication. The "information," the language of the dogma, is not nearly as important or as necessarily fixed as we might think. This is why there were a variety of creedal statements in the early church, a variety of the words used for the consecration of the Mass. Catholics accept the church's dogmatic teaching as indispensable illuminations and starting points for obtaining a deeper understanding of the meaning of being a Christian. When the entire church does teach and accept a statement of faith, then individual Catholics accept this as a valuable *guide* for the meaning of their Christian lives. They know that the statement has not captured the whole reality and that the understanding of this reality can grow, develop, and be modified as the church's experience of God (not the information) deepens.

This is why, historically, there have been different schools of theology, developed at Antioch and Alexandria in the early church, and by the Franciscans, the Dominicans, the Jesuits, and others in later centuries. They represent different ways of thinking about the same faith. As we shall see in a later chapter, it was only in the time of Leo XIII and Pius X that one school of theology (Thomism) was accepted over all others. These things remind us once more that the church is rooted in history, and that if the theologians are doing an excessive amount of questioning today (even on the most "untouchable" subjects), this does not necessarily mean that there is doubt. It means trying to see the dogma in a different light, trying to see what the historical conditioning was in the first place, and trying to see how much is "content" and how much is "context," or culture.

THE MESSAGE OF JESUS

We have yet to see the Reformation of the sixteenth century or the Modernist movement of the late nineteenth and early twentieth centuries. When we do, we shall see how the church's leadership reacted. For example, the Protestants extolled the Bible, so the church's leadership reacted by overemphasizing tradition. The Protestants viewed the church a little too spiritually, so the church's leadership reacted by emphasizing the external, organizational structure.

When Protestants took a different theological perspective on the sacraments and the notion of the Mass as a sacrifice, the church's leadership reacted by giving the sacraments heavy legal overtones and freezing the Mass in layers of rubrics. Beginning in the 1890s, the Modernists made attempts to break through all this when they put out feelers regarding the new ideas and the new science of their time. The church's leadership reacted by emphasizing papal infallibility.

The point is that today's church is seeing the historical process involved, is cutting through it all, and asking more ultimate questions, namely, what *is* the message of Jesus? Do our inherited expressions help or hinder that message? Does our language, our idea-wrappings, proclaim Jesus or the organization? What view, for example, does the old Baltimore Catechism give of the church and of Christ? Are those the views we want? How historically conditioned are they? Better still, is that the view of the gospels? These are some of the questions and reflections that a knowledge of history has promoted.

THE GREATNESS OF THE CHURCH

We must take advantage of these pages to make a final point. Because (by traditional definition) history is made up of the large world-moving events and personalities, we have no real record of the little people, the vast majority of humanity that lived and died in the Ages of Faith. As a result, we tend to dwell, inevitably, on the mass movements, the large passions, and the great leaders. These alone do not make history but we can write of them because their records are bold and open. But what about the average people in Western civilization? What did being church do for them? How did they respond as church? They were no more caught up in the dramatic events and personalities in their day than the average person is today. They quietly lived their own lives.

Life, to be sure, was often difficult in the early and late Middle Ages. Economic conditions were often harsh. People were exploited, as always, by the powerful—their nobles and lords, and even by some of their clergy and bishops. The times were barbarous. Yet the Catholic church did much and inspired much. We have no idea, for example, of how many people in small parishes were served well, or how many clergy gave sincere and humble service to the people.

Lutheran historian Martin Marty writes:

> Unfortunately, the general illiteracy of the times and the en-
> during edge of barbarism and violence made the people some-
> times superstitiously dependent upon the sacraments and sac-
> ramental objects and upon the parish priests who seldom
> measured up to their calling. Illiterate themselves, products of
> inadequate training and often warped cloistered environ-
> ments, grasping and greedy, many used the church and the
> fear of the masses to advance their own interests. But these
> generalizations have never done justice to the countless exam-
> ples of parish priests who quietly went about their business
> gaining the respect of their flocks and serving them with the
> sacraments and with Christian counsel. The conservative Ref-
> ormation never wishes to repudiate this continuity of evangeli-
> cal counsel in the centuries that preceded it.[4]

We know that the monasteries were havens of refuge and peace
for many. We know that the monasteries preserved our cultural heritage. We know that the church not only preserved and increased
social culture, but also developed the spiritual culture. People were
inspired to do great deeds, and they lived with a totally conscious
awareness of the supernatural that the modern secular world finds
difficult to comprehend. While there was greed, lust, and all the
other vices of the human condition, there was also virtue, answers
to the ultimate questions, and God, who is always just. Many a ra-
pacious and greedy nobleman wound up his days in a monastery.
Many an evil lord expiated his sins in magnificent acts of charity.
There was no pope, no matter how political or how immoral, that
did not understand that he, too, must answer to God.

People had a wholistic perspective on their lives. They might
(and often did) ridicule the errant monk or the drunken priest, but
they had a most awesome respect for the priesthood and the sacred
ministry itself. We have seen how capable people were to suddenly
rise to great religious fervor. Saints, mystics, visionaries, and plain
holy people nurtured in the church were a part of every age. People
were consistently conscious of God, and no matter how close to superstition they sometimes went, this consciousness remained a
powerful reality. How else is one to explain a most exquisite stone
carving in a cathedral in a position that could not possibly be seen
by the public? How else except that the hidden piece of art was

made, not for people to see, but "for the greater honor and glory of God"?

The church not only civilized and educated the barbarians, but also sanctified them. In the tenth and eleventh centuries, the church directed and promoted peace movements such as the Peace, or Truce, of God, forbidding fighting on certain days and giving immunity to certain categories of persons. The liturgy was a most powerful source of inspiration to those living in the Middle Ages. As Christopher Dawson describes it:

> Meanwhile throughout the West the liturgy was becoming more and more the center of Christian culture.... Whatever else might be lost, and however dark might be the prospects of Western society, the sacred order of the liturgy remained intact and in it, the whole Christian world, Roman, Byzantine, and barbarian, found an inner principle of unity.... It is almost impossible to convey to the modern mind the realism and objectivity with which the Christian of those ages viewed liturgical participation in the mysteries of salvation....[5]

In spite of all of its vast problems, the church as a whole never lost its sense of mission. We have seen that individual popes, bishops, and priests were sometimes corrupt, ignorant, and worldly, but faith remained very lively all the while. For example, in the tenth, eleventh, and twelfth centuries the founding of monasteries and the whole reform movement of Cluny and Gregory VII show that many were truly committed to the kingdom of God and to restoring the church to better image Christ. The personal guidance and ministrations given by the friars is beyond measuring. The schools, orphanages, and hospitals are beyond counting. The learning, theology, and synthesizing still compel our admiration. Beneath all the growing legalisms, the basic centrality of the gospel message was preserved. In its two-thousand- year history perhaps the greatest demonstration of the Holy Spirit's presence can be found in the church's ability to renew itself, to raise up its prophets, to withstand the purifying fires, to bend to the times, to reassess its identity periodically, and to admit its faults.

All of this must be said here at this midpoint. We are approaching the Reformation. We have to be reminded that all of the reformers were Catholics who were mightily concerned with restoring the somewhat obscured image of Jesus. The tragedy of loss and division is still with us, but we should recall that the reformers did not disparage the mighty work of the church throughout the centuries. Nor did they act out of hatred, but out of love for the church; they desired to see the church once more in its former spiritual glory. The original intent was reform of the church that nurtured them, not revolution.

These reflections have been offered to help the average Catholic realize that current developments in the Catholic church have a historical basis; they do not arise from shallow reasons (although inevitably all change produces some shallow by-products). Such reflections help us to see that the church is not bound to a particular cultural expression, such as the old Roman-Frankish model that most Catholics were brought up on. Such reflections show us that the church as a community of believers in the Lordship of Jesus has changed and developed; history is a valuable tool in distinguishing what is essential to the church from what is cultural.

Let us now return to our narrative. We left the church at the height of its political power, at the crest of the wave. But that wave is about to crash. The crash started when all those feudal counties began to conglomerate into what we today call the "nations."

CHAPTER 13

The New Nations

NATIONALISM

After East and West went their separate ways, other shadows were beginning to lengthen across Christendom. These shadows would very quickly become substantive. By the end of the fifteenth century, the Middle Ages were over and the church's influence was in decline. The modern secular age had begun. This transition was not without pain and disillusionment, similar to that experienced in our present day, as we move from the modern age to the technological age. The first element we might notice in the steady disintegration of the church's prestige and influence was the rise of nationalism.[1] Up to this time, we have spoken of "Christendom," that mystical half-reality that encompassed all baptized people of East and West. In the thirteenth and fourteenth centuries, the nation-states began to appear. People began to identify themselves as French or English or Spanish. As this consciousness grew, Christians would fight one another for national honor. The rise of such national spirit is attributable to the rise of the kingly monarchy. Formerly, as we have seen so often, kings were more like local mayors, petty magnates, whose own nobles might be more powerful than they. There was no centralized government as we know it today. But, as centralization began to appear, it grew at the expense of the church. Let us briefly survey the fortunes of England, France, Germany, and Spain to see how and why this happened.

ENGLAND

In 901, King Alfred the Great temporarily checked the advances of the invading Norsemen. But these hardy Vikings renewed their attacks and, for a time, attached England to Denmark.[2] When Edward the Confessor recovered the throne in 1042, the drama of England's rise began. Edward, however, died without heirs, which divided the Saxon nobles between two claimants for the throne. Harold, Edward's chief minister, claimed to have been named by Edward on his deathbed and, with the support of most of the court, was quickly crowned. Meanwhile, Edward's cousin by marriage, William, Duke of Normandy, pressed his claim, based on a supposed promise Edward made to him years before. Soon, William crossed the channel, and, in the famous battle of Hastings in 1066, he and his Norman forces defeated Harold and won the English throne. (We should recall the irony here: William and his Normans were themselves descended from Vikings (Norsemen) who had invaded France in the tenth century and settled in an area named for themselves—Normandy; yet, one hundred years later they defeated England as Frenchmen, not Vikings!) There was such disorder following his victory that William decided that a strong monarchy was the only means of preserving unity. He proceeded to keep his strict control over his subjects and his properties. (In his famous *Domesday Book*, he listed all his properties and chattel in England.) The local lords became his vassals, because there were no rival princes there to detract from the power of this outsider.

Keep in mind the ever-present reality that this new king of England, William the Conqueror, had come from Normandy in modern France. This meant that he was king in his own right as well as vassal to the king of France for his properties there. Understandably, as we shall see, the kings of France could not be long happy with this arrangement.

In time, Henry II, the first Plantagenet, succeeded to the English throne. Under this king, constitutional law was written. This introduced a more equitable system of trying legal cases based on evidence, and a fairer system of legal justice. In this new system of legal justice, Henry ran into conflict because of exemptions given to church clerics. This dilemma was brought to a head by the famous Council of Clarendon, whereby the king declared that, from that time on, clerics were bound by the same law as anyone else. To back up his decision, the king forbade appeals to Rome. Naturally, there was opposition from church leaders. This opposition was personally irritating to the king because his own chancellor and friend, whom he had made the archbishop of Canterbury, would not support him. This man was Thomas à Becket. Thomas refused to honor the Council of Clarendon and excommunicated those bishops who sided with the king. As the well-known story goes, Henry exclaimed one day in exasperation, "Who shall rid me of this miserable clerk?" A band of Henry's knights overheard this remark, and they murdered Thomas in his cathedral. This incident has been celebrated many times in literature, most particularly in T.S. Eliot's famous narrative poem, *Murder in the Cathedral,* and in Jean Anouilh's *Becket.*

The incident provided the nobles with a reason for resisting and then halting Henry's growing power. Henry eventually backed down on the Council of Clarendon. After Henry's death, the monarchial fortunes declined even more. Under Henry's son, John Lackland, taxes rose, English holdings in France dwindled and, most of all, King John and his country were handed a crushing defeat by the French in the battle of Bouvines in 1214. The king found himself in a very weak position. Stephen Langton, the Archbishop of Canterbury, took advantage of this to lead the barons and nobles to demand some of their rights back, rights which had been taken over by the previous king. They held secret meetings and plotted rebellion. In 1215, they confronted the hapless King John and wrung from him that milestone of human liberty, the Magna Carta. Although this document was a typical nobleman's document—it gave all the rights to the nobles, not the peasants—it was still important in that it declared that the law must be observed by all, including the king. No longer could he be above the law. Moreover, the king could levy no taxes without the consent of a Parliament. Parliament got its start under King John's son, Henry III. This king, in spite of everything, continued to levy taxes, and was faced with a resistance movement led by a Simon de Montfort. Simon, with two knights from every section and two burgesses from every town, faced the king with an impressive show of strength. Henry III took the hint, and the next time he wanted to levy taxes, he summoned the knights and burgesses on his own. Thus began the English Parliament, and under the next king it would become a permanent reality.

FRANCE

France's road to centralized monarchy was quite different from that of England's. In England, the nobles finally brought the king under the law. In France, the nobles were so jealous and divided that the king himself emerged as the referee and lawmaker above them. We might remember that the Capets had taken over the western part of the old Carolingian empire and settled in Paris. There they ruled so quietly and so long—some two hundred years—that the kingship slipped into a hereditary one. After a time Paris, the first permanent capital in Europe, became an important center. The court was there—in contrast to the still wandering courts of the other local kings. By the twelfth century, Paris had attracted an archbishop and a school. In 1163, the construction of Notre Dame cathedral was started.

Moreover, France had already begun to show signs of greatness even in her formative years. It was here that many religious orders were founded. Most of the crusaders came from these Franks. Gothic art had its beginning here. France became the center of theology, and every notable scholar of the times flocked to the new university of Paris. Paris was also an international marketplace, and the tolls collected there enriched a series of kings. By putting down banditry and maintaining order, the king caused the townspeople to look to him for support and redress, rather than to the feuding nobles. The French court thus became a center for justice. In brief, a very stable capital of growing prestige, a hereditary kingship, financial stability, and an open court of justice all contributed to the emergence of a strong monarchy.

Just as William the Conquerer might be called the founder of the English monarchy, so Philip II (1180-1223) might be called the founder of the French monarchy. By marriage, he extended his territories and sent out royal judges to try cases throughout the land. In addition, the French victory at Bouvines in 1214 had given him enormous power and prestige. Slowly, the king began to annex the smaller kingdoms and countries held by the local princes. As we have seen in another chapter, this was the time that the king took advantage of the Albigensian heresy to confiscate the lands of these heretics. Louis IX (1226-1270) was the beneficiary of all this growing power. He used it well. He founded hospitals, asylums, and homes of various kinds. Most of all, he had his goodwill ambassadors roaming throughout the land, redressing grievances in his name and bringing important matters to his attention. Soon, there was no part of France that did not have some contact with the king. Louis's peaceful policy was changed abruptly by his successor, Philip the Bold (d. 1285). Under him, France began an aggressive policy of external expansion. Taking advantage of the weakness of the German empire, France expanded its territories northward and eastward. France even established herself in Naples and Hungary, and coveted land in Spain. France was on the way to becoming a great political power.

Philip the Fair, inheriting all this power in 1285, contributed much to the developing monarchy. An administrative genius, he surrounded himself with competent civil servants and lawyers whose talent, not position or birth, brought them into his service. He carefully built a legal system on the foundations of the Roman theories of law (which were interpreted to remind all that the king himself was the chief lawgiver). Philip was the king who inaugurated the French equivalent of the English Parliament, the Estates-General. This was only an advisory body at that time, but would play a major role centuries later in the French Revolution (which began in 1789). He allied himself with the causes of the new merchant classes of the new towns. Slowly but surely, the kingship was beginning to rest on its own foundations. It would no longer need legitimation through the church. Not that there was any hostility—yet.

HOSTILITY BETWEEN ENGLAND AND FRANCE

Hostility between France and England was to be expected. One obvious problem was the fact that the king of England had property in France. Several French kings had made small skirmishes against the English to drive them out, but they had not sufficient strength to do so. But, when Philip II became king, a strong attack was made against the English. Philip found a pretext to confiscate English properties in France. War ensued, and even Germany was brought into the battle. The famous battle of Bouvines gave the French a great victory and resulted in the king of England's being compelled to sign the Magna Carta.

The hatred and rivalry between England and France did not end here. A century and a half later, the desires of the English kings to conquer the more populous and wealthy France led to the futile and unproductive Hundred Years War. All of Europe, as well as the two principals, were involved at one time or another. Before we see that sad spectacle, we must turn to the relations between the church and these newly emerging nation-states.

CONFLICT WITH THE CHURCH

If we would try to reduce the entire matter of the severe conflict between the emerging states and the church at this period to one word, that word would be *money*. With the growing centralized papacy, a whole new machinery was needed to run it. Financing this machinery required vast sums of money. Thus, in the eleventh century, Rome introduced the Peter's Pence. Next, Rome began to tax all local churches throughout Europe (thus unwittingly developing a refined system of international finance through her use of the Italian bankers). In any case, the various rulers resented this one-way flow of money from their kingdoms to Rome, especially when some of that money was used against them in warfare directed by the pope! But the real issue surfaced most forcefully when the emerging nations were just starting their rivalry and their military campaigns against each other. That cost money, and money meant taxes. Both France and England hit upon the same source to tax: the church. In this, both countries ran afoul of the then current church theory that its revenues were always traditionally exempt from civil assessments, because it was thought that only the church could tax her own clergy and her own property. The kings saw it another way. A showdown was in the wings.

THE PAPACY

In France, the contest of power was between the two antagonists, Philip the Fair and Boniface VIII. Philip was the possessor of a new and strong emerging nation. The papacy, up to Boniface's time, was once more the center of intrigue from outside rulers. Charles of Anjou, king of Sicily and brother to the King of France, had designs on all of Italy. He worked hard and successfully to get a majority of French and Italian cardinals to elect the kind of pope he wanted, Clement IV. This pontiff, in turn, made many more French cardinals. The very real influence on such cardinals by the French king and his brother was offset by Pope Gregory X, who, in 1271, mandated the "conclave" whereby the cardinals are shut up in a closed room for the papal election. This new procedure did not succeed. In 1280, a Frenchman, Martin IV, was elected. He was followed by two Italian popes.

By 1292, the intrigue and maneuvering were quite pronounced. The cardinals settled on that much used temporary measure: they would elect a compromise candidate. Thus, they got an old hermit, Peter Murrone, almost literally dragging him from his cell, and elected him as Celestine V. The old hermit was duly installed in the Lateran palace, and proceeded to amuse the sophisticated prelates by building a rude hut amid the splendor. He could put up with the luxurious surroundings this way, but he could not swallow the realization that he was expected to be the puppet of the French king. His only recourse was to remove himself from the scene. He, therefore, duly resigned the papacy. He went back to his old hermitage, and later took his place in the canon of the saints. In this highly unusual situation, the cardinals elected in his place a Roman noble, Boniface VIII.

BONIFACE VIII

Boniface was a man to be reckoned with, one determined to restore the dignity of the papacy in the style of an Innocent III. In light of the preceding circumstances, he lost no opportunity to assert the primacy of ecclesiastical power over the civil. He added a regal crown to the papal tiara and had his ministers carry two swords before him in procession—a sign of church and state.[3] At another time, this would have been impressive, but the sad fact was that Boniface was out of context. He was no longer dealing with Christendom. He was dealing with newly emerging independent nation-states.

This was the pope who had to deal with England and France's audacity in taxing church property to raise money for their internal exploits of consolidation and their external military rivalries. Boniface VIII dealt with the matter by immediately issuing his famous bull, *Clericis Laicos*. In it, he threatened the excommunication of any lay ruler who dared to tax the church. England and France were both unimpressed with this over-used penalty. Actually, the papal bull contained nothing new. It was the old traditional doctrine of the two powers of church and state that previous popes had proclaimed many times before. Long tradition had consecrated the doctrine and so, in perspective, it was the kings of England and France who were violating tradition. The pope was merely reminding them of this.

But, as we have said, the picture was different now. This was a new political situation, and the question at stake was really the sovereignty of the new national powers. Boniface's mistake was in his failure to recognize this new situation. He failed to sense a new spirit among the people, a new national pride which would defy even the church. Perhaps Boniface had visions of another solitary Henry IV at Canossa, or a humiliated Frederick Barbarossa at Venice. Such visions would never again materialize, because whole nations, even those willing to admit guidance in the spiritual realm, were not willing to admit any papal prerogatives in the political arena that would limit their new solidarity.

ENGLISH AND FRENCH REACTION

England had a history of bucking church interference. The Council of Clarendon tried to put clerics under the same civil penalties as everyone else. In 1279, England forbade the donation of land to the church. In 1351, some fifty years after the time we are considering, England prohibited the appointment of foreigners to the English bishoprics in order to prevent the Italian prelates from taking over lucrative positions in England. Thus, when Boniface issued *Clericis Laicos*, England retorted by decreeing that any cleric who did not pay the tax was to lose his legal protection and his temporal property.

In France, Philip hit where it hurt. He prohibited monies and letters of credit to leave France for Rome. Thus, he dried up a needed source of papal revenue at a time when the pope could ill afford it. Boniface backed down for the time being. He might have maintained that position, except that, in the year 1300, the first Jubilee year in the church was proclaimed. People from all over the world came to Rome. Boniface became so intoxicated by his show of numbers that he misread it as backing for his claims. He failed once more to realize that these people were not ready to transfer their spiritual allegiance to the political realm. He reprimanded King Edward of England immediately for his injustice and violence toward the Scots. Edward simply presented the pope's complaint to his people, and the whole nation rejected the pope's interference in their affairs.

Next came Philip. He had the boldness to have a French bishop imprisoned. Boniface demanded his release, and once more forbade church taxation. Philip responded to this the same way Edward of England had. He appealed to his people. He called the forerunner of the Estates-General, which backed Philip all the way. At this time even the lawyers and theologians got in on the act by repudiating papal claims to the right to interfere in political matters. The whole issue became one of public debate—which could not have served Philip's purpose better. Boniface was stunned. His only reaction was to come out with *Unam Sanctam* (1302), the most extreme statement on papal power that has ever been written, and which has provided material for anti-papalists—both Catholic and Protestant—ever since. He reasserted that the pope was supreme in all matters on earth, both spiritual and temporal and, in an oft-quoted passage of papal extremism: "We declare, state, define and pronounce that it is altogether necessary to salvation for every human creature to be subject to the Roman Pontiff."

Philip was not one to let the matter end there. He was determined to destroy Boniface. Knowing the unusual circumstances of Boniface's election (remember, he had replaced the retired Celestine), Philip pretended to call his legitimacy into question. Later, he included the charges of heresy, simony, and immorality. The pope must come to France to stand trial. Boniface, at age 86, had gone to the town of Anagni for the summer. Some French troops broke into his bedroom and verbally, and perhaps even physically, abused the old man. They kept him prisoner for several days until he was freed by the townspeople. He died three months later at Rome.

The issue appeared to be resolved in favor of the French king when, in 1305, the cardinals elected as Pope a Frenchman, Clement V, who considered himself first and foremost as a vassal of the French king. He filled the college of cardinals with relatives and followers of Philip and, as an ultimate blow, moved the papal court from Rome to the French city of Avignon. He and his successors were to remain there for seventy-two years, thus earning from their opponents the biblical epithet "the Babylonian captivity." Philip had won. The prestige of the papacy fell to a new low. Philip's new pope, Clement V, revoked Boniface's bulls, and Philip enriched himself by having his vassal pope suppress the great crusading order of Knights Templar. As we pointed out two chapters ago, people were scandalized, but the papal machinery went on in Avignon as easily as in Rome, because when it came to matters of administration and finances, which the papacy had come to represent, its location did not matter. People became cynical. Besides, they had other things to occupy their minds.

GERMANY

Germany was very slow to develop a monarchial government, because the emperors, seeing themselves as rulers of the Holy Roman Empire, were too busy pursuing the grand illusion of restoring the old Roman Empire of the Caesars. In addition, they were too busy fussing about Italy, and subduing the pope. As a result, Germany was left to disintegrate into a series of small municipalities, a mass of civil and ecclesiastical particles at the mercy of the strongest local lord.

Emperor Frederick Barbarossa was one such strong man, who used his time as emperor pursuing the myth of the empire. In pursuit of that dream, he turned once more to Italy and to Rome. To do this, he had to pass through the now independent Italian towns that had sprung up on the plains of Lombardy. He stomped through with terror and force. Eventually, Frederick even tried to choose the pope, since there were two contenders for the job, but no one would recognize his choice, his anti-pope. Moreover, Frederick was badly defeated by the Lombard towns, and found himself at Venice kissing the feet of the legitimate pope, Alexander III, in a scene reminiscent of Henry IV standing in the cold of Canossa begging forgiveness of Gregory VII. Frederick ended his career, we may recall, by drowning while on a crusade.

Frederick's grandson, Frederick II, was an interesting person. A free thinker, skeptic, and schemer, he was a man of talent, far ahead of his time in social legislation. His mother was a Sicilian, so he attempted to join Sicily to Germany. This could only mean putting the squeeze on the pope and his territories. He was excommunicated several times, and Innocent IV finally deposed him as emperor in 1243, and gave Sicily to France. Frederick died with the same problem he tried to solve: a divided empire and a neglected Germany.

So far had the fortunes of Germany declined, so leaderless had Germany become, that sometimes the princes elected children to be their puppet-emperors. By 1256, the princes had become so indifferent to the election of an emperor that they agreed to a constitutional document known as the *Golden Bull*, which left the naming of a new Germanic emperor to only seven electors. At one point, these electors sold the crown to two rival claimants at the same time. When one rival dropped off the scene in 1273, the electors gave the crown to the colorless Rudolph, who was important in light of the future. He was the first Hapsburg, a dynastic family that would dominate the stage of Europe for centuries. By and by, Germany became united with Bohemia and annexed some of the Slavic areas in the East, while some of its western territory spun off into the influence of France. Yet it remained divided, economically backward, and far behind the other emerging nations. Even here, the struggle of the popes with these emperors must be seen in the context of the times. Once more Henri Pirenne puts it in perspective:

It must be repeated that the motive which for two and a half centuries had determined the hostility of the emperors to the papacy was by no means their eagerness to defend the temporal power against the encroachments of the church. To envisage the question thus is to transport into the heart of the Middle Ages ideas and problems which belong only to our modern times. Neither the humiliation of Henry IV at Canossa, nor that of Frederick Barbarossa at Venice, nor that of Otto IV at Bouvines, was the humiliation of the civil power before priestly arrogance. In reality, the conflict was not a conflict between state and church; it was an intense struggle within the church itself. What the emperors wanted was to compel the popes to recognize them as governing the universal church, a right which they claimed was theirs from the time of the Carolingian empire, as the Ottos and Henrys had done, or from the time of the Roman empire, as the Hohenstaufens had done. Their pretensions thus imperiled, in every country, that temporal independence of which, by the strangest of confusions, they had been regarded as the defenders. The cause of the pope was the cause of the nations, and with the liberty of the church was bound up the liberty of the European states....[4]

SPAIN

Spain was somewhere between Germany and France in development. Since it had been occupied by the Muslim invaders from the seventh century, it did not yet have much of an identity. These Muslims were practically natives. They built beautiful cities and cultivated their civilizations. We must remember that it was through them that the Greek philosophers, such as Aristotle, found their way to the West. Normally, after six or seven hundred years, they would be expected to mingle with the natives and fuse a new culture as had been done so often before in history. One factor prevented this: religion. The Muslims were not Christian; they were the hated infidel. The Spaniards, on the other hand, were fiercely Christian; therefore, no compromise was possible. Extermination could be the only answer. To be a Spaniard was to be Christian, and national sentiment got inextricably tied up with religion. Thus, the relationship between the Muslims and the Spanish was that of a Holy War that prevented cultural fusion of any kind.

It is likely that victory over the Muslims could have been won sooner, except that Spain was divided internally, with Aragon often at odds with Castile. In 1195, the Muslims seemed on the verge of such a complete conquest that the pope intervened by getting the two kingdoms to combine their forces. In 1212, they shattered the Muslim offensive. From this point on, the Spanish Christians moved steadily ahead. They captured Cordova in 1226, Valencia in 1238, and Seville in 1248. They eventually left the Muslims with but a foothold in Granada, and only the internal quarrels of the various Spanish kingdoms kept them from expelling the Muslims altogether. The important thing to note is that as these victories were won, several Spanish areas tended to gather around the prominent cities of Castile and Aragon. The latter was better situated, since it was on the Mediterranean and could reach out to Europe and feel its influence. Barcelona was soon to become an important seaport, and, in a short time, this outlet to Europe was to be involved in the affairs of Sicily and Naples.

It was in the inland Castile, however, that the true Spain was finding itself. The Castilians fought most gloriously against the Muslims and gave rise to their popular local hero, El Cid (the counterpart to the French hero, Roland). It was in Castile that the national language and character were formed. Even so, all of Spain was beginning to find a national identity. Their commerce in wool was increasing and leading them to trade with the Low Countries. They were emerging as a strong seagoing people, and a Portuguese prince, Henry the Navigator (1394-1460), was even now outfitting ships that would venture far into the uncharted waters of the Atlantic.

THE HUNDRED YEARS WAR

We must include, in our secular survey of history during the thirteenth to fifteenth centuries, a mention of the Hundred Years War. This was, in reality, a series of on-again, off-again military campaigns. There were many reasons for the hostilities. The English, as we saw, held property in France. France and England were fighting over water rights and trade priorities. Perhaps most significant of all was the rivalry of nationalism. People were becoming conscious of their own traditions and language: they considered themselves to be English or French or Spanish. The monarchies were becoming focal points of national consciousness. A whole new spirit was abroad. Rivalry was paramount. It began with the English King, Edward III. When Philip of France's son died (thus ending the old Capetian line), Edward, a cousin, claimed the throne and promptly invaded France. In 1346, the English, armed with a new and devastating weapon, the longbow, crushed the numerically superior French forces, thus inflating English national pride.

All the evils of war followed, threatening to overturn the new national states. A major problem was raising money to finance the war. Another problem was national spirit that ebbed and flowed as battles were won and lost. Many uprisings of the common people occurred in both countries as a result. In 1356, the English again invaded France and captured the French king's son whom they took back to London. The people of France exploded. They mocked the Dauphin, ruling in his father's absence. Peasants rose up against their masters, but they were cruelly crushed and hanged. The Estates-General demanded that the king be more responsible to them as taxpayers. Such internal trouble only allowed England to advance further into France. With the loss of more and more property, the resentment of the French deepened.

England, too, was having internal problems for the same reasons. Taxation was quite burdensome because of the war. In 1381, English peasants revolted and were similarly cut to pieces by the nobles. Moreover, when England suffered certain military reversals at French hands, Parliament took the crown away from King Richard and gave it to Henry of Lancaster whose son, Henry V, renewed the offensive against France. At this point, France was about to be taken over completely by the English. Only the central and southern parts, entered by way of Orleans, remained to be subdued.

But it was at this time that history was altered. There was a maid in Orleans, Joan of Arc, who was convinced that she heard heavenly voices telling her to save her country. She won the approval of the Dauphin, who gave her some troops. Dressed in men's armor and riding a white horse, she so inspired her soldiers that the English were routed. Eventually, Joan was captured and turned over to the English. Under English pressure, a church court founded her guilty of heresy and, in 1431, abandoned by that same Dauphin whose coronation as king she had witnessed in Rheims cathedral, she was burned at the stake. Yet her spirit lived on, and in 1453 (the same year that Constantinople fell) the English, except for the area of Calais, were expelled from France. The Hundred Years War was at an end. As for Joan, twenty-five years after her death, the church reversed her sentence. In 1920, five centuries later, the church canonized her.

UPHEAVALS

This chapter has been almost entirely secular history. Almost, but not quite. People were still Christians, and the church was still in power. Yet, we cannot fail to notice the shift of emphasis and the basis of present and future conflict. England was Christian, but signs of strain with Rome were showing. The Council of Clarendon forbidding clerical exemption from civil law was a premature sally into hostilities with the church; it was a sign of the direction England would take. The introduction of Parliament and the desire of the people to govern their own national life boded little good for the international church. Forbidding papal episcopal appointees for English dioceses was another step in England's desire to run her own affairs.

France, too, showed the church that she intended to go into the future with or without her help. Philip the Fair had bested Boniface VIII, and had so captured the papacy that it was actually residing at Avignon, his town, as his puppet. Germany's Frederick had been subdued. Spain was too busy fighting for her identity against the Muslims to pose much of a problem. But the world was changing materially. The face of modern Europe was beginning to show. Rivalry between Christian nation-states became a reality with the Hundred Years War (1346-1453). Everything was in the process of change. Before long—only forty years later, in 1492—a whole New World would be opened up. The West and the church might have survived all of this were it not for the spiritual change that was also beginning at that time. There were changes in people's minds. New mystical leanings and movements outside the mainstream of Christianity were starting; the forerunners of the Protestant Reformers were making their voices heard in the land. What was coming to a head was what historian Henri Daniel-Rops described as "the crisis of authority, the crisis of unity and conditioning both, the crisis in men's souls, in their consciences and in their minds." To this we must now turn.

CHAPTER 14

Outside the Mainstream

UNREST

Underneath the external sameness, the structures of late medieval
society were tottering. New nations had arisen. France and England
were at each other's throats. The Germanic empire was disintegrat-
ing, and Italy was more divided than ever. The Muslims were about
to seize Constantinople. There was trouble in the towns, because riots and strikes accompanied the demand for free competition as
people sought to throw off the controls of the guilds. The new
towns, heavily taxed to subsidize the warfare of the new nations,
were wresting more and more privileges for themselves. Economic
depressions were severe. Parliaments and Estates-Generals were
signs of the unrest of the people and of their desire to have a say in
their rule. The nobility was becoming decadent. The knights no
longer had any practical loyalty to their lords, but sold their military services to the highest bidder. In addition, the church was
proving a haven for the sons of the nobility, and so more and more
nobles monopolized her upper ranks. Thus, the church was losing

much of her democratic character and considerably undermining her intellectual and moral vigor. As a result of this development, a new period of decadence and worldiness began to manifest itself in the church.

The old ideals of church and society still persisted but they were, as we shall see, being shaken, and they lacked any great vigor. Furthermore, there were no great leaders around: no Bernards or Gregorys or Innocents. If anything, the times were characterized by unrest, rebellion, and criticism permeating all strata of society. There was no lack of visionaries, mystics, and reformers. All the unrest described thus far would shortly affect the common person who, in turn, would shake up the church (we must remember that the real power of the church lay in the people who supported it). In a deeply religious society, people could only think of the church as eternal and necessary for salvation. Even a Frederick Barbarossa or a Henry IV would never have denied the church her spiritual mission. As long as leaders and common people thought the church was the visible kingdom of God and necessary for salvation, the church would continue to dominate. But when people's confidence waned and new and strange thoughts appeared in public (not just underground), then public support would weaken, and with it domination by the Catholic church. With this in mind, we now turn to one major event which shook that confidence in the church, the Great Western Schism.

THE GREAT WESTERN SCHISM

The Great Western Schism divided Christendom for forty years (1378-1417). Here is how it began. We recall that the popes were residing, not at Rome, but in Avignon. These popes were all French, somewhat captive to the French king, and unabashedly chauvinistic, that is, zealously patriotic. For example, of the 134 cardinals made by seven of the French popes in the fourteenth century, 113 were French. All this was as pleasing to the French as it was odious to the rest of the Christian world, especially to Italy, and most especially to France's archenemy, England. Sooner or later there had to be attempts to rescue the papacy and restore it to Rome. Finally, it happened. Under the prodding of Catherine of Siena and others, Pope Gregory IX returned to Rome in 1377 amid great rejoicing. Unfortunately, Gregory died the following year.

Then the expected happened. All around the terrified cardinals, meeting in Rome for the election, was an irate mob howling for an Italian pope. The cardinals, fearing for their lives, complied and elected Urban VI. Had not Urban been so irascible—he alienated even his supporters—no more would have been made of this forced election. When the election's validity was questioned, many of the cardinals returned to Avignon and elected Robert of Geneva as Clement VII. But Urban refused to step aside for this replacement and he replaced the cardinals who had fled with others who supported his election. Such was the uncertainty of the identity of the real pope that all of Christendom soon became divided (even saints of that day took opposite sides). However, whatever the theological issue, politics soon became involved. Now there were two popes, two headquarters, two sets of cardinals, two curias, and two sets of papal successors. To appreciate the situation, try to imagine two presidents of the United States, each with his own cabinet, his own senate, and his own congressional representatives, issuing conflicting laws and demanding separate allegiances. So it was then. In each country, whole hierarchies of rivals sprang up, making the situation quite unbearable and endlessly confusing.

France, Scotland, Spain, and Naples supported the French pope. Therefore, their rivals England, Germany, and Bohemia supported the Roman pope. There could surely be no better indication that the universal concept of Christendom was dead, because people were no longer rallying to the church, but to their respective nations. In any case, it took no time for sincere people to become disgusted with the whole matter. A solution was needed. Since the last traditional resort, the pope, was the problem, the only solution left was to call a council.

A general council was opened in Pisa in 1409 with kings and princes attending as well as prelates. Both popes refused to honor it or attend, in spite of the fact that it was called by the cardinals of both sides. The council in turn, feeling that neither pope was really worthy of the office, deposed both and elected a third! (This third pope died quickly and was followed by the infamous anti-pope John XXIII, who so dishonored the name that no pope till modern times would use it. Pope John XXIII, who called Vatican II into session, chose it deliberately as a sign of his hope to end disunity.) This situation dragged on for five more years. Finally, the Council of Constance was called by the Emperor Sigismund in 1414 (following the precedent of the first councils) and settled the schism. One pope was deposed (John XXIII for his scandalous life). The Roman pope, now Gregory XII, legitimized the council with a new bull of convocation, and then resigned in 1415. But the Avignon pope, now Benedict XIII, fled to Spain, when he remained a prisoner until his death in 1423 (but he had been deposed by the council in 1417). On November 11, 1417, the council elected Martin V, and the schism was over.

One result, conciliarism, stemming from the resolution of this schism, would agitate the Christian church for centuries. Simply stated, the theory of conciliarism held that a general council is superior to the pope. It was argued that the councils settled things in the early church. One of them, Constantinople III, in 681, had even condemned Pope Honorius. Conciliarists asked why not replace the monarchial structure of the church with a council rule? The situation that prevailed in the Great Western Schism only underscored the benefits of conciliarism. Not everyone agreed about this, of course, and much dissension took place within the Council of Constance itself. People like the famous and respected John Gerson theorized that the priests and indeed all the baptized were the real source of papal authority, that power resides in the church as a whole, and that only lawful election communicates such power. For the same reason, the whole church could correct, punish and, if necessary, depose a pope. Gerson held that, in a general council, every person really had a right to vote, whether clergy or laity. Elements of this theory are being discussed to this very day. Historian Philip Hughes made this observation about the Council of Constance and its discussions, which resolved the Great Western Schism:

> ...This same council that had brought the schism to an end had sown the seeds of much future dissension. Whatever the niceties of canon law that had safeguarded the legitimacy of its liquidation of a complex problem, the fact remained that the Council of Constance had judged two claimants to the papacy and condemned them, and that it had elected a new pope. And it also declared, in explicit terms, that general councils were superior to popes, and it had provided that every five years this general council should reassemble and the pope, in some measure, give to it an account of his stewardship. As far as the wishes of the Council of Constance went, a revolution had been achieved, and the church for the future was to be governed in a parliamentary way, and not by the absolute, divine-

ly given authority of its head. The forty years that followed the council were to see the successive popes—Martin V, Eugene IV, and Nicholas V—wholly taken up with the effort to destroy this new theory and to control the councils which it bred and inspired.[1]

Hughes was right. For the next forty years, the popes were engaged in various plots to lessen the force of the implications of the Council of Constance and its conciliar theories. However, we must insert a word of caution. The Council of Constance has often been described as having instituted novel theories concerning the pope and the general councils. But the fact is that, from the twelfth century onwards, there was a steady tradition about the limitation of papal powers; therefore, the Council of Constance "can no longer be seen, as people liked to think, as having taken an unheard-of initiative or having indulged in unseemly excesses stemming from hasty and unconsidered improvisations."[2]

The council that really tried to be novel was that of Basel in 1431. It was ready to master the pope and settle the matter of conciliar superiority once and for all. Unfortunately that pope, Eugenius IV, was a poor diplomat and only strengthened their resolve. He dissolved the council, which simply refused to be dissolved. The council, in turn, suspended the pope. Eugenius IV retorted by excommunicating the council. Finally, both met in compromise. The council wanted to set up a permanent watchdog committee over the pope and his curia, but the pope balked at this. So, the council once more deposed him.

Meanwhile, the imminent fall of Constantinople to the Muslims seemed to aid the cause of the pope. We have seen how the Muslims were threatening Constantinople, and how anxious the Eastern emperor was to get the support of the West. To achieve this end, the emperor and his prelates came to the Council of Basel to discuss the East-West theological differences. The pope shrewdly moved the Council of Basel to Ferrara and then to Florence, leaving a disgruntled rump council sitting at Basel. The anxious Greeks accepted all the terms of the West, even papal primacy. This was both the wedge and the support the pope needed. A council, made up of both East and West, had reaffirmed his primacy and that was that as far as he was concerned. The rump council still at Basel fulminated but finally fell apart and disintegrated, after weakly re-condemning the pope and electing an anti-pope—the last one in history (if "elect" is not too loose a word, since there was only one cardinal present at this "election"). The papacy, for the time being, had triumphed over conciliarism. Yet, on the other hand, the papal residence at Avignon and the Great Western Schism dealt an almost mortal blow to the papacy as an institution, and constituted a definite mark of its decline.

STRANGE VOICES

The Great Western Schism had surely shaken people's confidence in the leadership of the church. Such a catastrophe would now bring to public notice things that had been only whispered in small circles up to this time. Dangerous theories developed, and they would find echoes in a later age. True, there had been strange and prophetic voices before. There were individuals, for example, who protested the church's wealth. Poverty had a popular appeal in the twelfth century, but it had not provided a unifying force to achieve reform. Critics (then as now) could not reconcile the poverty of the primitive church with the pomp and power of the ecclesiastical organization of their day.[3]

At that time, Pascal II (1099-1118) tried to disentangle the church from its wealth, but he did not succeed. Arnold of Brescia (d. 1155), and others like him, felt that the church's wealth was a betrayal of Jesus' teaching.[4] His voice was muted, and his movement ended in failure. Another popular movement was the Poor Men of Lyons (Waldensians) headed by Peter Waldo. He was converted in the medieval style, gave away his wealth, and in 1173, gathered followers who dedicated themselves to living the simple life of poverty. Waldo and his group were met with suspicion and many attempts were made to silence them. Driven into more radical postures, they eventually endorsed heretical ideas and were condemned. It is interesting to note that Peter Waldo's life and conversion paralleled that of another man who, just a few years later, was to get his poverty movement approved by Innocent III (d. 1216): Francis of Assisi. Arnold of Brescia and Peter Waldo were but early voices outside the mainstream that would be repeated over and over. By the sixteenth century there was a chorus of reforming voices which brought the Reformation into being. There were three more influential voices that we must mention. One voice belonged to Marsilius of Padua. He wrote a pamphlet accusing the papacy of being incompatible with Scripture (a favorite theme of the Protestant reformers). The pope, Marsilius said, was merely another bishop; the church did not include only the clergy but also the laity. He declared that the church was not a monolithic structure, but a community of believers (a theme of renewed Catholics today). He held that the state alone should own property and wield civil power, and proposed that the clergy should, in effect, be in the employ of the state. He also held that supreme authority belonged to a general council rather than to the pope (conciliarism). Marsilius is significant both for what he anticipated, and also because he represented a growing number of believers who were critical of the church's leadership.

Another man who lived in England through the Great Western Schism, John Wycliffe (1329-1384), was to voice sentiments similar to those of Marsilius. Recall that England at that time was protesting papal interference in its internal affairs. The English government deeply resented the fact that a French pope was collecting English monies. Wycliffe personified the protest against the church and the papacy. He held that all people were equal and there was therefore no basic distinction between priest and laity. Each person's salvation would rest on his or her own faith. From this, Wycliffe concluded that neither the church nor the clergy were needed as intermediaries between God and the believer. People could consult the Bible directly for guidance. To this end, Wycliffe translated the Bible into English.

Because he lived at a time when the English nation was protesting the policies of the papacy, his views gained many supporters. In addition, he founded an order called the Lollards, who were intended to be a contrast to the friars who were not well respected at this time. Eventually, he slipped into heresy when he taught predestination, denied the transubstantiation of the eucharist, and held that the Bible was the sole arbiter in religious matters. Yet it is significant that Wycliffe died a peaceful and natural death in 1384, because the elements of English nationalistic feeling in his teaching were enough to insure him of immunity from church penalties.

But Wycliffe's immunity did not endure after his death. A new king of England, Henry IV, needed papal support. Accordingly, in 1415, he turned against Lollardism. He oversaw the condemnation of these heretics, burned them at the stake, and forbade the translation of the Bible. Lollards of nobility were overlooked, however, as the king's heart was not in this venture. It was his son, Henry V, who enforced it ruthlessly. Thus Wycliffe's influence persisted, and many of his radical ideas were resurrected during the Protestant Reformation. Even before that, however, his ideas were kept alive by being transplanted to Bohemia.

Jan Hus of Bohemia was a reformer of morals, upbraiding the luxurious and scandalous lives of the clergy. Strongly influenced by Wycliffe's ideas, Hus also accepted the heretical teaching about predestination. One particular issue that came to be a symbol of his whole movement was that Christians should be allowed to drink from the chalice at Mass (a practice restored to Catholicism after Vatican II). Centuries before, church leadership had restricted the chalice to the clergy in fear that the clumsy laity might spill it. Hus and his followers pointed out that Jesus had said, "Take and drink, all of you." This whole matter became a symbol of resistance to the kind of church leadership that seemed to interfere in the spiritual lives of the people. Hus added to the tension by castigating the practice of making indulgences available to those who performed good works of donating money to ecclesial representatives (money that ended up financing papal wars and paying for the construction of new churches in Rome).

In 1414, Hus was called before the Council of Constance (that same council trying to untangle the Great Western Schism). Actually, he was glad for the opportunity to express his views to a council. He thought his views would be understood and accepted. He was given the promise of safe conduct by Sigismund, the emperor who called the council. But shortly after his arrival, his safe conduct was revoked at the request of the council, and he was imprisoned. Hus was heard at the council, misunderstood, and burned at the stake for heresy in 1415. Hus's influence remained for a long time and factions sprang up around his name in Bohemia. There were the Utraquists, a more moderate and aristocratic group, who were willing to go back to Rome if the chalice were allowed to the people (hence their name: *utraque* means "both," that is, both bread and wine). The Taborites, a more radical and democratic group, would make no such concession. At first, the two factions worked together resisting several crusades against Bohemia. Finally, the Utraquists joined with the Catholics to defeat the Taborites. Catholicism was reestablished in Bohemia, but the anger and discontent remained.

THE BLACK DEATH

Any age has its religious mass movements. The late Middle Ages were no exception. Often, the twin evils of disease and despair led to such movements and there was no lack of either at this period. The lot of the average peasant was hard. Life and property were constantly at the mercy of the ever-present soldiers fighting their endless wars. The barbarous treatment of civilians throughout the Middle Ages is a sad commonplace of history. During the fourteenth century, at the start of the Hundred Years War (1346-1453), however, an even greater disaster struck. It was called the Black Death. It was a form of the bubonic plague brought from the East, probably carried by fleas on the rats of homebound Italian vessels. The plague hit Florence in 1348, and in the next fifteen years spread to the rest of Europe. It is estimated that Europe lost one-fourth of its population to the plague. With devastation and chaos everywhere, life came to a halt. There were simply not enough people to till the fields, work the crafts, sail the ships, and teach the schools. Economic depression set in. The pope gave charitably of money and land. The clergy aided, but in so doing they decimated their own numbers.

It is hard for us to appreciate what it must have meant for Europe to lose one-fourth of its population and to experience such utter devastation and despair.[5] Many people saw the plague as a punishment from God. Others claimed that the pestilence was caused by infected air and water. As often happened in the past, the Jews were accused of causing this disaster, and many Jews were slaughtered by the Christians. Movements of popular despair and religious frenzy were launched. We read of crowds of people, sick and diseased, crowding churches in spasms of prayer, begging for a miracle from heaven to save them. Only a sign from God could make their lives tolerable. Others joined the flagellating groups, who beat themselves bloody trying to appease God. They ran through the towns of Europe, drawing their own blood and singing their Our Fathers and Hail Marys. Traditional outlets and devotions did not suffice in such times of anguish and severe emotional stress. A whole new style of art featuring this preoccupation with death became immensely popular. The painters of the period produced art depicting the terrors of the Last Judgment and the tortures of hell. Immensely popular were the Dance of Death woodcuts and murals, depicting the immediacy of death and the dread of dying without the sacraments. The Black Death did much to crush the human spirit and make people look beyond the authentic devotional practices.

WOMEN ON THEIR OWN

We have seen in the early centuries that women as well as men were attracted to religious life—going off to a monastery, or for women, a nunnery. In some cases this was in response to a "call," while in other cases it might well have been seen as an escape for those women who refused to marry the men selected for them by their families. Yet, before the eleventh and twelfth centuries, women could inherit wealth, and thereby independence, from their fathers or husbands, so a nunnery was less used as a refuge. But with the acceptance of *primogeniture* (that is, inheritance by the first born son) in nearly all the kingdoms of Europe, there was no inheritance and little place in the families of the wealthy for unmarried women or younger sons. So the religious community became increasingly a haven and a place of possible prominence for young sons, and for daughters who chose not to marry.

Lest we think too harshly of this choice for women, let us remember the abbesses seen in Chapter 3, who ruled over some members of the male clergy. They were not subordinate to a bishop but, as abbesses of exempt orders, were directly responsible to the pope. These abbesses even appointed priests to their parishes and authorized them to preach and hear confessions. Occasionally, abbesses even excommunicated difficult priests. In short, these abbesses were like bishops in that they exercised ecclesiastical authority and jurisdiction and they were often upheld in this role by Rome. (There were similar exempted orders of religious men.)

For centuries, these abbesses wore the miter, pectoral cross, and ring, carried the crozier, and were invested with the pallium—all symbols of the episcopal office. It was the combined influence of the Renaissance (with its return to a Greco-Roman culture in which women had had lower status) and the Protestant Reformation (with its stress on patriarchy as found in the Hebrew Scriptures), as well as the conservative Catholic counter-reformation (as exemplified at Trent), that once more reduced all women in the church to a subordinate status. Yet it was not until 1873 that Pius IX, citing the change in civil society, relieved the last exempted abbess (in Spain) of her jurisdiction. Our point is that some women, though never in possession of full social equality with men during the Middle Ages, were nevertheless quasi-official members of the Catholic hierarchy until the late nineteenth century.

NEW "ORDERS"

We leave our mitered abbesses to turn to other people who were seeking some kind of religious life apart from the standard religious orders and structures. These men and women were seeking a religious lifestyle which, in reality, was a response to the new conditions of urban life and the changing times. The "Beguines" were an informal movement of women who wished to live life more religiously. Rather than take vows, the Beguines made a statement of intention to live a life of poverty, chastity, and charitable works. They had no founder, no rule of life, no official leaders, and no ecclesiastical authorization—and this was precisely what perplexed the church leadership.   Usually they lived together in small groups or alone with their families, supporting themselves by manual labor and seeking spiritual guidance from the friars. Obviously, there was no fault here. These women were doing nothing wrong, but rather were doing a great deal that was right in desiring to live a holy life. (Vatican II's Dogmatic Constitution of the Church devotes its entire fifth chapter to the concept that the call to holiness is given to every member of the church.) They could be accused of no heresy (although this was tried). They were just there, a source of inspiration to their admirers, an irritation to their detractors, and an enigma to the church hierarchy, who did not know how to handle a Christian movement outside the mainstream of traditional religious patterns. By the middle of the thirteenth century, the Beguines had doubled their numbers to nearly 37,000. There was a similar, but less popular, association of men, who were known as the "Beghards," because they supported themselves by begging.

    In due time, as vested interests continued their attacks, fervor waned and some absurdities crept in. Before long, the church leadership was investigating such fringe communities as the Beguines and the Beghards. The Council of Lyons II in 1274, for example, passed some legislation against such unauthorized religious orders. Thirty-seven years later, the Council of Vienne mentioned the Beguines by name, noting some of the good things they had done. Such kind words were significant, because they show the ambiguity of the official church's relationship with an obviously holy and exemplary movement whose members, however, did not conform to pre-existing patterns. The real problem was the tension (to use modern terms) between freedom and authority. By the middle of the fourteenth century, the Beguines as a movement had all but died out, while the whole experience left the church wondering about institutional religious lifestyles.

As the Beguines and Beghards were dying out, another more widespread and influential movement was beginning to blossom. It had all the characteristics of a free-lance religion and would further call into question the value of institutional religion. It had its origins in the Rhineland like the Beguines and Beghards, but it was from Gerhard Groote (1340-1384) in Holland that this movement, known as the *devotio moderna* (the modern devotion), took its form. He was a sincere layperson, uninterested in the formal religious life as provided by the great religious orders, but highly interested in the interior life of the spirit. Groote desired to have, as an individual, a reflective interior religious life, or, if you will, a personal relationship to God. He had no program, no articulated theories, no visions. He was no revolutionary; he was simply a seeker after God in his own heart.

A number of laywomen were the first to gather under Groote's direction, forming a religious community known as the Sisters of the Common Life. They were similar in many ways to the earlier Beguines, having no rule and no vows, while offering service to God and the world from within the secular society. However, by the fifteenth century, most of these women had entered monastic communities. It was a group of laymen, known as the Brethren of the Common Life, and organized by Groote's friend and disciple, Florentius Radewijns (1350-1400), who had a greater effect on the church as a whole.

The Brethren continued to increase in numbers, while living ordinary lives and strongly insisting on work in the secular world as a means of religious living. They dropped all the old penances, long rites, chants, and complicated rituals of the regular religious orders. They kept away from expertise in theology and any seeking after privilege. Rather, they devoted themselves to a simple life of useful work and prayerful meditation on Jesus' life and passion. In addition, the Brethren were composed of both clergy and laity. This was a most extraordinary and upsetting feature, because few concepts were as deeply imbedded in the medieval mind as the idea that the clergy and the laity were separate in every way. Again we see the recurring problem faced by the institutional leadership of the church: How could there be a religious order without vows or without a life-long commitment? Such unusual freedom seemed to pose a threat because:

If people could form associations without authorization, choose a superior in some unknown manner, adopt a monastic type of life without the sanction of a monastic rule, read the Scriptures together in the common tongue, confess their sins to one another and receive counsel and correction from no one knew whom, there would be an end to all order in the church.[6]

In summary, the existence of the Brethren was another symptom that this new age had new needs. Before we proceed to see how those needs were met, we should note that although the Brethren did eventually die out, they had a great impact on the church and the world. Besides their occupations of copying books and distributing religious literature, they taught in the city schools throughout Holland and Germany. Among their most famous students were Erasmus and Martin Luther. In addition, there was Groote's most distinguished follower, Thomas á Kempis, who wrote the spiritual classic, *Imitation of Christ*.

MEDIEVAL PIETY

The Brethren were a sensible relief from some of the excesses of their age. Late medieval life was full of the strangest contradictions. Deep and abiding piety often rubbed shoulders with the erratic and unusual, as one might expect in a society where the sacred and the profane were so intertwined. A host of special blessings, festivals, religious orders had sprung up.

Nowhere were the extremes of medieval piety more evident than in the cult of the saints. Popular imagination had a field day. The saints became as real and familiar as the trees and sky. They were invoked on every occasion, and assigned to every phase of human life and activity. Saints in charge of sickness, gout, headaches, shoe-making, motherhood, and impossible cases came from medieval piety. Obviously, the search for and the possession of relics of the saints turned for many into a fetish bordering on the barbaric.

It was inevitable that this pious attachment to material things should draw all hagiolatry into a sphere of coarse and primitive ideas, and lead to surprising extremes. In the matter of relics the deep and straightforward faith of the Middle Ages was never afraid of disillusionment or profanation through handling holy things coarsely. The spirit of the fifteenth century did not differ much from that of the Umbrian peasants who, about the year 1000, wished to kill Saint Romuald, the hermit, in order to make sure of his precious bones; or of the monks of Fossanuova, who, after Saint Thomas Aquinas had died in their monastery, in their fear of losing the relic, did not shrink from decapitating, boiling and preserving the body.... In 1392, King Charles VI of France, on the occasion of a solemn feast, was seen to distribute ribs of his ancestor, Saint Louis....[7]

To associate with a holy person was like having a living relic. In fact, St. Francis of Paul was literally purchased by a royal collector to live in his palace. Saints and visionaries were consulted by the high and mighty. This explains why some of the saints were always to be found in the royal entourage, or why a St. Bernard or a St. Catherine were at the sides of the popes. Actually, so profuse and so overdone was the cult of the saints that when the Reformation attacked this cult, many local Catholics did not resist.

The liturgy itself, under the influence of the Franks, had departed from its original simplicity. Everything in the Mass became dramatized and lengthened. New emphases were added to help a congregation that did not understand Latin. For example, the high point of the Mass became for some the double elevation of the host and the chalice. The laity were no longer permitted to carry Viaticum, communion for the dying. In time, many came to believe that it was sacriligious for a layperson to touch the host or the chalice.

One rather significant change regarding the Mass in the early Middle Ages was the growing tendency to dwell on the sacred species itself, and it was at this time that the feast of Corpus Christi was created to honor the Real Presence. As this interest concerning Christ reserved in the Blessed Sacrament became excessive, all kinds of legends about bleeding hosts arose, and a glass was put in the monstrance or the tabernacle so that Jesus could "see" out to the people. The notion of the sacrifice of the Mass began to overshadow the earlier understanding the Mass as *eucharistia*, the communal thanksgiving offered to God for salvation in Christ. In a very real sense, the extremes of the cult of the saints, the rerouting of so much of the liturgy, the new legal approach to the sacraments, and the introduction of the confessional box at the end of the Middle Ages—all these things were in reality "outside the mainstream." They were indicators (as were the moderate and sensitive spirituality of the independent Beguines and Brethren of the Common Life) that the Catholic synthesis was breaking up.

THE CHURCH

The fourteenth and fifteenth centuries saw not only the individual prophet and mystic who had always been around, but also a new prominence and publicity given to mysticism itself. In addition, there was a new public prominence given to greater individual freedom. This led to a reaction not only against the traditional way of doing things, but also a reaction against the hierarchical church. There was a distinct thrust toward the religious value of a purely secular life. The Brethren and the Beguines were examples of this. Several mystics of note at this time were Tauler, van Ruysbroeck, and Eckhart. Eckhart said that God and union with God was open to all people, not just to professional religious. The interior life was what counted. All these mystics wrote in the vernacular and not in Latin, the language of the church. Such mystical writings in the vernacular had the effect of undermining the monopoly in religious matters that the institutional church had taken to itself.

The church did recover somewhat after the scandal of the Great Western Schism, and reforms were made. New congregations were founded. Saintly people abounded during this period: the three Catherines, of Siena, of Genoa, and of Bologna; Saints Bernadine, John Capistrano, Colette, and Antoninus. Popes Martin and Eugene went out of their way to pick worthy cardinals. Popular piety increased, although much of it, as we have seen, centered around the aspects of the passion of Jesus and the sorrows of the Blessed Mother. Much of this was due to the Black Death, which had imposed on society a certain preoccupation with death, the after-life, salvation, and indulgences as they affected the rewards to come. Much of this preoccupation about salvation helps to explain the inner spiritual struggles of such diverse personalities as Ignatius of Loyola, the founder of the Jesuits, and Martin Luther.

Still, the influence of the institutional church was clearly waning. Many forces without and within were beginning to shake it to its very foundations: the rise of the nation-states and their conflicts with the church; the loss of the Eastern church; the humiliation of Boniface VIII; the rising skepticism of the schoolmen; and the rising merchant class with its yen for profit and progress and its impatience with the moral confinements of the old order. Then, too, other events occurred to disrupt and disturb. For example, in the fourteenth century, it was discovered that the *Donation of Constantine* document mentioned in a previous chapter was a forgery. The Apostles Creed was shown not to be the work of the apostles. Some early critical methods were being applied to the Bible. We have already taken note of the writings and activities of Marsilius, Wycliffe, and Hus. The Beguines and the Brethren challenged some long-held ideals and ideas. All these, as well as the writings of the mystics, exemplified the tendency to go outside the mainstream of ecclesiastical life. Many of these things, of course, had only a limited appeal to the formulas and practices of the institutional church. The externals were still important to the crowd. But discontent was brewing and, as we shall see, papal life and morals went into another decline. An era was about to come to an end. Before we see its demise, we must look at one more element in the changing scene.

THE RENAISSANCE

The Renaissance was partly built on the decline of the church's influence, which was no longer corresponding to the needs and realities of the age. It was also an embodiment of the physical and intellectual ferment that was going on. Many wanted freedom to experiment. As we have noted above, merchants wanted an end of political and moral limitations to their money-making and expansion. A New World across the ocean was opening up and the Old World did not have answers to the questions raised by the New World's existence and the possibilities it offered. Thus, the Renaissance became, in the context we have described, a kind of collective thrust into the whole area of human activity.

It is not mysterious that the Renaissance found its roots in Italy. Here, more than any other place, town life had developed with a high degree of sophistication. Italy was not united as were England and France. Italian towns were fiercely independent. Both nobles and commoners found themselves in a community of shared commercial interests. Such towns were quite ready to work out their fortunes free of political or ecclesiastical influence. The wealthy ran the towns; their wealth was often matched only by their unscrupulousness. They had little regard for the ideas and traditions of old. Since banking had started in Italy, many families and merchants became wealthy. With more leisure time, they began to dabble in the arts.

At the same time, the old ascetical ideals of the church were beginning to break down. Traditional asceticism did not set well with the new competitive commercial spirit, especially when that asceticism forbade charging interest on money loaned to others. Certain New Testament ideals, such as that we had not here a lasting city or that the wealthy could hardly be saved, were simply breaking down. A monk like Savonarola might still be able to preach doom and despair in the middle of wealthy Florence and move people to burn their works of art and frivolous books. But in the end they burned Savonarola.

The church, it must be admitted, did not do much to foster the old ascetical ideals. Many of the upper clergy were preoccupied with wealth, and the luxury of the papal court itself was becoming an open scandal. Even the monastic orders no longer offered an ideal for society (except for the cloistered orders), because they did not respond to the needs of the moment. Increasingly, therefore, the ignorant and rude members of society entered their ranks. As the new learning took root in society, the religious orders consequently became the butt of sarcastic comments and shady stories, such as those found in Chaucer's *Canterbury Tales*, written in the fourteenth century. It was not that the people of the time lost their respect for sanctity; they simply would not tolerate an asceticism intolerant and hostile to their way of life. This loss of the ascetic ideal had immediate consequences. With the loss of moral ideals, the history of this time is filled with endless assassinations, poisonings, infidelities, and crimes. The dark streets of Florence and many other medieval towns provided cover for the most unspeakable crimes.

We must mention that economic and social conditions elsewhere were nourishing the Renaissance. In fact, the age has been characterized by historian, Jacob Burckhardt, as "urban, commercial, and lay rather than ecclesiastical and feudal."[8] New merchants were to be found in other areas besides Italy. The great money lenders appeared at this time in the Low Countries and England. They were embarking on a vast amount of trade, especially with the New World, whose coffee, tea, and tobacco were enriching them. The discovery of the New World was the result of cautious navigational experiments such as those made by Prince Henry the Navigator in the early fifteenth century. The earliest discoveries were primarily adventures on behalf of the faith and in the interest of scientific curiosity.

The commercial implications of such discoveries were not at first obvious. But later the discovery of foreign lands would have a major impact on the economy of Europe. The Azores were discovered in 1431; Diaz reached the Cape of Good Hope in 1486; Columbus sailed to North America in 1492; Magellan encircled the globe for the first time in 1520. When the economic import of these discoveries began to be realized, the Italian cities would begin to decline as maritime trade centers. Their place was taken by Antwerp and other cities in the Low Countries.

So far we have spoken of the Renaissance without defining it. What actually was it? The Renaissance was a revival of learning and art. It nourished itself on antiquity, the rediscovery of Greek and Roman ways. The Europeans were always aware of antiquity since they lived with it, but they now saw everything in a different light. They ceased to see the world through ecclesiastical glasses. Now they were donning the glasses of the cultured pagan. Great interest in Greek and Roman art, language, and philosophy developed. The cultivated persons of the Renaissance spoke and read Greek and Latin. The pagan authors, not the Christian, were their sources of education. In short, antiquity was not only being imitated, it was also being assimilated into the vernacular languages of the time.

Thus, the Renaissance had its intellectual impact. It would, in effect, replace the church's dominance in the area of thought. Learning, previously the province of clerics and theologians, became the property of the layperson. The pages of pagan antiquity would nourish the mind and the spirituality of the laity as well as that of the clergy. In fact, the self-perfection of the human person and not the life hereafter would be the focus. The study of the human person became the abiding concern of those we have come to call the humanists, such as Thomas More and the famed Erasmus. According to the humanists, each person was to be prepared for *life*, not the monastery. Schools must be designed to impart not salvation, but learning. This is why the humanists attacked church schools, their methods and the old time asceticism. In his book, *Praise of Folly*, the most popular work of the time, Erasmus poked fun at the church and wanted to take education out of clerical hands. Thus, many colleges unrelated to the church were founded at this time. It was for the sake of universal education that Erasmus translated the Bible into classical Greek and Latin.

To this extent, the Renaissance was anti-clerical but not anti-religious. Art and science were no longer exclusively to serve theology, but were to be studied for their own sakes. The church, in the eyes of the humanists, should stay involved, but should no longer have a monopoly on all learning. They thought that the church should do everything in its power to create a truly human world and from this human world people would wend their way to God. The church, in short, was also to be guided by reason and devoted to the humane. It was this attitude that underlay the horror that Erasmus displayed to Luther and the Reformation. As much as these humanists criticized the clergy, they also saw a need for the church. They were appalled by the violence that Luther unleashed, and they resented the substitution of force for reason. In this respect, Luther was far more a medieval man than a Renaissance man. His dogmatism and use of force were more akin to the wars of religious extermination waged by the German princes against the Slavs than to the reasoned persuasions of the leaders of the Renaissance.

It must be stated again that the Renaissance of itself was not consciously hostile to the church or organized religion. The Renaissance simply went beyond the church's activities. In fact, many of the popes patronized the Renaissance and were Renaissance men. This presented its own problems. The popes became too preoccupied with the new learning and did not give enough time to the spiritual side of the church. Nicholas V (1447-1455), who succeeded Eugenius IV after the Great Western Schism, was devoted to the Renaissance. It is to him that we owe the fabulous Vatican library and other monuments in St. Peter's. But even the Renaissance popes took time out for the chronic game of playing power politics among the nations. Wars in Italy were still commonplace, and they sapped the energy that the popes wanted to spend elsewhere. Elsewhere still meant fighting the Muslims. The popes wanted to regain Constantinople. Unable to rouse the princes of Europe, Pius II himself planned to set off on a crusade—the last one in history—and died before it really got underway.

Sixtus IV (d. 1484), the builder of the famous chapel named after him, the Sistine Chapel, returned to the unsavory practice of handing out cardinals' hats to unworthy relatives. This had the net effect of breaking up the college of cardinals into factions each jockeying to get its own man elected as pope. After Sixtus IV came the unworthy and scandalous Callistus VIII, who frankly bought the papacy. He was the first pope to publicly acknowledge his bastard children and give them a place in the church's administration. He was succeeded both in title and sin by Alexander VI, another Borgia pope, who went even further in providing for his bastard children as well as his evil relatives, who were cutthroats and murderers. Alexander VI died in 1503 and was succeeded by the vigorous Julius II, who was both a diplomat and soldier. He did not hesitate to lead the papal armies into battle himself. He was the one who pressured Michelangelo to paint the ceiling of the Sistine Chapel. Julius also, unfortunately, continued the practice of nepotism. Yet he did manage to keep off balance his current enemies who might be a threat to the papal states. Julius II was succeeded by a Medici, Leo X, who had become a cardinal at the age of thirteen, and who would sit on the papal throne for eight and one-half years. Leo X, too, never lost an opportunity to further the interests of his family. It was also his misfortune to be the pope when Luther began what Leo called a mere "monkish squabble."

As we close this section, we must emphasize strongly that the Renaissance, for all of its intellectual intoxication and artistic activity, did not go into profound philosophical questions. The Renaissance, in fact, operated well within the old Christian finalities. This explains why, in the midst of all of this enlightenment, magic could revive and witchcraft trials be renewed. Another point of strong emphasis is this: The Renaissance was essentially an elitist movement. The wealthy few were its patrons, and there was a marked disdain for the illiterate or those engaged in mundane mechanical tasks. It was the leaders of the Renaissance who coined the pejorative term "Gothic" for the cathedrals of Europe. It was these Renaissance elite who could be rather indifferent to the lower classes.[9] Thus, although all levels of society could be caught up in the spirit and adventuresome times of the Renaissance, the time and the wealth to pursue and encourage it belonged to the few. There was no telling how far the Renaissance might have taken this period of history, before it was suddenly checked and restyled by another powerful force that appeared in its midst, that of the Protestant Reformation. At long last the seeds planed by Marsilius, Wycliffe, and Hus had flowered.

CHAPTER 15

The Reformation

ABUSES

In spite of all that we have seen in the past chapters, the church continued to hold sway over Europe. No one seriously considered its overthrow. The very idea would be civilly as well as religiously unthinkable to the medieval mind, because society and church were as one. Yet, in the space of fifty years or so, that is precisely what happened: millions of Catholics were wrenched from the church and new churches were founded that were radically different from the old one. To understand how this happened, we must look at both the abuses prevalent in the early sixteenth century and the circumstances that brought society to the forefront of this revolution.

There were, of course, the elements already mentioned: Wycliffe's ideas and his Lollard group; Marsilius of Padua and his proroyalist teaching that Henry VIII would use; Jan Hus of Bohemia, who had religiously disturbed that land; the Great Western Schism that weakened papal authority; the theory of conciliarism that placed a general council superior to the pope. Then there were the daily chronic irritations: too many clerical exemptions from civil law; worldly clergy and absentee bishops; unlettered and uncouth lower clergy; the scandalous rivalry between the Franciscans and Dominicans; ineffective and spiritless monasteries; the low estate of clerical celibacy and the very use of the term "cleric" or "monk" as an insulting word among the laity. But over and above such chronic scandals we might list five major causes of the Reformation: spirituality, money, the papacy, the power of the kings, and the new learning.

SPIRITUALITY

There were indeed many reformers active in the church. Although new and fervent orders were rising up and a wave of idealism was spreading over Europe, these elements only aggravated the need for a better spirituality. The experience of the Black Death drove people to a greater preoccupation with salvation and death. Groups like the Brethren of the Common Life and the Beguines had whetted spiritual appetites and thereby increased the dissatisfaction with the packaged (and costly) piety of the church. For many, their personal experience of dissatisfaction with what was offered by the Roman church was the turning point. For some, the Protestant Reformation was basically a religious quest for a new spirituality. The Reformation came out of a common desire to renew and perhaps redirect Christian spirituality from external routine to inner involvement. The Reformation was thus a concern for the entire church, that it get back to the gospel. People were looking critically at the old Constantinian concept of the church, which identified it too much with the political order. People were asking whether the kind of institutional church that responded to the needs of people in a violent barbarian age was fulfilling in the present age its basic role as a mediator between God and humanity. In the estimation of many, spiritual needs and evangelical virtues had taken second place to a preoccupation with rights and privileges.

For these reasons, many of the reformers' denunciations of the church were made to purify it, not destroy it. They wanted the church free from the practice of using almost mechanical and automatic means to attain salvation, especially those means that had price tags attached to them. To that end there was always the vague presumption that this new spirituality could somehow be subsumed into the Catholic church. Genuine doctrinal differences came later as the result of misunderstanding and the hardening of opposing positions. Most of the people who thronged to the reformers "did not consider themselves in opposition to the Roman church. Even if they were against the clergy or ecclesiastical prerogatives, they were not really against the church. The resolute mood of separation came much later. The Reformation was a filial revolt; in other words, a prodding to get the church to undertake certain changes...."[1]

Not all were so interested in such pure motives, but for many the Reformation began with a crisis in their hearts, a holy dissatisfaction with the externalized sanctity offered by the church, a dilemma between church authority and the freedom of the gospel.

MONEY AND THE PAPACY

The burdensome taxations (imposed under penalty of excommunication for failure to pay) fell largely on the backs of the middle class artisans and the peasants. What was particularly galling was the widespread suspicion that such tax monies were underwriting the scandalous and luxurious lives of the Italian prelates. Besides, why should the faithful in Germany pay for the siege of Bologna by Julius II? Why should England pay for the rebuilding of St. Peter's? Why should France finance the wars and politics of the pope?

Thus, for money reasons alone, there was strong anti-papal feeling in many countries. Roman expenditures and the upkeep of the papal bureaucracy were so great, however, that the quest for money and its attendant corruptions went on. (Pope Innocent VII [1404-1406] at one point even pawned his tiara.) Graft became a way of life. Church positions were bought and sold almost on the open market. Dispensations were costly. From pardons to candles, from Masses to the papal office itself, nothing seemed free of a price tag. Nor did the papal office-holders themselves help. During Luther's lifetime (1483-1546), the popes were Alexander VI, who flouted his bastard Borgia children to the public; Julius II, more at home on the battlefield than at the papal court; and Leo X, more Renaissance prince than pope.

However, the popes could hardly bring reform, not only because they lacked the will to do so, but because they had lost to power to do so. The new rising nations had eroded that power considerably.

In spite of past victories, papal dominance in international affairs had dwindled. Kings and local lords won more and more rights to dispose of many of the highest clerical offices in their territories as they saw fit. Thus, churchmen became more loyal to prince than to pope. When Pope Urban called for the first crusade in 1098, all of Christendom had responded. When Pius II called for a crusade against the Muslims, Europe did not respond, even when Pius took the crusader's cross himself, and died in 1453 while embarking on the Holy War. Not only did the papacy lose its power in other lands, it became more and more embroiled, as a sovereign power, in protecting its territories in Italy. Because of this immediate local Italian need, all the popes of the fifteenth century, with two exceptions, were Italian, and from 1522 until the election of John Paul II (1978) have remained such. The papacy had come to require its incumbents to be Italian princes to protect its own interests; the papacy became a home-grown interest and the curia provided high jobs (and pay) for the popes' families.

THE POWER OF THE KINGS

The kings were forging strong centralized nations. It is not difficult to see that the international power of an international church must necessarily be a threat to them. Never far from their minds, therefore, were plans to dominate the church, to nationalize it, and make it a department of state. Already, as we have noted, they had secured rights to appoint the higher clergy. As the popes became weaker and the kings became stronger, the popes had to resort to the new invention of having papal ambassadors (nuncios) at the various courts. Such ambassadors, like any other diplomats, had to cajole, flatter, and bargain with the kings. The day of the direct papal thunderbolt was over, even though the pope still retained considerable prestige and power. Because the pope did have prestige and power, the kings were not entirely displeased with Italians possessing their dioceses. Such an arrangement also gave the king his man at the papal court, and his ambassador could press the king's interests. In this way, the kings, wanting to reward their loyal followers, could secure papal approval of their appointees. Of course, such papally approved royal appointees were really the king's men in church robes; when a crisis arose, they were loyal to the king and not to the pope. In short, because of the weakening of the papacy and the growing power of the monarchs, the Reformation, when it came, would succeed only where the king wished it to succeed and would fail where he decreed it would fail. At no time was the Reformation apart from the political power.

The relation between this [the king's forging of strong nations] and the success of a Protestant revolt is undoubted but not easy to define. It might be said broadly that in England and in Denmark, the Reformation was necessary because limitation of the power of the church was necessary to the future development of efficient government. Efficient government demanded restraint upon papal intervention, upon ecclesiastical privilege and exemptions, upon the legal right of an authority outside the country to levy taxes.[2]

When the time came, the reality of the king's strength and the pope's weakness would lead the reformers to look to the king for redress and support.

THE NEW LEARNING

This was the time when a new quest for learning was abroad. Sophisticated scholars like the great Erasmus (d. 1536), pained at seeing learning, the great civilizer of Europe, stranded on forms and vested interests, and distressed at seeing the discrepancies in both church and society, set out by his writings to provoke reform. Erasmus used ridicule in particular, as seen in *Praise of Folly* (1509). Perhaps more than anyone else in Europe, he lowered the reputation of the popes and the clergy, the monks and the friars, and especially the nit-picking theologians who had become too rationalistic and too unacquainted with critical scholarship. In his efforts to spread learning, Erasmus translated the Bible into Greek so that more people might read it.

Along with new scholarship was the cry for simplicity in contrast to the convulsions of the church devotions, relics, cults, madonnas, bleeding hosts, indulgences, and more. In fact, there was a looking back to the "Golden Age" of the apostles when people thought that all was harmony and peace (in spite of ample evidence to the contrary, as we have noted before, in the Pauline epistles). Many wanted accretions of the church at that time to be stripped away. This thought explains why the reformers were always looking backward rather than forward. This desire to discover and reproduce the supposed purity of the early church was not new. It was behind the Waldensians, Wycliffe, and others. The trouble was that up to this time there were really no texts or documents to use in finding out what that church was really like. Thanks to the Renaissance, however, there were many more discoveries of early Christian literature. There was an increased knowledge of Greek and Christian Scripture studies, and new critical methods were being applied to Scripture. For the first time, scholars were able to look directly at the Scriptures, not merely through official church documents or the liturgy. In other words, the new scholarship turned society more than ever to the Bible, especially to Paul and his moral teachings. The early church became more of a reality.

The sixteenth-century church provided a contrast with the church of the first century. In the eyes of people like Erasmus and the reformers, this contrast was most apparent in the rampant and pervasive clericalism. That is why, from the very beginning, people like Erasmus simply ignored the privileged clerical class. The new learning was meant to bring a literate people in direct contact with Jesus as he was seen and known in the sacred writings. "Let us consider," wrote Erasmus, "who were the hearers of Christ? Were they not the common, willy-nilly multitude?...Is Christ offended that such people should read him as he chose for his hearers? In my opinion the husband-man should read him, along with the smith and the mason and even prostitutes, bawdy people, and Turks." The disgust that the humanists had for clerical domination over the means of salvation is at the heart of their turning directly to the Bible. Both the humanists and the reformers were anxious to do away with such intermediaries. It is no wonder that a popular saying of the day was "Erasmus laid the egg and Luther hatched it."

The predominance of the Bible from the beginning of the reform movement, then, was not only the result of its easy accessibility and new translations but, symbolically, it was the result of direct anti-clericalism. To all of this must be added other factors, such as the adventuresome spirit engendered by the Renaissance and the invention of printing, which could quickly spread ideas. In a word, everything so far mentioned coalesced into what we might call the "ripeness of time." Luther would succeed where other reformers had failed because the time was ripe for reform and revolution.[3]

LUTHER

Luther was of peasant stock, subject to strong emotions and impulsive actions and speech. At twenty-two, he left the pursuit of law to enter an Augustinian monastery. No one is certain why he made this sudden decision. Emotional anxieties were always present in him. He did say that while caught in a severe thunderstorm, he cried out to St. Anne for help and vowed to enter a monastery if he were saved. In 1506, he made his profession as a monk and remained so for the next twenty years. Yet, all during this time he was subject to great scruples about his unworthiness, his guilt, the pressure of his sins, and the fear of God's punishment. Modern psychoanalyst Erik Erikson in his book *Young Man Luther* suggests that Luther's stern father was the prototype of his stern and demanding God. In any case, Luther could not rid himself of guilt. He would confess his sins for hours on end "...yet for all this my conscience could never be fully certified, but was always in doubt and said: this or that thou hast not done rightly; thou wast not contrite and sorrowful enough; this sin thou didst omit in thy confessions."[4]

Through his Bible studies, Luther came upon his theory of justification by faith alone. He felt that Paul said it all in Romans 1:17: "The righteous shall live by faith." A person, then, is not made holy by works or ritual, but by faith in God. Each one must simply believe that God forgives him or her. A person is saved only if one ceases to rely upon self and totally accepts God's goodness. This reliance, this trust, this total confidence is the faith that makes a person holy, that justifies the person. Luther felt a weight lifted with these thoughts that attributed little merit to good works, relics, statues, and all the other rituals and superstitions of the church. However, Luther had no thought of going further, no intent of breaking with the church.

He went on to become a teacher and lecturer at the University of Wittenberg in 1512. Then the appearance of the Dominican Tetzel led to Luther's emergence into the public limelight. The background was this: Albrecht of Brandenburg, a twenty-four-year-old cleric who already held several church offices, aspired to become the Archbishop of Mainz (and thereby one of the electors of the emperor). He needed a papal dispensation to obtain yet another office which, according to the custom of that time, he had to pay for. Albrecht borrowed the money from the Fugger banking family, and the pope in turn allowed him to sell indulgences, with part of the profit going to repay the Fuggers and the other part going toward the rebuilding of St. Peter's basilica in Rome. The Dominican Tetzel was chosen to hawk these indulgences near (not in) Wittenberg. Luther was incensed that people were being told they could buy an indulgence—a remission of the punishment due for their sins. It is said that on October 31, 1517, he posted his ninety-five theses on the town bulletin board (as was customary), and sent copies to Tetzel's superiors and to Albrecht, who forwarded his copy to the pope. Luther's ninety-five theses, although quite Catholic, included a direct challenge to the pope's use of authority. He also called for a reinterpretation of the teaching on indulgences, a matter not yet defined by the church.

What should have been a minor irritant became a hornet's nest, because Luther had simply nudged too many vested interests at that time: the whole elaborate money-indulgence system, big names, a banking family, the rebuilding of St. Peter's. Luther seemed to be under the impression that if only the pope knew what was going on he would be shocked enough to put a stop to it. Instead, Luther received a reprimand from the pope's censor, and Tetzel himself replied vigorously. Then the controversy began to spread in very small circles. By the next year, however, Luther's ninety-five theses were more widely publicized, and by this time the German nationalists, always ready to needle Rome, were applauding his stand. The church leadership now proceeded to make its biggest mistake: they did not take Luther seriously or give him a decent hearing. In 1518, proceedings were opened against Luther, and he was ordered to appear in Rome. Luther was not sure that he would return alive from Rome and so, in one of the most symbolic acts of the Reformation, he appealed to his political superior, the Elector Frederick of Saxony.

FREDERICK OF SAXONY

Luther's appeal was that he should be heard in his native Germany; Frederick supported this request. Why he did so is a moot question, since he did not know Luther and did not share his religious views. Perhaps it was because Albrecht of Brandenburg was his rival. Perhaps it was because Tetzel was cutting in on his own revenue-producing relics, for Frederick's church at Wittenberg had cases containing some 17,443 fragments of holy relics, including, it was claimed, the corpse of one of the Holy Innocents. Perhaps it was just that, like any good German, he wanted to show the Roman Curia that it could not proceed in the way it wanted to. For whatever reason, Frederick intervened and this, in effect, saved the Lutheran Reformation from extinction. Because the old emperor lay dying, and the pope did not want the contenders from Spain or France to get the imperial crown, the pope granted Frederick's request that Luther be examined in Germany. Thus, the meeting took place in 1518 at Augsburg, where Luther held to his rejection of the selling of indulgences before the famous Cardinal Cajetan.

The following year, Luther met with John Eck at Leipzig, which lay near the Bohemian border, the land of the burned heretic, Jan Hus. Eck goaded Luther on, getting him to admit that in some areas Hus was right and that the general council that had condemned him was wrong in doing so. Luther was also led to say that the councils were not infallible. That was the turning point. Luther had actually gone so far as to identify himself with a man condemned by the leadership of the church.

Still, matters were not irreparable, because the church had tolerated many who disagreed with it, like Erasmus. There was as yet no official teaching on justification. In 1520, a papal commission rendered a rather mild verdict on Luther's writings. However, at John Eck's instigation, a papal bull of June 15, 1520, condemned forty-one of Luther's propositions. Luther, meanwhile, was not idle. He wrote three of his most famous political pamphlets appealing to the nobles to bring about reform and attacking the sacramental system, reducing the sacraments to three and then to two, baptism and eucharist. On December 10, 1520, Luther burned the papal bull before some students who took it as a lark. He also burned a copy of canon law, symbolically rejecting church authority, which he replaced with Scripture alone. Finally, on January 3, 1521, he was excommunicated. Four months, later he was banned in the empire by the recently elected emperor, Charles V. For safe keeping he was "kidnapped" by the Elector Frederick and spirited off to the castle of Wartburg where he stayed for a year.

At this time, he translated the Bible into colloquial German. (He was not the first to do so, for there were some eighteen other translations.) Nor was his work accurate or literate. He was not above correcting St. Paul or St. John. He criticized the epistle of James with its heavy emphasis on good works: "You see then that a man is justified by deeds and not by faith in itself" (James 2:24). His translation, however, was an immediate success. With his pamphlets he became the most popular writer in Germany.

THE MOVEMENT SPREADS

The man was becoming a movement. Nothing was formed yet: no doctrine, no church, but power and politics were gathering their forces to keep Luther's position alive. Many, for various reasons, were gathering around his cause. Some joined for noble, religious reasons. In other instances, "it is surely noteworthy that at some place the demand for the discontinuation of payments to the church for evangelical ministers was made in the same breath as that for greater popular participation in governmental affairs."[5] Some, however, did not join his cause, and others left it. The humanists, for example, were on his side at the beginning. Luther and Erasmus, because of their criticisms of the church, were identified with each other, though neither admired the other. In any case, Erasmus broke with Luther over what he considered Luther's violence and wildness. He called Luther the "Goth." In 1523, Erasmus took up his pen against Luther, provoking the expected and characteristic wrath as Luther, in turn, dubbed Erasmus a "viper and a piece of dung" and the "insane destroyer of the church" who "walked arm in arm with the devil of Rome." Understandably, the universities, theologians, and higher clergy were cool to Luther, but the lower clergy eagerly joined him.

THE PEASANTS' REVOLT

Simultaneous with Luther's message, the ever-restless peasants were stirring against their cruel local lords. (We must remember that there was no central government in Germany.) In 1524, the peasants revolted and some hundred thousand of them were most cruelly crushed. Luther figured in the incident indirectly, because some peasants felt that his insistence on Christian freedom and the priesthood of all believers was a clarion call to political freedom and equality. Luther, a political conservative, deplored violence and deplored the peasants using the gospel to justify it. He therefore urged the princes in a famous pamphlet "to slay, stab and kill" the peasants. "These times," Luther exclaimed in a typical overstatement, "are so extraordinary that a prince can win heaven more easily by bloodshed than by prayer." Feeling betrayed, the common people, especially in southern Germany, abandoned Luther. The Peasants' Revolt had two other results. One was that Lutheranism thereby tended to become more tied to the state, since the state (read: the princes) had gained more power by the revolt's failure. The second result was the politicalization of Lutheranism. On the one hand, Catholic princes rallied together to prevent another peasant uprising, since it was popularly thought that Luther had inspired the Peasants' Revolt. On the other hand, the Lutheran princes banded together for mutual protection. From 1525 on, Luther's movement was largely out of his hands and into the hands of the power play between the Catholic and Lutheran princes.

THE COMMUNION CONTROVERSY

Other matters began to go badly for Luther. One was his distress for his fellow Protestants. He claimed that he could more easily handle the Catholics than his Protestant adversaries. One early controversy concerned the eucharist. Luther taught that the Catholic notion of transubstantiation was inadequate, and that the Mass was not a sacrifice, for it could not be so verified in Scripture. However, in words that echoed Thomas Aquinas, Luther believed in the Real Presence, but other reformers disagreed. Karlstadt, an old professor colleague, took a different point of view. Most significant of all, Zwingli, the great Swiss reformer, disagreed. Before long, everyone was debating the matter concerning the eucharist. Finally, the two major protagonists, Luther and Zwingli, met at Marburg in October 1529, to settle the matter. They left their encounter still in basic disagreement—which had far-reaching results.

> The Marburg colloquy was a failure. Theologically, it had confirmed that Protestantism was a divided house. This fact, bitter though it was, gave lie to the exuberant Protestant assertion that men everywhere would agree to the meaning of Scripture if they were only of good will. Now it turned out that evidently such good will was absent among some Protestants or that Scripture did not quite lend itself to the easy interpretation that had been assumed. And which of these two options to favor was surely a painful decision.

The failure to attain agreement meant that both sides clung to their respective theological positions with unwavering determination. The consequences were both far-reaching and disastrous. Protestantism remained a divided house, a fact that influenced the Reformation era no less than subsequent centuries.[6]

THE FAILURE OF REUNION

Remember that Luther was still under the emperor's ban. Yet, because Charles V was usually out of Germany, the ban was ineffective. As a matter of fact, the emperor was away so long, thereby delaying any Lutheran-Catholic settlement, that the truce, which merely tolerated the Lutherans, became a way of life. Germany was in reality already split. When Charles V did meet with his princes in 1529, he was still not ready to enforce any uniform solution for the simple reason that he was still pressed by many enemies, particularly the ever-present Muslims, who were invading the eastern parts of his empire. There Charles needed all the allies he could get, and this included the Lutheran princes. So, in one of history's frequent ironies, Protestantism owes its survival to the Turks. Therefore, all that Charles asked for in 1529 at the Imperial Diet of Speyer was for help against the Muslims, and that everything should return religiously to the old all-Catholic way until a general church council should be called. (Charles was continuously calling for a church council, but it was not forthcoming for reasons we shall see; when it did come, Charles did not want it at that inopportune moment.) The minority Lutheran princes *protested* against such an arrangement, thus earning their name ever after: Protestants. The real problem, as we mentioned above, was that too much time had elapsed to allow for a reversal of religious positions.

Both sides were to be heard at another meeting held at Augsburg in 1530. The problem was that there were already several divisions. Therefore, there was no one Protestant side, since there was no one Protestant church. Philip Melanchthon drafted the famous creedal statement that has become the classic statement of Lutheranism, the Augsburg Confession (though his purpose was to stress agreement with Catholicism). The Catholics denounced the confession with another statement the emperor asked the Protestants to consider (he still needed their aid against the Muslims). But some of the Protestants could not even accept the Augsburg Confession, and some of the Catholics were definitely disinclined to be conciliatory. Thus, nothing came of the 1530 meeting.

There was one tangible result, however: Lutherans feared that the time had come for the emperor to use force against them. They quickly banded into the League of Schmalkald in a defensive alliance. The emperor, however, had need of this very alliance against the Muslims. Meetings continued to be held, even though the reality of a divided Germany was evident.

Meetings of reconciliation were still going on in 1546. They ended in failure. War was declared, and the emperor ultimately defeated the League in 1547. The emperor, still trying for a middle course, did not restore Catholicism. Political considerations still kept Lutheranism alive. Another meeting was held in Augsburg in 1555. Here, the famous agreement was reached that all subjects must adopt the religion of their princes, whatever that might have been, in the year 1552. Dissenters might leave the territory. Only Lutheranism and Catholicism were established (the others were not tolerated). Germany was now officially a divided country. Meanwhile, at one of the meetings in 1546, news arrived that on February 18 Luther had died.

SPREAD OF LUTHERANISM

By 1555 Lutheranism was a reality. While it had official status, it soon fell into subdivisions. The gentle Philip Melanchthon was a leader so agreeable to the restoration of some Catholic ways that he offended the more rigid adherents. Thus, Lutheranism split into a moderate party (known as the Philipists) and the strict party (known as the "true" Lutherans). Soon, each side was verbally attacking the other. This intra-church strife left the way open for the growth of the reformed (Calvinist) churches in Germany.

Meanwhile, Lutheranism moved into other territories through the election of Protestant bishops for those areas. Then, according to the Augsburg agreement, the bishop's territory would have to follow suit. Thus, we read of the inevitable jockeying for control that led to such extremes as the election of two Protestant youths under the age of twelve as bishops, in order to get that episcopal territory into their religious camp. Complications arose when some important areas became Protestant of the reformed type, which worried the Lutherans. Thus, in the Lutheran areas they would allow neither the Catholic Mass nor Calvinist worship. In their areas the Calvinists reciprocated. Much bitterness ensued and at times each side was not sure if it did not prefer the Catholics to the other. It would only be in the seventeenth century that both sides reduced the essentials to some kind of common ground and thus reduced the tensions.

ZWINGLI

Luther was only one of several independent reformers, for "the Reformation did not all spring from Luther; it sprang from those conditions of the church and those states of mind which made Luther possible."[7] Thus, Zwingli represents the reformer who, although a contemporary of Luther, disclaimed any dependency on him. Zwingli had been much more influenced by Erasmus. Zwingli was a Swiss pacifist and patriot who was more rigid than Luther, and felt that nothing was religiously valid unless specifically mentioned in the Bible. Therefore, in his Swiss city of Zurich, he removed relics, organs, pictures, and smashed religious objects of art (something Luther would not have done), thus paving the way for English Puritanism. Like Luther, he rejected papal authority, clerical celibacy, and the Mass as sacrifice. In 1525, he abolished the Mass and replaced it with a simple communion service (the idea was to oppose ecclesiastical superstition with primitive simplicity). However, Zwingli was unable to get all of Switzerland to accept this new religious outlook, and this led to the formation of political alliances.

In time, matters went badly for Zwingli. He could not agree with Luther about the eucharist, and was excluded from the Diet of Augsburg and the League of Schmalkald. By 1531, he had formed an economic blockade against the Catholic cantons and war was imminent. Zwingli, the pacifist, entered battle and was killed. Peace was arranged and each canton was permitted to determine the religious preference within its own boundaries. Thus, the new faith received a measure of toleration but remained a minority community of Christians.

CALVIN

Calvin, a Frenchman who had left the Catholic church at twenty-four, was one generation removed from Luther. Thus, he grew up in an environment quite concerned with the religious issues that Luther had raised. He had his starting point, therefore, not in a crisis of conscience like Luther, but in the religious upheaval created by him. It was Calvin's task to bring order and system to this upheaval, and he thus became the mentor of the Presbyterian and Reformed churches. Calvin had fled from his persecuting France to Geneva. Geneva, which had become a haven for such religious refugees, was already Protestant due to men like Zwingli, Bucer, and Farel.

Calvin had already written his famous *Institutes*. While most of the *Institutes* conformed to traditional Catholic theology, his work gave Protestantism its much needed systemization, and contained Calvin's teaching on predestination. This teaching was based on the absolute majesty of God and the logical conclusion that people are saved by grace alone. God, in the words of Calvin, "ordains some to eternal life, and others to eternal damnation." No one knew for sure who was saved or damned, but there were certain fallible signs of the elect: acceptance of the gospel, the reception of the Lord's Supper, and living a decent life. In due time, Calvin saw to it that Geneva was militantly governed in such a way that everyone fulfilled these three signs of election. This was another instance in which papal authority was replaced by state or civic authority. There was little that was democratic in Calvin's ideal community, and the state board or consistory, as it was called, controlled the town in godliness.

The consistory met weekly to consider matters such as blasphemy and dancing, and to check on the obligatory church attendance. Worldly songs met with punishment, theaters were closed, and gambling forbidden. In six years, the consistory excommunicated more than 1,300 persons. Heresy was most intolerable, and when Michael Servetus, the erratic Spanish Unitarian, fled to Geneva for Calvin's protection, Calvin had this denier of the Trinity burned at the stake "in the name of the Father and of the Son and of the Holy Ghost." "This act makes the blackest page in Protestant history"[8] and did not increase Calvin's popularity. Calvin lacked Luther's flair and warmth and good humor. He did not enjoy nature, and married out of principle, not for love. It was he who gave the uncompromising color to Protestantism, stressing that the road to heaven was straight and narrow. He gave Protestantism its hardworking, no-nonsense ethic, and inspired the early Calvinists to believe that they were the elect of God. Such Calvinists, so inspired, became fearless and hard-working; life was short and much remained to be done for God. Like the monks of old, however, they often fell into the same problem: they were successful and soon became prosperous, middle-class citizens.

Yet it was Calvinism, not Lutheranism, that would become widespread. Lutheranism remained a somewhat German phenomenon and, except for Scandinavia, never succeeded in developing large memberships in other countries. To this day, Wittenberg holds no place in history or in the popular mind comparable to Rome or Geneva. It was Calvinism and its reformed churches that became international and free of the patronage of the princes. People were drawn to the Calvinist discipline rather than to its doctrines. The Calvinist became the hard-working, fearless rearguard of Protestantism and created a spirit that worked well with political agitation and expansion. The lay people were taken with the novelty of collaborating in the running of their churches; they grew close together and formed strong (and at times fanatical) proselytizing groups. The clergy, thanks to the Academy of Geneva, founded by Calvin in 1559, were trained and capable, in contrast to the ignorance and apathy of the Catholic clergy. Calvinists grew bold, spread the faith, and met death with great courage. It was their blood, shed by Catholics and other Protestants alike, that kept the reformed faith moving.

SPREAD OF REFORMATION

The reformed pattern of church formation took the lead in Europe rather than the Lutheran (considered too "popish" by many). This meant perceiving the eucharist as a memorial, having an austere worship ritual, observing a strict moral discipline, striving to get every person to read the Bible and freeing religion from any subjection to the state (though the state should work on behalf of religion). Yet, for the new faith to succeed, it had to involve itself with politics, because in the medieval mind the ruler still determined the religion of his subjects. Thus, the drive was on to convert the ruler or depose him for a more favorable candidate, or get him to legally permit all Christian denominations to coexist within his country. In most places, force and attempts at deposition prevailed. The cause of religion was joined to the cause of politics—and vice versa.

SWEDEN AND THE NETHERLANDS

In Sweden, there was the usual tension between church and ruler. The Reformation there was a political movement to achieve imperial consolidation. In 1523, the king's newly appointed chancellor filled the king's mind with Lutheran ideas. By 1525, a decree was issued ordering all church income to go to the crown. In the following year, all clerical matters were placed under the king's jurisdiction. Catholic rebellion was crushed. In 1529, a Protestant was appointed to the important see of Uppsala, and all Catholic practices were purged by 1544. But, in 1575, a new king made up a new liturgical order and even went so far as to open secret negotiations with Rome. In 1592, the Catholic Polish king, Sigismund, succeeded to the Swedish throne but was opposed by his Protestant uncle. This uncle called a meeting, condemned Catholicism as well as the teachings of Zwingli and Calvin, and adopted a form of Lutheranism as the state religion. Thus, the initial political dissatisfaction led to Sweden's joining the Reformation. In 1604, all Catholics were deprived of offices and banished from the realm.

Reform ideas spread quickly in the Netherlands among the merchant people who were prosperous and educated. But the ruler was Philip II, the Catholic king of Spain. Political resistance to Philip became identified with religious dissent. In 1566, a mob broke stained-glass windows, desecrated churches, and sacked monasteries, thus pushing the country toward civil war. In 1568, William of Orange, former Catholic, former Lutheran, and present Calvinist, became the leader of the anti-Spanish forces, and thus automatically became the leader of the pro-Protestant party. The result was civil war which, with the help of England, resulted in a divided country. The Calvinist northern section (which one day would become Holland), and the Catholic southern section (which one day would become Belgium).

POLAND AND FRANCE

Poland was a more religiously pluralistic society, and the arm of the government was not used to establish any religion. Moreover, there was really no political issue at hand, for the nobles in general were content. They already possessed considerable power over the Catholic church and the king. They had no special grievance to which the reform movement could attach itself. Protestantism did come to Poland, and some of the lower nobility espoused it. The Catholic king even petitioned the pope for a married clergy and a vernacular Mass. He was refused. Nevertheless, the king and the people remained loyal to the church and so "the Reformation in Poland failed because Protestantism was unable to make its political case."[9]

In France, King Francis I had too many privileges and controls over the Catholic church to relinquish that church lightly. Therefore, if Protestantism was to make headway it had to align itself with and become a political issue. Protestantism had come to France by way of Luther's and Calvin's writings. Furthermore, France had its own native reformers who were actively seeking change at the precise time the king needed national unity to face his many problems. Besides, Francis I was suspicious of the new version of the faith: He had seen some of its political excesses elsewhere. So, in 1540, he acted by making heresy a matter for suppression by the state. In 1551, the next king, Henry II, persecuted the French Protestants, or Huguenots as they were called, and made glorious martyrs out of them.

Henry II died in 1559. Then Cardinal Guise ruled through Francis II, Henry's fifteen-year-old son. It must be noted that the Guise family was staunchly Catholic, while the rival Bourbon family was pro-Protestant. Huguenots therefore rallied to the Bourbon side and involved themselves in political maneuverings that they hoped would bring them to power. After Cardinal Guise, the real ruler and regent was the queen mother, Catherine de Medici. Faced with so many hostile voices on all sides, she became surprisingly tolerant. In 1562, she permitted the Huguenots to hold services outside the fortified cities. Even with this concession, however, Huguenot and Catholic hostilities continued and religious warfare raged for the next nine years. Catherine tried again to heal the breach by marrying her daughter to Henry of Navarre of the Bourbon house, a Huguenot and heir to the throne.

One of those attending this wedding was Admiral Coligny, a Calvinist, who had considerable influence over Catherine's royal son and who was, moreover, seeking an alliance with Protestant Elizabeth of England. Catherine apparently planned to have the admiral assassinated (he was wounded, not killed) and, fearing a religious backlash for this action, decided to murder all the Huguenots who had gathered for the wedding. Thousands of them were slaughtered on what has become known as the St. Bartholomew's Day

Massacre. Reflecting the typical lack of gospel values of that time, Pope Gregory XIII sang a hymn of thanksgiving in the Sistine Chapel when he heard of the slaughter of the Huguenots.

The martyrs of St. Bartholomew's Day, and other martyrs, went to their deaths singing hymns and thus became symbols of resistance for the living. Pro-Protestant and antiroyalist tracts began to appear and tensions grew. At this point, a new factor entered the political picture. The last Valois king, Henry III, who was assassinated in retaliation for having the Guise family leaders assassinated, died without children. On his deathbed, he pronounced Henry IV, Bourbon and Protestant leader, to be his successor. Henry IV turned out to be more French than Protestant. He knew he could never rule a basically Catholic country from Catholic Paris, so he promptly converted to Catholicism, supposedly commenting that "Paris is well worth a Mass." The Protestants were aghast. However, King Henry did not forget them. On April 13, 1598, he issued the famous Edict of Nantes, a milestone in religious toleration (for that time), and granted religious liberty to the Huguenots.

This edict permitted religious freedom only to those Huguenots living in certain towns and fortified cities. To this extent, they were separated from the mainstream of French life, and somewhat independent. Such an arrangement was all right for a while, but later a monarch was to become so absolute in France that he would not tolerate such independence. Cardinal Richelieu, the real ruler of France, saw that the Huguenots were really a state within a state and was determined to deprive them of their fortified cities. He attacked their strongholds and reduced their castles (most of the castle remnants seen in France today testify to the cardinal's work). However, the cardinal confirmed their religious freedom, and the Huguenots thus submitted and became quite loyal to the crown.

We might carry the story ahead a little and observe that the Edict of Nantes would be revoked under Louis XIV (1643-1715). The church in France had regained real strength and was becoming independent of Rome. In 1682, the great preacher Bousset drew up the famous Gallican Articles proclaiming the king superior to the pope and the French church possessor of its own inviolable liberties. Louis, of course, reveled in this, and felt that with the church in his pocket the whole land should once more be united under one faith perspective. In 1685, he revoked the Edict of Nantes with terrible vengeance on the French Huguenots. As a result, some two hundred thousand exiles fled to Switzerland, Berlin, Holland, and North America.

SCOTLAND

Scotland also went to the Reformation perspective by way of politics, the pro-French Catholics of the government versus pro-English anti-government Protestants. Entering this political climate was the arrogant and rude John Knox (d. 1572), who was totally convinced that God had called him to proclaim the Protestant message in Scotland. He became chaplain to a group of nobles who assassinated the Catholic leader, Cardinal Beaton, causing Knox to flee to England and then to Geneva. Meanwhile, the queen, Mary Stuart, had married the Catholic king of France in 1558, thereby agitating the Protestant political factions. The violently anti-Catholic Knox returned to Scotland to urge that country to disobey Mary. In 1559, in retaliation, Mary issued laws against the Protestants. In opposing her, Knox carried Scotland to the brink of civil war. Finally, the English government stepped in (Queen Elizabeth I could not afford a Catholic and pro-French Scotland) and sent assistance to Knox.

In 1560, Parliament adopted a confessional statement made up by Knox and passed several laws against Catholic practices. Mary, Queen of Scots, having been accused of murdering her Scottish Catholic second husband, was forced to abdicate in 1567. She fled to England, where she gave herself to the protection of her cousin Elizabeth. There, while in captivity, she foolishly plotted to seize the throne, and Elizabeth had her executed. (This unusual woman and her intrigues, her several husbands, her relationship to Queen Elizabeth I, have always made for high drama. Countless movies, plays, and television programs have depicted her life and death.) In due time, because of Knox's influence, a Calvinistic type of Protestantism known as Presbyterianism became the religion of Scotland. There is only one more country to consider, the England that produced Queen Elizabeth, and that is a story by itself.

CHAPTER 16

Dissent: Radical and Established

REFORMING THE REFORMERS

Before we take a look at the color and drama of England's road to Anglicanism, we must to look at a movement mentioned in Chapter IV of this book, the radical churches. In every reform movement, there are always those who want to reform the reformers. Such were the radical Protestant sects that arose at the time we are considering and that proved to be such an irritant to Luther. The radicals—sometimes called "believers"—were fundamentalist in outlook, often rooted in medieval mysticism, and particularly enamored of what they considered the simple "Golden Age" of the apostolic era:

> Earnestness, witness, covenant (signing their names), discipline, mutual aid, simple pattern of worship—these are the hallmarks of the believing people. The tragedy of Protestantism is that when such groups did emerge in history, Luther and his colleagues could see nothing in them but enthusiasts,

fanatics, and rebels. This prejudice has not been completely overcome to this day.[1]

The radicals had the habit of going one step further with Luther's principles. If a person is saved by faith alone, they asked, why baptize infants who cannot have faith? If Scripture was the sole guide and the Spirit was needed to interpret it, did this mean in the last analysis that the inner Spirit is more important than the written word? The radical desire to have freedom from all externals made them impatient with all forms of organized religion. Thus, because of some extremes, they threatened not only the foundations and principles of the church, but civil stability as well. Both the government and established religions (Catholic and Protestant), therefore, persecuted them.

The major radical group was known as the Anabaptists (or rebaptizers). They did not believe in infant baptism, and were dedicated to restoring the church to its supposed scriptural purity. They branched off in many directions since they lacked a single body of teaching. Some of their extensions were quite susceptible to lunatic leadership. Thomas Munzer had led the disastrous Peasants' Revolt in Germany (the one Luther was involved in). John Batenburg believed that the unconverted must be killed, that polygamy was moral (as it was for the patriarchs in the Hebrew Scriptures), and that he himself was Elijah the prophet. A group of Anabaptists got political control of the town of Munster. Attempting to turn it into the New Jerusalem, they declared that polygamy was moral, called for the extermination of the ungodly, and proclaimed the imminent second coming of the Lord (a favorite theme). They led raids on nearby towns where they ran naked through the streets. In 1535, they were invaded and slaughtered. The whole episode had the net effect of setting back any practice of religious toleration and gave the radical sects a bad name.

At the Diet of Speyer in 1529, both Lutherans and Catholics agreed to kill the Anabaptists. The Anabaptists had to flee. In so doing, they broke up into several groups. One group, known as the Hutterites, settled in Moravia (today, central Czechoslovakia) to live a communistic life. Their work, industry, and honesty won them a good reputation and wealth. In 1874, they had to flee Moravia for the wilds of South Dakota. Another group, called the Mennonites, withdrew into very simple living patterns. Their exclusivity went so far as to lead them to divorce unbelieving spouses and excommunicate the unworthy. They split into factions, and their descendants are to be found in the Pennsylvania Amish who to this day do not wear buttons since they are ornamental.[2] A third group gave rise to the Unitarians, who revived the old Arian heresy of denying the Trinity. Michael Servetus was one of them. So also was a man named Sozzino, who gave Unitarianism its basic form. There were other groups too numerous to mention, many of them extremists. They were usually proclaiming the second coming. England, for example, was so rife with these groups that generations of the English would always harbor suspicion for religious enthusiasm of any kind.

We might mention that one of these English groups survived as the Religious Society of Friends (or Quakers, a derogatory name used to describe their "quivering" with religious emotion). Its founder, George Fox (1624-1691), sought God at nineteen in the fields and within himself. Around 1648, he became an evangelist, preaching common radical messages such as the repudiation of oaths and military service, a suspicion of external forms, and the inspiration of the Spirit who could speak to the humblest peasant. The silent prayer meetings of the Mennonites and the writings of the medieval mystics influenced Fox into believing that no external guide, ministry, or authority was needed, because there was always the "inner light" to teach the devout. This "inner spirit" led him and his followers into eccentricities. Fox, for example, would not take off his hat (at the direction of the inner spirit).

What eventually saved the Friends from possible extinction was Fox's own maturity in being able to distinguish the practical from the absurd. Following his marriage to one of his early converts, Margaret Fell, he proceeded to organize the Society of Friends (a name he took from the words of Jesus, "You are my friends, if you do what I command" [John 15:14]). By 1670, the Quakers found stability while holding on to their quiet ways and teaching of the indwelling light.

The radicals or believers' churches have continued to the present day, but many Catholics have little knowledge or appreciation of them. The Catholic convert, Ronald Knox, in his book *Enthusiasm* describes their origin:

> You have a clique, an elite, of Christian men and...women, who are trying to live a less worldly life than their neighbors; to be more attentive to the guidance...of the Holy Spirit. More

and more, by a kind of fatality, you see them draw apart from their co-religionists, a hive ready to swarm. There is provocation on both sides; on the one part, cheap jokes at the expense of over-godliness, acts of stupid repression by unsympathetic authorities; on the other, contempt of the half-Christian, ominous references to old wine and new bottles, to the kernel and the husk. Then while you hold your breath and turn your eyes in fear, the break comes; condemnation or secession, what difference does it make? A fresh name has been added to the list of Christianities.[3]

Such a list in the United States includes the Hutterites, Baptists, Quakers, Church of the Brethren, Methodists, Disciples of Christ, the Plymouth Brethren, Mennonites, and others. Some of these sects would startle Catholics by arguing, as we pointed out in Chapter IV, that they are descendants of a long line of "heretics" who have always kept the torch of Christianity alive while the corruptions of the organized church grew. Yet they, too, like their more "established" Protestant counterparts, have fallen into divisions. In the United States alone, denominational handbooks list twenty-seven Baptist, four Brethren, three Disciple, eight Plymouth Brethren, nine Quaker, fifteen Mennonite, and twenty-two Methodist bodies. All these are sharply divided among themselves along ethnic and doctrinal lines. However, since the late 1960s, some of these groups have been able to heal their differences through ecumenical unions.

If these sects have erred, they have done so on the side of enthusiasm, as Knox points out, and that is preferable to erring on the side of indifference. We might also note a parallel with the turmoil of the 1970s in the Catholic church. Groups such as the Charismatics and the Pentecostals are precisely such enthusiasts looking for a more basic and fundamental Christianity. Whether they will find it, whether they will survive, whether they will break away is another matter. However, they have a kinship with Christian enthusiasts of the ages.

ENGLAND

England is the simplest example of the religious issue being determined by the ruler. Chronic anti-Roman antipathy toward papal taxations and foreign appointments existed there. England was the home of Wycliffe and his Lollard followers. Although England had both Tyndale's translation of the Bible and the ideas of Erasmus, these elements were not decisive factors. Henry VIII, like other rulers, took advantage of the church's influence. Henry would use highly placed clerics like Cardinal Wolsey to control church property and keep the clergy in line. Henry was not ready, therefore, to cast off the church. When Lutheranism reached his realm, he wrote a treatise against it in 1521, earning from the pope the title "Defender of the Faith."

Yet the break with Rome came from Henry himself. In 1527, he sought a divorce from his wife of seventeen years. With his wife, the aunt of the emperor, Charles V, Henry had only one living child, a daughter, Mary. During the War of the Roses (1455-1485), his Tudor family had fought too hard for the throne to lose it through lack of a male heir. Thus, Henry sought a divorce for five years on the grounds that for a few months his wife had been the wife of his deceased brother. This meant that the papal dispensation for Henry to marry her was invalid. He should, therefore, be free to marry Anne Boleyn. Similar annulments had been granted to other monarchs in the past, but Henry's request was complicated by the pope's hesitancy to incur the wrath of the emperor, Henry's nephew-in-law.

By 1529, Henry gave up trying to persuade the pope and turned to pressure tactics. He resurrected old laws to harass the clergy and force them into recognizing him as the national head of the church. In 1532, he made Parliament pass a law forbidding the annual payments to Rome. In 1533, abetted by Thomas Cromwell (whom he later beheaded), Henry restricted appeals to Rome. In 1534, all the pope's rights were transferred to the king, and the Act of Supremacy was passed, This law declared the king supreme head of the church in England. As such, there was a quick divorce trial presided over by Archbishop Cranmer (warmly recommended by Anne Boleyn), and Henry married Anne a week later.

To support his break with Rome, Henry needed theological underpinnings. Protestant tracts began to appear in England, but Henry insisted that the propaganda be only anti-papal, not anti-Catholic. Those who offended the faith were executed. It came to be a strange choice in England: death to the Protestants who dissented from Catholic doctrine, and death to the Catholics who dissented from the Act of Supremacy. John Fisher and Thomas More were beheaded because they would not submit to the Act of Supremacy.

The following year, 1536, Henry, always in need of money, dissolved the English monasteries, and by 1540, these centuries-old monasteries ceased to exist. Trumped-up charges were made against the moral lives of the monks, yet "whenever the time came to confiscate the glebes of a monastic house, its monks were charged with gross immorality and then were pensioned as if they had been altogether respectable."[4]

True, the English monasteries had lost much of their vitality, but their suppression caused major social problems, not only in the discontinuances of many hospitals, orphanages, and almshouses, but also in the plight of former monks, nuns, and teachers. In England, as elsewhere, the suppression of such monasteries was a long-range mistake, because the Protestant rulers of Europe

...in their need for money, missed a unique opportunity of converting these charitable resources to truly charitable ends like education, hospitals or the relief of the poor. It would not be so severe a charge if it could be shown that the endowments were diverted to truly national ends. Some of the endowments were so diverted. In other cases, the effect of the dissolutions was to put money and land into the hands of the lay lords.[5]

From the scholarly point of view, many fine libraries and works of art got scattered all throughout England, and many were forever lost.

ENGLAND UNDER EDWARD AND MARY

In 1547, Henry VIII died, leaving behind him a hybrid church. It was not a Protestant church, but it was a church without the pope, Catholicism without Rome. This was the case because, in 1539, Henry had issued the Act of Six Articles, decreeing punishment for anyone denying Catholic doctrines concerning the Mass, clerical celibacy, and more. The regent for Henry's sickly nine-year-old son, Edward VI, was the Duke of Somerset. He persuaded Parliament to repeal the heresy laws as well as the Six Articles. By 1548, the vernacular and the chalice were ordered to be used in the communion service. In 1549, the famous *Book of Common Prayer* (compiled mostly by Cranmer) was issued. It was a book of lovely prose, ambiguous theology, and half-Catholic ritual that offended the radicals, Puritans, and other rigorist dissenters. After six years of Edward's rule, Protestantism was in England, yet not very deeply; the masses of the people were unconcerned by it all.

Mary Tudor, the daughter of Henry and his first wife, and the soon-to-be wife of Catholic Philip II of Spain, came to the throne in 1553 at the age of thirty-seven. She, who had been rejected by her father and shunted aside all these years, was determined to restore Catholicism. She was in many ways noble, idealistic, and pious. Her failure was that, not knowing the temper of her people, she was hasty and impatient. Had she lived long enough and been more prudent, she might have been able to restore Catholicism on the precedent established at Augsburg, that a nation went along religiously with its ruler. For the few years that she did reign, she brought England into conformity with Rome.

> One marvels that the English, if they loved Rome should have permitted the Protestant Reformation, and if they loved the Protestant Reformation should have been willing to return to Rome. Evidently they did not greatly care what happened to monks, whether priests were married or celibate, and whether the Mass was in Latin or in English. Rather than incur civil disorder, they were ready to return to the old ways.[6]

To be fair, however, such reversals created much confusion in the minds of the people. Anyway, through Parliament, Mary did restore Catholicism to England. Henry's Act of Supremacy was repealed and the persecution of Edwardian reform-minded bishops and priests begun. In this, Mary

> ...showed herself thereby a true child of the age, for religious diversity was, for sixteenth-century man, a pill too bitter to swallow. Diversity seemed to entail the disruption of order which was feared as much as the possibility that the dissenter might infect others with his heretical venom. Since criminal law was severe, the capital punishment an all-too common matter, the Marian persecutions were in a way neither particularly unique nor ruthless. The number of victims was less than three hundred, but was substantial in a country that for more than two decades had experienced gradual alienation from Catholicism.[7]

Mary not only burned the rabble-rousers or unpopular figures, she also had people of repute and integrity, like Archbishop Cranmer, put to death. This was her mistake, because, in doing so, Mary created Protestant martyrs and forged an association between ecclesiastical tyranny and Rome in the minds of the English. The English began to associate loyalty to country with resistance to a half-foreign government. Books like John Foxe's *Book of Martyrs*, telling tales of the chilling tortures and the brave resistance of Mary's victims, became very popular. After reigning only five years, Mary died and left the throne to her half-sister, Elizabeth.

ELIZABETH

No one will ever know what Elizabeth's religious convictions were. She preferred a celibate clergy and the Real Presence in the eucharist. The Protestants, she claimed, drove her further than she wanted to go. Realistically, however, there was no doubt that this daughter of Anne Boleyn, considered illegitimate on that account by the Roman church, must be Protestant. In 1559, she was not the head but the "governor" of the English church. *The Book of Common Prayer* was restored with some changes, especially those presenting the Lord's Supper as a compromise between the teaching of Luther and Zwingli. The Catholics, understandably, were not pleased. But their lot was made most difficult when Pope Pius V excommunicated Elizabeth in 1570 and released her subjects from obedience to her—one of the greatest blunders in the whole Catholic reaction. In effect, this act made traitors of Catholics. Furthermore, the Jesuits were infiltrating into England, and the Catholic Mary (Stuart), Queen of Scots, was plotting to seize the throne. All this forced Elizabeth to persecute the Catholics, thereby arousing the hostility of France (which she placated) and Spain (whose famous Armada she defeated).

The Jesuits were not the only ones sneaking back into England. English Catholics trained on the Continent, and armed with pamphlets and the English Catholic Douay version of the Bible, returned to re-Catholicize their native land. More than two hundred priests were apprehended and killed. Although Catholics were not involved, the Guy Fawkes Plot of 1605 to blow up Parliament became associated with Catholic activity. Soon, the queen's ministers were seeing treacherous Catholics everywhere. A papal brief did arrive assuring the English that they could obey the queen. Certain Catholics became more radical politically, but they were few and did not pose any serious danger to the crown. "That this Catholic political threat was ever serious may be doubted,"[8] but it was never absent from the minds of those who thought it so.

The radical Puritans were more furious than the Catholics over Elizabeth's religious settlement. In their eyes, the church in England had too much "popery" in it. Vestments and bishops upset the Puritans. In reaction, the Anglicans (as we might call them now, though the term did not come in until 1836), began to argue that bishops were indeed authentic expressions. By 1590, the Anglicans were seriously concerned that their bishops be in the line and succession of bishops of the Middle Ages. In fact, scholarship of the time was revealing that the office of bishop was evident in the early church, much to the chagrin of the radicals. There was even a distinct move on the part of the Anglicans to appropriate the best of Catholic devotions and traditions. Meanwhile, in 1593, Elizabeth passed a law forcing dissenters to leave the country.

THE STUARTS AND CROMWELL

After Elizabeth, the Virgin Queen and the last of the Tudor line, came the Stuarts of Scotland, whose flirtations with Catholicism would assist in their undoing. Under the Stuarts, the cry arose to curb the powers of the king. The first Stuart king, James I, gave in to Puritan demands by authorizing the King James version of the Bible. On the other hand, he offended those same Puritans by asking for money, by favoring Anglican practices in Calvinist Scotland, by permitting games on Sunday, and by negotiating to marry his son to a Spanish Catholic princess. The chronic fear of a Catholic restoration was raised.

James was succeeded by his son, Charles I, in 1625. Charles, in the minds of many people, was even more associated with the Catholics because he had married a Catholic. Then there was his Archbishop of Canterbury, William Laud. Laud insisted on uniformity in the Anglican liturgy, vestments, and the surplice (which became something of a symbol). He backed up his wishes with punishment by using the Star Chamber, a kind of Anglican Inquisition, to induce uniformity. Laud only succeeded in aggravating the radicals: the Congregationalists, the Baptists, the Quakers, the Unitarians, the Puritans, and a hundred other radical sects so numerous at this period.

Since Scotland and England were now joined as the United Kingdom, Laud's efforts extended to Scotland as well. Riots broke out in Scotland and war was imminent. King Charles made a temporary treaty while he obtained money for an all-out offensive. Parliament, however, was not ready to allocate him money unless he redressed certain religious grievances. Charles disbanded Parliament, but after his defeat by the Scots he was forced once more to recall a now Puritan Parliament. This Parliament had Archbishop Laud unjustly executed. When the king attempted to arrest some of the Parliament leaders, civil war broke out between Parliament (the Puritans) and the king (the Round Heads).

The leader of Parliament's forces was Oliver Cromwell, a strict Puritan and firm believer in the concept of a Holy War. He gave the king's forces several stunning defeats and Charles was ultimately captured. When Charles would not agree to the changes wanted by the Puritans, Cromwell purged Parliament of all Presbyterians, pronounced Charles guilty of treason and had him beheaded in 1649. (Charles, who believed in the episcopal tradition, contributed to the ultimate Anglican victory over the Puritan ways. His execution turned him into a hero, martyred by fanatics.)

Cromwell next turned to Catholic Ireland, which had conspired with English and Scottish loyalists to restore the Stuarts to the throne. He treated Ireland brutally, deporting priests and slaughtering many. Then he proceeded to push the Catholics into the least productive areas of Ireland and parceled out the rest of the confiscated land to English Protestants. In time, this group created "the Ascendancy," that is, a Protestant aristocracy that governed the island and denied civil rights to the Catholic majority.

Having defeated the Scottish Presbyterians, Cromwell became virtual dictator of England. Catholics, Quakers, Anglicans, and Unitarians were not allowed to worship publicly but they were tolerated. Blasphemy was punished by torture but not death. *The Book of Common Prayer* was suppressed. Actually, these enactments were rather tolerant for those times. To pay for his wars, Cromwell had to resort to selling church land and levying taxes. He imposed military rule and initiated government censorship under John Milton, who is known to us as a poet and advocate of free speech.

Cromwell died in 1658, and Charles II, son of the martyred king, was summoned to rule. With him returned a conservative Anglican church, though Charles was always suspected of Catholic leanings. In 1685, King James II succeeded his brother, Charles. James *was* a

Catholic. Although he granted tolerance to all Christian denominations, he did favor Catholics, and his son was baptized a Catholic. This alarmed the English, and so James was deposed and the throne offered to William and Mary of Orange, because Mary was the oldest daughter of James II. This bloodless change of power is usually referred to as the "Glorious Revolution."[9] William and Mary were Calvinists. Under them, in 1689, laws were passed whereby Presbyterians and others had to subscribe to certain religious articles, Catholics and Unitarians were forbidden to practice their religion, and by law only Protestants could ever sit on the English throne. Many Puritans fled. Some went to Holland, while others sailed to the New World to join the descendents of those Puritans who had arrived on the Mayflower in 1620.

THE THIRTY YEARS WAR

We have seen that while individuals did not have religious liberty, some territories did. Most northern European countries had adopted the Reformation perspective, while southern countries stayed Catholic. The Thirty Years War broke out in 1618; as always, such wars were intimately bound up with politics, economics, and religion. It began in Bohemia, a part of the German empire, which had granted toleration to Lutherans but not to Calvinists, who thus fought the arrangement. The Bohemians, therefore, disregarded the Peace of Augsburg, brought in another king to replace the Catholic emperor, Ferdinand II, and war involving many nations resulted. The Bohemians were crushed. The Danes intervened and were repulsed. The Swedes came into the war under Gustavus Adolphus. He felt he must protect all Protestants against the Catholics, and thus, as a Lutheran, he assisted his religious enemies, the German Calvinsts. Yet, if Ferdinand's war were successful, he would unite Germany under the Catholic faith. Ironically, neither the pope nor France would tolerate a united Germany. For the pope, it was the perennial fear, ever since the German Ottos, of German interference. For France, it was to their political advantage to keep Germany religiously divided. Thus, Catholic France, under Cardinal Richelieu, with the pope's approval, supported the Lutheran Swedes to prevent a united Catholic Germany. This alliance demonstrated once more the subordination of religion to politics.

The war ended in 1648 with the Treaty of Westphalia, which established the religious lines of modern Europe. Both Catholics and Protestants received a measure of toleration in each other's territories, and Calvinists were given an equal footing in the empire with Catholics and Lutherans. The pope, relieved on the one hand at the failure of a united (and now wrecked) Germany, was on the other hand provoked by the anti-Catholic clauses in the treaty and the concessions to the Protestants. His feeble protests gave ample evidence that, from this point on, the papacy was no longer even to be considered in the political settlements of Europe. No one paid any attention to him—especially the growing absolutist monarchies of Spain and France, the former now broken and poor and the latter emerging from the war as the most powerful nation of the time.

The era of the Thirty Years War and of the peace of Westphalia is highly important in the history of modern Europe. The Thirty Years War itself was the worst but the last of the so-called religious wars. While it began as a fight between Protestants and Catholics, its chief stakes were ever economic and political, and it closed a major conflict between Hapsburg and Bourbon dynasties, both nominally Catholic but chiefly concerned with statecraft. That a Protestant prince of Brandenburg should give assistance to the Catholic emperor and that a cardinal of the Roman Church should incite Catholic France to aid German Protestants were clear signs of a noteworthy transfer of interest, in the first half of the seventeenth century, from religious fanaticism to secular ambition. The Thirty Years War paved a rocky road toward the eventual dawn of religious liberty.

The Thirty Years War likewise prepared the way for the emergence of the modern state-system of Europe, with its formulated principles of international law and its definite usages of international diplomacy. Modern diplomatic usages had originated among the Italian city states early in the fifteenth century and had been adopted early in the sixteenth century by the monarchs....Yet the modern state-system could not emerge as long as one European state—the Holy Roman Empire or the dynastic empire of the Hapsburgs—claimed to be, and actually was, superior in power and prestige to all other states. What the Thirty Years War did in this respect was to reduce both the Holy Roman Empire and the Hapsburg empires to a position certainly no higher than that of the national monarchies of France, Sweden, England, Spain, or that of the Dutch Republic. Indeed, from the negotiations and treaties of Westphalia truly emerged the modern state-system of Europe, based on the novel principle of the essential equality of independent sovereign states, though admitting of the fact that there were great powers as well as lesser powers....[10]

OBSERVATIONS

From 1517 to 1648, the religious face of Europe (and subsequently America) was changed. Religious pluralism was now a reality, and so were the hostility and polemics that would last for the next three hundred years. Even at that time, some Christians—not all, for some did believe in a visible church, and others saw in sectarianism a sign of vitality—began to feel the disgrace of disunity of those who, after all the anger and violence was said and done, had much in common. A new phase would begin among Protestants at Edinburgh, Scotland in 1910. The Catholic church would officially join the ecumenical movement with the Decree on Ecumenism promulgated by the Second Vatican Council in 1964:

> From her very beginnings there arose in this one and holy Church of God certain rifts...but in subsequent centuries more widespread disagreements appeared and quite large communities became separated from the full communion of the Catholic church—developments for which, at times, men of both sides were to blame.... Catholics must joyfully acknowledge and esteem the truly Christian endowments from our common heritage which are to be found among our separated brethren.... Nor should we forget that whatever is wrought by the grace of the Holy Spirit in the hearts of our separated brethren can contribute to our own edification (3, 4).

Protestantism has brought many things to the edification of the world. It gave impetus to religious instruction and the centrality of the Bible. Many sincere Protestants would work their days around the Bible, reading it frequently, knowing large sections by heart. It was Protestantism that took sanctity out of the exclusive hands of the religious, the monk, and the friar, and said that it was the common vocation for the common person. It was Protestantism that contributed a greater dimension of unity and spirituality to family life. Luther himself had no intention of marrying, but when a whole nunnery closed down and all nuns except one, were placed in homes he married her, not out of romance "but out of a sense of duty,"[11] and with her he established the forerunner of the Protestant parsonage. Protestantism gave participation to its laity and called into question too much reliance on external forms.

In many ways, the whole Protestant Reformation came down to the rejection of mechanical Christianity. Neither Catholic nor Protestant has ever really appreciated that, at the beginning at least, the desire of the Reformers was to reform, not break away from the church. The real theological differences between Catholics and Protestants did not come until relatively late, and even at that the theological differences need not have brought such great separation. As we have noted, one of the crucial points of Luther was that of justification by faith. While this was not initially a Catholic dogma, there was still room for free discussion. It was the heat of controversy that generated the emotional words that urged not only the more daring declarations, but also the radical and dangerous ones.[12]

Rather than a theological matter, the Reformation was a religious one, seeking to renew and even redirect the church. The Reformation was concerned about an authentic spirituality for the church, a spirituality that many corruptions, superstitions, and externals had obscured. There was a desire for new forms of piety. There was genuine hope that what the Protestants initially said could be taken into the church, just as the church tolerated many dissenters (such as Erasmus) and forms (such as the religious orders). That is why most of the people who thronged to Luther and supported his cause did not consider themselves in opposition to the church as such. They might be against the clergy and against clerical privileges, but not really against the Catholic church. That anti-Catholic stance and the need for separation came much later. At that moment the Reformation was a prodding for change. In this matter, according to the Lutheran historian, Hans Hillerbrand, the leadership of the church was to blame:

> If anywhere, the fault of the Catholic church in the schism we call the Reformation lies here—not in its neglect of reform or in its toleration of abuse, but in its failure to afford the notions of Luther a full hearing....Such was the setting that caused the reformers to be dismayed and then turn adamant. The case can

be made that they emphasized their insight only after they had become persuaded that they had not been heard....[13]

It was that they rejected infallibility and papal authority. The reformers felt that they would rather be heretics than be untrue to their understanding of the gospel. Once more, the real issue at stake came to be that of authority. The Catholic tradition had been one of both the church and the individual; both the papacy and conscience. However, the official response given to the Reformers made it seem that it was a matter of either the church or the individual; either the pope or conscience. Luther himself insisted in his later writings that he was not contesting the authority of the pope as such, but rather the abuse of that authority. In summary:

...The Reformation was above all a fundamental crisis of confidence in the authority of the church's teaching office. It was for this reason that a different emphasis was placed, in Protestant teaching, on the meaning and function of the apostolic office. What was stressed above all was that the gospel, as bearing witness to the saving event of Christ, always transcended the institutions of the church and that all ecclesiastical institutions were there to serve the gospel.[14]

PLUSES AND MINUSES

It is important to note how many of the items considered so important by the reformers have been accepted by the Second Vatican Council (1962-1965). The church now permits the sharing of the chalice. Parish councils and the pope's synod of bishops reflect congregational overseeing. The use of the vernacular, which always distinguished Protestants from Catholics, is now present in Catholic worship. Scriptural studies and scripture reading are undertaken by Catholics as well as Protestants. Joint Bibles have been published. Clerical celibacy is once more a point of debate within the Catholic church. The simplification of rites reflects the initial drive of the reformers for simplicity in worship. In many ways, then, the demands of the reformers have found their way, four hundred years later, into the Catholic church.

However, Protestantism has had its share of troubles and has bequeathed certain problems to its followers. Many of the practices rejected by the reformers are being reappraised by their spiritual descendants today. For example, in reaction to the magical approach that Catholics often seemed to place in the sacraments, the reformers stressed that the sacraments had no objective reality apart from faith. Yet, they continued for four hundred years (except for the Baptists) to baptize infants who could not make an act of faith. For this reason, some Protestant theologians are beginning to admit some objective reality to the sacraments as traditionally understood by Catholics.

Furthermore, Luther taught the concepts of the priesthood of all believers and the freedom of each individual conscience: "Therefore I declare that neither pope nor bishop nor any other person has the right to impose a syllable of law upon a Christian man without his own consent." Yet Luther was too much a child of his times. He could not be democratic in his churches. He would not give the lay congregation any authority. When confronted with a plan for a congregational type of church rule, Luther rejected it. Nor would he ever accept the congregation choosing its own pastor. Accordingly, in 1525, he forbade the celebration of the Mass; in 1527, he promoted uniformity by organizing state ecclesiastical visitations; in 1529, he denied freedom of conscience; and in 1531, he agreed that Protestant extremists like the Anabaptists should be put to death.

Perhaps the reformers' biggest disappointment was in reference to their famous "Scripture alone" as the basis for Christian knowledge and belief. Luther and the other reformers

...miscalculated in their assumed ease of united affirmation on the basis of New Testament authority. Protestantism was never to overcome its difficulties in this respect; it appealed to the Scriptures, but men of different birth and land and tradition and experience read them differently.... If every man was to be his own judge, if every man was to be of the universal priesthood, standing before the Scriptures as his own pope—what would prevent the growth of as many churches as there are men or factions or parties? The experience of Europe in the half-century following 1517 certainly seemed to thunder corroboration.[15]

Or again, as Hans Hillerbrand puts it:

The hopeless and apparently insoluable division [of Protestantism] called into question the basic Protestant affirmation that Scripture was clear and self-evident, and that men of good will could readily agree on its meaning. Luther, who had first voiced such sentiment, was to learn its weakness in his controversy with Zwingli over the interpretation of Communion. His increasingly rigid view of Scriptural interpretation may well have been influenced by his dismay over the inability of men, even men of goodwill, to agree on the interpretation of Sacred Writ.[16]

Furthermore, Luther's alliance with the German princes did not render the best service to Lutheranism. The princes, of course, were ready to listen to Luther in his attacks on Rome, because religion could be brought under national control and church wealth appropriated. With such princes leading, with the emperor preoccupied elsewhere, and with the absence of any vital Catholic leadership, the Reformation easily moved ahead in Germany. It persisted because it had no particular hardships to endure. In fact, so political did the religious issue become, that the Catholic emperor could induce Lutheran princes to wage war on their co-religionists, much as later on Cardinal Richelieu would have Catholic France side with Protestant Sweden against the Catholic emperor.

As the old order fell before Lutheranism, there arose the question of who should fill the authority vacuum; the princes were the most likely candidates. In fact, many of them acted as did the Catholic bishops of old. Frederick appointed parish visitors. This system of state visitation tended to become institutionalized. The appointment and removal of ministers thus became dependent on the state. Even the ministers' salaries were paid out of the income of secularized church property. "Under such circumstances Luther's dictum that the minister should be the mentor of the magistrate sometimes was difficult to realize."[17] In fact, "by the time of Luther's death the secular leaders were well poised to assume spiritual functions and make the church in many respects a lackey in their temporal pursuits."[18] Right up to modern times, the closeness of Lutheranism with the state had unhappy results.

The oldest, largest, and in a geographical sense most catholic Protestant body, Lutheranism, has suffered most in times of catastrophe and suppression. Sorely tried in its German stronghold by the First World War and post-war disillusion, it was handicapped by a long tradition of accepted paternalism on the part of the state. Never working out a detailed approach to church-state religions, it held largely to a doctrine of acquiescence, always uncertain when the moment would come when one must forget penultimate for the superior: "We ought to obey God rather than men." Much of Lutheranism in Germany was therefore quiescent in the rise of Hitler. The extreme element rallied around the Nazi puppet, Reichsbischof Mueller. Some theologians tragically sold themselves to the German Christian Movement.[19]

Finally, we must acknowledge that the religious crisis of the sixteenth century was, in reality, basically an educated, upper-class phenomenon. They were the ones with the crises; they were the ones with influence; they were the ones who stood to gain the most politically and economically; they were the ones sufficiently secure and educated to call for change. The rest of society in the sixteenth century were largely spectators, or followers, or victims. As we have seen, whenever the prince or king moved decisively (for example, as in England), the rest of the society followed without too much protest. The Reformation was not, by and large, a popular movement any more than the Renaissance was a popular movement. Nor would the Counter-reformation be a popular movement. Public opinion alone never determined the issue in any state in those days. The will (or whim) of the ruler or, more likely of the ruling class, was the most important single factor as to how the Reformation fared, the direction it took, and whether it survived or not.

THE ECUMENICAL SPIRIT

The great political significance of the Reformation was that no longer would the Catholic church, or any church, have control over the state as it had in the Middle Ages. It was more the other way around in the seventeenth century. In some powerful monarchies (for example, England), religion was reduced to a department of the state. As we shall see in the next chapter, some people were still of the medieval mindset, whereby they thought that political and religious uniformity were intertwined. In their counter-reformation, the Catholic leadership cleaned house and defined "church" so as to exclude Protestants. In a similar manner, the Protestants held firm to positions that would exclude Catholics.[20]

No informed Catholic or Protestant thinks that ecumenism means to convert the other to its side. Today, Christians of many denominations are working for unity, wherever that may lead. Both Protestants and Catholics have a common Christian tradition. Now that much of the polemical fighting has calmed down, each can look at what the other is really saying with less passion and more charity. A full discussion of some of the fruitful harmonization that has taken place between Catholics and Protestants is beyond the scope and purpose of this book. Yet we might take a few pivotal examples to demonstrate how far the dialogue has come.

For instance the Roman Catholic explanation of the eucharist was summed up in the scholastic term of "transubstantiation," a term many Protestants felt was too much philosophical, too much of unbiblical rationalization.[21] When the Catholics explained the intent of this doctrine, namely, that God really does something and that the risen Christ really is present in the Lord's Supper, then Protestants saw that this was *their* intent as well and most of them could give agreement. When a joint committee of Roman Catholic and Lutheran theologians met in 1966-1967, the Lutheran conclusion was as follows: "It becomes clear...that the dogma of transubstantiation intends to affirm the fact of Christ's presence and of the change which takes place...; when the dogma is understood in this way, Lutherans find that they also must acknowledge that it is a legitimate way of attempting to express the mystery...." Most Catholics are surprised to learn that most Protestants believe in the Real Presence and that many of them can accept the eucharist as Catholics understand it. This is why, on July 7, 1972, guidelines were issued by the Secretariat for Christian Unity permitting Protestants, under certain strict conditions, to receive the eucharist in a Catholic church.

Protestants, too, have come to recognize that there is no really pure distinction between the Bible and tradition, that "Scripture alone" does not operate in a vacuum, but in the context of *their* tradition. As Lutheran Michael Rogness expresses it:

The fact of the matter is that although Protestants claim "Scripture alone" as the source of their doctrine, the historical tradition of each Protestant church has been decisive in determining its doctrinal outlook. For about 400 years Lutherans have accepted the Book of Concord documents as their doctrinal statements, that is, writings from their north German situation which they believe accurately define biblical doctrine. The "39 Articles" of the Anglicans and the various catechisms of reformed churches are all doctrinal statements growing out of particular historical traditions and circumstances. Every Protestant church must acknowledge that it is shaped doctrinally by its tradition, and it ought not to fall into the temptation of imagining that its tradition is the only one striving to be loyal to the Bible.

The irony is that a Protestant who is immovably loyal to his church's tradition and refuses to budge one iota from his church's inherited doctrine has surrendered the basic Protestant principle of sola scriptura. He has fallen victim to precisely that sin of which he accused the Roman Catholics, namely becoming trapped in his own tradition, failing to see the biblical truth might demand a new kind of proclamation than the thought forms of past centuries. To be truly Protestant is to be not only true to one's heritage, but to allow our doctrinal concerns to be molded by the Bible's message for today's world.[22]

Even on the basic issue of justification, one of Protestantism's leading theologians, Karl Barth, in commenting on Hans Küng's explanation said, "All I can say is this: If what you have presented in Part Two of this book is actually the teaching of the Roman Catholic church, then I must certainly admit that my view of justification agrees with the Roman Catholic view."[23] It has been said that if the Council of Trent's decree on justification (beautifully and economically set forth) had been decreed at the Lateran Council V in 1512, the Reformation would not have occurred.

In the final years of the twentieth century, disunity has no valid place. We are no longer in an age where the question is "What is the most valid form of Christianity?" We are in a time where the question seems to be "in the light of fantastic technological advance, is Christianity valid at all?" In the light of a threatened planet, the possibility of nuclear war, genetic control, organ transplants, and interplanetary exploration, partisan differences in Christianity are obscene. The minds of both sides which accept "Jesus Christ, the same yesterday, today and forever" (Hebrews 13:8) are called to join forces to make him credible to the modern world.

CHAPTER 17

Catholic Reform

SOURCES OF REFORM

Prior to and during the Protestant Reformation, the Catholic church was beginning to reform itself. Later, this reform took on some of the characteristics of an offensive against Protestantism, which still had its own independent wellsprings. Catholics, such as Erasmus, together with their fellow Catholics like Luther, Calvin, Zwingli, and others, had always complained about abuses in the church. There was no local or national meeting that did not bring the matter up. Hostility toward church leadership was indeed a characteristic of the fifteenth and sixteenth centuries. Dante had put cardinals in hell, and Erasmus depicted St. Peter driving some popes from the gates of heaven. Art and literature ridiculed grasping prelates and immoral popes. We have seen that Catholic monarchs tried to use the church for their own national ambitions. There was, then, *within* the church much pressure for reform, and the church was able to tap its wellspring of spiritual vigor that lay deep within.

There was, for example, the revival of Thomism, a revival that equipped the church for its intellectual renewal. Cardinal Cajetan, who debated Luther early in his career, was a noted commentator on St. Thomas. There were many devotional books in the Catholic tradition, the most influential being *Imitation of Christ* from the Netherlands. There were the writings of the mystics: Peter Canisius, who based his spirituality on Tauler, a fourteenth-century mystic, Peter Alcantara, and the famous duo, Teresa of Avila and John of the Cross, who are only two towering figures among a whole mass movement of Spanish spirituality. There were the writings of the Franciscan spiritualists, the example of the Carthusians, and a still-living spirit of Francis of Assisi. Each country had its outspoken Catholic reformers whose names are unknown to the average Catholic of today. There was the great Cardinal Ximenes in Spain who fostered a kind of religious purity based on blood and who, therefore, in his vision of things, permitted the genocidal practices against the Moors and Jews. In France, there was Jean Standonck who organized a college in 1499 to train priests. Colet tried to do the same thing in England, and there were also Reginald Pole (Cardinal), Bishop John Fisher, and the better known Thomas More. Italy had the pious Bishop Gian Matteo Giberti (its own Savonarola), who assiduously visited his parishes and reformed their liturgies; there was Cardinal Sadoleto who gave up his tenure at Rome. In Poland, there were outstanding prelates, such as John Laski and Peter Tomicki.

RELIGIOUS ORDERS

In spite of general decline, several religious orders were being renewed and others were being founded. The Franciscans branched off into an Observant Order which favored a stricter way of life. The Carthusian Order influenced many of the laity to add their considerable support for Catholic renewal. There was the new Theatine Order that attracted holy men and formed many who would become worthy bishops. There were the famous Oratories, the best known being that of the gentle Philip Neri. There were the Barnabites, founded by laymen in 1533, who were known for their open air meetings in the cities of northern Italy. A group known as the Somaschi were noted for their examples of practical charity. The Capuchines, founded by Maria Longo to restore the spirit of St. Francis, did much to hold the masses to the church.[1] In 1535, Angela

Merici founded the Ursulines, one of the earliest teaching orders of women. Finally, there was the outstanding Society of Jesus—the Jesuits.

The Jesuits were founded by Ignatius Loyola, a contemporary of Luther. Ignatius also had an inner struggle, but he found his answer within the church in inner meditation. He wrote his renowned *Spiritual Exercises*, and his new order was approved by Pope Paul III in 1540. The Jesuits made their first great impact in Italy, where they founded their first colleges at Bologna, Messina, Palermo, and Rome. In Ignatius's native Spain, the Jesuits encountered the jealousy of the Dominicans; in France, they were not at first very successful; they did not penetrate England until the middle of Queen Elizabeth's reign. But the Jesuits grew in number (there were one thousand members by the time Ignatius died, and 13,000 five years later). Through their excellent schools for the sons of the nobility and kings, they became very influential and, in time, were associated with the politics of the royal courts. As time went on, their influence became increasingly resented, fearful legends grew up around them, and, in the eighteenth century, the whole order was suppressed.

THE DELAY OF A COUNCIL

All of these outstanding people and movements urged not only reform, but also a general council that might achieve reform effectively and universally. But, for many reasons, no council was called until it could no longer be denied. First, when Luther's critique became known, communication with Rome was poor, and the popes detected neither the enormity of what was happening nor, subsequently, the need for a council. Second, Luther's new ideas were still being assessed, and there was not a consensus that they were radically opposed to Catholic doctrine. Third, the popes, as was often the case, were too engaged in Italian politicking to be bothered with a council. Fourth, there were tremendous outside distractions. France did not want a council, lest it suddenly clear up the Protestant Reformation, thereby bringing about the unification of the German empire. Fifth, Henry VIII was pressing for his divorce, while his nephew-in-law, Emperor Charles V, harried the pope by sacking Rome in 1527. In addition, Clement VII did not want a council, lest he be deposed, because he had been born out of wedlock and his election had been tainted with simony. Finally, there was the fear of conciliarism: another council might again raise the question of the superiority of a general council over the pope.

It was the pope following Clement VII who would eventually call a council. This was Paul III, who made his teenage grandson a cardinal and gave his disreputable son the dukedom of Parma and Piacenza. Yet, Paul III also raised to the cardinalate such men of quality as Fisher, Contarini, Caraffa, Sadoleto, Pole, and Morone. Moreover, it was this pope, much to the dismay of Charles V, who called for a council in 1537. The emperor, who had probably wanted a council, by then felt it would be inopportune, because he feared that the council might affirm Catholic teaching and prevent a sorely needed unity in Germany with the Protestants (remember Charles still needed the Protestant princes to fight the Muslims).

In 1536, a commission appointed by Pope Paul III[2] to study church reform came up with the startling document, *The Council of Cardinals on Reforming the Church.* It became famous as the most direct and blunt condemnation of abuses ever written by a papal commission. So critical of the church leadership was the document, that even Luther had it published in German, adding scurrilous margin notes. But the document's very frankness regarding church abuses prevented its public use, and so many of its striking reforms were not put into effect. Yet this document did mark a change in outlook.

In May 1542, the bull of convocation was issued summoning the council. Since Germany and France were currently at war, both sides forbade their bishops from attending. Finally, on December 3, 1545, the first session was held. Only thirty-one bishops attended[3] and none of them was from Protestant territories; the majority were Italian. All the sessions (there were three main sessions stretching over eighteen years due to enforced recesses) had a majority of Italian bishops. Of the 270 bishops attending at one time or another during those eighteen years, 187 were Italian, 31 Spanish, 26 French, and two German. Of the 225 bishops who signed the final Acts of Trent, 189 were Italian.

There were, however, high caliber theologians, religious, and bishops at the Council of Trent. During the first eight meetings of the first session, the council set the tone for doctrinal conservatism. This was precisely the retrenchment of Catholicism that the emperor feared. This doctrinal conservatism prevented dialogue with his German Protestants. A few Protestants appeared during the second series of meetings, and the emperor ordered the council to allow them to speak. However, most bishops were not interested in anything they had to say.

The council approved the medieval term "transubstantiation," and reaffirmed the sacraments of extreme unction and penance (now called the sacrament of the sick and reconciliation, respectively). In 1552, the council was recessed for political reasons—war (the council fathers feared capture by the French). This recess lasted ten years. The third and final session was recalled in 1562. By this time, the Spanish contingent was working to form a national hierarchy and was talking about the divine rights of bishops (and, therefore, their independence from the pope). At this session, the issue of offering the chalice to the laity was rejected; the Mass was reaffirmed to have a sacrificial character, and was to be celebrated only in Latin. The use of the vernacular and the question of clerical celibacy brought about heated debate (not to mention political considerations), but the very divisions of the bishops failed to provide a consensus that would change these issues. In reaction to the reformers' insistence on "Scripture alone," the council also placed tradition alongside of Scripture as a source of revelation.

The Council of Trent did an excellent job. Its decrees were models of clarity and directness; they were not as hostile as they sounded to the Protestants of the time.[4] "The decrees of Trent were framed with care; their language was designed to allow more liberty of opinion than their Protestant critics believed. The care with which they were framed has only been fully evident during the twentieth century."[5] Trent produced a feeling of general well-being and practical achievements, such as the catechism (which was originally intended for use as a handbook by parish priests), the reform of the missal and breviary and, above all, the establishment of seminaries. Modern Catholics have generally been more impatient with Trent than modern Protestants because they have failed to see the difficult political circumstances surrounding this council. More seriously, a Catholic appreciation of Trent has suffered for two basic reasons: Its interpreters did not teach the nuances and refinements built into its decrees, and most of its ideas were not allowed to mature in subsequent centuries.

Of course, the council was not perfect. Its defensive attitude toward Protestantism led to some shortsightedness (later to be corrected by Vatican II). For example, the Council of Trent, in spite of the biblical interest of that time, failed to encourage biblical studies. Nor did the council encourage the laity to read the Scriptures, or provide a scripturally oriented catechism. In fact, the Baltimore Catechism that many older Catholics still remember reflects almost entirely Trent's preoccupation with precise doctrinal statements, which were framed as a counteraction to the reformers' teachings.

The Council of Trent also failed to encourage teachers to go into the natural philosophies and sciences. This set a conservative tone for many centuries. Trent's close-mindedness to science was a reaction to the reformers who, it was felt, went awry in unguided speculation. Finally, the bishops at Trent, although reflecting much previous tradition, could be criticized for their defining matters that were not universally held throughout the Christian world. Perhaps it was a mistake in some cases to close matters that were still speculative and under discussion at the universities. The conservative cast given by Trent provided the basis for the future suppression of ideas in the Catholic church. The barbs of Voltaire (d. 1778), and the reopening of old questions at Vatican II in our own century, serve as potent critiques to the Tridentine mindset. Yet, even with these critiques, A.G. Dickens points out:

These strictures are easy to make in the context of our own society, which so long ago decided to pay the price for freedom of thought; they will give little offense at a time when Catholics themselves are increasingly critical of Tridentine habits of thought. Yet in its own period-context, Trent corresponded with the demands of many men, who may well have been right in believing that a far larger measure of doctrinal definition had become a critical necessity for Catholic survival. And even those who judge Trent to have defined too sweepingly, and to have reacted too automatically against anything remotely savoring of Protestantism, may still think that the sheer weight of its intellectual achievement entitles it to a place of honor in Christian history. The canons and decrees remain one of the greatest monuments of committee-thinking in the whole history of religion. Given their general purpose and outlook, their technical perfection and consistency are worthy of the highest admiration. In form and language they are models of clarity and care; they are serviceable documents well abreast of the modern idiom of their day; whatever their debts to scholastic theology, their language is uncluttered by the scholastic habits which had so little relevance to the needs of simple priests and literate laymen. To study them can be a fruitful, almost a moving experience, and this even for readers who normally inhabit very different worlds of thought.[6]

REFORMING POPES

Pope Paul III, who eventually called the first session of the council, was succeeded by a series of reforming popes who did as much as anyone to interpret Trent strictly and lend their sometimes fanatical housecleaning crusade to the council itself. Paul was succeeded by Julius III, who reconvened the council in 1551 and continued Paul's reforms. He was succeeded by Paul IV who, at 79, saw the council as hazardous. Thus, he scattered his own reforms like wildfire. He was the one who, as Cardinal Caraffa, had advocated reform through fighting the Protestants, in contrast to Cardinal Contarini, who favored conciliation and concession. Contarini met with the Protestants in 1541 and obtained considerable agreement with them, despite skepticism from the absent Luther, the annoyance of his pope, Paul III, and the hearty disapproval of Cardinal Caraffa. This meeting came to naught because of French political fears (of a united Germany). Contarini died under suspicion of collaboration with the Protestants, and Caraffa's hard-line approach became the alternative. This was the cardinal who persuaded Paul III to establish a Roman Inquisition. When Caraffa became Pope Paul IV, he showed no mercy. He bore down on permissions, dispensations, and the nominations of bishops. On one day, he rejected 58 nominations—all that were proposed. He was ready to use torture and punishment to weed out what was considered dangerous. In Rome itself, he filled criminals with terror, sent wandering monks to the galleys or to prison, and, in 1559, created the Index of Forbidden Books, an indiscriminating list mercifully later modified by Trent.

Paul IV was succeeded by Pius V, a man of no outstanding qualities. He had three illegitimate children and showed concern for this family. (Fortunately, one of his nephews, Charles Borromeo, the bishop of Milan, who had been made a cardinal at twenty-two, was destined to become a shining light of reform.) This was the pope who summoned the final session of Trent in 1562 in the hope of stopping the spread of Calvinism in France. (Calvinism had been ignored in the first two sessions.) Pius V (d. 1572), who supported the Roman Inquisition, stamped out any vestiges of Protestantism in Italy, stopped financial abuses in the Curia, supported the fierce persecutions of the Netherlands by the Spanish Duke of Alba, and aided Charles IX of France by ordering the death of the Huguenots, on the grounds that they were heretics. His biggest blunder, as we have seen, was to excommunicate Queen Elizabeth in 1570 and urge her subjects to disobey her. His successor was Pope Gregory XIII (d. 1585), who rejoiced when Henry of Navarre, the Protestant king of France, became a Catholic so that he could have an ally against the Spanish. The next pope, Sixtus V (d. 1590), set up the papal Congregations (the Curia that we know today) to take care of church matters. He also revamped the city of Rome in a huge urban renewal. All of these popes of the counter-reformation had one thing in common: a determination to renew the church no matter what the cost.

AFTERMATH OF THE COUNCIL

In the long run, the Council of Trent was only as effective as the Catholic kings and princes wanted it to be. The rulers hindered Trent's reforms because they wanted to dominate and nationalize the church. Diplomacy and concession crept back into church procedures. The church had difficulty, especially with Philip II of Spain. On the one hand, he protected the church and on the other, he was determined to rule it. Philip controlled his clergy, forbade his subjects to appeal to Rome and, from his territories in Naples, pressured the pope to accede to his wishes. Much of the papal activity of the time consisted of efforts to offset domination by the Spanish Hapsburgs. Yet, outside of the political entanglements, the time after Trent did see several results.

Since the Council of Trent besought the pope to confirm its decrees (which he did in 1564), it implicitly recognized the primacy of the popes. Conciliarism, for the time being, had been put to rest. The papal monarchy was reenforced to such an extent that the pope was able to do without a council for the next three hundred years. Even then, when such a council was called (Vatican I), it concluded by declaring the pope's primacy and infallibility. Trent thus elevated the papacy to an absolutist style and a form of isolationism that was to last until the election of Pope John XXIII in 1958.

Furthermore, as we have noted with the reforming popes, conservative trends set in. There followed an intolerance, a certain hostility toward unauthorized learning, and a suspicion of science. The case of Galileo's condemnation in 1633 is a good example of an obscurantist spirit that fell upon Catholics and Protestants alike.

The pile of books condemned by Protestant censors reached as high towards heaven as those condemned by Catholic censors. The defenders of orthodoxy were slow to realize that where they once cut manuscripts to pieces, the printed book was bound to escape their clumsy scissors. Pope Urban VIII and his advisers who condemned Galileo (it has been said by Giorgio de Santillana) were not so much oppressors as the first bewildered casualties of the scientific age.[7]

Still, for all the censorship, some scholars managed to speak out and move ahead. The Roman catacombs were discovered in 1578, and the pope set up a printing press for Oriental literature in 1584. In 1582, Pope Gregory XIII reformed the calendar. (Protestant countries were among the last to accept this change: England in 1752, and Russia not until 1917.)

Nevertheless, only those countries like England and the Netherlands, which broke away from religious restrictions, made cultural progress. Censorship was least enforced in the Netherlands. Thus, that country published books that were permitted nowhere else. Furthermore, in spite of more respectable scholarship, witch hunting began to flourish again in the Protestant countries, especially in Germany and England. England influenced the witch trials among the Puritans and Congregationalists in the famous Salem witch trials in Massachusetts.

ASCENDANCY OF MORAL CONCERNS

Another result of Trent was that it had fashioned dogma so definitively that doctrinal speculation more or less ceased. The focus among Catholic theologians, therefore, began to shift to moral questions and concerns. Did not Trent in its pronouncements on the sacrament of penance insist that sins be confessed according to number and kind? Soon, whole new schools of moral theology arose, complete with many theories and systems on sin and its divisions. The use of confession increased. Manuals assessing the gravity of sin, advising the confessor, and offering complex moral cases became common. Texts were written that weighed the moral implication of every human action. Nothing was too big or, unfortunately, too small for the attention of the casuists. Thus, moral theologians discussed how much meat one could eat on a Friday before it was a question of mortal sin; how much of the Mass one could miss before a person committed sin; if lipstick or chewing gum broke the eucharistic fast; if lipstick rendered invalid the anointing on the lips at the sacrament of extreme unction (sacrament of the sick); whether pregnancy was an excuse for missing Mass; whether the fasting time from midnight was computed on natural time, man-made time, local time, or universal time; whether sexual thoughts were mortal or venial. During the centuries after Trent, there were endless discussions (and manuals) on moral minutiae, the net effect of which was to produce the sin-conscious, scrupulous mentality that was the lot of many a Catholic prior to Vatican II.

The beautiful medieval formulas for absolution gave way to the legalistic, declarative forms of post-Tridentine wordings. Certain sins were taken out of the priest's hands and were reserved for the absolution of the pope or the bishop. The priest moved from the role of community reconciler and representative to that of judge. The confessional became, not the locale of an encounter with the forgiving Jesus, but a tribunal where one's case was heard, tried, and pronounced upon. Attention was given to the "five steps" in order to make a good confession: examining one's conscience, being sorry for one's sins, having a firm purpose of amendment, telling one's sins to the priest, and being willing to do the penance the priest gave. Elaborate rules were devised for dealing with the sin a person forgot to confess, deliberately kept hidden, or the penance a person forgot to do. The legal moralist replaced the prophetic figure.[8]

Needless to say, the reaction to all of this was either a morbid preoccupation with sin or a reactive laxism. There were some very disedifying public quarrels among casuists, religious orders, and others over what was right and wrong. The Jesuits acquired a reputation for moral laxity, and some suggested that the Jesuit confessors could find a reason for doing whatever one wanted to do. Purists, such as the Jansenists, tended toward a stricter code. No one really gained from the frequent and offensive debates that followed.

THE MASS

In reaction to the reformers, the leadership of the church after Trent continued to emphasize those devotions most under attack. This meant the veneration of the saints, devotion to the Blessed Virgin Mary, and the adoration of Christ in the Blessed Sacrament. In reference to the sacrament of the eucharist, the trend toward distance and away from participation continued. Since the reformers had stressed the priesthood of all the faithful, post-Trent Catholicism felt it was necessary to emphasize the distinction between priest and people.

Mass was the one public place that this could be taught. The people came to watch the priest "effect" this great drama. No longer was there even any thought that the laity had a part to play. The eucharist was shrouded in mystery. The laity were to stay at a distance, preparing their hearts by acts of faith, hope, and charity for what they had been taught was the great moment of the Mass, the elevation of the host and chalice. They were taught to bow their heads and strike their breasts in profound adoration during the elevations. Popular prayers, such as the rosary, were thought to be the best acts of piety during Mass. People were not permitted to use missals.

In 1661, the Roman Latin missal was forbidden to be translated into the vernacular under pain of excommunication. Missals in the vernacular did not appear in Europe until 1897. In the United States, there was no vernacular missal until 1927, when the St. Andrew's Daily Missal was published in St. Paul, Minnesota. The biggest impetus given to missal use in our country came during World War II, when Father Stedman produced pocket-sized missals that the service men and women took all over the world. With World War II, the missal in the United States became commonplace, and small beginnings were made of the laity's participation. The Constitution on the Sacred Liturgy, promulgated during Vatican II, has provided the liturgical principles for the laity's full and intelligent participation in the eucharistic celebration.

POPULAR DEVOTIONS

Meditations on Christ's passion and death continued to play a large role in Catholic piety. The rosary, with its joyful, sorrowful, and glorious mysteries, was encouraged. Receiving communion was more frequent after Trent, but it was still looked upon as an "extra," as an action the truly devout would do out of devotion, not something necessarily connected with the Mass. With the loss of the intrinsic connection between the celebration of the Mass and the reception of the eucharist, communion was often received after Mass or outside of it.

In a related deviation, the tabernacle, especially after it was fixed to the altar, became more important than the altar (table) around which the community gathered. The adoration of Christ in the Blessed Sacrament, visits with the eucharistic Lord, came to be considered the high point of devotion. It was said that the parish church existed to house the tabernacle instead of being the place where the community gathered to worship. Forty Hours was seen as a high point of eucharistic devotion, and, at times, Benediction began to rival the Mass for popular attention.

THE BAROQUE PERIOD

The slow but steady change in the Catholic church began to manifest itself not only in such devotions, but also in its architecture and music. A note of triumphalism appeared and the baroque made its appearance. At first, the baroque style was cautious and restrained, but it later broke out into some glorious and some wild fantasies. The baroque style soon became the sign of the Catholic counter-reformation as well as a genuine sign of genuine faith.

The last stone of the dome of St. Peter's was put in place in 1590, a few months before the death of Sixtus V. The long period of austerity and consolidation was almost over, and in that decade were born the three men who were to make visible the victory of the Catholic church: Bernini, Borromini, and Pietro da Cortona.

How had that victory been achieved? In England most of us were brought up to believe that it depended on the Inquisition, the Index and the Society of Jesus. I don't believe that a great outburst of creative energy such as took place in Rome between 1620 and 1660 can be the result of negative factors, but I admit that the civilization of these years depended on certain assumptions that are out of favor in England and America today. The first of these, of course, was belief in authority, the absolute authority of the Catholic church. This belief extended to sections of society which we now assume to be naturally rebellious. It comes as something of a shock to find that, with a single exception, the great artists of the time were all sincere, conforming Christians. Guercino spent much of his mornings in prayer; Bernini frequently went into retreats and practiced the spiritual exercises of St. Ignatius; Rubens attended Mass every morning before beginning work. The exception was Caravaggio, who was like the hero of a modern play, except that he happened to paint very well.

This conformism was not based on fear of the Inquisition, but on the perfectly simple belief that the faith which had inspired the great saints of the preceding generation was something by which a man should regulate his life. The mid-sixteenth century was a period of sanctity in the Roman church almost equal to the twelfth. St. John of the Cross, the great poet of mysticism; St. Ignatius of Loyola, the visionary soldier turned psychologist; St. Teresa of mystical experience and common sense; and St. Carlo Borromeo, the austere administrator—one does not need to be a practicing Catholic to feel respect for a half-century that could produce these great spirits. Ignatius, Teresa, Filipo Neri, and Francis Xavier were all canonized on the same day, 22 May 1622. It was like the baptism of a regenerated Rome.[9]

Indeed, the seventeenth century has been rightly called a century of saints and spiritual vigor. There were, in addition to the saints mentioned above, Bossuet, Fenelon, John Eudes, Peter Canisius (Jesuit missionary, reformer, founder of colleges, preacher, and author of a famous catechism), Jeanne de Chantal, Cardinal Berulle, Jean Jacques Olier, founder of seminaries, and Vincent de Paul (d. 1660) who inspired retreats, disseminated humane ideas, and founded the Ladies of Charity and its numerous offspring of the Sisters of Charity. One of the most influential saints was Francis de Sales (d. 1622). He was a friend to the Jews, conciliatory toward Protestants, and founder of his famous Oratory. He initiated modern spirituality by providing the laity with a rationale to seek and practice sanctity in the world. His famous book is the *Introduction to the Devout Life*, one of the most widely read spiritual books in the seventeenth and eighteenth centuries; it is still reproduced today. Scholarship moved ahead with the likes of Suarez and Robert Bellarmine. In 1592, the first Congregation of Christian Doctrine was founded (forerunner of our modern religious education programs).

THE BEGINNINGS OF TOLERANCE

We have seen much evidence of intolerance and suppression during the wars of religion that ended with the Peace of Westphalia in 1648. Intolerance existed between Catholic and Protestant, between Protestant and Protestant, and between Christian, Muslim, and Jew. Catholics had their Inquisition, Calvinists had their Consistories, and the Anglicans had their Star Chamber. As time went on, each side saw some good in the other. Cultural exchanges were made when Protestants composed Catholic Masses and Catholics sang Lutheran hymns. Devotional literature was exchanged. Protestants of those times could not shuck off their Catholicism easily. Many still continued to bless themselves, celebrate Palm Sunday, and honor statues. Only gradually did cultural differences grow, as seen in a sterner Sunday inspired by the Puritans; the destruction of musical instruments and objects of religious art led to bare churches. Yet, in the aftermath, Protestants picked up simple music (though by no means universally or willingly) and gave birth to the chorale.

Catholics, for their part, stressed the old devotions and added new ones, such as the Angelus. Catholics focused on the altar, while the Protestants focused on the pulpit. In spite of this, toleration was beginning, for the simple reason that too many countries had several denominations within their boundaries. Persecutions and killings could not go on indefinitely. The simple expediency of living together, and the desire for a unified country, tended to bring about a measure of toleration. While the medieval mind could not conceive of a people and its ruler having different religions, the concept of freedom of conscience was developing during the seventeenth and eighteenth centuries. It had received some theoretical foundations in the writings of Sebastian Castellio, whose pioneering book of 1550 helped to influence the thinking of many.

Catholics found themselves in a different church after Trent (a point some Protestants have been quick to point out). They even mark Trent as the beginning of modern "Roman" Catholicism in the sense of a Roman-directed church. In contrast to the more freewheeling speculations permitted in the past, a stricter party line became the norm. In contrast to the more pliable and contestable maneuvers of other bishops and kings, an uncontested papacy, monarchial and absolute, dominated the church. In contrast to the variety of local customs and traditions, there was a universal conformity to what Rome would henceforth decree. In contrast to the many international influences before Trent, Italian-Roman coloring would dominate the church. Four centuries later, these developments would be contested and, to some degree, overturned by Vatican II.

THE MISSIONS

We do well to close this chapter on reform and renewal with a word about the great missionary activity of the church in the period after Trent. When the Catholic Europeans went to settle the New World (before the Reformation began), they did so with the medieval presumption that the faith was to be propagated. Colonists planted both colonies and churches. The long list of Portuguese and Spanish holy names in the Americas attests to this fact: San Francisco, Los Angeles, Corpus Christi, San Antonio, St. Augustine—to mention just a few on the mainland United States. Soon, schools were built. The first university in the New World was in Mexico, and the first diocese, San Domingo, was established in 1511.

Europeans looked upon their colonizing as a holy crusade. This was especially true of the dominant power of that time, the Spanish. They set out to civilize and evangelize the heathen, and they brought to that task the fierce crusading spirit honed to a fine edge through centuries of conflict with the Muslims in their own country. With this Spanish history in mind, one might understand the reasons for the forced conversions, the extermination, and the exploitation of the heathen Indians in Mexico and Latin America. In 1519, when Cortes landed in Mexico, the native population was some fifteen million. By 1575, only about two million were left. The Portuguese, Dutch, and English were to prove no better when their colonizing began.

Yet there were several outstanding voices who spoke against such cruelty and who fought mightily for the interests of the natives. One of these was the first priest ordained in the New World in 1519, the Dominican, Bartholomew de las Casas. He spent his whole life getting legal protection for the Indians, and reminding his fellow Spaniards that the Indians were human beings and must be treated as such. His persistence and work laid the foundation for international justice and law. Moreover, "it is to the credit of the popes of the counter-reformation that they steadily condemned the doctrine of slavery for the Indians."[10] Peter Claver worked among the Negroes and opposed the slave trade in Colombia. Another spokesman for the oppressed was the great archbishop of Peru, Turibio (later canonized), who passed laws to defend the rights of the Indians and Negroes. He even educated them. The most famous of all helps to the Indians were the Jesuit reservations, known as the Paraguay Reductions, which provided protection for the Indians (from the white men), schooling, and a measure of civilization. (*The Mission* is a film telling the story of the Jesuit reservations and their suppression brought about by greed, political intrigue, and jealousy.) Civilization meant, of course, becoming Spanish, and mass baptisms were as much geared to make the Indian Spanish as Christian.

THE EAST

We have already alluded to the work of Francis Xavier in the East. Here we must emphasize how the missionary experience in the East was entirely different from that in the Americas. Here the Catholic missionaries ran into the great Eastern religions such as Hinduism and Buddhism. In India and China, the missionaries were stunned to find genuine virtue, mysticism, and asceticism. They began to acquire a respect for these religions and, therefore, held back on the heavy-handed methods of forced conversions, such as occurred in the Americas. The more daring and insightful missionaries allowed the converts to continue those Eastern practices not incompatible with Catholicism. In Peking, the famed Jesuit, Matteo Ricci, learned Chinese, dressed in mandarin clothes, studied Chinese science, and presented Christianity as the fulfillment of what the people already knew from Confucius. As might be expected, he was not without his shocked conservative critics. His successor, Adam Schall, a priest, became a scientist and even Minister of State at the Chinese court. By 1650, there were Christian congregations scattered throughout the main Chinese cities (however, there were no Chinese priests yet).

The same respectful approach was used in Japan, but Christianity was doomed when Dutch and Spanish ships appeared, raising fears that Western imperialism was at hand. In 1614, Christian missionaries were expelled from Japan and the worst persecution in all of Christian history began. In some twenty years, over 40,000 Christians were martyred. By 1638, Japan was officially closed to foreigners. Thus, if by 1614 there were some 300,000 Christians in Japan, by

1697 there were hardly any left.

In India, another great missionary, Robert de Nobili, a Jesuit, adopted the Brahman way, dress and lifestyle, and liturgy. He, too, was denounced by jealous conservative Catholics and brought before the archbishop of Goa. Counter-reformation conservatism perhaps did most harm in the area of the missions. Henri Daniel-Rops, in his volume, *The Catholic Reformation*, gives a telling example:

> If there was one country where the missionaries had made the mistake of trying to impose the framework and methods of European Catholicism upon native converts, that country was India... The Archbishopric of Goa, with its suffragan bishoprics of Meliapur and Cranganor (not to mention Macao in China), presented a handsome facade behind which there was little spiritual reality—dioceses administered on European lines, and more Portuguese than Hindu. In 1559, however, Catholicism won a notable success: the 200,000 descendants of the "Christians of St. Thomas" in the region of Cochin, who were subject to the heretical and schismatic Jacobite patriarch of Mesopotamia, but who retained vivid memories of a visit paid to them by St. Francis Xavier, determined to submit to the Holy See. Unfortunately, they were soon led to regret their decision by the stupidity of a few Western missionaries who wished forcibly to Latinize the age-old Syro-Chaldaic, and to forbid them to pray in the popular tongue of Malabar. The resulting tension produced a new schism in 1633.[11]

In 1662, Pope Gregory XV created the Congregation of the Propaganda to assist the missions. (This was to be the forerunner of the Society for the Propagation of the Faith, which was founded in Lyons in 1822.) However, with the coming colonial ascendancy of the Protestant Dutch and English, many Catholic missions disappeared.

Much of the decline and disappearance was already in the making. This was due to the inability of Christianity, in all of its denominational forms, to shake off the traditional conviction that conversion and European culture were inseparably linked. This led to four fatal defects in the whole missionary enterprise. First, the Franciscan, Dominican, and some of the Jesuit missionaries (with notable exceptions, as we have seen) did not follow the advice of Gregory the Great to build on the natural culture and symbols of the natives.

Instead, the missionaries steadfastly sought to replace native talent and genius with European models. In those cases where the missionaries were flexible and innovative, they were reported to the Holy Office and their work was undone. Second, most missionaries were consistently condescending and chauvinistic, that is, nationalistic; they did not want, and would not permit, a native clergy. The newly Christianized peoples were somehow always to be treated as children and regarded as incapable of any status in the church. Furthermore, the missionaries were not sophisticated enough to make the proper anthropological distinctions between the people and their culture. The result was that the missionaries did not provide a self-sustaining home-grown Christianity, but a caste system of white missionary and subservient foreign people. Third, the terribly scandalous rivalries among the missionary religious orders sapped concentrated effort and often mutually undermined any effective work. Fourth, the mission enterprise was overly entangled with the crown, the inevitable trade, and the economic merchants. Christianity became identified with Western colonialism, imperialism, and exploitation. Forced conversions left bitter memories, especially when coupled with westernization.

It is also true that the missionaries were often victims of the church-state system. For example, Spain from the beginning assumed extraordinary control over the church. In 1508, with papal consent, the Spanish government was granted the right to approve the establishment of any new religious institutions. It also acquired the right to make commendations to ecclesiastical posts in the colonies. The conflict between the Spanish civil authorities and the religious clergy was protracted and harsh.

In spite of their auspicious start, the Catholic missions gradually declined. By 1815, the missions had almost come to a standstill, especially after some 3,000 Jesuits were pulled from the field when that order was suppressed in 1773. By the early nineteenth century, there were fewer than 300 Catholic missionaries in all the world. After 1815 and the restoration of the Jesuits, the missions again picked up steam. New missionary orders were founded, such as the Oblates of Mary Immaculate in 1816, the Marists in 1817, the Salesians in 1859, and the White Fathers in 1868.

The Protestant mission activity was very late in coming. Not until the eighteenth century did they seriously engage in missionary work. The Dutch, Germans, and English then began to work abroad in earnest. The United States Protestants, including women missionaries, began to take a leading part in missionary activity in the Far East. But the Protestant missions suffered from the same defects as did the Catholic ones. They were tied to the crown, to colonialism, and to commerce. An Anglican divine wrote, "...In every progressive step of this work, we shall also serve the original design with which we visited India, that design so important to this country—the extension of our commerce." Even the famed Dr. David Livingstone admitted in a private letter to a friend:

> That you may have a clear idea of my objects, I may state that they have more in them than meets the eye.... All this machinery had for its ostensible object the development of African trade and the promotion of civilization; but what I can tell to none but such as you, in whom I have confidence, is that I hope it may result in an English colony in the healthy highlands of Central Africa!...

The missionary was successful in spite of these limitations, as is evidenced by the spread of Christianity everywhere on the globe by the mid-nineteenth century. Nevertheless, it is perhaps significant that Christianity had its greatest successes among the primitive people. Little progress was made where Islam, Confucianism, or Buddhism were already firmly established.

It should be noted that this missionary activity gave Christians new and disturbing thoughts. For the first time, they traveled to new parts of the globe where they met strange animals. Had all these animals also been on the Ark? Did the Indians descend from Adam and, if so, how did they get to these distant lands? These people seemed to be living happy and virtuous lives in the East. How, then, was Christianity unique? People's minds were stretching beyond the narrow confines of Europe. Explorations were being made. Scientific discoveries (such as those of Galileo) were reshifting the Christian worldview. A certain skepticism was on the horizon, the beginning of a period which has come to be known as the Age of Enlightenment.

CHAPTER 18

Reason and Reaction

THE ENLIGHTENMENT

While wars of religion were being fought, each side trying to defeat or dominate the other, another revolution of far greater consequence was happening. It was a revolution in thought, in emphasis, and in science. The seventeenth and eighteenth centuries produced philosophers like Descartes, Spinoza, Leibnitz, Locke, and Montesquieu; scientists like Newton, Linnaeus, Lavoisier, Boyle, Fahrenheit, Halley (Halley's comet), and Adam Smith; writers like Pope, Milton, Defoe, Swift, and Fielding. Their works and ideas laid the foundations for the modern age. These, and many others like them, helped in one way or another to shift the world's spiritual axis from heaven to earth. They created a thirst for knowledge, a scientific mentality, and a keen desire to throw off all restraints and traditions of the past by following wherever knowledge would take them. This was the age, too, when new worlds, new cultures, new peoples were being discovered. Those who were filled with disgust at the vices and follies of Europe would profess to see in the pagan savages (the "noble savage," as Rousseau said) more goodness and nobility than in the Christians of Europe.

People, like the great genius Isaac Newton and others, were demonstrating that the universe was not a haphazard puppet on divine strings, but a universe controlled by its own laws. The universe was an accurate, programmed clockwork with discoverable and knowable laws. These scientists declared that the world was self-sufficient, dynamic, and as closed to divine intervention as it was open to rational inquiry. Naturally, this sudden shift in worldview raised some crucial questions. If, for example, the world was running on precise and immutable laws, what part, if any, did God have to play? Did these natural laws allow for miracles? If there is a common natural law governing the physical world, does this apply to humanity as well? If it does, does it mean that beneath all the religious sects, beneath the beliefs of the Protestants, Jews, Catholics, Muslims, and American Indians, there lies a natural common universal law applicable to all human beings? Does this further imply that morality, therefore, rests on a much broader foundation than Christianity?

Could not reason even sit in judgment on religion itself? Must not religion and its teachings and its miracles come under reason's scrutiny? Was revelation, in fact, even necessary? With reason to explain everything, there was no *need* for God to reveal. And why should religion have anything to say about politics? If there is a sub-Christian natural law, it is to that law that society must look for reasonable conduct among all people, Christian and non-Christian alike. From this perspective, there is no need for divine guidance in political matters.

It must be said that the early scientists like Newton were reverent toward religion and were anxious to reconcile religion and science. But later, less reverent thinkers would raise the above questions, and deliberately challenge not only superstition and intolerance, but also authentic religious beliefs. War was waged against religion under the banner that declared that the natural must be substituted for the supernatural, and that reason must be the measurement of all things.

Thus began the Age of Enlightenment, or the Age of Reason. In many ways, therefore, the Enlightenment was opposed to Catholicism and the Protestant Reformation, because the Enlightenment struck at the very roots of revealed religion by denying the authenticity of the Scriptures and the existence of the supernatural. With this idea of the superiority of natural reason, a new "religion" was born. It was called "progress" and it was supposed to free society from the "superstitions" of the ecclesiastical Middle Ages. It should be noted here that by the time the Enlightenment was over, having reached its extreme expression in the French Revolution, Christianity would have slipped from center stage. Religion as such would now be separated from secular and civil life. One's profession of faith would no longer be an affair of the state, but a very private affair of free citizens. From ancient times, long before the birth of Jesus, the governments of society and religion had always been interdependent. With the advent of the secular society (pertaining only to this world), something radically different was at hand.

This eventual development was not the result of some concerted plot of evil people. It was partially the long-term result of an intolerant Christianity. The religious wars drove increasing numbers of educated and intelligent people away from the churches. In addition, there was a growing tendency to work out life's affairs apart from organized religion, especially in the areas of economics and culture. Those who took such a course were not irreligious by any means. Indeed, while they faithfully read their Scriptures, they had little tolerance for the mutual intolerances of Catholicism or Protestantism. They wanted to seek reason, peace, accord, and ecumenical harmony. But even this desire for ecumenical harmony grew faint by the mid-seventeenth century, when we detect a distinct loss of faith in institutional religion by the educated upper classes. Their conclusion was that Christianity was hopelessly divided and would always remain so. Any hope that a total Christian society could be reconstructed was abandoned. People turned their attention and energies to other (commercial and scientific) enterprises. A secular and pluralistic society became solidly established. The only place left for religion would be in the voluntary consciences of private individuals. Religion, science, and education began to go their separate ways. Voluntary organized religion, falling into formalism, ironically became as mechanical and off-hand as the old pre-Reformation church.

The upper-class clergy, both Protestant and Catholic, especially in France and England, eventually became little more than ordained sophisticates keeping themselves busy, as was the general custom among the aristocrats, by dabbling in the arts and sciences. As part of the secular scene, they had no inclination to engage in any discussion over irrationalities such as sin or hell or any other "nonscientif-

ic" nonsense. They were the learned, rather than the pious clergymen of the plays and novels. Their forte was secular, not spiritual,
excellence.

DEISM

Deism was one result of all the preceding attitudes—that reason
and natural law were co-partners in discovering the validity of
everything. Deism came to be seen as a compromise between the
God of Christianity and the Law of Reason. It held that while a person can reasonably believe in God (because reason could argue back
to a Prime Mover or an Uncaused Cause), this God was not personal. He is rather the God of the Newtonian laws, a Divine Architect
who, like a watchmaker, wound up the world and lets it run according to the immutable laws built into it. God is thus enabled to withdraw from the scene. Thus, Deism was a natural religion.

    Deism and its philosophical foundation, the Enlightenment, had
its start in England, but found its home base in France, where the
French took Deism to its logical course. Voltaire, the perfect example of the scientific skeptic, was its chief exponent.[1] More than any
other, he made Deism, cynicism, and religious skepticism respectable. Linking Christianity, miracles, and superstition, Voltaire led the
attack on all of them. He pioneered many of the enlightened reforms still in use today, such as popular education, humanitarian-
ism, and anti-war movements. Voltaire contributed to the famous
Encyclopedia of Diderot, a compendium of all knowledge of the time,
and permeated by deistic principles. However, his attack on organized religion continued until it became an obsession. Historian
Philip Hughes writes:

> The French Deists and atheists availed themselves of every
> possible literary weapon, and they secured a hearing in thou-
> sands of minds where no serious work of theology or apolo-
> getics would ever gain entry. The Jansenist had been a solemn
> and serious opponent and could be fought off, intellectually,
> and without any great difficulty. But the mockery of these new
> foes, the pioneers of the modern popular assault on traditional
> faith and conventional morality, could not be met with the
> weapons of learning. They had the first laugh, and the crowd
> that laughed with them was already beyond the reach of the

dialectic. For the hour when the crowd turned to reflect, the movement provided a great compendium of knowledge, the first Encyclopedia, and there the civilization of the eighteenth century found a kind of universal popular educator by which to initiate itself into all the sciences and general history, and so written that at every turn the universality of human knowledge was made to tell against religion, and especially against the Catholic church.[2]

Most of the intellectuals of Europe and America fell under the Deist spell. Thomas Paine, Benjamin Franklin, and Thomas Jefferson all held Deist ideas. The English poet, Alexander Pope, and the historian, Edward Gibbon, promoted Deism in their works. Deism became the official religion of the fast- growing Freemason lodges that spread rapidly throughout Europe and America. Benjamin Franklin and George Washington were such members. (Some Freemason lodges, abandoning Deism for atheism, were heavily anti-clerical and anti-Catholic. Some former Catholics became Freemasons. This partly explains the church's condemnation of them.)

THE ENLIGHTENED DESPOTS

Many of the rulers of Europe were dedicated to the Enlightenment, and rivaled each other in introducing liberal reforms. They were bent on ideas of toleration, popular education, and freedom from past traditions and superstitions. However, in the process, they often trampled on the freedom of those with different perspectives.

Many of these countries had several religious sects. This, plus the skepticism of the times, the indifference to church teaching, and the desire of such religious minorities for a place in the sun, led the enlightened rulers to be champions of religious toleration. They had no enthusiasm for maintaining any organized state religion. Anti-Protestant laws in France and anti-Catholic laws in England began to be relaxed. The Inquisition was considerably curbed in Spain, and even Benedict XIV, an enlightened and witty pontiff, was praised by Voltaire for his tolerance because, according to Enlightenment standards, tolerance was reasonable.

Hand-in-hand with such toleration went the desire of enlightened people for humane treatment of all minorities, not only religious, but also racial minorities. Negro slavery came under attack.

The Quakers condemned slavery as early as 1696 and, in 1761, forbade their members to engage in its practice. In America, a society for the abolition of slavery was founded in Philadelphia in 1774 by an enlightened physician, Dr. Benjamin Rush. Many enlightened fathers of the American Revolution, such as Washington and Jefferson, even though they themselves owned slaves, hoped slavery would disappear.

All these things were positive legacies of the Enlightenment. The rulers who sought these ideals could not, however, achieve them without the cooperation or the subordination of the church. Thus, while enlightened rulers did not seek the church's annihilation, they sought to control it and to purify it of "unreasonable" elements, thus bringing the clergy into the status of civil servants in the interests of Enlightenment programs. We should also note that many of the reformed Catholics (Catholics anxious to reform the church following the spirit of Trent) were in agreement with the rulers' aims, and each side used the other for its ends.

AUSTRIA

Austria, under Maria Theresa, pursued a moderately enlightened policy that included popular education and protecting the church. Her son, Joseph II (1765-1790), felt no such compulsion. He introduced compulsory education, granted religious toleration to all denominations, took over seminaries, put the clergy under civil control, suppressed some monasteries, regulated the holy days, determined what prayers were to be said and what songs could be sung, forbade the rosary, and even determined the number of candles to be lit on the altar for Mass (for which he has been called the "Imperial Sacristan"). Joseph II was determined to make Catholicism into a national church by putting the bishops under his care and resisting all papal decrees. (This tactic is called Josephism; we shall later meet its French counterpart, called Gallicanism.) In 1782, Pope Pius VI made an unprecedented journey to Vienna in an attempt to get Joseph to reverse his policies, but to no avail. However, Joseph's overkill only succeeded in triggering a reaction. Ultimately, his work was undone, but for the time being, he helped keep the church powerless. It was the same story in Spain, Denmark, France, and Portugal. There was not a single Catholic country where the Catholic church could operate without interference from the government.

FRANCE

France, the home of Voltaire, merits our special attention. It was during the Enlightenment that the stage was set for the French Revolution and the church's role in it. Louis XIV, the Sun King (1643-1715), had made France the cultural and social arbiter of the world. He was the perfect absolute monarch, even in religious matters. We have seen how he revoked the Edict of Nantes in the interest of national unity, and then tried to control the church. There were the Four Articles of 1682, but they are not as important as the spirit known as Gallicanism that they engendered. Gallicanism wanted both the Catholic church and the pope, but rejected control from Rome and papal claims to infallibility. In short, papal power was to be ineffective in France. Every school in France, including the seminaries, was required to convey the spirit of Gallicanism. But it was not just the anti-papal spirit that was present. The church's wealth and its almost full control over education and charitable institutions also caused resentments. Most irritating was that, while the nation experienced financial stress, the church did not pay taxes or even offer to help carry the financial burden.

France was full of other conflicting forces. Some of the French did not want Gallicanism and the resulting curtailment of the pope's power. They were called the "Ultramontanes," which literally means that they looked "across the mountains" to Rome for guidance. Among the Ultramontanes were the Jesuits, who were very powerful. They were mentors to the sons of nobles and the spiritual guides and confessors to kings and princes. They were considered by many to be too accommodating in their moral opinions and they gained the reputation for finding legalistic loopholes that permitted doubtful moral actions. There was also a conflict among the clergy. As in other countries, the clergy was sharply divided into upper and lower clergy, the latter living in ignorance and abject poverty, the former living as if they were well-endowed nobles. Many of the upper clergy were so much the children of the Enlightenment, so free-thinking, that even tepid King Louis XVI said about a certain candidate, "No, the archbishop of Paris must at least believe in God." The upper clergy, which meant largely the episcopacy, was too tied to the monarchy and too much at home with the nobility.

JANSENISM

France was divided also by the differences between the reformed

Catholics and the Jansenists. The reformed Catholics were progressive, wanting the church to move ahead with Trent's reforms, to free itself of the monarchy, and to reduce the church's wealth. The Jansenists also started out as Catholics dedicated to the ideals of Trent. They, too, wanted to get back to the older and stricter practices of the church, and thus advocated the equality of all bishops with the pope. They were Pietists (which we shall describe below), in that they wanted more simplicity, less theology, a greater dependence on God's grace, and less dependence on the sacraments, ritual, the cults of the saints, and a more severe and stricter moral code. In short, they were Catholic Calvinists. Politically, they wanted more state authority and less church authority; they desired more modern and secular administration. In those times, they were allied with the aims of the state. Although the Jansenists were condemned at various times, even by the papal bull *Unigenitus* in 1713, Jansenism continued to flourish. Even some of the cardinals in Rome were in favor of the Jansenist movement.

Needless to say, the morally strict, papal-decentralizing Jansenists had the Jesuits for their archenemies. As long as the Jansenists served Louis XIV's ambitions against the church, they were unmolested. However, when Louis made peace with the pope (for reasons of expediency), he began, in the interests of unity, to persecute the Jansenists. Still, the Jansenists continued to draw people. To the nunnery at Port Royale came some famous names such as Blaise Pascal and the Abbot St. Cyran (who popularized the Netherlands-born Jansenism in France).

The hostilities between Jansenist and Jesuit continued. The Jesuits were able to obtain from the weak King Louis XV a concession that no one could receive the last rites unless they accepted *Unigenitus*, the papal bull condemning Jansenism. This, then, became a matter involving the French Parliament as well. Having lost all support from both the king and the French Parliament, the Jansenist movement eventually died (except for some "old Catholics"), but not without causing much agitation in the church.

This victory over Jansenism demonstrated to many that reforms of any kind were impossible to achieve without the support of Rome. As a result, many of the progressive members of the clergy would come to support the French Revolution. "After the disappointments with Rome and with enlightened absolutism it was widely felt that the ideals of reform Catholicism could only be realized with the help of the Revolution and in close alliance with the democratic movement."[3] Yet, such an alliance was to crumble because of the excesses of the French Revolution. Catholic reform had become associated with such excesses and revolutionary terrors. Thus, the Catholic reform movement perished, and Rome emerged victoriously conservative. In 1794, Rome was strong enough to condemn both Jansenism and reform Catholicism without fear of resistance.

QUIETISM

There was another heresy afflicting the church in France during the seventeenth and eighteenth centuries: Quietism. It was a reaction to the rationalism and formalism of the times. Quietism was propounded by a Spanish priest, Michael Molinos, who taught that people must suspend all of their human power and become passively resigned (quiet) to what is good or evil. Thus, temptations, and the sins that resulted, must be simply accepted since they were, for the moment, God's will. Each person must be passive; even vocal prayer was unnecessary. Famous French bishops took sides: Fenelon favored Quietism, while Bossuet opposed it. Quietism was condemned in 1694, but the movement left many people suspicious of contemplative life.

Thus, there was France: the seat of the Enlightenment, the home base of the devastating Voltaire. There was the church upset by Quietism, stunned by Jansenism, and dishonored by the infighting between the Jesuits and Jansenists. The whole position of the church in France is summed up by Philip Hughes:

In this France, where Catholicism lay helpless, racked with the Jansenist controversy, cut off from Rome by its Gallicanism, shackled by its long connection with the state, oppressed by a hierarchy too often incompetent and not infrequently worldly, a France whose ruling classes were more and more given over to immorality, the mockery of Voltaire, in a single generation, put the church in the position of the defendant, Catholicism was summoned to explain what right it had to live. Hated, derided, it was henceforward, for the best intellect of France and therefore for the intellect of the world, an infamy, and not to be endured.[4]

SUPPRESSION OF THE JESUITS

One of the indirect results of the Enlightenment was the suppression of the Jesuits. There were many reasons for this suppression. The Jesuits' undue influence over the nobility and royalty caused much jealousy. In addition, they were associated with the pope's interests; they were among the "Ultramontanes" who looked to Rome for leadership rather than to the state. They were to some extent anti-royalist and dangerous to national interests. Since this was an age of toleration, and the Jesuits were champions of a monolithic church, they were considered by many in France to be hostile to tolerance and freedom. There were also the continued hostilities of the Jansenists and others who thought that the Jesuits' moral teaching was too permissive. Finally, the Jesuits were too often affiliated with the politics of the times and tended to overplay their hand. Many powerful enemies plotted their downfall.

The attack on the Jesuits began in Catholic Portugal. There a strong, very able, and self-seeking minister named Pombal saw that the Jesuit influence on the royal family might obscure his own. Pombal came up with some flimsy evidence that the Jesuits were somehow involved in an assassination attempt on the king by the jealous husband of a woman who had had an affair with the king. In 1759, the king confiscated the Jesuits' property and expelled them from the country.

In France, enemies of the Jesuits included not only the Jansenists and Calvinists, but also Louis XV's mistress, Madame de Pompadour, "minister in petticoats," and the real ruling power. Angry because the king's Jesuit confessor had chastised the king for his affair with her, Pompadour was determined to have revenge. When the Jesuits' mission on Martinique became a financial failure due to the loss of cargo to English raiding ships, she found her opportunity. The creditor tried to recoup his money, but the Jesuits claimed that they had no responsibility for this loss. The Society then appealed to France's highest court. A hostile Parliament was glad to have a pretense to investigate all Jesuit activities. Their decision was that the Jesuits should be expelled. In 1764, the weak Louis XV signed the decree. Pope Clement XIII protested, but could do no more. Spain followed suit in 1767, by expelling the Jesuits with great suddenness and surprise. Next, the king of Naples and the duke of Parma did the same. By 1769, all of the Catholic rulers were demanding the suppression of the entire order. The pope held out and tried to conciliate by making Pombal's brother a cardinal. Pressure still continued to mount, with the Bourbon powers threatening to invade the papal states. Finally, on July 21, 1773, Clement XIV gave in and the Society of Jesus was suppressed. Father Ricci, the General of the order, was put into prison where he died a year after the pope.

Ironically, non-Catholic rulers Frederick II of Prussia and Catherine the Great of Russia refused to publish the bull of suppression, and thereby kept the Jesuits in existence in their countries. Moreover, we should note that the pope was forced to suppress his most ardent supporters and the most vocal upholders of a centralized papal power as against the power of the state. By this action the pope, in effect, was telling the world (or at least those who were anxious to read into his act) that he repudiated the former teaching of the supremacy of the church over the state.

PIETISM

Pietism is the name for the general reaction of many people to the tedious infighting among the various denominations, the heavy theologizing, the cold rationalism. It took many forms. We saw it in Quietism and Jansenism in Catholic France. In the Protestant countries, however, it appeared in the form of revivalism, a Protestant phenomenon. Pietism had a strong hold among the Lutherans in Germany. P.J. Spener created a form of Pietism that was more of a personal religion, in which the interior life of the spirit was more important than doctrine. Through Count Zinzendorf, Pietism broke away from its native Lutheranism to find a new home among the spiritual descendents of Jan Hus. Zinzendorf associated himself with some Moravians, who later migrated to Pennsylvania and founded the city of Bethlehem. They became known as the Unity of Brethren or the Moravian Church.

Pietism in Germany was very popular, yet it had some drawbacks that eventually caused it to disappear. It did not keep spiritual and intellectual vitality in balance, and so it became theologically sterile and too emotional, too subjective, and too introspective. There is an interesting sidelight to German Pietism that historian Roland Bainton points out:

> The suggestion has been made that when Pietism kindled the emotions of many in the nation and the Enlightenment dimin-

ished the intensity of faith, emotion was transferred from God the Father to the fatherland. It is at least plain that the romanticists who saw a special divine afflatus in the German soul had been reared in the Pietist tradition.[5]

Pietism was bound to spread to England for much the same reasons that Jansenism got a foothold in France. The more the Anglican upper clergy became infected with Enlightenment ideas, the more the church became tied to the state. This resulted in a church that "became politically useful and theologically insignificant."[6] The upper Anglican clergy lived like well-to-do nobles, while the lower clergy languished in poverty. It was under these circumstances that an Anglican priest, John Wesley, and his brother Charles, founded at Oxford the Holy Club which developed a disciplinary "method" for spiritual improvement—hence the name Methodism. Having been impressed with the Pietism of the Moravians, they decided to regenerate society through individual preaching and congregational singing. No one ever wandered more throughout village and town to preach the word than Wesley. The Wesley brothers never left the Anglican church, for they were determined to purify it; yet their successors broke off into the Methodist church. John urged piety, sobriety, and chastity. He had a great concern for the working man, the very person neglected by the German Pietists—and this would make a difference in time to come. Wesley's Methodists shared pietistic concerns with the English evangelicals who, while they reacted to the tepidity of the Anglican church, nevertheless remained within it. They were very humanitarian, battled against slavery, founded schools for children, and established missionary and Bible societies.

Before we leave England, we might mention the status of the Catholics there. Catholics in eighteenth-century England were a small minority. With the overthrow of the Catholic king, James II (which Louis XIV's revocation of the Edict of Nantes in 1685 in France stimulated), they lost their ability to influence national affairs. Yet, in the minds of most of the English, Catholics continued to be viewed as a political threat. In due time, however, Irish immigration swelled their numbers and, by 1791 (the very year Wesley died), it was generally thought safe to grant privileges to Catholics and free them of many legal disabilities. By the 1830s, the English Oxford Movement would see a revival of Catholicism, a "second spring" as it was called by its most illustrious member and convert to Roman Catholicism, John Henry Newman.

ENLIGHTENMENT AND THE CATHOLIC CHURCH

Because the Enlightenment did not distinguish between superstitious practices and authentic faith, religion in general and the church in particular were dealt a severe blow. The Enlightenment cast the church in the role of a force that shackled people's minds, and depicted Christianity as something totally irrelevant to the modern world. Protestants, wrestling with Enlightenment ideas, were succumbing to its onslaught. The Catholic church had no leaders who could effectively refute its detractors. The papacy itself had been forced into the embarrassment of suppressing its own spokesmen, the Society of Jesus.

The Catholic church then began to take a reactionary stance, retreating into the realm of authority. By identifying itself more and more with the old order of things, Catholicism would not and could not come to terms with the new learning. Retreating from the new science, the Catholic church resorted to censorship and obsolete apologetical methods that were out of touch with the mental tenor of the times. By not coming to terms with the data supplied by advances in the emerging fields of anthropology, literary criticism, geology, astronomy, and others, data that called revealed religion into question and which challenged the way the Bible was understood at that time, the church merely postponed the inevitable confrontation. This confrontation took place in the late nineteenth and early twentieth centuries, when the movement called Modernism would force the church to take a second look at what science and critical studies were saying about Christianity.

But more was at stake than the church's failure to come to intellectual terms with the Enlightenment. The Enlightenment only added to the general disintegration of the old European unity which was centered in the church. Feudalism had declined, and the centralized monarchial powers were busy depriving the church of its international character by weakening the bonds that held their nations to Rome. The Italian Renaissance had rejected the barbarism of the Middle Ages and was looking for cultural purity. The Germanic Reformation was seeking gospel purity. The humanists were finding fault with what they saw as the culture of the "Dark Ages."

Although piety in the seventeenth century was remarkable, religious skepticism fostered by the philosophers of the Enlightenment was growing. "The greatest religious genius of the century, Pascal, was already acutely conscious that it was this easy-going, lighthearted skepticism, and not Protestantism or metaphysical error, which was the great danger that Catholicism had to face."[7]

Of course, as so often happens, the actual result of the Enlightenment turned out to be a far cry from the toleration it preached. The real result was to replace one unity with another. They substituted the universal reign of science and reason for that of religion and authority. There was no real sympathy for political or social revolution, for the leaders of the Enlightenment were squarely on the side of vested interests, on the side of property and order. The Enlightenment, like the Renaissance, was an elitist movement, allied with the powers that be, and determined to give only what they perceived as "good" for the people. As Voltaire admitted, "We have never pretended to enlighten shoemakers and servant girls...." It is ironic, for example, that the enlightened elite succeeded in getting the Jesuits suppressed, only to substitute themselves as "confessors" and advisors to the rulers of Europe.[8]

Up to this point, the rulers and their advisors shared a common faith. Now, of course, the enlightened philosophers felt that Christianity was only good as a means for controlling the lower classes. The net result was to sow discord and beget division between the upper and lower classes. Thus, the average person turned away from the sweet reasonableness of Voltaire and turned toward a new star on the horizon, Jean Jacques Rousseau (1712-1778). He was the one who took the high-flown liberal ideas, clothed them in religious terms, and popularized them for the masses. He vocalized themes that pitted the individual against society, religious sentiment and intuition against the rationalism of the philosophers, and the poor against the rich. He filled the minds of the lower classes with the idea of democracy as a way of life for everyone, not as a mere system. Thus it was that the abstract, elite, and enlightened rationalism met head on with the strong romantic feelings expressed by Rousseau. In many ways, this led to the French Revolution.

Meanwhile, there were some signs of quiet religious vitality among the people during this era. The Age of Voltaire was also the age of Wesley, Tersteegen (a Protestant mystic and religious poet), Paul of the Cross, the founder of the Passionists, Margaret Mary, Leonard of Port Maurice, and the great Alphonsus Liguori who founded the Redemptorists, and whose spiritual writings, verses, music, and sympathetic moral theology guided the hearts of many. There were the Moravians and Pietists in Germany, the Methodists in England, and the Great Awakening in America. There was the building of the great Catholic baroque monasteries. In fact, "Nothing shows the divorce between the bourgeois rationalism of the Enlightenment and the religious traditions of popular culture better than the figure of the beggar saint Benedict Joseph Labre (1748-83), who lived the life of a medieval ascetic and miracle worker in the age of Gibbon and Adam Smith."[9] Yet, all in all, the eighteenth century was not a good one for the Catholic church. The French Revolution was about to begin. The church would be further shaken, then recover, and then oppose liberalism and the democracy that came forth from that turning point of modern history.

CHAPTER 19

Liberalism and Conservatism

THE FRENCH REVOLUTION 1789-1799

Before we get into the immediate story of the French Revolution, we must first realize that we are dealing with an idea, an ideology, and something that was almost a religion. The Enlightenment had had its effect. Some, at least those of the intellectual elite, were prepared to jettison and replace Christianity with a new enlightened, humanitarian, natural religion. There was an almost mystical enshrinement of humanity in the Freemason lodges. The so-called Rights of Man were to be upheld. According to those thinkers, all kings, popes, and bishops who enslaved people must go. The appeal for freedom, democracy, and equality became a real spiritual problem, a genuine ideological force that was at the bottom of the French Revolution and all the succeeding revolutions that were inspired by it. Just as Communism in its early days presented itself as a true religion, with its hierarchy and promise of liberation, so, too, the French Revolution was based on a precise ideology that was supposed to change the world. (Like the Russian Revolution, it was conceived in a bloodbath, had its purges, fell far short of freedom, and wound up with a dictator.)

We must keep these thoughts in mind as we turn to the immediate factors that unleashed the revolution in France. There was in France, as elsewhere, a chronic agitation for reform, both of church and state. People wanted the Catholic church to remain the established church, but they wanted it renewed and reformed. It is interesting to note that Gallicanism had done its work well, because in all their aspirations for reform, the people and clergy looked not to the pope, but to the king.

There were many matters in France that cried out for relief. The cost of wars was heavy; taxes were galling and oppressive. More annoying was the fact that there was such a wide gap between the lifestyles of the lower clergy and peasants and the lifestyles of the nobility and upper clergy. In France, the upper clergy and nobility owned one-fifth of the land. The old caste divisions of clergy, nobility, and commoner had become irritating since the enlightened aristocracy had become vain social parasites at the royal court, living on the shallow resources of a bankrupt state. (It is no wonder that they fell like a rotten tree at the first struggle, and resigned their rights and privileges without a whimper.)

The middle-class bourgeoisie was getting restless. These, we recall, were the very ones imbibing the ideas of the Enlightenment from Rousseau; they were also chafing at the moral restrictions of the church on their commercial interests. The leadership of the church, even down to the eve of the revolution, was opposed to the new capitalist philosophy and commercial view of life which had triumphed in Protestant England and Holland. With its ideals of poverty and its condemnation of the greedy and competitive spirit that the new commercial society was acquiring, the church was an irritant to this middle class. However, because of their interests in capital and commerce, the middle class held the real power and was ready to throw off the restrictions of the church. Ultimately, just as capital and commerce played a real role in the Puritan American Revolution, so they would be radical factors in the French Revolution.[1]

On top of all this, the kings of the time were incompetent. Louis XV (1715-1774) was pleasure-loving and dominated by his mistress, Madame Pompadour. It was she who got France into the financially disastrous Seven Years War. Louis XVI (1774-1792) was no improvement. He was lazy and untalented. The one man who might have saved France from bankruptcy was the king's minister, Necker, but the queen, Marie Antoinette, had him dismissed. The nobles and upper clergy could have shared the tax burdens in France's grave financial straits, but they were unwilling. Louis had no choice but to call on the Estates General which had not met for one hundred seventy-five years.

The three orders of the Estates General met at Versailles: the clergy, the nobility, and the numerically superior commoners. Each order was originally supposed to vote as a separate bloc, which meant that the first two related orders, the clergy and the nobility, would always outvote the commoners' bloc two to one. But this was not to be. Many humble parish priests were there as delegates to the clerical order, but they insisted on voting with the commoners. After much maneuvering, it was agreed that those present would form a National Assembly with each member having an individual vote. This was most significant. It meant that the higher clergy and nobility had been defeated by this blending of the three orders into one vast democratic assembly where the commoners had the most members. Although reform of state and church was the aim at first, revolution was in the making. The king tried to cower this National Assembly but the people of Paris identified with it and rose up to storm the fortress of the Bastille on July 14, 1789. Thus, Paris became the seat of the Revolution.[2]

It was a revolution that was more important for the energy it released to build a new world from the regime that fell apart than for any immediate ushering in of democracy. In reality, the Bastille was almost empty when it was stormed, feudalism was practically over, and any vaunted "Rights of Man" were drowned in the horrendous bloodbaths of the Terror only five years after they were proclaimed. The revolution was born in violence and the September Massacres of 1792, an orgy of killing that took the lives of more than one thousand persons, were like a secular Last Judgment. All tolled, those terrible years took about 17,000 lives.

The irony here is that, true to the Enlightenment, reason was supposed to rule. Mathematical precision was imposed on everything, even to changing the calendar to ten days a week, three weeks to a month and twelve months to a year. Ordinary days received new names which suggested rational progressions; day one, day two, day three, etc. The metric system was adopted. Notre Dame cathedral was renamed the Temple of Reason. Yet, within this context a bloodbath engulfed the revolution, making one think of Chesterton's observation, "A madman is one who has lost everything *but* his reason."

REVOLUTION AND THE CATHOLIC CHURCH

The National Assembly set out to construct a new government, and they did it with a vengeance. When their work was finished, they claimed that they had undone fourteen centuries of abuses in three years, that the constitution they had made would last forever, and that their names would be blessed by all humankind. Yet, in only a few months their work was wrecked and their leaders exiled or imprisoned. "They had destroyed what they could not replace and called up forces that they could neither understand nor control."[3] Being influenced by the Enlightenment, most of the National Assembly wanted to abolish class privilege and distinction. Financial stability was to be restored through the seizure of church lands. Because this was done, the priests were to receive a stipend from the government. But the class that actually profited from all this stripping of the church was the monied class, who made fortunes from the purchase and resale of confiscated church property. Monasteries were disbanded except for those engaged in teaching or running orphanages. The government reduced the number of dioceses from 134 to 83—to coincide with the 83 newly-created provinces.

Then a novelty was introduced whereby the government would make bishops and notify the pope later. Even the French kings had not done this; they would nominate men to be bishops, but always sought papal confirmation. So far, the parish priests were agreeable with these changes, because such arrangements could only improve their lot. However, they were soon to learn that if the state paid their salaries, the state could also interfere in the realm of doctrine. The aged pope, Pius VI, wrote and told Louis XVI not to approve the new laws, but Louis had already done so when the pope's letter arrived a day late. Soon, the clergy saw themselves being reduced to mere civil functionaries. They, along with the reformed progressive Catholics, had desired to integrate the church into a new pattern of society and to make the church and state a harmonious unity. Now they were being required to take an oath supporting a new civil constitution which did not accept Catholicism as the state religion.

About half of the lower clergy took the oath, but only seven of the bishops did. It was easier for the bishops to refuse to take the oath because they could go into exile, which would be comfortable for most of them. This alternative was closed to the lower clergy. There was much confusion about this oath, and a word or directive from the pope would have been most helpful. But the pope delayed until the clergy were forced to make their own decisions without his advice. This resulted in a divided clergy, the "Romanist" clergy (who refused to take the oath), and the government-approved constitutional clergy (who had taken the oath). Only the latter were able to perform weddings and celebrate the sacraments. As a result of this confusion among the clergy, rioting, often involving sacrilege, broke out among the people.

Matters took a turn for the worse when Louis XVI tried to flee his country at the same time as the pope condemned the civil constitution in 1791. Because the king had broken with the revolution, and the pope was against it, the Romanist clergy became suspect. This suspicion escalated after the new government became involved in a war with Catholic Austria. To offset this danger a second oath was imposed on the clergy in 1792. Those who refused were to be deported. Those too ill to be deported were placed in prison, where many died. Death, deportation, and exile severely reduced the number of clergy obedient to the pope. The whole church-state relationship was deteriorating quickly. There was for all practical purposes a schism. Carlton J.H. Hayes summarizes it this way:

> The ecclesiastical policies of the National Assembly were perhaps the least efficacious and the most fateful achievements of the revolution. Yet it would be difficult to perceive how they could have been less radical than they were. The church appeared to be indissolubly linked with the fortunes of the "old regime"; the clergy comprised a particularly privileged class; and the leaders and great majority of the Assembly were filled with the deistic or skeptical philosophy of the "Enlightenment." In November 1789, the church property was confiscated. In February 1790, the monasteries and other religious communities were suppressed. In April, absolute religious toleration was proclaimed....In December, the Assembly forced the reluctant king to sign a decree compelling all the Catholic clergy in France to take a solemn oath of allegiance to the "civil constitution."[4]

The remaining constitutional clergy, those who took the oath in obedience to the state, did not long enjoy their privilege. A new and more radical leadership had taken over the revolution. This new leadership sought to de-Christianize religion, making marriage a civil contract, not a sacrament. Clerical marriages were made legal, as well as the remarriages of divorced persons. Meanwhile, the marriages of priests were actually encouraged. By 1793, any clergyman who did not agree with such legislation was deported. Austria and Prussia were threatening war in order to protect and restore the king of France. The revolutionary government reacted to such foreign threats by imprisoning the king and executing him in January 1793. Soon France was being invaded from all sides.

SUBSTITUTES FOR CATHOLICISM

The deported French bishops and other clergy hoped these invaders would be victorious. Their open encouragement served to make the French government even more anti-clerical. In 1792 and 1793, an effort was made to discredit Christianity entirely. In the spirit of Voltaire, violent denunciations of the Catholic faith were made. A Feast of Reason was held in Notre Dame cathedral on November 10, 1793. An actress, a "Goddess of Reason," was enthroned on the main altar to preside over an orgy. Vestments and statues were destroyed. Donkeys wearing bishops' mitres were paraded through the streets. Churches were closed. Yet, while such church-hating people as Hebert and Marat were urging violent anti-Catholic measures, others, like Robespierre and Danton, saw that it was a fruitless venture. Some lessening of the anti-church laws was granted.

When Robespierre came to power as a virtual dictator, he substituted a more personal Supreme Being for the God of Reason. But Robespierre was soon beheaded in the Reign of Terror that sent thousands to the guillotine. By 1795, under the rule of a five-man Directory, some toleration was evident, even though anti-Catholic measures were still being carried out. It was at this time that the abbey church of Cluny was leveled to the ground, as were the lovely cathedrals of Arras, Liege, Cambrai, and Bruges.

By 1795, permission was given to the Romanist priests for partial use of some of the churches, if they made a full act of submission to the laws of the government. Many refused. Two years later, they were required to take the "Oath of Hatred" against the monarchy.

Refusal meant deportation. In 1796, failing to get rid of Christianity, the government created a new religion. Its liturgies included hymns to nature and readings from the pagan philosophers, the Koran, and the gospels. Still, the people flocked to those priests offering Mass, even though the government had severely limited the time allowed for each Mass.

Yet, for all of this harassment, the faith lay deep in people's hearts. Many were impressed by the fidelity of those clergy at home and those in exile. It was only natural, of course, that those exiled clerics found the revolution repulsive, and longed for the restoration of the monarchy. (This clerical reaction will have more significance later.) The papacy would look with suspicion on revolutionary ideas and liberalism, because its initial contact was with the excesses of the French Revolution.

If some of the Romanists were more preoccupied, in their exile, with the fate of the monarchy than with the fate of the church, if some of the bishops were blind adherents of the ancien régime, and if many of the constitutional clergy dishonored their calling, it is right that the sacrifice of the devoted, during a period of extreme trial, should be remembered, for without it the remarkable revival of the church in France, in the following century, is unintelligible.[5]

PIUS VII

One of the failings of the papacy during the French Revolution was that it did not make clear to the clergy where their duty lay. The clergy, divided into constitutional and Romanist groups, was unable to present a united front. The papacy hesitated too long and was too indecisive. Pius VI (d. 1799) delayed too long in condemning the civil constitution of the clergy. He did sympathize with Louis XVI and the political aspirations of the French deportees, but this only made the lot of the loyal clergy in France that much harder. The power of the papacy in general was at a low ebb. In addition, the spirit of Gallicanism led the clergy to seek redress from the king rather than from the pope. Yet, in spite of all this, there were a few perceptive people who felt that if Rome could ever give a clear-cut directive to the church in France, that directive would solve many problems and give the unity so sorely needed by this troubled nation.

The situation had so degenerated that a French general invaded Rome in 1798, carried off the eighty-two-year-old pope to Siena and then to Florence. When the Austrians tried to rescue him, "citizen" pope was taken to France. The aged invalid, paralyzed in both legs, was dragged over the snow-covered Alps. He got as far as Valence before he died. A conclave met in Venice in a place set aside by the Holy Roman Emperor, who hoped to obtain a pontiff agreeable to himself. In 1800, Pius VII was elected but this choice did not please the emperor, who refused to allow him to be crowned in Venice, or to pass through northern Italy to Rome. The new pope had to travel by boat for four months before he arrived in Rome.

NAPOLEON

Meanwhile, the ruling Directory of the revolutionary government in France had been overthrown by one of its generals, Napoleon. He took the title of First Consul, but in reality he was the dictator. More than anyone else, he spread the ideals of the French Revolution[6] over the Europe he conquered. The whole feudal system and the hierarchical society on which medieval Christianity rested were permanently swept away by Napoleon. Even when he fell from power, other countries took up those ideals and fanned the liberalism that would be perceived as threatening by the papacy. For the present, however, Napoleon had to deal with the church. One of his first acts was to allow the Romanist priests full freedom in religion. Napoleon knew the depth of Catholicism and saw that the persecution of the church was a source of internal weakness. He, therefore, reestablished the Catholic church in order to fulfill his own ambitions. His cynical frame of mind was summed up in his own words:

My political method is to govern men as the majority of them want to be governed. That, I think, is the way to recognize the sovereignty of the people. It was by making myself a Catholic that I won the war in the Vendee, by making myself a Muslim that I established myself in Egypt, by making myself an Ultramontane that I gained men's souls in Italy. If I were governing a people of the Jewish race I would rebuild the Temple of Solomon.

In the beginning, Napoleon suppressed the anti-clericals of northern Italy.[7] He then had to make peace with the new pope, Pius VII.

Pius was ready enough to yield on the material property of the church in France, but in spiritual matters he proved difficult. His famous and notable minister of state was Cardinal Consalvi, who had to work with the redoubtable Talleyrand, Napoleon's minister of state. The result of their negotiations was the famous Concordat of 1801 (which lasted till 1905). The Catholic religion, while not the state religion, was allowed to be practiced openly, but with some government regulation. All bishops were required to resign and new bishops were to be nominated by Napoleon. These bishops would then be invested only by the pope, who had the option of *refusing* to do so, and who even afterwards could depose them. We must take note of the novelty here: for the first time in the church's history since Constantine, there was no state intermediary. The pope and the pope alone could invest or refuse to invest bishops. He and he alone could depose them. No governmental intervention was to be a part of this. We can see that this gave the death blow to Gallicanism in France and its equivalent elsewhere when this Concordat was copied by other countries.

By this concordat, a different church came into being (the one modern Catholics know). The bishops were no longer to be allied with the government. The negotiating parties were the bishop and the pope and his curia, as in the United States today. Henceforth, there was no other authority in religious matters than Rome. Local hierarchies were discounted, since they now had to look to Rome, not to the government. Note that for fifteen centuries the ruler had rights over the episcopacy; recall Constantine, Charlemagne, the Ottos, Henry IV, and Louis XIV. Even when Gregory VII humiliated Henry IV at Canossa and won the right to invest bishops, he still had to invest those bishops nominated and approved by the king. Even during the period of centralization under Innocent III and the other jurist popes, the national rulers rewarded their loyal followers with a bishopric. With the Concordat of 1801, the bishops were invested only by the pope. He could even deprive the bishops of their office. All state mediation had been eliminated. Surely this was one great triumph for the pope's able secretary, Cardinal Consalvi, who participated in the concordat. By fighting for an international centralized papacy, Consalvi was bucking the trend toward separate national independent states.Yet, he felt that local nation churches were too much of a danger for the Catholic church. In spite of the apparent victory for the Catholic church, there was an undesirable and unforeseen drawback. The episcopacy suffered a loss of prestige and authority, as dioceses came to be regarded not as local churches, but as administrative units of the universal church. These "administrative units" were governed by a bishop who appeared to be only a functionary of the pope.

The remainder of the concordat stipulated that the lower clergy were to be nominated by the bishops. No longer were priests to be presented for ordination by lay sponsors. This, too, tightened up the chain of command right up to the pope. Historian E.E.Y. Hales puts it so well:

> One result of lasting consequence to the church in Europe, and ultimately to the whole world, which flowed from the reorganization involved in the concordat, was the appearance of a new centralization within the church itself. No longer were the lesser clergy nominated by private patrons, they were nominated by the bishops, and any promotions they gained they would owe to those same bishops.... This strictly hierarchical organization which is characteristic of the church today, is doubtless now a source of strength; but it is interesting and perhaps significant to notice that, in its modern form, it dates from the Napoleonic Concordat with Pius VII, and that it owes something, at least, to Napoleon's determination not to allow too much independence to the local curés [parish priests]. For he knew very well that the curés, in 1789, had launched the Revolution.[8]

Finally, by the terms of the concordat, churches and cathedrals were to be restored to the church for its use, although the state retained ownership. The state was also to pay clerical salaries (which was not to the pope's liking). Thus the constitutional church of the revolution disappeared.

Napoleon chose not only most of the old Romanists to be bishops but also a large minority of constitutionalists. (There was some bitterness among the exiled bishops that caused a schism, since they would not deal with an "anti-Christ" revolutionary like Napoleon.) The concordat, which was destined to be copied by other countries, helped put the church back on its feet again, not only in France but in its dependencies, such as Belgium, the Rhineland, and part of Germany and Italy. The concordat showed, moreover, that the church need not be tied to the old regime, but could survive under Napoleon or any form of government if it were permitted to function without government interference.

Yet, Napoleon was determined to get concessions. Without telling the pope, he published with the concordat the "Organic Articles" which, in effect, were designed to regulate the affairs of the church in the spirit of Gallicanism (which, incidentally, he made mandatory in all the schools and seminaries in France). Napoleon insisted on one form of liturgy, one catechism, a civil ceremony prior to the church wedding, and refused to permit the observance of religious feast days. But Napoleon was pragmatic. Because he wanted the church to teach obedience to the state, he saw to it that the church was efficient. Thus, Napoleon even forced the constitutional clergy to make their obedience to Rome.

NAPOLEON AND PIUS VII

In 1804, Napoleon was given a new title, Emperor (a title not likely to please the other rulers). He wanted the pope to come to Paris to crown him. The pope was in a bind. Such an act would not only be an affront to the legitimate Bourbon king in exile, Louis XVIII, but also an insult to the Holy Roman Emperor. Neither did the pope want to give the crown to the French nation that had so recently persecuted the church. Cardinal Consalvi, however, felt that there would be more advantages in doing as the Emperor asked. Pius VII was "accidentally" met by Napoleon, who appeared to be hunting in the forests of Fontainebleau. This was Napoleon's way of paying homage to the pope in private rather than in the public limelight of Paris. At Notre Dame cathedral Napoleon, who had recently married Josephine in a religious ceremony (there had previously only been a civil one), would not go to confession or receive communion, and refused to receive the crown from the pope. Thereupon Napoleon placed the crown on his own head.

Despite criticism, the pope's going to France was a measurable success. The people in the streets of Paris pressed in on him with unbounded adulation. His visit helped the French to look once more to Rome. He demonstrated that the papacy was not tied to the old regime. But real friction developed when Napoleon, on his own initiative, instituted the feast of St. Napoleon (a doubtfully authentic saint). He rewrote the catechism, inserting his name frequently as the object of loving obedience and veneration for the school children.

The last straw came when he began to conquer all of Europe. He made himself king of Italy, kept the northern papal states and wanted the pope to close the shipping ports of the remaining papal states to the British (Napoleon was trying to starve out the British during his war with them). The pope not only refused, but also asked for his northern papal states back. In 1809, Napoleon responded by confiscating the pope's territories. A general then arrested the pope. After forty-two days of travel, the pope arrived at Savona, where he was held a prisoner. Although Napoleon did not allow him to communicate with the outside world, the pope had a trump card. It was necessary that he invest the newly appointed bishops in their dioceses, but he refused to do so. Pius was cajoled, threatened, and drugged, but he held out. This encouraged the clergy.

In 1812, when Napoleon had the pope removed secretly and by force to a prison in Fontainebleau (south of Paris), Pius VII almost died. He was to stay in prison while Napoleon set out to defeat the Russians, after which Napoleon would come back to deal with the pope. But the Russians defeated Napoleon and destroyed his armies. Because he wanted to raise a new army, Napoleon needed a settlement with the church, and so he sent envoys to the pope. Later, Napoleon himself went to see the prisoner and stayed six days. No one knows what passed between them. There were rumors of hair-pulling and dish-smashing. In any case, the pope agreed to invest the bishops in return for his freedom and the right to exercise his papal powers in France. But Napoleon abused the concession and issued a new concordat. The pope promptly denied it. Napoleon imprisoned him once more.

However, within two years, Napoleon was defeated again, at Waterloo, and the Bourbon king, Louis XVIII, was restored in 1815. The pope was taken in triumph to Rome at the very moment Napoleon was being secretly taken to his exile on the island of Elba. Yet, even after all of the indignities done to him, Pius VII wrote on Napoleon's behalf, asking consideration and easement of his trials on Elba. Napoleon died on May 5, 1821, on the isle of St. Helena. (There is a story that he was slowly poisoned by his jailer.) With supreme illogic, the French soon forgot Napoleon's ambitions, the devastation of property, and the enormous loss of life he wrought all over Europe. His memory soon became the "Napoleonic Legend" and this legend soon became powerful enough among Frenchmen to seat another Bonaparte on the French throne in the future.

AFTER NAPOLEON

A new spirit of liberalism had been unleashed by the French Revolution and spread by Napoleon. Liberty, equality, and justice, although much abused during the past years, were potent ideals which helped to abolish class distinction and opened the way towards democracy. From 1815 to 1870, the church leadership was in a position to adopt these more liberal tenets and to harmonize her old policies with them. But the church did not do so, bringing upon itself considerable chastisement from future historians. However, the context of the times did not warrant such a move. In 1815, Rome was besieged with many problems. In the devastating aftermath of the revolution, the church was looking for stability and peace in order to find solutions to many problems. During the five years of Pius VII's imprisonment, a large number of dioceses in France and its dependencies remained vacant because the pope had withheld his approval of the bishops. The pope's cabinet, the Curia, could not exercise many ordinary duties since the ecclesiastical archives had been removed from Rome to Paris.

Furthermore, after Napoleon was finally defeated, the Treaty of Vienna made many territorial adjustments that vexed Rome. The traditional Catholic Rhineland, as well as parts of Catholic Poland, fell into the hands of Protestant Prussia. In Italy, an army general was trying to build a kingdom south of Rome; Catholic Austria (under conservative Chancellor Metternich) had occupied the northern papal states in order to observe what was happening south of Rome. Revolutionary forces were expelling not only Spanish rule in South America, but also the Catholic church, which was associated with it. Rome was in no mood to embrace liberal ideas. Political conservatism reigned in Rome as it did in Russia, Austria, Sweden, and Holland, nations that extolled "law and order" government.

Besides the political preoccupations of the time there were the spiritual. Monasteries had to be reopened. Religious orders had to be restored. Influenced by Cardinal Consalvi, newly reinstated as his secretary, Pius VII restored the Jesuits in 1814. Seminaries had to be renewed. The Napoleonic wars had taken the lives of millions of young men and a severe shortage of priests resulted. With all of these things on his mind, the pope tended to work with the monarchies (the old regime) at the Congress of Vienna. In principle, Rome by no means gave sanction to such monarchies. It remained neutral. Yet for the life of the church to resume, law and order had to be reestablished. In the eyes of both civil and church leadership the horrors and excesses of the revolutionary forces underscored the need for the old traditional monarchies as the restorers of stability. The Catholic leadership, of course, was under no illusion. It had suffered a great deal from the kings but was inclined to feel that they were not as dangerous as the revolutionaries. This prevailing attitude of favoring monarchies brought the Bourbons back to France and Spain and returned other princes elsewhere. It was with these monarchs that the pope, through Cardinal Consalvi, had to deal at the Congress of Vienna.

CONSALVI AND THE PAPAL STATES

Rome made no attempt to recover its European properties confiscated during the revolution and Napoleonic era; it only insisted on recovering its own papal states. Most of them, thanks to Consalvi, were restored and were allowed to keep some of the reforming changes in administration introduced by Napoleon when he held them. Consalvi, an able diplomat, had no real position from which to bargain. But there was an almost universal admiration for Pius VII, who had withstood Napoleon and whose integrity and strict neutrality induced the other great powers at the Congress of Vienna to restore the papal states to him.

But this was not solely due to admiration. The restoration of the papal states was due more to mutual jealousies and fear among the great powers. Neither the British nor the French wanted Austria (or each other) to possess the papal states. It was, therefore, due to their insistence and diplomacy that these states were returned to the neutral pope. We shall see shortly how the papal states became a severe bone of contention when the liberals wanted to unite Italy. Note that this problem had its immediate origin, not in papal domination, but in European politics which restored the papal states to the pope, because national leaders considered that to be the lesser evil.

There were compelling reasons at that time why Consalvi wanted the pope to possess the papal states. To begin with, the northern papal states were an economic necessity if the pope's office was to function. Furthermore, on another front, Austria had already taken over Venice and Milan and controlled other duchies. Since the pope had barely escaped domination by France, he did not intend to fall into the hands of Austria. Possession of the papal states seemed to be the best protection at the time. We say, "at the time," for we have observed before that the papal states increasingly became more a hindrance than a help. Pepin's gift of these lands initially gave the pope some temporal independence from warring barbarians in Italy. The papal states were also a good buffer for subsequent encroachments. Yet, by the fifteenth and sixteenth centuries, these states became a liability. They kept the popes locked into the role of Italian sovereigns rather than spiritual leaders. It made them Italian princes involved in Italian politics, thus confining their truly Catholic view. When the new nation-states arose in Europe, the papal states had even less value as a source of protection and independence. We have seen how easily the major powers or dictators could take them over. Yet, Consalvi felt that the keeping of the papal states was, at the moment, an advantage to the papacy.

ROME'S ANTI-LIBERALISM

We have noted how both the kings and the leadership of the church tended to become suspicious of liberalism. To them it meant havoc, excess, and political and religious upheaval. The result was, as far as the church was concerned, that wherever liberal movements and revolutions took place, they did so without the approval of the pope. At this time there were several countries where Catholics and liberals collaborated to throw off the government and obtain freedom. Still, Rome disapproved and even opposed them. Consider, for example, what happened in England. By 1800, Ireland and England were joined, the Parliament of Dublin was dissolved, and the Irish members could sit at Westminster. The king, however, insisted on privileges over the Irish Catholic church, since he was supreme head of the English church. He wanted to be able to veto clerical appointments and censor communications with Rome. The British Catholics were ready to accept this, but not the Irish Catholics. Led by Daniel O'Connell, they did not want their church subjected to a Protestant Parliament that had so long oppressed them. O'Connell, therefore, waged a successful nonviolent campaign, got elected to Westminster, despite his ineligibility as a Catholic, and got a seat in Parliament.

The government eventually gave in and, in 1829, removed all the disabilities which had prevented Catholics from taking part in public life. Here was a great victory for the church in this alliance of

Catholics and liberals, but the victory was achieved without the cooperation of Rome.

A similar event happened in the Netherlands, where Catholics and liberals fought side by side to obtain freedom. The Catholic church not only refused to cooperate, but even negotiated with the opposition. Belgium, with a great Catholic majority, was joined to Protestant Holland under the kingship of a Protestant king who proceeded to discriminate against his Catholic subjects. Here again, the liberals and the clergy joined forces to effect the revolution of 1830, by which Belgium gained its independence.

Poland was the most notorious example of this papal rejection of a liberal cause. For years the Poles, thanks to the Jesuits, had remained Catholic. But Poland was partitioned among the powers of Prussia, Austria, and Russia. In 1825, Czar Nicholas I wanted to unite his territories into one land with one sovereign, one law, and one faith. He abolished the Greek churches in union with Rome, and tried to bring the Polish Catholic church into the Greek Orthodox camp. He even intercepted the pope's letters. Yet, in the face of all of this, everyone was astounded when, during the Polish revolt against the czar in 1830, the pope counseled the Polish clergy to tell their people to submit to Russia. After the czar crushed the Polish revolt, the pope sent a letter to the bishops urging their submission to legitimate authority. Liberals everywhere were dismayed at both the pope's lack of support for the oppressed Catholic Poles and his apparent support for the absolutist policies of the czar. Rome had failed to support the Catholics in England, Belgium, and Poland. This lack of support cast a pall over the democratic and liberal movement among Catholics.

Because Rome was either hostile or indifferent to democratic liberal ideals, the church soon ceased to be a formative influence on the age. Rome was reduced to the role of a church upholding the old order of things and producing citizens obedient to the lawful monarch. This was the sort of attitude that led to a certain passivity, made the church a useful tool of despotic kings, and occasioned Karl Marx's well-known statement that religion is the opiate of the people.

This political conservatism of the church had its counterpart in theological conservatism. The Enlightenment and the Napoleonic wars caused great suffering for the religious orders. Catholic or papal universities had been replaced by state universities. This so reduced the church's ability to produce priests and scholars that the formal teaching of theology was relegated to seminaries isolated from the larger intellectual communities, much to the harm of the church. The defects of an isolated religious training apart from the university led to the great efforts of Cardinal Newman of England to found a Catholic university. Similarly, the bishops of the United States were stimulated to establish the Catholic University of America in Washington, D.C.

The net effect was that Rome cut itself off from the intellectual influences of other countries, like Germany, England, and Holland. Rome fell back onto the most sterile area for doing theology, namely Italy. Such political and theological conservatism led succeeding papal administrations to issue a long series of condemnations, excommunications, and suppressions of various theologians and theological schools. The newly shorn-up papacy became the sole arbiter of what was theologically correct (in a departure from the ages where theological ideas were freely critiqued and exchanged). All unfamiliar thinking was uprooted—or perhaps it would be more correct to say, driven underground. Some of these "condemned" theological ideas would later reappear in the aberrations of Modernism (1890-1910) and in the authentic developments of the Second Vatican Council (1962-1965).

RELIGIOUS REVIVAL

Despite the severe efforts to eradicate religion during the French Revolution, there was a revival of religion. In spite of the anti-religious onslaught of the revolution in France, in spite of the attempts at control of the church in places like Austria and Germany, and in spite of the fact that the Enlightenment had greatly influenced the upper class prelates, religion revived or, rather, remained as strong as ever in the hearts of the masses of people. Many clergy, after all, had met death with honor and heroism. While some had denied the old religion, there were others, like the Abbé Pinot, who mounted the scaffold saying, "I will go unto the altar of God." The liturgies celebrated in secret and the devotion of the Romanist clergy contributed a great deal to the prestige of the Catholic church. Many recovered their faith in Christianity. Those groups of people called the "Romantics" were inspired by a new spiritual revolution. They greatly admired medieval Catholicism and its great unifying role. Many of these romantics, such as the Schlegels, Clemens, Brentano, and others, found their spiritual home in the Catholic church. The greatest orator of the time, the Dominican Lacordaire, gave dramatic sermons extolling Catholicism for its social and moral contributions to civilization. Thousands who had lost their faith returned to the Catholic faith because of his sermons.[9]

Along with this religious revival and desire to return to the traditions of the medieval church was the attempt, made by such people as Lacordaire, to reconcile the modern liberties with the church, in spite of the papacy's conservative reaction. There were others who looked to the papacy itself as the one stable guardian of both orthodoxy and political stability (remember, for example, that the Jansenists and the reform Catholics were allied in wanting to reform the church). They believed that nothing could succeed unless the popes were for it. Some went so far as to suggest that, if any future government were to succeed, there must be a union of church and state, but with the papacy dominant. These were the super-Ultramontanes.

LAMENNAIS

Among the super-ultramontanes was a famous name, the Abbé Lamennais. He was an upholder of papal centralization and hostile to the resurgence of Gallicanism in France. At the same time, he saw that the ideas of the French Revolution, though tarnished, were not disappearing. He also observed that the monarchy to which the church was uniting itself was only another form of despotism. The church, he held, should be free of any state association. When Lamennais witnessed the struggles of the Catholics in Ireland, Belgium, and Poland, he began to see the value of democracy and developed new ideas. In 1819, he called on the church to ally itself with all peoples who were striving for independence. He concluded that the church would flourish better in a liberal social order and that the pope, therefore, should not engage in concordats with kings, but should put his faith directly in the people. In Cavour's celebrated phrase, there should be "a free church in a free state."

In 1830, Lamennais began his little review *L'Avenir;* it was to be the most important Catholic journal of the century (though it lasted only a year). He advocated freedom of conscience, religious worship, instruction, opinion, open assembly, and popular elections. He was interested in what was happening at that time in the United

States, where there was no connection between church and state. In fact, the United States Constitution forbade any established church. So, argued Lamennais, let it be in Europe. Let all churches compete privately for people's allegiance. Let them run their own affairs, free of the government.

Lamennais, who was highly respected by some in Rome, felt that if he could get to speak with him, the pope would listen and embrace these ideas. But Lamennais, of course, had his enemies. And then there was Pope Gregory XVI, an honest, reactionary, conservative monk who ran the church like an abbot ran his monastery. Gregory was the pope who disliked trains, refused to back the English and Belgian Catholics, and supported the Russians against the Catholic Poles. He might have been willing to concede to America the things Lamennais said, but in America there was no Gallicanism and no prior traditions of state interference. He could not imagine the same arrangement in Europe. Gregory, an advocate of strict, hierarchical obedience, was not about to give credence to wild revolutionary statements like "power to the people." So when Lamennais and his two companions, Montalembert and Lacordaire, went to Rome, they were coolly received. They had a polite audience with the pope and left Rome in 1832, not expecting immediate approval but not expecting condemnation either.

Lamennais was stunned when the pope issued the encyclical *Mirari Vos* which totally condemned his teachings. Gregory wrote: "From this poisonous spring of indifferentism has also flowed that absurd and erroneous doctrine or rather, the delirium, that freedom of conscience is to be claimed and defended by all men." In 1834, at a time when Lamennais's contemporaries, the Curé of Ars was drawing souls to God, and Bernadette Soubirous was beginning her visions at Lourdes, another encyclical was issued that condemned liberal ideas. Lamennais lost faith in Rome. He left the priesthood and the church. He died in 1852, bitter, unreconciled to the church, and so poor that he was buried in an unmarked pauper's grave. Rome had thus laid the groundwork for the even more anti-liberal Syllabus of Errors (1864) of Pius IX.

It goes without saying that Lamennais's ideas are accepted today by most modern nations and can be found in the Second Vatican Council's Declaration on Religious Liberty (1965). Yet, his ideas were too novel for the pope who, like most of his contemporaries, Catholic and Protestant alike, could not conceive of a government by the people, a free press, toleration, and the disestablishment of the church and state. Unfortunately, in condemning these democratic ideas, Gregory used such strong language that he offended even those well disposed to the church. As for those hostile to the church, Gregory's condemnation led to the conclusion that to be liberal meant that one was also anti-clerical. To fight for freedom was automatically to be against the church. It is no wonder that the church would take a long time to shake off the image of being a friend to tyranny and a foe to freedom. Only with Leo XIII (d. 1903) and Pius XII (d. 1958) would the papacy begin to understand and address, very cautiously to be sure, the social and scientific problems of the time. Only with Vatican II would the leadership of the church officially and openly embrace the liberal aspirations of humanity.

The church would remain a cautionary force against that tyranny which claimed the title of revolution and reason. The church would be wary of any system that merely substituted one repression for another and that would denigrate religion as peripheral. If one's inner moral persuasion is not motivated by religion, then one can more easily be manipulated by external forces. This is the reason why external control and conformity become primary objectives of totalitarian governments. Arnold Toynbee says of the era we have just covered:

The revolution's supreme paradox was that, in the act of deposing the traditional Christian "establishment," it opened the way for an atavistic return to pre-Christian religion: the worship of collective human power which had been the religion of the pagan Roman empire and of the Greek city-states which the Roman Empire had incorporated. This worship of human power is about ninety per cent of the religion of about ninety per cent of the present generation of mankind. Shall we succeed in shaking it off? And, if we remain enslaved to it, whither will it lead us?...[10]

CHAPTER 20

The Age of Pius IX

LIBERAL TO CONSERVATIVE

When the ultra-conservative Gregory XVI died in 1846, a compromise candidate was elected—a young man of fifty-four who has had the longest reign of any pope to date. This man was Pius IX,[1] who set the tone for the church until the mid-twentieth century and gave the image of the papacy that the contemporary Catholic knows. Pius was a man of much personal charm, though of no great intellect. He was also a home-grown product, in that he had been outside the papal states only once. This drawback did not prepare him well to deal with the world problems unleashed by the French Revolution that confronted him.

At the beginning, there was promise. He became the instant darling of the liberals by granting amnesty to thousands of his predecessor's exiled enemies, and he displayed many other liberal trends. His name was on everyone's lips. The big question was whether Pius would show such a liberal spirit in politics. There were several revolutions in the making, not the least of which was the one in Italy itself. We might recall that the conservative Austrians had stationed themselves in the northern papal states to offset the liberal revolutionary forces in southern Italy. Everyone wondered which groups the pope would back. At first, the pope seemed to side with the liberals, for he set up a form of representative government right in his own papal states. This alarmed Metternich, the conservative Austrian chancellor, who occupied another papal state, until the pope forced him to withdraw. The liberals' admiration for this papal act knew no bounds, and Catholics and Protestants alike heaped praise on the pontiff—but not for long.

Pius IX granted other liberties in the papal states, giving Rome its own elective government, freedom of the press, and a constitution with the power to veto his own proposals. This last step went a bit beyond where he wanted to go in temporal matters and put him in a dilemma. Suppose, for example, that the papal states voted to oust Catholic Austria altogether? Could the pope go along? If he did, could he thereby condone the inevitable war between his Catholic children? Could he afford to support a war against his prime mainstay, his protector in time of crisis? This was the dilemma that broke Pius's liberal cause against the Austrians. Liberals everywhere immediately disapproved, and the pope's huge popularity dwindled as quickly as it had arisen. Later, when an invading army had been routed by the Austrians, the pope's lack of support was blamed for the defeat.

PREMATURE ITALIAN REVOLUTION

Reaction to the pope showed itself in the increasingly liberal demands made by the citizens of Rome. A series of Roman leaders could not bridge the growing gap between papacy and the city's inhabitants. Unfortunately, the one leader moderate enough to be acceptable to both the pope and the people of Rome was murdered by Italian army volunteers. This event ended the rapport between the pope and the liberals. Tension grew until, on November 24, 1848, a mob surrounded the pope's palace and murdered the papal prime minister, Rossi, at the Cancellaria Palace. Pius IX, dressed as a simple priest, then fled to southern Italy (near Naples). In his absence, a new assembly convened in Rome and, in the hope of advancing an Italian revolution, summoned the non-Roman and anti-clerical Mazzini and his guerilla leader, Garibaldi. Pius IX sought help from the Catholic countries of Europe. At first, these Catholic powers were slow to move (mired in old jealousies and competition), but Louis Napoleon of France finally ousted Mazzini. Pius was restored to Rome in 1850. It is understandable why he wanted no more representative government in the papal states. The bloodshed, power struggles, and intrigues were, unfortunately, Pius's personal experience with liberal politics. Equally unfortunately, he had to deal not only with liberals but also with the most extreme and anti-clerical liberals. Even if Pius had stayed in Rome, "...it is hard to believe that he could have collaborated for long with the more extreme Italian liberals like Mazzini and Garibaldi. Their religious positions were irreconcilable, and Pio Nono was above all a man of religion."[2] The net effect was to make Pius forever suspicious of liberal ideas and movements. He did not condemn them outright, but he had been deeply frightened by what he had experienced. Under the influence of his ultra-conservative secretaries of state, such as Lambruschini and Antonelli, Pius could find no good in liberal causes, even the liberal Catholic movement.

THE PROTESTANT COUNTRIES

We have noted that the efforts of Daniel O'Connell of Ireland led to the passing of a Catholic Emancipation Act passed in England in 1829. That act removed most of the political disabilities for Catholics. Irish emigration continued to flood England. The time had come for considering the restoration of the Catholic hierarchy in England, a prospect most agreeable to England in 1848 (for Catholic England had been a "missionary" country overseen by Apostolic Vicars). While Pius IX was preparing for such a restoration, the Italian Revolution began. When Pius sought to resume negotiations regarding England in 1850, he met an entirely different mood. The English detested Pius as a tyrant because the Roman Revolution had been suppressed. For that reason the old hatreds of the "foreign and immoral" pope, which were nourished during the days of the Reformation, were revived. It was the least opportune moment to negotiate the restoration of the Catholic hierarchy. Riots broke out in England. Pius was burned in effigy.

Galling restrictions were placed on the proposed Catholic restoration. For example, the pope could not choose dioceses that were already Anglican. (Thus the major Catholic diocese in England is not Canterbury, but Winchester.) With bitter sadness, English Catholics had to forego historical places like Canterbury, York, Lincoln, and Salisbury, all of which played significant parts in Catholic medieval history. Saints' names and titles already used by the Anglicans could not be used for Catholic parishes. Catholic public processions were banned, and the clergy could not wear clerical clothes in public. Yet, in spite of all these restrictions (many of which were soon left unenforced), the Catholic hierarchy was restored.

The same routine occurred in Holland, where Pius restored the hierarchy in 1853. Again public outrage was expressed against Catholics. At one point, the people even toppled the local government. The objections to Catholicism decreased in time. The same was true in Prussia, where the church was permitted freedom. Surprisingly, the church was freer to fulfill her mission in Protestant Holland, England, and Prussia than in the Catholic countries, especially in Hapsburg Austria and Gallican France.

IMMACULATE CONCEPTION

When Pius IX returned from exile in 1850, he attributed his restoration to the intercession of the Blessed Mother (he had always had a great devotion to Mary). He was, therefore, predisposed to listen to the petition from his theological commission and others to define her Immaculate Conception. While in exile, he had asked the bishops for their opinions on this matter. Most of the replies were favorable. On December 8, 1854, the dogma expressing the church's long-held belief in Mary's special holiness was proclaimed. Devotion to Mary thereby received a great spur. (Less than a hundred years later, in 1950, another pope, Pius XII, would proclaim the doctrine of the Assumption.) It is important to note that Pius IX acted on his own authority in proclaiming the Immaculate Conception, even though he had consulted the bishops. He proclaimed the dogma alone without waiting to call a council. This had the effect of elevating his authority, which was further elevated with the First Vatican Council's declaration of papal primacy and infallibility in 1870.

LOSS OF THE PAPAL STATES

Despite the premature revolution of 1848 in Italy, which caused the pope to equate liberalism and rebellion, the liberal spirit still flourished. The liberal spirit found its nationalistic outlet in the *Risorgimento*, or the movement for the unification of all Italy. Naturally, this implied the absorption of the papal states, the end of the church's control of education and marriage, and the abolition of all monasteries. All eyes were turned toward the state of Piedmont whose leader, Victor Emmanuel II, had an army that might be able to expel the Austrians. Pius IX might have gone along with a program of Italian unification by urging Austria to leave Italy, if the nationalists would guarantee that the church would be left in peace. But there was every indication that the government of Piedmont was anti-clerical. In its own territory it had abolished church courts, feast days, and clerical immunities. Under the very able minister, Cavour, a proposal was made to suppress monasteries not engaged in "useful" work. What most upset the pope was that there were no negotiations on these church matters; they were done unilaterally and portended a continued anti-clerical policy.

We mentioned that unification implied the absorption of the papal states. Actually, some of the papal states in the north had experienced a better, more democratic, and more efficient government with Napoleon. They were displeased to be back under the antiquated regime of the pope. The educated classes resented that canon law had weight in civil matters and that the courts might impose fines and even imprisonment for "crimes" such as eating meat on Friday. Such states were already on the edge of revolt. Most of the papal states were run poorly, though not as badly as the nationalists' anti-papal propaganda suggested. The pope tended to look on these states as his little papal family. Initially, there were some attempts to find an honorable place for the pope (as pope-president) in an Italian confederation. But Lambruschini and Antonelli blocked any attempts to reform the economic and political situation, and they refused to listen to any proposal in which the papal states would be incorporated into an Italian confederation.

In July 1858, a secret meeting was held between Cavour and Napoleon III to liquidate the papal states. Once the Austrians were driven out, the northern papal states invited Victor Emmanuel to take over—which he gladly did, with Napoleon's approval. The pope realized that he could no longer rely on Austria or France to protect his property. He decided to raise his own international army in spite of the protest of his secretary of state, Antonelli, who saw this as a move that would annoy France. While France allowed a takeover of the northern papal states, it had no intention of letting

Rome fall to the nationalists.

In 1860, Garibaldi arrived in Sicily and advanced to Naples. Not wanting Garibaldi to advance far enough to take all of Italy, Cavour, with his Piedmontese troops, headed south to forestall Garibaldi. To do so, Cavour had to invade the papal states, in his words, "to restore order." The international papal army was soon routed and the papal territory was reduced to a narrow strip of land. At the same time, France was engaged in war with Germany and was forced to withdraw her troops from Italy. Ten years later, on September 20, 1870, the army entered Rome, and the papal states disappeared forever.

The new government went out of its way to be respectful of the pope. It was seeking recognition from abroad and could not afford to estrange the Catholics in Italy and elsewhere. The pope was given the rights of a sovereign; he could maintain his own postal and diplomatic services. In hindsight, it would seem that the pope was better off without these temporal territories, which had sapped the time and energy of many popes in past centuries. But it was a disaster to Pius IX, and one which he protested by making himself a "voluntary prisoner of the Vatican" and refusing to recognize the new government.

THE SYLLABUS OF ERRORS (1864)

To understand why the Syllabus was disastrous, we must remember that the pope had just lost the papal states to those who felt that they were acting in the name of progress, liberalism, and civilization. These same catchwords were being used by revolutionaries in France and elsewhere. The pope and his advisors came to see political issues only in terms of black and white. The pope equated liberal with being anti-church—and this in spite of the fact that some liberals were devout believers, such as Prime Minister Gladstone of England (a devout Anglican) and the Italian author, Manzoni, who wrote the most famous novel of the time, *The Betrothed*. However, Pius elevated reaction to liberalism (as he understood it) to a theological principle. The Syllabus of Errors, which was contained in the encyclical *Quanta Cura* (issued in 1864), comprises eighty theological and political statements that condemned such concepts as progress, liberalism, and modern civilization. Most of the Syllabus was taken from previous encyclicals and therefore should have been read in their context, but few did so. The Syllabus itself carried the signature of Antonelli, not Pius IX. Still, many thought that it was an infallible pronouncement, despite Bishop Dupanloup's efforts to demonstrate that this work needed to be seen within its Italian setting.

The Syllabus was second only to Gregory's *Mirari Vos* as the papacy's clearest rejection of the movements and ideas of the nineteenth century. The language of the document was not only extreme, but it also gave the impression that it was intended for the whole world when, in reality, the pope was thinking of the local Italian scene. What were Protestants and Catholics to think of a pope who condemned liberalism, a free press, freedom of conscience, civil rights, and even modern civilization? Prime Minister Gladstone and President Lincoln were perplexed, to say the least. Those less favorable to the pope gave the Syllabus the widest publicity. Lamennais's old friends in France, Lacordaire and Montalembert, were disturbed, and the Syllabus led Montalembert to end his campaign (which he shared with Frederick Ozanam) for a "free church in a free state."

The Syllabus also dealt a stunning blow to the Catholic intellectual movement and widened the split between Catholic conservatives and Catholic liberals. In Germany, the Syllabus depressed the great Catholic historian, Dollinger. The Syllabus pleased Ultramontanes, such as Louis Veuillot, Archbishop Manning of England, and W.G. Ward (who said he would be happy to have a "papal bull with his breakfast every morning"). In any case, the popular mind interpreted the Syllabus as an official and infallible teaching indicating that the church was opposed to modern liberties. In this light, it is easy to see why the campaign to promote papal infallibility raised such alarm for some. If the pope, who had just condemned modern liberties and reasserted the superiority of the church over the state, was declared infallible, where would that leave the modern governments and their subjects? The infallibility issue could only increase political tension.

VATICAN I

Pius IX had considered calling a general council for some time. In 1869, he did so. The previous council of Trent had defined its dogmas to counter another Christian alternative. Now, because the Enlightenment had denied the very idea of divine revelation, the church had to define itself anew. It had to look at its relationship to the new democratic governments. In addition, there was much agitation about papal authority and infallibility, both promoted by the Ultramontanes. In fact, the conservative Jesuit weekly *La Civilta Cattolica* suggested that, when the bishops met,[3] the First Vatican Council would define by acclamation the doctrinal points in the Syllabus of Errors as well as papal infallibility. Progressive church leaders were especially distressed with this linking of the Syllabus with the concept of papal infallibility, because it made infallibility seem like another bulwark against modern democracy.

There were other things, too, that bothered the progressive wing of church leadership. They disliked the very conservative tenor of the proposed constitutions (schema) that would be discussed. In the schema dealing with "faith," the liberal bishops disliked the contempt that the conservatives had for all Protestant thinkers. At one of the early sessions, the liberal Croatian bishop, Joseph Strossmayer, protested their attributing all of the church's ills to Protestants or Protestantism. He reminded his listeners that rationalism had taken root in Catholic France, and that many Protestants had good will towards the church. The conservative majority, objecting to this soft talk about Protestants, warned Strossmayer about expressing his high regard for Protestants. The bishop defended his right to be heard but was shouted down with cries of "He is another Luther! Throw him out!"

Another major schema proposed for discussion dealt with the church in general, papal primacy in particular, and the relationship of church and state, a topic which had been much debated since the French Revolution. Through the "requests committee," which allowed the bishops to suggest topics other than those on the council's official agenda, many amendments about papal infallibility were added to this document, so that it was sent back to committee for revision. What resulted was a shorter document dealing only with the papacy: its origin and history, as well as papal primacy and infallibility. (It was expected that the issue of "church" would be dealt with at a later session.) No one was surprised at this development, because of all the preconciliar predictions and the strong pro-infallibility majority at the council. In addition, Pius himself let it be known that he favored the ultramontane perspective on infallibility.

But there was also a strong anti-infallibility minority at the council. Some bishops were outright opposed to the doctrine. Others however emphasized that this was an inopportune time for such a definition, and that a definition was unnecessary because the infallibility of the church was already generally accepted. Many of them believed that this definition would set back Protestant-Catholic relations. The bishops of the United States felt that any definition of papal infallibility would discourage persons from joining the Catholic church. The greatest thinker of the day, John Henry Newman (who had been invited to the council by personal letter of Pius IX, but declined because of ill health), characterized the definition as premature, unnecessary, and a concession to the Ultramontanes. He wrote, "...What have we done to be treated as the faithful never were treated before? When has a definition *de fide* been a luxury of devotion and not a stern painful necessity? Why should an aggressive and insolent faction be allowed to 'make the heart of the just sad, whom the Lord hath now made sorrowful.'"[4] He was irritated because the Ultramontanes were pushing the infallibility dogma for personal and political reasons. He felt that the whole community of the church should be consulted: "We do not move at railroad pace in theological matters even in the nineteenth century. We must be patient and that for two reasons, first in order to get at the truth, and next in order to carry others with us. The church moves as a whole; it is not a mere philosophy, it is a communion."[5]

Others suggested that infallibility would be terribly misunderstood. It might imply mind-control by the pope, the abolition of all liberties, and that all words from the pope, even the most off-hand utterance, might be construed as infallible. Most German theologians thought the matter indefinable and feared more Roman centralization. Some bishops were not impressed with the low level of the theological education of the Spanish and Italian bishops who were pro-infallibility. Dollinger, Newman, Lord Acton, Ketteler (the founder of Catholic Social Action), Dupanloup, Montalembert, and other notables all opposed the definition. Ultramontanes like Manning, Veuillot, Ward, and others were for it. They and their sympathizers, particularly the Ultramontane press, spread slanderous and inaccurate stories, implying that those who were against the definition of papal infallibility were not good and loyal Catholics.

The debates on infallibility took place during May and June of 1870. Some objected to the proposed declaration on the grounds that nothing was said about the power of the bishops. They pointed out that each bishop was autonomous in his own diocese and his authority was derived from God and not the pope (which is the view held today). Pius IX and others disagreed, stating that the pope had full power in jurisdiction all over the world. Some of the minority bishops, about eighty of them, rather than embarrass the pope by voting negatively, left Rome the day before the vote was taken.

Finally, the day arrived. It was July, and a summer thunderstorm made St. Peter's so dark that the pope needed a candle to read the constitution, *Pastor Aeternus*, in which papal infallibility had been overwhelmingly approved by the 535 bishops present. Only two voted *non placet*, and afterwards they called for another vote that the issue might be passed unanimously. (One was Bishop Fitzgerald of Little Rock, Arkansas. Later the wits commented how the Little Rock submitted to the Big Rock.) Meanwhile the Franco-Prussian war became more intense. France pulled its troops out of Rome. The Italian army moved in and Pius had to suspend the council indefinitely. Vatican I was never officially reassembled, so the first act of Vatican II was to close Vatican I.

The final decree on infallibility reads:

The Roman Pontiff, when he speaks ex cathedra, that is, when exercising the office of pastor and teacher of all Christians, defines with his supreme apostolic authority a doctrine concerning faith or morals to be held by the universal church, through the divine assistance promised to him by St. Peter, is possessed of that infallibility with which the divine Redeemer willed his church to be endowed in defining doctrine concerning faith and morals: and therefore such definitions of the Roman Pontiff are irreformable of themselves and not from the consent of the church.

The last clause is still subject to misinterpretation. This statement was inserted at the last moment and was intended to deal a death blow to conciliarism. The final clause did not imply that the pope could define something in opposition to the whole church. We must also note that the definition of the pope's infallibility is linked to that of the church's infallibility, which has never been defined.[6] Once the definition was given, Newman, for example, accepted it, and in his famous *Letter to the Duke of Norfolk* explained the definition satisfactorily to many. On the other hand, Dollinger and some of the German Catholic intellectuals refused to submit, denying that the council was ecumenical or that the definition was freely made.

They remained faithful to the "old" Catholic church (meaning pre-Vatican I) and today they are known as the Old Catholics.

RESULTS OF THE DEFINITION

Many conservative trends started before Vatican I were confirmed by the conciliar definition of infallibility. The old scholasticism in the spirit of Thomas Aquinas had been revived by the Jesuits. After Vatican I, this conservative neo-Scholasticism became the dominant school. Other schools of theology were looked on with suspicion, especially the forward-looking German schools. Recall that, after the destruction of the Catholic universities during the wars of religion, joint Catholic-Protestant theological faculties were founded in the universities. Among these were Tübingen University, founded by Drey and Mohler, Munich University, which housed Dollinger, the greatest Catholic historian of the day, and Bonn University. Such German experimentation and thought were considered too liberal by Rome, which sought to protect Catholic theologians from Protestant "contamination." With chastisements from Pope Gregory XVI, Pius IX's predecessor, and the pronouncement of papal infallibility, such liberal German schools declined, and the German conservative, neo-Scholastic schools gained the ascendancy. It was the same with liberal Catholic thought in France and England. The proclamation of infallibility was a victory for neo-Scholastic conservative forces and Thomism was on its way to becoming (as it did under Leo XIII) the "official" theological system of the church. Intellectual vitality dried up, and there soon were no intellectual links between the papacy and the liberal middle class. Rome alone became the source of theological approval. This meant that the curia became more powerful, because this official papal cabinet often spoke in the pope's name. The curia was notoriously conservative and saw to it that no new theological developments were approved. This attitude explains the theological explosion at Vatican II in the 1960s. When the lid that kept theological expression in check was removed, ninety years of repressed thoughts forced their way to the surface.

Politically, we have already noted that the papacy viewed any Catholic political party as potential national bodies capable of separating themselves from Rome, just as the national hierarchies had done in the past. The Vatican felt that Catholic liberals might side with their national leadership rather than with Rome. After Vatican

I in 1870, liberal Catholic leaders found themselves in a position of less influence than ever before. They witnessed their cherished dreams practically condemned by Rome. (This was one result of the excesses of those Ultramontanes who identified the Syllabus with infallibility.) In such countries as France and Germany, political issues could not help but involve Catholics, yet Rome did not and would not give any support to them. In Italy, Catholics were forbidden to vote or take part in political life. Their absence created a vacuum which was filled by the anti-clericals. In Germany, Bismarck's *Kulturkampf* (struggle against the church) tried to pry Catholics from Rome, but it only succeeded in creating a Catholic political party that Rome was forced to recognize.

Rome retreated more and more into itself. Rome—the pope and the curia—took on the aura of standing apart from the world, as if it were the last citadel of truth. Thus, Rome backed the old monarchies and suspected any social reform. Catholic social reformers, such as Buchez in France (the father of French trade unionism), and Gorres in Germany, had no support from the Vatican. So, while some Catholics were working hard for social reform and democracy, most Catholics, because of the attitude of the papacy, withdrew from the field. In such isolation, no one could really help Rome to understand the real problems in the church. The church's image became that of the closed corporation, one hostile to democratic freedom and to the world at large. Pius IX placed the church in a ghetto, and it was not until Pope John XXIII that it emerged.

CULT OF THE POPES

Pius IX, a man of great personal charm, enjoyed great prestige among Catholics. He was admired for his courage when he was being persecuted by the Italian liberals. To the Ultramontanes, he represented the one stabilizing force in Europe after the excesses of the French Revolution and Napoleon. Extremists began to look on him almost as an eighth sacrament. Thus, the Jesuits, in their conservative newspaper, would depict the pope's function in these words: "...treasures of revelation, treasures of truth, treasures of justice, treasures of charismata, coming from God are deposited on the earth in the hands of a man who is their sole dispenser and guardian...this man is the pope...and in respect to us he would seem to be

Christ, if he were himself and visibly here below to govern the church."

After Vatican I, the mystique of the pope grew even more. Groups were dedicated to his cause. The revival of Peter's Pence gave him financial independence. The almost mystical awe that modern Catholics associate with the pope began with Pius IX. He was accessible to all Catholics. He was the first pope to give many audiences to groups and individuals. He introduced the practice of *ad limina* visits, which required bishops to make regular trips— about once every five years—to see the pope. He widely conferred the papal title of monsignor, which served to link the lower clergy, priests, directly with Rome, and saw that the Roman liturgy was adopted everywhere. In reaction to Victor Emmanuel's seizure of Rome, he made himself a "voluntary prisoner of the Vatican" and won the sympathy of many.

ASSESSMENT OF THE AGE

The biggest failure of Pius IX was his inability to read the signs of the times. He treated Catholic liberals as less than loyal and favored the conservative Ultramontanes. This is not to imply that progressives of every type were guiltless. Some liberals tended to naivete. Others felt that if humanity had the chance to be educated, to be free of all authority, then progress would be inevitable and the millenium would arrive. But most governments of the time wanted to keep things as they had been, and so did most Catholics. Pius IX was a child of his time and could not be expected to suddenly drop old traditions in order to embrace the new liberalisms; he had personally experienced the consequences of the excesses of these new movements. He and his successors were faced with rapid change and tremendous challenge. Robert Cross comments:

> The problem [of reconciling the church with a new era] is most severe in periods of rapid cultural change like the nineteenth century when traditional policies are satisfactory to neither the cautious nor the confident. Through the preceding century, the rationalism of the Enlightenment had been reconciled, to the satisfaction of most Catholics, with the trusting faith demanded by Christian orthodoxy. But the problems presented to the church by Newton, Locke, and Voltaire were trivial compared

to the challenges of scientists like Lyell, Darwin, and Virchow, of philosophers like Bentham and Spencer, of historians like Strauss and Renan. The collapse of the old regimes during and after the French Revolution also drastically affected the church. Catholic leaders, accustomed to dealing with anointed monarchs, were confronted with governments conceived in revolution, and dedicated to the rights of man and the sovereignty of the people. Social relationships were also in flux. Moral theologians, therefore, had to turn to such novel problems as the ethical responsibilities of factory owners and industrial laborers. Parish priests had to learn how to care for a flock not scattered over a countryside, but jammed into urban tenements. And the immense migrations from country to city, from nation to nation, even from continent to continent, taxed the ingenuity of bishops to build diverse classes and nationalities into a unified church.

In the face of these confusing developments, the prevailing confidence of eighteenth-century Catholicism gave way to fear and suspicion. Catholics began to demand greater vigilance in distinguishing and defending the City of God from the City of Man.

...The Society of Jesus, which in the eighteenth century had supplied many spokesmen for the Catholic rapprochement with modern tendencies, now took the lead in combatting the age.... Catholic doctrine should be taught in its full stringency, allowing no concession to the predilections of the age of "liberty of conscience."...Many who preached in this way were avowed traditionalists, who refused to acknowledge that they advocated the slightest modification of historical Catholicism to fit the new circumstances of the age.... By 1860, these activist conservatives had almost unanimously subscribed to two such developments: the increased centralization of the church under a papacy of unlimited power; and an intensified devotionalism.[7]

Still, Pius IX should have noted that education was rapidly taking place in Europe and that he would have to deal with this transformation of minds and increase of knowledge in ways other than suppression. He was helped neither by his curia, which boasted no intellectuals, nor by the church in Rome, which was at a low theological ebb. Much of his thought has since been disregarded. Vatican II reversed much of what Pius IX taught. The 1965 Declaration on Religious Liberty, for example, has reversed Pius IX's policy as expressed in the 1864 Syllabus of Errors. The Second Vatican Council also adopted many of Newman's ideas, which so distressed the Ultramontanes of his time: "It is Newman's profoundly historical mind which places him in the tradition which has finally reached recognition in the Second Vatican Council; and it is that historical attitude which commends this council to English-speaking peoples of today."[8] Perhaps the best conclusion to the age of Pio Nono is expressed by the historian von Aretin:

> The history of the papacy from 1831 to 1878 is a story both significant and depressing. Except for the short interlude from 1846 to 1848, the papacy grew ever more confident in its antagonism to the age. This reactionary attitude became an inherent part of the church and ultimately prevented it from exerting any kind of positive and formative influence.
>
> The reign of Pius IX certainly had its impressive aspects. But his many widespread condemnations affected such varied issues as liberalism, pantheism, naturalism, absolute rationalism, indifferentism, communism, secret societies, bible societies, freedom of worship, free speech, and many more besides. Ultimately, Pius made no contribution to the social problems of human society, nor to any of the great issues of his age.[9]

Yet, for the sake of balance, there is another perspective on the church's reaction to the times. The nineteenth century was indeed a time when all churches lost confidence in themselves and were faced with the choice of withdrawing from the modern world or accommodating themselves to it. Pius IX, as we saw, chose the former and has been greatly criticized for that choice. Most Protestant churches chose the latter and have, in recent times, come in for their share of criticism as well. The result of their marriage to that age was a decline of creedal certitude and moral fervor. Historian R.R. Palmer writes:

> Church attendance among Protestants became increasingly casual, and the doctrines set forth in sermons seemed increasingly remote. Protestantism traditionally trusted their own private judgment and regarded the clergy as their own agents, not as authoritative teachers placed above them. Protestants

also had always set especial emphasis on the Bible as the source of religious belief, and as doubts accumulated on the literal truth of Biblical narratives, there seemed no other source on which to rely.[10]

Interestingly, those historians who hold such a view maintain that of the two choices of withdrawal or accommodation, the Catholic church under Pius IX and his successors made the wiser choice in the long run. In their eyes, Catholicism more effectively resisted the secularism of the times and insulated itself from the disasters of the twentieth century. Thus, instead of criticizing Pius IX's choice, it can be said:

...many secular historians, accepting the premise that Christianity and culture truly were incompatible in the nineteenth century, regard the strategy of ultramontanism, however reactionary it might appear, as eminently sensible and astute. Through the trials of the period the Catholic church, unlike its Protestant counterparts, remained true to itself and occupied a powerful defensive position from which it could reemerge as a political and social force when the energies of modernity had played themselves out in the catastrophe of the twentieth century.[11]

CHAPTER 21

The New Governments

THE WORLD SCENE

As we move into the twentieth century we must give a quick survey of the world scene and the reactions to it of the popes of that time. The popes we have in mind must be considered as a unit, because their reigns together form a pattern of the church's activity during these times. The three popes are Leo XIII (1878-1903), Pius X (1903-1914), and Benedict XV (1914-1922). It was these popes who had to deal with a rapidly changing world in which the church was playing a less and less important part.

OVERSEAS EXPANSION

The end of the nineteenth century and the beginning of the twentieth was the period of what is called the "Europeanization" of the world. With every European nation scrambling for more outside territory, the overriding concern soon was for a "balance of power,' so that one nation would not be more powerful than any other. Spain was forced to give Cuba independence and to cede Puerto Rico and the Philippines to the United States as a result of the Spanish American War of 1898. Japan, as we have seen, was opened by the missionaries, closed to foreigners, and then reopened in 1854. In due time Japan became industrialized, Europeanized, and imperialist. It engaged in the Sino-Japanese war of 1894 and obtained Korea and Formosa (today's Taiwan). In the Opium War of 1839-1842, China was forced to admit Britain, and soon other Western states tried to parcel it up. By the early 1900s, three-fifths of the entire area of Asia was ruled by the European powers and the United States. By 1914, for example, the British Empire took in one-fourth of this earth's land and one-fourth its population, including India, Hong Kong, Cyprus, and parts of Africa. In 1914, Europe owned almost all of Africa.

One result of all this imperialist ferver was a new and intense spirit of nationalism, economic competition, and rivalry. Nations tried to outmaneuver each other as they were "arming for peace." Historian Carlton Hayes provides a good description of the situation that was building up to World War I.

In 1913 the international situation was extraordinarily perilous. Recurrent crises in Morocco and in the Near East had cost every Great Power some measure of prestige. Germany had been outplayed in the Moroccan crisis by France and Great Britain. Yet France had been forced to cede African territory to Germany, and Great Britain to yield predominance in the Ottoman Empire. Russia had been outplayed in the successive Near Eastern crises by Austria-Hungary and Germany. Yet Austria-Hungary had been flouted by Serbia and held in leash by Italy and Germany had to face the fact that instead of exercising an hegemony in Europe, as she had done in the days of Bismarck, she was now "encircled" by a ring of potentially hostile Powers.

...Naval rivalry was in full swing.... Imperialistic rivalry...was intensified for all these Powers...Nationalism in an aggravated form, was everywhere rampant; it was dictating to governments an emotional, rather than a reasoned, behavior; and, quite triumphant now in the Balkans, it threatened speedily to become so throughout east-central Europe.[1]

INDUSTRIAL REVOLUTION

Besides the political revolutions taking place during the lifetimes of these popes, there was also the industrial revolution. After the 1830s, mechanization and industry spread quickly. Fulton invented the steamboat in 1807, and Morse gave us the telegraph in 1837. By 1870, the world had seen the coming of the Gatling machine gun (then regarded as the ultimate weapon and as such was supposed to herald the end of warfare), the Bessemer steel furnace, and dynamite. By the turn of the century, the world had witnessed the birth of a practical submarine, the wireless, the refrigerator, the sewing machine, the bicycle, the diesel engine, and the automobile. The Wright Brothers of Dayton gave us the airplane in 1903.

What was of chief importance for the church and for society was the introduction of the factory system and the rise of a new propertyless, moneyless class—the proletariat. Those people had only their labor to sell and were easy targets for exploitation. At the same time, governments abandoned the idea of liberal self-determination for the sake of new national priorities and national conformity. This was done because nations were competing both financially and industrially. As each nation sought to consolidate its identity and to subordinate all interests to the state, the church was increasingly regarded as something to be likewise brought under state control—or at least made impotent so as not to stand in the way of "progress."

INTELLECTUAL REVOLUTION

Science was advancing and soon made its impact felt in the life of the average person. Advances were being made in natural history, botany, and geology. The earth's surface was being studied as never before. The geologist Lyell demonstrated that the earth was millions of years old. Perhaps the high point of intellectual and popular awe was the theory of Charles Darwin, who shook the world in 1859 with his explanation of evolution, and shook Christian believers in their interpretation of the Bible. The result of all the new knowledge culled from anthropology, archaeology, and the other sciences was to bring into vogue the educated skeptic. Karl Marx issued his famous *Communist Manifesto* in 1848. Philosophers like Huxley, Haeckel, and Spencer formulated materialistic theories. Schopenhauer and Nietzsche extolled the human will and natural instinct with its consequent tendency to trample on the weak for the sake of the survival of the elite. Such ideas were eagerly received in an age of growing militarism, imperialism, and nationalism.

As we have indicated, the new theories concerning human origins and the age of the earth deeply affected biblical understanding and the faith of believers. D.F. Strauss wrote his *Life of Jesus*, denying the possibility of miracles and the supernatural nature of Christ. In 1862, J.E. Renan published his *Life of Jesus*, which portrayed Jesus as a self-deluded prophet and Christianity as a fabrication. Among the intelligentsia, religion was falling further into disrepute. The industrial revolution and the new city life were loosening the ties people had with their traditional religious affiliations. The nations promoted the new nationalism as if it were a religion. It was this nationalism that accused the denominational Christian (especially Catholics) of being less than a good citizen by reason of their religious commitments.

This, then, was the world inhabited by the church in the early 1900s. It was a world of contrast and contest. The church was alternating between resistance and accommodation to the new governments; anti-clerical governments were bent on subduing and emasculating the church in their drive for the self-determination, nationalism, and imperialism, all of which would eventually lead to World War I. It was also to be a contest between the church leadership's conservative theological approach to the new discoveries in scholarship and those who sought some kind of rapport with the modern world. We must now see how the popes and other church leaders acted in such times.

FRANCE

After the defeat of Napoleon (1815), the monarchy had been restored in France, but it did not last long. Louis Philippe, who succeeded King Charles X, acquired Algeria for France, but could not withstand the various resisting factions. Many, particularly the clergy, wanted the restoration of the Bourbon monarchy. But in 1848, a revolt forced Louis Philippe to flee to England, and a Second French Republic was founded with Louis Napoleon as its president. However, in 1852, he established a new empire with himself as Napoleon III. We have also seen that he was entangled in the attempt to unify Italy. Napoleon III came to the aid of Victor Emmanuel but, when the latter was victorious, Napoleon's fears of a united Italy returned. He tried to withdraw suggesting a compromise that would leave Italy still divided. The Italian patriots were duly outraged and forced Napoleon to recognize their achievement. He lost much prestige in France because of this, and his later failures to take over Spanish Mexico and to defeat Bismarck in the Franco-Prussian war of 1870. A Third Republic, born of humiliation and defeat in the war of 1870 with Prussia, replaced him. This new government was liberal, imperialistic, and anti-clerical.

ANTI-CLERICALISM

At the time of the Franco-Prussian War, Rome's attitude was definitely pro-monarchy; Pius IX was deeply suspicious of any liberalism or democracy such as that represented by the Third Republic of France. The new government retaliated with anti-clerical measures. The Jesuits were expelled, a divorce law was published, and education was secularized. The next pope, Leo XIII (1878-1903), was quick to understand the problem. He perceived that Rome's persistent support of the old monarchies, such as in France, and Rome's hostility to the newer liberal democratic forms of government, had to change. Leo set out to show Catholics that they could live in a liberal world without sacrificing their Catholic principles. He asked French Catholics to support the Third Republic. Even though Leo was at pains to affirm the union of church and state as an ideal, he shocked many of the French clergy with this sudden turnabout. But Leo's words came too late and his approach failed. Many of the French clergy could not be expected to turn from ardent monarchists to fervent republicans. They continued their hostility to the Third Republic. Conservative groups resisted the pope; they met and prayed for his enlightenment. Thus, Catholics in France were divided into conservatives and liberals. But the worst was yet to come.

The conservative French Catholics made two major blunders. First, they backed the ill-fated General Boulanger, who tried to take over the Republic and establish a dictatorship. Second, they, along with many of the liberal Catholics, were on the wrong side of the sensational Dreyfus affair. Dreyfus was a Jewish officer of the French army who was accused of selling military secrets to the Germans. Although found guilty, he was later proven innocent by further investigation.[2] The army, riding a wave of nationalism and anti-Semitism, was against Dreyfus. Unfortunately, the Catholics were also against Dreyfus, and their nationalism and anti-Semitism were as strong as any. The Catholic press shared in the anti-Semitism and presumed the guilt of Dreyfus. The leading Catholic paper of the day, *La Croix*, declared "Dreyfus is an agent of international Jewry which has decided to ruin the French people." The nearly universal anti-Semitism among French Catholics—with only a few exceptions such as the young intellectual, Charles Peguy—was a disaster for the church. Catholic anti-Semitism cost the church much prestige and promoted a whole new wave of severe anti-clericalism from the government. "Because the Catholic church, and especially a large number of militant priests and monks from such orders as the Assumptionists, had taken an active and verbally violent part in the bitter campaign to deny justice to Dreyfus and discredit the troubled Republic, the church now had to face the consequences."[3]

In 1901, the French government suppressed all religious orders, driving many into exile. Under Emile-Combes, over 13,000 schools were closed. By 1904, the government had broken off relations with Rome, and in 1905, the final step was taken. Church and state in France were officially separated. The "eldest daughter of the church," the heir of Clovis and Charlemagne since the eighth century, now broke away. To many contemporaries, this must have seemed gloomy indeed. They had witnessed the fall of papal Rome, and now Catholic Paris was no longer Catholic. Church property was handed over to a lay board, and the church lost control over her own buildings and churches. With this in mind, Pius X, who was now pope,[4] simply handed over all church buildings to the state, although he condemned the separation. The church rented its own old and glorious cathedrals for Mass.

It was not long before the church in France recovered. With the separation of church and state, the pope was at least free to run the church without interference. Bishops were consecrated. Money was raised and new seminaries, churches, hospitals, and schools were built. Although anti-clerical attitudes continued to be taught in the state schools, the church moved ahead. Catholics were also nourished by new devotions to the Blessed Mother and the Sacred Heart. The great Sacred Heart Cathedral, completed in 1912, is a monument to the revival and was built in reparation for the excesses of anti-clerical France.

ITALY

The situation in Italy tended to color the pope's outlook for the rest of Europe and America. The Italian government was anti-Catholic. Religious orders were dissolved, clerics were forced into military service, and the government even attempted to seize the funds of the church's Propagation of the Faith. Feast days were abolished, education secularized, religious processions were banned, and clerical criticism of the state was punishable by law. Pius IX reacted by forbidding any Catholic to take part in such an anti-clerical government either by voting or by holding office. Leo XIII unwisely held to the ban against the wishes of his more perceptive advisors. He even tried to get Bismarck and William II of Prussia (who was also the German Emperor) to abandon Italy as an ally and to side with France. This could hardly have pleased the Italian government. Thus, the struggle continued, and each side lost no opportunity to harass the other. The government held jubilees and public events designed to embarrass the pope. When Pius IX's body was being transferred in solemn procession to the basilica of San Lorenzo in 1881, fanatical crowds abused the processional and almost threw the pope's body into the Tiber. There were many times when Leo was ready to flee Rome. Yet, he countered with harassment of his own. He made a flourish of church festivals and played up the Holy Year of 1900, losing no opportunity of telling visitors to Rome of the persecution by the Italian government.

Pius X (1903-1914) began to relax the ban on Catholics taking part in the Italian government. However, he would permit no Catholic political party to form because he and his conservative curia wanted the laity to be submissive to the Holy See and take their political orders from the Vatican. The Vatican leadership did not want any threat of independent action from the laity, nor did it want the laity to be strong enough to deviate from the party line of the curia. Pius X condemned the writings of anyone who suggested otherwise and sought to protect seminarians from "dangerous" ideas by forbidding them to read newspapers. Even the beginnings of Catholic Action, founded by Leo XIII and furthered by Pius X himself, was simply meant to be an organ of the hierarchy, not an independent movement. Pius's successor, Benedict XV (1914-1922), was likewise unhappy with the anti-clerical Italian government, but found it wiser not to offend it. During World War I, he remained strictly neutral so as not to offend Catholics on either side. Afterwards, in 1919, he did permit Dom Sturzo to found a People's Party, and withdrew entirely the ban forbidding Catholics to take part in politics. Until 1919, the Italian situation caused the Vatican's continued suspicion of any democratic government and the ban on Catholics to share in them. The papacy was not able to make distinctions from country to country, because the pope felt that he could not condemn democracy in Italy and support it in France.

GERMANY

When the new anti-clerical, nationalistic government established itself in Italy, it was but the forerunner of several similar forms of government throughout Europe. Each nation became highly nationalistic, and to that degree anti-clerical, because clericalism was perceived as a threat to nationalism. Moreover, the Enlightenment had done its work, and the church had lost many members of its intelligentsia. A whole new working class was being raised in an increasingly secular world, and the new nationalism was not about to tolerate any check on its conscience from the church. In Germany, this feeling of nationalism was especially marked. Prussia had just defeated France and the chancellor, Bismarck, was seeking to absorb the other German states into a new Germanic empire, or reich, with Prussia at the helm. German Austria had been the dominant power heretofore, but Bismarck defeated Austria in 1866, and put it in a subordinate position. The new Germany became, in effect, an expanded Prussia, with its headquarters at Berlin. By 1870, the only resistance to German pride (racial and intellectual) was the Catholic Church (the Lutherans, always tied to the state, were delighted with Protestant Prussia's leadership).

Since the new Germany (the "Second Reich"; Otto I was the head of the First Reich and Hitler would call his empire the Third Reich) was about one-third Catholic, Bismarck knew he must dominate the Catholics and control the church as Napoleon did. By 1872, he had passed the Falk laws subjecting all schools to the state, expelling the Jesuits, and putting the clergy under state control. Fortunately, Germany possessed a remarkable Catholic leader named Windthorst, who led a Catholic Center Party that was able to offset some of the *Kulturkampf* of Bismarck. Nevertheless, by 1875, the *Kulturkampf* had deprived millions of Catholics of the sacraments when thousands of priests were sent into exile or imprisoned. However, by

1878, political pressure caused Bismarck to retreat, and some of the offensive laws were relaxed. He had been making no headway against a loyal clergy and laity or against the skillful work of Windthorst's Center party. In 1888, the new emperor, Kaiser William II, came to the throne. He needed the church's support against the socialists, and thus dismissed the "iron chancellor" under whom the church had suffered so much.

Another feature in Germany was that, after Bismarck's time, Catholic associations began to appear and flourish. Catholicism grew strong again. Leaders like Bishop Ketteler, the father of social action, created strong workers' associations. The Germans received Leo XIII's social encyclical *Rerum Novarum* (1891) with enthusiasm. Yet, under Pius X and his conservative curia, the old suspicion of Germany returned. Germany was intellectually superior to Rome even in Pius IX's time. Protestant-Catholic faculties taught in the German universities. Germany was also the home of Dollinger, who was suspected by the Vatican for his theological opinions. The books of Hermann Schell, who tried to wed Catholicism to German modern culture, were put on the Index. Rome—and some German bishops themselves—did not like the independence of the German associations, did not like the interdenominational character of the trade unions, and did not like the clergy's lack of control over the trade associations. German Catholics, as a result of Pius X's disapproval, were split on these issues. Only the outbreak of World War I prevented further polarization.

BRITAIN, SPAIN, PORTUGAL, AND AUSTRIA

Recall that the Catholic hierarchy was restored in England in 1850. But there was no noticeable "second spring." Although there were impressive conversions among the intellectuals, the Catholic population grew mostly through the birth rate and Irish immigration. There was no mass movement among the Anglicans to return to Rome. On the contrary, whatever thoughts of reunion there might have been between Anglicans and Roman Catholics were aborted by Cardinal Vaughan. It was he who, in 1896, persuaded Leo XIII to issue a bull declaring that ordinations to the priesthood in the Anglican church were null and void. This was a gross insult to the Anglican community and to Protestants in general. Any attempts at further reunion after this were brought to a standstill. Even worse, many of those who had returned to Rome left. Cardinal Manning's hope that Vatican I would present a compelling Catholic church went unfulfilled. A lingering anti-Catholicism and the materialism and secularism of the day also took its toll. However, as often happened in the Protestant countries, the Catholic schools fared better. In England, Holland, and Scotland the state assisted the parochial schools and worked out solutions to financial problems that still vex the United States. In 1927, Britain revoked the anti-Catholic measures and established diplomatic relations with the Vatican.

The main problem in Spain and Portugal was that the church and state were united. Therefore, as pro-church governments fell, so did the church. Succeeding governments were thus extremely anti-clerical and passed humiliating anti-clerical measures. In Spain, the king fell from power in 1931. When the new republican government ruthlessly carried out anti-clerical measures, it provoked a reaction which supported General Franco. In 1936, Spain was plunged into a bloody civil war.

By 1901, religious orders in Portugal had been suppressed. After the king was expelled and the republic proclaimed in 1914, there came the official separation of church and state. After World War I, Salazar took over and opposition to Catholicism declined.

In Catholic Austria, a *Los von Rom* (Freedom from Rome) movement developed. But much had changed in Austria. Once head of the German confederation, she had been reduced to a secondary role. She had been expelled from the papal states and northern Italy. After World War I, Austria's influence and territories were further reduced. Vienna seemed to have become a capital without a country as communist leaders gained control of the provinces.

SOCIAL PROBLEMS

Much of the church's relationship to France and the other countries revolved around two major points: the first, the social problems brought about by the Industrial Revolution, and second, recognition of the new democracies. We have seen how profoundly the Industrial Revolution spread, and it is commonplace to acknowledge the plight of the landless workers and the social ills it brought. The problem for the church was that Pius IX had foolishly prohibited the Italians from taking part in the new republican government of Italy and had disapproved of Catholic political activity in any country. Associations of workers of any kind were suspect. Leo XIII, however, recognized some of the pressing social problems and accepted such organizations as those of the French industrialist Leon Harmel. Not only did Harmel allow his workers to organize, he also led them on pilgrimages to Rome!

In 1890, Leo felt it was time to issue an encyclical on the worker, as the plight of the wage-earner was becoming more and more urgent. He had certain encouragements to do so. For example, in 1887, in the United States, Cardinal Gibbons defended the Knights of Labor as a legitimate association; in England, Cardinal Manning had so successfully intervened in the dockers' strike that they carried his picture, along with that of Karl Marx. Thus, in 1891, Leo issued his encyclical, *Rerum Novarum*. In it he stressed the right to private property and the workers' rights to form associations and to receive a just wage.[5] He criticized exploitation and unchecked competition. He warned against extreme socialists and other societies hostile to both state and religion. Significantly, although he did not fully recognize it, Leo was laying the foundation for a different relationship between church and state. In essence, he took the position that the church was not committed to any particular form of government (a blow to the monarchists), as long as the church was free to function. In 1885, Leo began to accept the independence of Catholic political parties who could act on their own (something his successor Pius X did not like). In short, Leo was trying to face the fact that the new democratic governments were here to stay, and that the old regimes were either dead or dying. However, if the papacy was somewhat ambivalent about its attitudes toward the new democracies, when it came to the new modern scholarship, the papacy under Pius X and his successors definitely did not favor it.

MODERNISM

The theology of Thomas Aquinas had been revived under Pius IX. Under Leo XIII Thomism was made the basis of study in seminaries and colleges though by no means exclusively. Still, the ever-conservative curia (especially under Pius X) began to use Thomism (as they conceived it) as an absolute norm and even as a weapon with which to attack those who used different theological and philosophical systems.

Though basically conservative, Leo did disturb the curia by trying to reconcile the church with modern times. He supported scholarship, opened up the Vatican archives, and encouraged historical research. Most important, he set guidelines for studying the Bible in his encyclical, *Providentissimus Deus* (1893). By the late nineteenth century, the Bible in particular was under much scrutiny. There was such an explosion of knowledge in archaeology, geology, and critical scholarship that people were looking at the Bible in a new light. Scholars were questioning the traditional interpretation of the Scriptures. They wanted to know if the details contained in the Bible were historically and scientifically accurate. They wanted to know more about Jesus himself. Who was he? What did he teach? Was Jesus or Paul responsible for the development of Christianity? Leo's encyclical tried to guide such questions. He set up the Pontifical Biblical Commission for this purpose, but the conservative curia soon used the commission as a means to stifle scholarship and intimidate scholars.

A handful of Catholic scholars were impatient with such restraint. They felt that the Bible must be subjected to the same kind of scrutiny as secular works. Thus, a new quasi-intellectual movement called "Modernism" appeared between 1890 and 1910. Actually, Modernism was more of an attitude than any precise system of thought. Basically, it was the attitude that urged the church to come to terms with the modern world. Those who were called Modernists

> ...had first been struck by the incompatibility between many traditional tenets of Catholicism and the findings of modern scholarship, and they had felt bound to use scientific and historico-critical methods of study and to follow arguments wherever it led...What they had attempted to do was, while remaining sincere and loyal Catholics, to forward such a revision and fresh presentation of the church's teaching as would acclimatize it in the modern world.[6]

There were three well-known persons associated with Modernism. First, there was Alfred Loisy (d. 1940). Loisy was a Biblical scholar and was knowledgeable about the new critical and scientific methods which he applied to the Bible. In 1902, he published *The Gospel and the Church*, which claimed that Jesus came to bring a "spirit," a religious movement, not truths for humankind, and that Jesus was only one point in a development. Then there was George Tyrrell (d. 1909), a Protestant who became a Catholic, and then a

Jesuit priest. He also proposed that the church's theological system needed overhauling. Finally, there was Baron von Hugel, who played the role of international go-between. He introduced Tyrrell to Loisy and sent articles back and forth to various other friends.

PIUS X'S REACTION

Pius X, who became pope in 1903, was politically naive, superstitious, narrow-minded, and totally aligned in philosophy with his conservative curia. Together they became convinced that there was an international conspiracy, originating in France, to destroy the Catholic church. They called this conspiracy "Modernism." Pius was not long in reacting. He issued his encyclical *Pascendi* in 1907, which condemned many of Loisy's statements, though not mentioning him by name. Insofar as Loisy and Tyrrell had written articles under assumed names, the pope was convinced that there was some kind of international conspiracy, and his language was almost violent in his denunciations, which resembled the tone of Pius IX's 1864 Syllabus. Those who were trying to update the church and were labeled "Modernists" by *Pascendi* objected because the Modernism described by Pius existed nowhere but in his mind. They were correct because Modernism, as we have said, was no single concept or teaching, but an attitude. Pius crystallized that attitude in several propositions, called it Modernism, and condemned it. But, as indicated by Roger Aubert, the pope had a point:

> It was undoubtedly the merit of biblical Modernism that it called attention to the law of development of dogma and the need of including the historical method in dealing with the texts of Scripture. But its principle was to leave entirely out of account the supernatural and inspired character of the scriptural testimonies, and also the interpretations suggested by tradition and the magisterium of the church. Further, historians are now becoming more and more alert to the fact that the notion of history used by Loisy and many of the modernists was dependent on the positive notions of the end of the nineteenth century, which are today undoubtedly outdated in many respects.[7]

Loisy and Tyrrell would not submit and both were excommunicated. Von Hugel stayed because he had seen that, although some new thinking was necessary for the church in the modern world, that thinking had to take place within the context of the tradition of the church, not in opposition to it.

The results of Pius's extreme denunciations, however, were disastrous. His encyclical had the effect of intellectual witch-hunting. Catholic scholars backed down on their investigations. Pioneer scholars like the famous Pierre Batiffol and Pere Lagrange were unable to continue with their biblical studies and writings. A "reign of terror" set in and Modernism became a catch-all word for all that the pope or his curia thought was harmful in modern scholarship. Many careers were ruined on the hint of "Modernist" leanings as professors were removed from their teaching positions. No theologian of note was safe from the curia's suspicion. An oath against Modernism was made obligatory for all professors, teachers, and priests—an oath which few had trouble in taking, since the term itself was so nebulous.

Even this was not enough. The conservative Catholics were still determined to uncover all "Modernists" wherever they were lurking. Catholic journals were suppressed and a veritable censorship was in force. A secret service organization was set up with a thousand agents to keep files on professors, teachers, and even bishops. When the Germans captured some of these files in 1915, they thought they had uncovered some international espionage ring. We might note that this secret organization was not formally dissolved until 1921.

One of the suspects in the secret file was a professor at the Bergamo seminary named Angelo Roncalli. He only discovered this in 1958, when he was elected Pope John XXIII and demanded to see his file in the Holy Office. The only respite from all of this harassment was obtained when the German cardinal was able to get the professors of theology at the German universities excused from taking the oath against Modernism.

We recognize today that such a vehement overreaction by Pius to Modernism and its severe suppression was due to the grip that the pope, curia, and conservative Catholics had on the church. There was no question that some of these so-called Modernists were too much blinded by current fashions of thought and that some of their views could not be reconciled with traditional Christianity. Yet, the leadership of the church could have handled the situation more calmly and without panic. Ironically, the ecclesial leadership alienated the very scholars who could have helped the whole church understand the problems that sooner or later it would have to come to terms with. Meriol Trevor, in her book *Prophets and Guardians*, puts it well:

> The usual defense of Pius X and his advisers is that they were acting on behalf of the "little ones" whose faith was threatened by the Modernists. Christ's warning, addressed to those who mistreat children, was taken by ecclesiastical rulers to include adult but simple members of the church. But were Loisy's exegetical studies a terrible danger to the fishermen of Brittany? Would Blondel's philosophy, almost incomprehensible to his friends, upset the peasants of Provence? If the little ones were the bourgeois capable of reading books of criticism, was a condemnation the best way of answering the questions raised? If it was necessary to crush Modernism in order to preserve the faith, what sort of faith, what sort of faithful were envisaged? When Cardinal Richard censured L'Evangile et L'Eglise, Loisy's sales doubled. After Tyrrell was dismissed from the Society of Jesus, his books commanded a wider public than before. People wanted to know what the fuss was about—they always do. Suppression of criticism and of new ideas, never easy since the invention of printing, was quite impossible by the beginning of the twentieth century. No one in authority would admit the questions, let alone provide what could have subdued Loisy's influence—better answers than his. Persistent refusals to face these questions surely meant that it would become harder for educated Catholics to remain believing Christians. And if Rome was willing to jettison the educated in order to preserve the faith of the simple, it was shortsighted not to realize that as more and more received education, so the problems would be revived on a wider scale and would not be less difficult to solve for the passage of time.[8]

Pius X thus set the tone that would prevail until John XXIII. Pius XII, for example, acted in the tradition of Pius X when, in 1950, he issued his encyclical *Humani Generis* condemning many propositions of the "New Theology." Although no one individual was named, many theologians were removed from their teaching positions.[9]

One of these, Yves Congar, a French scholar and advocate of ecumenical dialogue, was so much under a cloud of suspicion as being one of those whose actions were condemned by Pius XII, that he found himself unwelcome in his own Dominican community in France. We can sense, then, what happened at Vatican II. Under Pope John's more congenial attitude, the lid was taken off and the world was surprised at the sudden expression of thought, differing opinions, and theological questionings expressed during the council. (Congar was personally invited to participate in the council by John XXIII, and later became an advisor to Paul VI.) It is not without merit to suggest that the explosion of Vatican II was in direct proportion to the suppression begun in the time of Pius X.

THREE POPES

We saw that the new democratic governments of Europe were anticlerical, and not one failed to go through the motions of expelling religious orders, closing monasteries, and taking over the Catholic schools. This helps explain the reaction and resistance of the popes and many Catholics. Yet, as we have seen, Leo made an attempt to come to terms with the new governments and the new social ills of the age. His social encyclical mapped out a program for practical attitudes and action. It encouraged labor unions and associations as long as they were open and not hostile to religion. Leo had almost condemned the Knights of Labor in the United States, the predecessor of the American Federation of Labor (AFL). The Knights of Labor had many Catholic members, and was established for the purpose of collective bargaining. Thinking that the organization was a secret, revolutionary Freemason type, Leo had his reservations. Only the courage and explanations of Baltimore's Cardinal Gibbons saved the Knights of Labor from condemnation.

Leo did fail in his attempts to restore even partially the papal states, and he failed in preventing a clash between the Third Republic of France and the church. Yet he established Thomism as the official theology of the church, established the Pontifical Biblical Commission, opened the papal Catholic University in Washington, DC, and filled the college of cardinals with capable and sincere men, including Cardinal Newman, to whom he had given the red hat at the request of the Duke of Norfolk and the Marquis of Ripon.

Pius X was less than a political and diplomatic success. It was under him that church and state were separated in France, and Modernism was given too much significance. It was under Pius that strict control from Rome became a high art and modern thought was repressed. It was under him that the papacy and curia reached its point of power and control, and witch-hunting took over. It was under him that Theodore Herzl, a key Zionist leader, was refused any church support for the founding of the State of Israel. In Herzl's interview with Pius's secretary, Herzl was told that, before the pope would declare himself for the Jewish people, they must first be converted. Since they were not about to do that, Pius said, "We cannot favor this movement." In the church's internal and spiritual realm, Pius X restored Gregorian chant in 1904, reorganized the seminaries, reformed canon law, and curtailed the power of the Roman congregations. He also revised the breviary, encouraged Catholics to receive the eucharist daily, and permitted first communion at the age of seven. Pius X was canonized by Pius XII in 1954.

And that canonization was significant, for Pius XII was in reality blessing a new form of a papal and curial mystique that began with Pius X, a mystique properly called "Catholic Fundamentalism," meaning that one treats the magisterium in the same manner as Protestant fundamentalists treat the Bible. That is to say, papal or curial pronouncements, disconnected from their context and history—and indeed the pope himself—are regarded as sure bulwarks against relativism and modernity, against any new or old Modernist heresy. A variety of movements from then to the present would use loyalty to the papacy and the Vatican as the litmus test of fidelity and orthodoxy. In the 1980s and 1990s, the papacy's stance and the power of the curia which were honed and refined in that period from 1870 to 1950 would be considered normative and would overshadow a much richer and much longer tradition. Movements such as *Opus Dei* (which sees itself as "the immaculate remnant of the true church"), *Communione e Liberazione* (Italy), Catholics United for the Faith, the True Catholics, the Remnant, the Wanderer Forum (all USA) would emerge. All could rightly be described as Catholic fundamentalists who could trace their origins to the Modernist times of Pius X and the response he created.[10]

Benedict XV (1914-1922) was the pope who guided the church during World War I. Naturally, he was accused of favoritism by each side, but he remained neutral throughout the war. He gave the papacy new prestige by his efforts to alleviate the suffering of people and to assist prisoners of war. He was willing to accept the new governments and saw the resumption of diplomatic relations between France and the Vatican. At the war's end, the rampant anti-clericalism of Italy prevented the papacy from any voice in the treaties or any part in the League of Nations.

As one surveys the period of the First World War and its aftermath, one has the impression that even less than in the days of Napoleon did the governments of Europe pay any serious attention to Rome, that Benedict was even less likely to achieve anything to influence Napoleon or Metternich. Napoleon had tried to bend the church to his service, but at least he had recognized its power. And at the Congress of Vienna, unlike the Conference of Versailles, a papal delegate had not only been present, but had been offered the presidency.[11]

Yet, as so often happens during times of great disasters such as World War I, the church's enemies saw much to admire: the priests in the trenches, the nuns in the hospitals, the important part that the Mass and the sacraments played in the life of the Catholics. Lost (though not altogether) were the fears of the Catholics' supposed "divided allegiance," and lost also was the violent brand of anti-clericalism of the previous hundred years.

Nevertheless, in the larger view, much was lost to Christianity as a whole through World War I. There was no escaping that this was largely a war among Christian nations. It meant, therefore, that Christianity did not transcend national boundaries, and that Christians did not and could not unite on matters of principle. On the contrary, each side equated Christianity with patriotism, and so urged the slaying of the opposite side in the name of Christ. When the neutral United States entered the war, it took on the same Christian-patriotic trappings and saw its involvement as a Holy War—much the same way that General Eisenhower would call his post-Second World War book *Crusade in Europe*. Christianity in any event was seriously undermined as a universal force whose main interest was the gospel rather than political chauvinism.

CHAPTER 22

Toward Vatican II

AFTERMATH OF A WAR

The end of World War I had many frustrations, not the least of which were those of the Germans themselves. In that war, we should realize, the Allies never fought a battle in Germany nor marched into Berlin demanding surrender. The German people had been kept in ignorance about their military defeats, and were unaware that von Hindenburg himself had insisted on surrender because the German armies were exhausted. When the German people, therefore, learned about the terms of the Versailles Treaty, they thought that they had been betrayed. Anti-Semitism and other biased notions led the German people to blame their betrayal on the machinations of the communists, the liberals, the socialists, and especially the Jews. The German nation found it particularly hard to sign a document that was indeed untrue: that they and they alone were responsible for the war. They were stunned when they were saddled with a most humiliating peace treaty containing vindictive financial arrangements that were impossible to pay. The Allies later found themselves unable to collect the amount Germany supposedly owed.

France went so far as to invade Germany's Ruhr valley, taking the rich mining region as payment for Germany's war debt. This only served to solidify German morale and hostility. Many unworkable financial plans were offered, until a general economic depression erased all debts and left behind hardship, dissatisfaction, and bitterness for all the nations involved. The seeds for World War II were literally planted in the unjust peace terms that ended World War I. In spite of the fact that unrestrained imperialism and nationalism had led to World War I, nationalism continued to grow after the war. While democratic governments were in vogue, ironically, more and more countries succumbed under the iron hands of dictatorships. They posed a problem both to the world and to the church.

THE POPES AND THE NATIONS

The old troublesome allies of the papacy, the monarchies, had all but disappeared. The aftermath of the "war-to-end-all-wars" left the papacy with the challenge of dealing with each new situation as it came along. The popes were wary of any political organizations composed of Catholic laity although they allowed them and gradually sacrificed them to the more manageable "Catholic Action" groups which were under the control of the hierarchy which removed them from any form of political action. All Catholics were forbidden to exercise any autonomous, independent action. With the rise of the totalitarian powers, these restrictions on Catholics were disastrous. Forbidden to act independently, or curbed by hierarchical leadership, Catholic laity could hardly be expected to know how to deal with a Hitler or a Mussolini. Without firm directives, or the strength of unity found in free political parties, Catholics tended to collaborate with the current political system. Some resisted, but they did so without church support. The popes, by acting unilaterally with the heads of such regimes, gave no guidelines for the ordinary citizen.

Note that this forbidding of any independent lay social action resulted in identifying social harmony with the official concerns of the institutional church. Leo XIII said as much when he wrote, "Let it become more and more evident that the tranquility of order and the true prosperity flourish especially among those people whom the church controls and influences." This meant that any Catholic social action was subordinate to concrete ecclesiastical interests. General Christian principles, such as the dignity of the human person, were ignored, especially in reference to those outside the church. That led philosopher Sidney Hook to write, "In any crucial situation the behavior of the Catholic church may be more reliably predicted by reference to its concrete interests as a political organization than by reference to its timeless dogmas." Guenter Lewy in his book *The Catholic Church and Nazi Germany* commented similarly that "the church's opposition was carefully circumscribed. It was rooted in her concern for her institutional interests rather than in a belief in freedom and justice for all men." It would be an almost impossible task for the priests and laity, except for those few driven to radicalism, to take the social issues from the hierarchy's exclusive organizational preoccupations.

THE CONCORDATS

The popes acted unilaterally with the various heads of state by making concordats, or agreements, with them. By this means, the church obtained certain legal freedoms (often confined to the paper they were written on). The concordats were a government-to-government diplomatic arrangement that preserved the rights of the church at the level of hierarchical diocesan leadership. The biggest defect of the concordat manner of dealing with governments was that such agreements did not take into account the needs of ordinary Catholics. Concordats were made without the laity's consent, and bound them to a course of neutrality or inaction. In short, fascist governments granted legal safeguards to the institutional church, but, at the everyday level of Catholics having to live, act, survive, and resist, there was no plan and no agreement. In practice, this meant that a Hitler could gladly sign a concordat with the Holy See (which he did), and then blithely violate the agreement and do what he wanted (which he did). The church's leadership, however, felt bound to the concordat even when it was violated. Vatican officials and bishops might protest, but they had no other means of enforcement. If the laity had been gathered into strong organizations, church authorities might have had a means of enforcement. The concordats proved to be more of a burden to the church since they tended to substitute high level arrangements for daily Catholic participation. The papacy failed to see that the new regimes of Hitler and

Mussolini were not merely indifferent to religion, but hostile to it.

ITALY

In Italy, the democratic government was faltering. Upon his election, Pius XI was anxious to come to some kind of agreement with the government, but he did not include the new People's Party of Don Sturzo in his plans. If Pius XI had, there would have been a strong party to support the old government. Since he did not, Italy was susceptible to the many forces that wanted to take over after the Great War. Such forces included the communists, the socialists, and the fascists of Mussolini.

Mussolini, rising on the wave of division and depression, became Italy's prime minister in 1922 and then obtained dictatorial powers, with the approval of the king. He quickly initiated much-needed reforms, suppressed dissent, and established a fascist dictatorship in 1925 with himself as "Il Duce." As did the wily Napoleon, Mussolini realized that to solidify Italy and to get the support of the masses, he must make some peace with the Catholic church. Accordingly, in 1929, he concluded the Lateran Treaty and Concordat with Pius XI. By the Lateran Treaty, the papacy was given 108 acres in the heart of Rome as the sovereign state of the "Vatican City." It included the Vatican and Lateran palaces, the villa of Castel Gandolfo outside of Rome, two buildings in Assisi, and the catacombs. This was in return for the pope's recognition of the kingdom of Italy. In addition, the concordat stipulated that the pope was to be paid the equivalent in bonds of one hundred million dollars as payment for the seizure of the papal states and property in return for the church's neutrality in the political affairs of Italy. Additional parts of the treaty dealt with the regulation of marriages, the repeal of all anti-clerical legislation, the rights and duties of clergy in Italy, and state salaries for all priests and bishops. Catholicism was proclaimed the state religion. (This and other items were eliminated through renegotiation of this concordat in 1985.)

After the agreement of 1929, Mussolini continued to harass the church. So, Pius XI, in the 1931 encyclical, *Non Abbiamo Bisogno* (written in Italian rather than the traditional Latin), warned against Fascist ideals and condemned Mussolini's attitude and oppressive actions. Yet, Pius still kept the Catholic Action groups out of politics and prohibited the clergy from engaging in any political activity. As the more pagan aspects of Mussolini's regime appeared, especially after his association with Hitler in 1936, the Vatican and Mussolini drifted further apart. As Pius XI neared the end of his life, he began to denounce Mussolini more strongly.

GERMANY

After World War I, Kaiser Wilhelm II had fled to the Netherlands and the German Weimar Republic came into being. Some progress was made, especially in getting payments for the war reduced. Business picked up, and Germany was admitted into the League of Nations. But all was not well. There were many pressures from both the old line conservatives and the communists. The former were successful in getting the aging von Hindenburg elected president of the Republic. Meanwhile, the Nationalist Socialist German Workers Party was gaining in strength. This was Hitler's Nazi party. Advocating totalitarian government, state control of industry, and Aryan superiority, Hitler's real opportunity came in 1929 when a series of economic depressions shook the country. Von Hindenburg appointed von Papen as Prime Minister. He, in turn, in order to achieve anything, needed the support of Hitler's Nazi party in the Reichstag (the German parliament). Von Papen, however, was unsuccessful in his policies, and von Hindenburg appointed Hitler as chancellor in 1933. When a Nazi conspiracy set fire to the Reichstag and then blamed it on the communists, democracy was snuffed out, and the Weimar Republic gave way to the Third Reich, a revolutionary dictatorship.

A drive was immediately put on to oust the communists. Propaganda recreated Germany in a Nazi image. All dissent was crushed, and the Jews were persecuted. To further crush dissent, Hitler launched his infamous purge of 1934, whereby some of von Papen's associates and certain Catholic labor leaders lost their lives. The notorious concentration camps, such as Dachau, were started at this time. After von Hindenburg's death, Hitler was elected President and Imperial Leader of the Third Reich. The SS, which in 1929 was a small group of Hitler's bodyguards, was expanded to a million persons who took charge of national security, policing action, and the operation of the death camps that were to implement Hitler's "Final Solution," i.e. the destruction of all Jews and others labeled as "undesirables."

It is at this point that we come to the incredible fact that both Catholic and Protestant Christian leaders in Germany came to terms with Hitler. With very few exceptions, they supported him even in the face of each growing and evident horror of his Third Reich. For the Catholic church, as for the Protestant ones, it was basically a question of politics. Rome did not want another *Kulturkampf*, and did not want a separatist church under the German state. Furthermore, Catholics feared the return of the Lutheran leaders, who had fallen from power with the fall of the Weimar Republic. Not wanting them to regain their ascendancy, Catholics saw an alliance with Hitler as the best way to foil this. Although some German Catholic bishops, like Bishop Preysing of Berlin, opposed Hitler, the majority of the bishops openly supported Hitler, and Pius XII, on his election, sent him a friendly letter.

Hitler even made a concordat with the Vatican. Up to this time, the Catholic bishops had forbidden the people to join Hitler's party because of his anti-Christian attitudes and racial intolerance, but with the concordat, they withdrew this stricture. Again, the issue was that the Catholics, like many other Germans, feared the communists, and thought that Hitler was the only one strong enough to subdue them. Although many did not like Hitler's atheism or militancy, both laity and hierarchy thought that Hitler could be kept in his place under the influence of von Papen and von Hindenburg. The Vatican's Secretary of State, Eugenio Pacelli, the future Pius XII, signed a concordat that was more beneficial to Hitler than to the church. Hitler now had an agreement with the Vatican that he could parade before German Catholics, as well as new prestige that he paraded before the world. He never intended, of course, to keep the agreements of the concordat. During the years of 1933 to 1937, the Vatican protested his disregard of the concordat. But the Vatican was hamstrung, because the church's leadership felt itself morally bound to carry out the concordat's provisions, while Hitler felt himself free to act in whatever way gave him an advantage. The concordat was thus useless to average German Catholics, who had to live with the ambiguity of an agreement made by church leaders without their participation.

Finally, in 1937, Pius XI issued his exceptional encyclical (written in German rather than the traditional Latin), *Mit Brennender Sorge* (With Burning Anxiety). The pope condemned outright the Nazi regime and the racist underpinnings of National Socialism, but Hitler easily suppressed the encyclical that German bishops smuggled into Germany and boldly had read out in all Catholic churches. The Nazis were livid and for days the German press and radio vilified the pope. But Hitler eventually backed off from this press campaign, deciding that he did not want a direct confrontation with the church lest the morale of the armed forces on which he so depended for power and expansion suffer. Pius XI had another encyclical prepared by two Jesuits, an American and an Australian, with the title *Humani Generis Unitas*. It was even stronger than its predecessor in condemning racism, anti-Semitism, and the persecution of the Jews in Germany. The Jesuits submitted the encyclical in July 1938, but it was delayed and Pius XI died before seeing it. His successor, Pius XII, read it but declined to approve it and it was never issued. One wonders if it had been, Hitler too might have backed off somewhat as he did with its predecessor.

In any case, both the hierarchy and the new pope, Pius XII (1939-1958), were trying to appease the Nazi regime, because they feared open persecution of Catholics in Germany and the church's loss of its tax-exempt status. This appeasement reached its extreme in the fact that neither the hierarchy nor the pope publicly protested the extermination of the Jews being carried out in the death camps all over Nazi-occupied Europe during the 1941-1945 period. Although the pope's silence became a scandal, Pius XII sincerely thought that any public protest would not only not have changed matters, but would have made them worse. (Others, like the International Red Cross, followed the same reasoning.) On June 2, 1943, for example, Pius XII wrote to the Sacred College of Cardinals, "Every word that We addressed to the responsible authorities and every one of Our public declarations had to be seriously weighed and considered in the interest of the persecuted themselves in order not to make their situation unwittingly even more difficult and unbearable."

At the time, many of the Jews themselves agreed. One Berlin couple who came to Rome after being imprisoned in concentration camps declared:

None of us wanted the pope to take an open stand. We were all fugitives and fugitives do not want to be pointed at. The Gestapo would have become excited and would have intensified its inquisitions. If the pope had protested, Rome would have become the center of attention. It was better that the pope said nothing.[1]

The Polish cardinal, Prince Sapieha, begged Pius not to make public protests, as they only increased the persecution of his people. There was truth to this. The Archbishop of Utrecht in Holland was warned by the Nazis not to protest the deportation of the Dutch Jews. He did anyway, and in retaliation the Catholic Jews of Holland were sent to their death. One of them was the Carmelite philosopher and mystic, Edith Stein. It was this reality that made Pius cautious. Still, Pius spoke when he could, publicly on occasion, privately, and indirectly when needed. The records show, for example, that the papal nuncio to Berlin had protested over 300 times against the actions of the Third Reich. It was this sort of thing that led *The New York Times* (12/25/42) to editorialize the pope as "a lonely voice crying out of the silence of the continent" and Golda Meir, Israeli Foreign Minister at the time of Pius's death, to declare, "When fearful martyrdom came to our people in the decade of Nazi terror, the voice of the pope was raised for the victims."

But none of this was remembered in later years. Moreover, it is regrettable that Pius XII never gave an open explanation to the world for the reasons behind his conduct or his silence, and never voiced any public regret afterwards. This left the field open to slanted popularizations such as the much publicized play, *The Deputy*, by Rolf Hochhuth. Coming as it did at the same time as the Eichmann trials and the publication of the diary of Anne Frank, the play renewed bitter charges of an indifferent pope and church and the "usual" politicking by the church, if not actual anti-Semitism.

Indeed, as reported by the Vatican on April 4, 1973, the pope's aides knew of the Nazi slaughter of millions of Jews. Certainly Archbishop Roncalli, then Apostolic Delegate in Istanbul (and later Pope John XXIII), reported to Pius XII's substitute Secretary of State, Monsignor Montini (later Pope Paul VI), about the killing of the Jews in Nazi-occupied eastern Europe, and presumably this information was relayed to the pope. What we do know is that, in 1966, Pope Paul VI opened the Vatican archives, and from these records have so far issued ten bulky volumes concerning the Nazi period. They refute the implications of *The Deputy*, and show beyond a doubt the Holy See's humanitarian efforts to save all peoples, and the basis for the praise from Jewish leaders mentioned above.

Archbishop Roncalli enabled hundreds of Jews to escape by providing them with passports. Pius XII himself quietly helped thousands of Jews escape the Nazis by providing them with forged papers identifying them as Christians. He also provided funds, such as to the Romanian Jews, to help them escape. In his classic work on the martyrdom of Hungarian Jewry, Eugene Levai writes: "From that day on, acting in accordance with the instructions of the Holy See and always in the name of Pius XII, the Nuncio never ceased from intervening against the disposition concerning Jews."

Many Vatican officials were involved in an "underground railroad" that helped Jews escape across the boarders to freedom from Nazi-occupied Italy. (It has been estimated that 90 percent of Rome's Jews were helped to escape.) Priests and religious were also encouraged to use church buildings to shelter Jews and political refugees. After the war, Chief Rabbi Isaac Jerzog of Jerusalem, who had traveled to Constantinople seeking aid for the Jewish Aid Fund and received more than he asked for, sent a "special blessing" to the pope for "his lifesaving efforts on behalf of the Jews during the Nazi occupation of Italy." In 1945, the World Jewish Congress made a gift of $20,000 to Vatican charities in recognition of the work of the Holy See on behalf of the Jews.

It is often forgotten that besides aid and help, a more striking witness against the Nazi horror was lodged in the suffering and martyrdoms of many clergymen. The records show that 2,579 priests, lay brothers, and seminarians were interned at KZ Dachau, of whom at least 1,034 died in camp. In the first 16 months of their war, 600 Polish priests died at the hands of the Nazis and 3,000 more were sent to concentration camps. More than half did not return. In France, by February 1944, the Gestapo had arrested 163 priests, of whom 123 were shot or decapitated before ever reaching any camp.[2]

Just as the Catholic opposition to Hitler was limited, so too was the Protestant opposition. This was, in part, due to Lutheranism's traditional alliance with the state. Thus, even those Protestants who rejected the totalitarian claims of the state in religious and political matters did not want a separatist church, and so while they sought to defend orthodox Christianity against the distortions and innovations of the Nazis, they made no open resistance. Only a few, like Dietrich Bonhoeffer, went so far as to actively resist Hitler—and many of these paid the ultimate price. Some American Jews themselves knew of the atrocities but, outside of a relatively few voices raised in protest or who sought intervention from President Roosevelt, most remained silent or indifferent.

Beyond the countless heroisms of many people, nevertheless, most Protestants and Catholics supported Hitler throughout most of his Third Reich. This revealed the vested interest of the churches, which did not want their tax status threatened or their social positions devalued, or their seats of power undone. World War II showed more than anything else that some clergy on both sides put politics and self-preservation before gospel values. It was a shameful record at times, relieved only by the unnumbered secret heroisms of many and the few public solitary voices, such as the Anglican bishop George Bell, the Catholic Archbishop Preysing of Berlin, Cardinal Faulheber of Munich, Bishop van Galen of Munster, and those many Catholic priests, brothers, and sisters who died for supporting the rights of Jews or even for merely praying for the Jews.

FRANCE, SPAIN, AND MEXICO

After the war, there were several factions vying for governmental control: the communists, the socialists, the democrats, and the monarchists. The papacy rejected communism outright, was wary of socialism and democracy, and tended to favor monarchy. In fact, resistance to the French government brought renewed anti-Catholic measures in 1924. During World War II, when the Nazis occupied France, Pius XII recognized the Petain regime, but he also negotiated with DeGaulle. The church's collaboration with the Vichy regime brought protests from DeGaulle. On a theological level, in 1942, Pius XII sent conservative scholar Reginald Garrigou-Lagrange to France in order to quell the efforts of the Jesuits at Forviére and the Dominicans at Le Saulchoir. Garrigou-Lagrange, a master in the abstract scholastic outlook, was effective in discouraging the scholastic use of patristic theology and the historical-critical method in biblical studies.

Spain, after World War I, was still a constitutional monarchy. The disastrous defeat of Spain in Morocco in 1921, however, led to a revolt against the king. The king permitted and encouraged the dictatorship of Primo Rivera in 1923. Rivera ruled until 1930. In the first election, Zamora headed the new Republic as its first president, and a strong anti-Catholic majority pushed for the complete separation of church and state, so that Catholicism was no longer the state religion. In 1932, the Jesuits were expelled and the schools were secularized. In 1933, all church property was transferred to the state, and clerical privilege was abolished. Subsequent elections brought some redress to the church. This, in turn, infuriated the communists and others. They led an insurrection during which many churches were burned and priests were terrorized. Anarchy was beginning to sweep the country. Suddenly, in 1936, a general from the Spanish army in Morocco, Francisco Franco (1892-1975), landed at Cadiz. He established a government with himself as dictator. A fierce civil war broke out, and Franco emerged as victor in 1939. In 1941, agreements were made with Franco by the church. In 1953, Catholicism was restored as the established religion of the Spanish state.

Across the Atlantic in 1917 a radical revolutionary movement called for complete Mexican nationalization. This meant the expulsion of every foreign influence in the interests of the native Indian culture. The Catholic church felt the full brunt of persecution. In 1926, laws were passed forbidding the church to own property and conduct schools. All foreign clergy were expelled or executed, and the Mexican clergy was required to register with the government. Out of protest, and with agreement of the pope, the bishops and priests conducted no religious services in Mexico for three years. Finally, in 1929, a truce was reached with the government, and the laws were more leniently applied. However, in 1931, a new and more vigorously anti-clerical government persecuted the Catholic church. Under a new president in 1934, this persecution abated and church services were tolerated.

WORLD WAR II

The Second World War was really a continuation of the first. By 1938, the League of Nations had almost ceased to function. France feared Germany. England distrusted France, and was soft in its approach to Hitler. Germany was still smarting over the terms of the Versailles Treaty. Japan entered Manchuria in 1931, and Germany began to rearm in 1935, the same year that Italy seized Ethiopia. In 1939, Italy seized Albania as Hitler seized Austria and Poland. At first, Russia was on Hitler's side, since it historically distrusted France and England. Thus, Russia signed a non-aggression pact with Hitler in Moscow in 1939. With such support from Russia, Hitler felt free to march into Poland, and on that occasion France and England declared war on Germany. It was a terrible and costly war.

After the war, the United States and the Soviet Union emerged as the world's two super-powers. As Pius XI and Pius XII had foreseen, communism became very strong in Italy and France. As the communists gained control of governments, even in predominantly Catholic countries, they skillfully persecuted and out-maneuvered the church. Oppression followed in Poland, Czechoslovakia, Rumania, Yugoslavia, and Hungary—wherever communism became the ruling power. It was no wonder that communism became the all-pervading, preoccupying concern of the church's leadership. Both laity and hierarchy came to view communism as the implacable foe, and took a rigid and uncompromising stand against it.

PIUS XII

Pius XII was as authoritarian as Pius XI. They both had issued several exacting encyclicals that gave rise to a controversy about the binding authority of such letters. There was a distinct danger that twenty centuries of tradition and Scripture would be ignored by those who felt that papal encyclicals were the final authority for their particular points of view.

It was during Pius XII's long reign (1939-1958) that Marxism (or communism) spread and World War II took place. We are still too near the events for an objective judgment of his reign, both as to his political and ecclesiastical efforts, but we might mention a few significant events in his pontificate. Pius XII tried in vain to keep peace between Mussolini and the church, and attempted to keep Italy out of World War II. After the war, when Italy was in political turmoil, the communists were able to make strong gains. There was the possibility that the monarchy might be restored once again as the political system in Italy, but Pius XII took no definite stand on this, and the monarchy was rejected in 1946.

We have mentioned before how the church became somewhat alienated from the rest of the world because of its narrow theology. At times, Pius XII would seem to accept some of the newer thoughts that emerged after World War II, especially those that originated in France—but he would not follow them through. In 1943, he issued the letter *Divino Afflante Spiritu*, which permitted biblical scholars the freedom of inquiry, and encouraged them to use the newly-developed methods for interpreting Scripture. He encouraged missionaries. For example, in 1939 he issued a decree tolerating the honors paid to Confucius and the dead in China, honors which, we recall, Ricci had tolerated at the end of the sixteenth century, but which Rome had condemned in 1704. In 1947, in *Mediator Dei*, he gave a great impetus to liturgical reform. He relaxed the regulations about fasting before receiving the eucharist, permitted evening Masses, revised the Holy Week liturgy, and gave the world the "dialogue Mass."

Yet Pius, as we saw, was too politically cautious. He did not speak out publicly for the Jews of Europe as Hitler systematically murdered them. By 1950, Pius XII retreated into conservative positions again. He knew that the church had to open itself to what was going on, as many of his speeches indicated. He even considered calling an ecumenical council. But he could not break out of the mold of authoritarian teacher because he feared the direction that the bishops might take the church. He was concerned that things would get out of hand. So he retreated. After consultation with the world's bishops regarding the belief of the faithful about Mary's assumption into heaven, he defined the dogma of the Assumption in 1950. This exercise of infallibility is the one and only *ex cathedra* pronouncement since 1870. He beatified Pius X, and considered beatifying Pius XI, thus giving support to the policies of these two conservative popes. In 1950, he issued the encyclical *Humani Generis*, in which he rejected the new trends in theology and caused a smaller version of the intellectual witch-hunting that Pius X caused with his encyclical on Modernism. The priest-worker movement in France, whereby priests took ordinary jobs during the week in order to show concern for the workers, and to better understand the situation of ordinary people, was brought to an end by Pius XII.

Pius XII was almost an absolute benevolent monarch. Being too astute and experienced to let the curia take over, he ruled the church by himself. He pronounced on many things: some profusely, some timidly. His was a one-man rule in the firm absolutist tradition of a Gregory VII, or a Boniface XIII. He ate alone, walked alone, and kept his own counsel.[3] He was his own secretary of state. We might say that he was the last of the total papal monarchs, ruling in almost total political isolation, the supreme example of the fortress mentality. Nevertheless, because of the nearness of his time, his place in church history has yet to be adequately assessed.[4]

PRELUDES TO A COUNCIL

In order to understand the brief reign of Pope John XXIII (1958-1963), we must recall once more the ecclesiastical atmosphere of the times. At least six of the seven previous popes can be described as very authoritarian. Less than a hundred years before John XXIII, in 1870, infallibility had been proclaimed, and this seemed to put a stop to theological questioning. From 1907 to 1910, Pius X's condemnation of Modernism had cast a pall over all theological speculation. Yet, in spite of this, small groups of intellectual leaders were determined to ride out the tide of suspicion. We have noted how the Dominican Father F.M. Lagrange retired to Jerusalem and founded a famed biblical school to prepare the next generation of scholars to face the problems so long ignored. Investigations were going on quietly at the universities, such as Louvain in Belgium, Nijmegen in Holland, Frieburg in Switzerland, Innsbruck in Austria, the Catholic faculty at Tübingen in Germany, and others. There was Romano Guardini (d. 1968), who promoted liturgical reforms; Jacques Maritain renewing Thomism; Erich Przywara, Hugo and Karl Rahner. In France, there were Congar, de Lubac, and Danielou. In Holland, there was Schillebeeckx. These scholars were helping the church to return to the ancient patristic and biblical roots of the faith. They helped the church, and eventually the papacy, to get out of their narrow vision of things, which was confined to the Western world, and to see matters in more universal terms. They were awaiting an opportunity to come out into the open, as it were. Still, they dared not. The Roman curia, with its continuous presence and its far-reaching control, was keeping watch. Xavier Rynne describes it thus:

In the government of the Catholic church over the course of the last two hundred years or so—at least since the French Revolution—the congregations of the Roman curia achieved a startling supremacy, so much as evidently to have given many members of these administrative organs the impression that, for all practical purposes, they were the church. Bishops, priests, and faithful were dealt with as a sort of mass appendage to the Vatican. Many of these officials seem to have felt that they were the effective executors of absolutist papal power over the clergy and faithful, and their decisions should not only be law, but that their opinions on doctrinal, moral, and political matters were manifestations of papal infallibility. In the appointment of bishops all over the world, the creation and apportionment of dioceses, the surveillance of faith and morals, the authorizing and control of religious orders and congregations, the dispensing of church funds for missionary enterprises, and the safeguarding of tradition and orthodoxy affecting every aspect of Catholic life, they gradually came to have the final say.[5]

JOHN XXIII

It was into this atmosphere that Pope John XXIII came. He was supposed to be an interim pope until the cardinals could come up with someone to better fill Pius XII's shoes. Pope John was 77 years old, moderate in his views, and at the mercy of the curia who really ran things in the beginning of his papacy. Thus, under Pope John's name, a new warning was issued to New Testament scholars, Latin was reaffirmed as the language of the church, and warnings were given against any new theological trends. Yet, John realized that the curia's hold would have to be broken. He knew that new thoughts could not be repressed forever. His own personal experience had given him a certain sympathy to what was going on. In 1925, he was the apostolic delegate to Bulgaria, where he ministered to a small and poor Catholic community in an Orthodox country. In 1934, he was apostolic delegate in Istanbul, Turkey, a newly-secularized Muslim state, where he was bishop to Latin, Greek, and Syrian Catholics. In 1944, he was apostolic nuncio in Paris, and in 1953, was appointed Patriarch of Venice. While he was in France, he had observed the experiments going on there with the priest-workers, and he felt the impact of the new theological perspectives that had developed from 1946 to 1950, when Pius XII's encyclical brought an end to the flourishing "new theology" of France. He knew something had to be done. That "something" was an ecumenical council.

CHAPTER 23

Vatican II and Beyond

THE COUNCIL BEGINS

Pope John XXIII's advisors were not happy with his decision to call an ecumenical council. (John referred to them as "prophets of gloom.") When the members of the curia saw that the pope was determined to go ahead with his plan, they set up a strategy to control the council by placing men of their own mindset in the key positions on the planning commissions. Together, they worked out the draft documents that would be placed before the gathered bishops when the council began. The proposed documents were backward-looking, heavy-handed, and legalistic. They contained condemnations of the various "evils" of the preceding hundred years.

Pope John, however, was prepared for the curia's conservative, even reactionary, agenda. In his opening talk at the council, on October 11, 1962, he encouraged the bishops to take seriously the task of updating the church so as to bring it into the mainstream of what was happening all over the world. When Cardinal Lienart proposed that the prepackaged, curia-dominated agenda be put aside, thunderous applause greeted his suggestion, and a fresh, new spirit moved through many of the gathered bishops.

Of the seventy prepared draft documents drawn up by the curia before the start of the council, sixty-nine were rejected by the bishops. The only one that was worthy of immediate attention was the document on the liturgy. Indeed, this was a prophetic point of departure for the council, because it was liturgical reform that underscored the real meaning of the council for ordinary Catholics throughout the world. One particular item, the idea of using the vernacular language in the celebration of the eucharist instead of Latin, may have signaled the beginning of a truly world perspective on the church, one that might replace the European-centered view of church. The African bishops and many other progressive prelates, such as Alfrink (the Netherlands), Leger (Canada), Doepfner (Germany) and Meyer and Ritter (United States), consistently urged such development of the manner of Catholic worship. They were opposed by those who wanted to continue the status quo, particularly by Cardinal Alfredo Ottaviani, Secretary of the formidable Congregation of the Holy Office. His personal motto, *Semper Idem* (always the same), sufficiently expressed his mindset, as well as the mentality of his allies, Cardinals Bacci, Staff, Vagnozzi (Italy), Browne (Ireland), and McIntyre and Spellman (United States).

By the end of the first session in December 1962, it was obvious that a great change had taken place. For the previous two hundred years, the popes had tried to shield Catholics from the rest of the world. John XXIII had unleashed an *aggiornamento*, a new spirit of openness. But, by June 1963, Pope John was dead. The world mourned the death of this joyful old man who had recently addressed his encyclical, *Pacem in Terris*, to all persons of good will, appealing to the whole human family to build a better world by working together. It was also John who, in his 1961 encyclical, *Mater et Magistra*, was the first pope to declare that the church was in favor of democracy. John moved the church away from local Italian politics to a consideration of the rest of the world. The siege mentality, dominating the church since the conclusion of the Council of Trent in 1563, seemed to be coming to an end.

THE COUNCIL CONTINUES

The Second Vatican Council might have ended with the death of

John XXIII, but for the election to the papacy of Giovanni Battista Montini, the Archbishop of Milan. Taking the name of Paul VI (1963–1978), Montini continued the council begun by his predecessor. Once more in its nearly two thousand year history, the church was ready to meet a new challenge—that of adapting to a world that had become a "global village."

For three years, Paul VI presided over the council, and for another twelve years, he shepherded a church in which tremendous changes were taking place as a direct result of that council. He faced tremendous challenges as the first post-Vatican II pope, many of them without precedent. Paul VI often agonized over a divided church, polarized by conservatives, who tried to do whatever they could to resist the conciliar developments, and by liberals who wanted to take the new conciliar directions to their logical destinations as fast as possible.

Caught in the middle, Pope Paul appeared to vacillate between moderate positions, which was his personal inclination, and conservative positions, which he seemed to embrace for the sake of that part of his flock who were trying to be the kind of Catholics that they had been spiritually and doctrinally prepared to be. There was, for example, his encyclical, *Humanae Vitae*, promulgated in July 1968. Four years earlier, in June 1964, Pope Paul had created a special commission of some sixty experts to study the issues of the morality of artificial birth control in light of the new technological developments in the area of fertility control. The results of their research were given to fifteen theologians who were to advise the pope in light of the conclusions of the work done by the full commission. Eleven members of that committee recommended that the church's teaching against artificial birth control be modified, while four theologians urged the pope to hold the line on the traditional prohibition. For more than a year, Paul prayed and agonized about what to do. Then he upheld the traditional teaching. It is likely that he did so for the sake of those Catholics who saw the church changing at such a rate as to leave them feeling not only bewildered, but perhaps even abandoned, by the church whose teachings they accepted and obeyed at great personal cost. Nevertheless, a careful reading of this "hard line" document reveals that, in the final section, Paul VI bequeathed to the church a sensitivity to the personal conscience of the faithful and a trust in the action of the Holy Spirit in their lives. And just as well, for a sizable majority of Catholics have rejected the conclusions of *Humanae Vitae*:

In 1971 [three years after the encyclical] Catholics said by 58–31 percent that a good Catholic could ignore the pope's condemnation of artificial birth control. In the 1977 CPA study, 73 percent said that Catholics should be allowed to practice artificial means of birth control; eight in ten Catholics under fifty took this position. Some observers [notably Andrew Greeley] believe that *Humanae Vitae* has been responsible for declining church attendance, and it is clearly a major factor cited by unchurched Catholics. But the size of the Catholic population has grown since 1968, and the decline in Mass attendance has been stable for a decade. It is not likely that people are turning away from the church today because of the birth control issue; more likely, they reject the church's teaching, practice birth control as a matter of conscience, and go to church or not for other reasons.[1]

HIGHLIGHTS OF THE SECOND VATICAN COUNCIL

At Trent, 225 bishops, 189 of whom were Italian, signed the final acts of the Council in 1563. Some four hundred years later, more than 2500 bishops participated in the Second Vatican Council. The representation was global: 1089 bishops were European; 489 were South American; 403 were from North America. Nearly 300 bishops came from Africa, and 375 came from Asia. From Australia came 75 bishops, and from Central America 84 participated. Nuns, clerics, lay Catholics, and Protestant and Orthodox observers were also invited.

For more than three years, the bishops met during four long sessions. By December 8, 1965, sixteen official documents had been drawn up, debated, modified, voted upon, and promulgated. The bishops had produced more than 600 pages of official teachings, a compendium of the Catholic church's contemporary self-understanding, including the church's view of itself vis-a-vis the world at large.

There were amazing advances in perspective with regard to the church's relationship with the human family, with the Jews and members of those world religions that were once referred to as "pagans," and with the Protestant denominations now recognized as "the separated churches and ecclesial communities in the West." The relationship between the bishops and the papacy, unfinished at the First Vatican Council, was clarified, and the ancient view of "all the bishops with pope as their head" acting together as a college (collegiality) was restored. The role of the laity in the mission of the church was recognized as its baptismal prerogative and responsibility. The principles for a thorough-going revision of the eucharist and the other sacraments were drawn up. Religious liberty was recognized as a God-given right; thus, the triumphalistic teaching that "error has no rights" was laid to rest. The tools of modern biblical scholarship and the fruits of biblical interpretation were recommended to laity as well as clergy. The leadership of the church expressed to the world at large what the church believed and how the church could help meet the common problems facing the entire human family.

Pope John XXIII's *aggiornamento* (updating), and Pope Paul's continuation of the same, swept through the whole church. Many theologians who had been silenced or held under suspicion for their innovative theological perspectives suddenly became the council's theological "experts." The Catholic lay people were surprised and sometimes threatened by the sheer volume of theological concepts and perspectives, many of them never heard before, because the hierarchical leadership had kept tight control on both theologians and the airing of theological opinions. Now the restraints were off. There was an explosion—some say it was in direct proportion to the suppression before the council. While many Catholics enjoyed this opening up of their church, others feared that the church was losing its identity by becoming "too Protestant." They were those who had enjoyed the security of belonging to an institution that possessed unchanging truth, sound doctrine, and divinely-guaranteed hierarchical leadership.

THE FIRST CONCILIAR DOCUMENT

The four key documents of the council are its four constitutions, *Sacrosanctum Concilium* (The Constitution on the Sacred Liturgy), *Lumen Gentium* (The Dogmatic Constitution on the Church), *Dei Verbum* (The Dogmatic Constitution on Revelation), and *Gaudium et Spes* (The Pastoral Constitution on the Church in the Modern World). Approved on December 4, 1963, *Sacrosanctum Concilium* called for a revision of the rites of the seven sacraments, provided for the celebration of the eucharist in the vernacular language (S.C.

36), recognized that the liturgy "is made up of unchangeable elements divinely-instituted, and elements subject to change" (S.C. 21), called for the adaptation of the liturgy to the spiritual and cultural condition of each particular nation, provided for a revision of the liturgical year, and advocated the centrality of the Word of God proclaimed during the eucharistic celebration. Many of the issues and reforms called for by the medieval reformers, especially Martin Luther, were found in this constitution. In particular, the principle of meeting the needs of the people was paramount. Throughout the document, bishops and priests were called to fulfill their duty to provide the kind of liturgical celebration that would enable "the faithful to take part knowingly, actively, and fruitfully" (S.C. 11).

When the liturgy was revised after the council, Archbishop Marcel Lefebvre, of Econe, Switzerland, refused to accept the new rite on the grounds that it was not Catholic. He also rejected ecumenism and began what some have called the "traditionalist movement." After years of negotiation with the Vatican, he was excommunicated in 1988 after consecrating four priests as bishops to serve in what is now a schismatic church.

VATICAN II'S REDISCOVERY OF THE LOCAL CHURCH

Lumen Gentium (The Dogmatic Constitution on the Church) represents the climax of centuries of reflection on the nature of the church. While this document is cast in almost entirely universalist terms (it was written from the perspective of church as a worldwide institution), the document pertinently addresses the ecclesial reality of the local church:

This church of Christ is truly present in legitimate local congregations of the faithful, which, united with their pastors, are themselves called churches in the New Testament (L.G. 26).

This recognition of the dioceses united under its bishop, or a group of churches united under the archbishop of a particular region, restores a long-neglected balance to the Catholic understanding of church. For a thousand years, an ecclesiology had been developing that had stressed the church only as a universal institution headed by the pope and governed from Rome.

Examining the period in which the Christian Scriptures were

written, one finds that the understanding of the local church in a particular place, such as Jerusalem, Antioch, Corinth, Phillipi, and Galatia, as well as Rome, preceded the view of a universal church as the totality of all believers. As the monarchical papacy developed, so did the idea of the importance of the view of the church as a universal entity. After the Reformation split the Western church, and after the hopes for reconciliation faded, Cardinal Robert Bellarmine, S.J. (1542–1621), devoted himself to developing a Catholic ecclesiology that would clearly indicate the nature and location of the "true church." He wanted a definition of "church" that would exclude all who were not members of the Roman Catholic church. He achieved this by defining the true church in terms of visible, institutional characteristics. The true church was, according to Bellarmine, the "community of men, bound together by the profession of the same Christian faith, and by the communion of the same sacraments, under the government of legitimate pastors, and principally under the one Vicar of Christ on earth, the Roman pontiff."

From the end of the sixteenth century to the promulgation of *Lumen Gentium* in 1964, Bellarmine's understanding of church had been the basic Catholic definition of church. For nearly four hundred years, in order to deny any ecclesial validity to the Protestant communities, the Catholic church taught that there was only one true church, the church Jesus built on the rock of Peter (Matthew 16:18). The practical implications of this view meant that dioceses came to be regarded as mere administrative units of the universal church, as convenient divisions for Rome to oversee with the help of the bishops. In mission territories, what should have been the local church was merely "a faceless, passive community, a kind of dependency of the mother church, a scaled-down version of a European church."[2]

As a result of the conciliar teaching in *Lumen Gentium*'s twenty-sixth article, one can approach the meaning of "church" from both the universal and the local perspectives. The universal perspective begins with Rome. The local perspective starts with the local, concrete community, where the word of God is preached and where Jesus' saving death is proclaimed at the eucharistic table. As Karl Rahner declared: "From this starting point one can come to understand the church as a whole, because it is truly there in the local church."[3] Such a recognition has enormous implications for the way the Catholic church can proceed in the years ahead. With regard to the relationship between Rome, the local churches, and the national episcopal conferences, the recognition of the local church leads to the discovery of new ways in which both unity and diversity operate in the worldwide communion of local churches. The bishops of the local churches are united with one another because they are all in communion with the bishop of Rome, the principle of unity of the Catholic church. The recognition of the local and universal poles of the church opens the way for two-way communication, with the Roman center being able to benefit from the various experiences of the local churches throughout the world. This rediscovery relates to two other significant conciliar teachings, collegiality and ecumenism.

COLLEGIALITY

By its teaching on the collegiality of the body of bishops, the council corrected the long historical development toward papal centralization. At Vatican Council I (1869–70), the Constitution *Pastor Aeternus* only dealt with the pope, defining his universal jurisdiction and infallibility. Although other documents were being drafted, the outbreak of the Franco-Prussian War brought the council to a close before the assembled bishops had time to provide a fuller expression of the hierarchical makeup of the church. For the next ninety years, the church had a definitive statement of papal power and no statement regarding episcopal power. *Lumen Gentium* restored a balance through its teaching on collegiality. This meant that the bishops of the local churches constituted a college of bishops who, together with the pope, exercised a role in leading the church. Thus, the Catholic church is seen for what it is—a worldwide network of churches, each in communion with one another in virtue of every bishop's being in communion with the bishop of Rome. In this way, the Catholic church is not only seen as simply one, universal church, but as a communion of the world's local churches or dioceses headed by their bishops:

> Just as, by the Lord's will, St. Peter and the other apostles constituted one apostolic college, so in a similar way the Roman pontiff as the successor of Peter, and the bishops as the successors of the apostles are joined together (L.G. 22).

In 1965, Pope Paul VI established a worldwide episcopal synod, the first instrument to help make the concept of collegiality effective in the post-conciliar church. Although bishops met in local synods as early as the second century, only in the twentieth century was there the opportunity to have regularly scheduled synodal meetings involving all the bishops of the world. Whether the synods are an effective exercise of the concept of collegiality is still in the process of being resolved. This lack of resolution stems from the fact that the bishops of the Second Vatican Council also reaffirmed the doctrine of the First Vatican Council that papal definitions "need no approval of others, nor do they allow an appeal to any other judgment," because the pope acts "as the supreme teacher of the universal church" (L.G. 25). Thus, there was no clear teaching regarding the way in which the pope and the bishops were to interact with one another. While the conciliar teaching on collegiality gave the bishops a consultative role in the administration of the Catholic church, the pope was left free to make the decision to consult the bishops or to act on his own. A case in point occurred at the second synod of bishops, meeting in the year following Pope Paul's controversial encyclical *Humanae Vitae*. The bishops had an opportunity to seek a more effective form of co-responsibility in the church. However, they meekly reaffirmed the pope's freedom to act on his own, stated that the full implications of collegiality would take more time to be worked out, and timidly expressed their hope that the pope would accept their collaboration in the future.[4]

Also interesting is the fate of the statement regarding the church's social mission made in the 1971 synodal document *Justice in the World*. The bishops declared that:

> Action on behalf of justice and participation in the transformation of the world fully appear to us as a constitutive dimension of the preaching of the gospel, or, in other words, of the church's mission for the redemption of the human race and its liberation from every oppressive situation (Intro., 6).

In the many papal statements and encyclicals regarding social justice promulgated after 1971, the assertion that social action is a "constitutive dimension of the preaching of the gospel" has never been repeated.[5]

NEW POSSIBILITIES FOR ECUMENISM

In 1928, Pope Pius XI wrote *Mortalium Animos*, an encyclical that gave a resounding "no" to possible Catholic participation in the Protestant effort to overcome the scandal of Christian disunity. Because Rome's chief desire was "to recall her erring children"[6] (the Protestants), and because the Protestant bodies would not accept the primacy of the pope, Rome declared that:

It is clear that the Apostolic See can by no means take part in these assemblies, nor is it in any way lawful for Catholics to give such enterprises their encouragement or support. If they did so, they would be giving countenance to a false Christianity quite alien to the one church of Christ. Shall we commit the iniquity of suffering the truth, the truth revealed by God, to be made a subject for compromise?[7]

Thirty-six years later, in *Unitatis Redintegratio* (The Decree on Ecumenism), the bishops of the Second Vatican Council called for a thoroughly new orientation toward those who were now recognized as "separated brethren." No longer were Protestant and Anglican Christians regarded as heretics and schismatics whose only hope of unity was to be found in their contrite return to Rome. Recognizing the Protestant peoples as "separated churches and communities" (U.R. 3), the council recommended common prayer, and called for dialogue to take place between the Catholic church and the Protestant churches, the Anglican communion and the Eastern Orthodox churches. While warning against a false spirit that would compromise belief to achieve an easy unity, *Unitatis Redintegratio* pointed out that those who compare doctrines "should remember that in Catholic teaching there exists an order or 'hierarchy' of truths, since they vary in their relationship to the foundation of the Christian faith" (U.R. 11). Such an official recognition of the relative placement of Catholic teachings opened up new paths for those engaging in dialogue. Now the church offered a way to distinguish between those teachings that are basic to Catholic faith and those that are subject to different interpretation due to a shift in historical, theological, or philosophical perspective.

The recognition that the church of Christ is broader than the Roman Catholic church (see L.G. 8), coupled with the concept of the Catholic church as a communion of local churches, opened up a new way of envisioning the future unity between the Catholic church and the other churches. As a communion of churches herself, the Catholic church could join with the Protestant, Anglican, and Orthodox churches to form a communion of Christian communions. Each of them would then be united with the others in their common baptism and mutual belief in Christ.

THE CATHOLIC CHURCH RECOGNIZES ITS SINFULNESS

The Catholic church has not been a stranger to sinful actions. This book has alluded to the massacre of the Jews by the crusaders, the silence of the papacy during the time of Hitler's "final solution," the imperialistic imposition of European ways upon Far Eastern converts, the eradication of "heretics" in the alignment of ecclesial courts with secular executioners during the times of Inquisition, and the crushing of people's careers by the silencing and ostracizing of prophetic leaders and faithful theologians. But there has never been a public recognition of the institutional church's sins. The conciliar bishops broke with that precedent. In The Decree on Ecumenism the bishops declared:

> Christ summons the church, as she goes her pilgrim way, to that continual reformation of which she always has need.... Therefore, if the influence of events or of the times has led to deficiencies in conduct, in church discipline, or even in the formulation of doctrine...these should be appropriately rectified at the proper moment (U.R. 6).

Regarding the schisms and division in church history, the council stated that persons "of both sides were to blame" (U.R. 3). As for sins against unity, the leaders of the church stated, "...in humble prayer, we beg pardon of God and of our separated brethren, just as we forgive those who trespass against us" (U.R. 7).

With the same kind of historical consciousness, the bishops, in the document *Dignitatis Humanae Personae* (The Declaration on Religious Liberty), admitted that "In the life of the people of God...there have at times appeared ways of acting which were less in accord with the spirit of the gospel and even opposed to it" (D.H.P. 12). At the level of the local church and episcopal conferences, twenty-three bishops in the Caribbean Islands asked "pardon and forgiveness" from their people as they admitted in a pastoral letter that they had acted in ways opposed to "the spirit of the Gospel":

We want to confess here in all frankness and humility, that the record of our church has not always been as good as it should have been...In spite of the example of many dedicated priests and religious who have lived among the poor...too often the church we represent has seemed to be on the side of the wealthy and powerful.... In order to maintain a position of privilege, [the church] has sometimes closed its eyes to wrongs and injustices crying out for redress.... Our church has also been guilty on occasion of acts of racial discrimination and of perpetuating social and class divisions.[8]

GROWTH IN UNDERSTANDING GOD'S REVELATION

Dei Verbum (The Dogmatic Constitution on Divine Revelation), completed in 1965, encouraged all Catholics to read the Scriptures, and provided them with an introduction to the historical-critical tools of scriptural interpretation. The long-standing Catholic-Protestant debate over Scripture and tradition was settled in *Dei Verbum*'s assertion that there are not two sources of revelation (Scripture and tradition), but only one—God. The council provided a dynamic understanding of the Scriptures, referring to the "growth in the understanding of the realities...handed down" and advocating Mary, who pondered over the meaning of the events she experienced, as a model for those who seek to understand the word of God (D.V. 8).

One result of the Reformation's exultation of the Bible was the Catholic tendency to exalt church doctrine while subordinating the Scriptures to the role of providing "proof texts" for the doctrinal teachings. When the bishops declared that the church's "teaching office is not above the word of God, but serves it" (D.V. 10), they called for a new situation in which biblical revelation would have its own unique authority.

The bishops also provided a balanced response to the Modernist theories circulated at the beginning of the century. The council recognized that the gospel accounts, while having a basis in history, were never intended to be biographies of Jesus. Rather, the gospel accounts were written by those who based their work on the traditions they had received. Each evangelist structured his account in light of the needs of the particular believing community for whom the gospel account was being written (D.V. 9). In summary, the council promoted an approach to Scripture that is soundly rooted in the historical process in which God gradually became known as the God of Abraham, Isaac, and Jacob. That process culminated in the Christ event.

BIBLE AND CATECHISM

About a year after the promulgation of *Dei Verbum*, the bishops of the Netherlands gave to the Dutch people *A New Catechism*, a book written for adults, and exemplifying the fresh approach to revelation that is contained in The Constitution of Divine Revelation. Starting with the human search for God, *A New Catechism* moved through the development of Judaism, the advent of Jesus of Nazareth, the founding of the church, and culminated in the mystery of the one God who is Father, Son, and Holy Spirit. But Rome objected to *A New Catechism* because of certain doctrinal ambiguities—one such ambiguity being its treatment of Mary's lifelong virginity. Since the Bible does not clearly assert more than Mary's virginal conception of Jesus by the power of the Holy Spirit,[9] this issue and others were integrally related to the methods of biblical interpretation advocated in *Dei Verbum*. When a papal commission called upon the Dutch bishops to revise *A New Catechism* so that it would be in line with the magisterium's position on such disputed points, the Dutch bishops refused to do so.

Although *A New Catechism* survived Vatican censorship through a compromise in which a Vatican statement about the disputed points was added in an appendix to the book, the spirit of the Dutch church which produced the book did not survive. Within twenty years of the appearance of *A New Catechism*, the liberal leadership of the small Netherlands church was gone. They had been deemed too progressive and so, whenever a Dutch see became vacant, the Vatican appointed a bishop of a conservative cast.

Nearly twenty years later, at the extraordinary Synod of 1985, another kind of catechism was called for. The proposed catechism will function, according to Pope John Paul II, as a "point of reference" for the church's bishops and for their national and diocesan catechisms. The pope encouraged the commission writing the catechism by telling them of "the necessity and the urgency of a concise and clear exposition of the essential and fundamental contents of the faith and of Catholic morality." This catechism, written under the direction of Cardinal Joseph Ratzinger, Prefect of the Vatican Congregation for the Doctrine of the Faith, should be completed by 1990.

THE CHURCH SPEAKS TO THE WORLD

Gaudium et Spes (The Pastoral Constitution on the Church in the Modern World) originated in an intervention made from the floor of the council by Cardinal Suenens of Belgium in December 1962. He urged the council to consider the needs of the poor people of the world, to propose a practical theology of the rich nations' responsibility toward the impoverished people in the Third World, and to answer this hypothetical question put to the church by the world-at-large: "Church of Christ, what do you have to say of yourself?" In December 1965, the leadership of the Catholic church gave its answer in the longest and perhaps the most significant document of the council. That answer began by identifying the joys and the sorrows of the people of the world with the joys and sorrows of the church itself:

> The joys and hopes, the griefs and the anxieties of...this age, especially those who are poor or in any way afflicted, these too are the joys and hopes, the griefs and anxieties of the followers of Christ. Indeed, nothing genuinely human fails to raise an echo in their hearts (G.S. 1).

This Constitution has a most positive attitude regarding the church's relationship with the world. The model of church underlying *Gaudium et Spes* is that of the church as the servant of the human family: "...the church seeks but a solitary goal: to carry forward the work of Christ.... And Christ entered this world to give witness to the truth...to serve and not be served" (G.S. 3). The conciliar bishops advocated a worldview that sees the human race passing "from a rather static concept of reality to a more dynamic, evolutionary one" (G.S. 5).

Gaudium et Spes is divided into two sections. The first part, "The

Church and the Human Calling," expresses the way the Catholic church understands itself in the context of the human condition and in relationship to the human family in the contemporary world. Answering those critics who have accused the church of escapism and of avoiding responsibility for the world, the document pointed out that the church's hope for life beyond this "must not weaken but rather stimulate our concern for cultivating this one" (G.S. 39). Earthly progress, "to the extent that [it] can contribute to the better ordering of human society,...is of vital concern to the kingdom of God" (G.S. 39). "They are mistaken," the council declared, "who, knowing that we have here no abiding city but seek one which is to come, think that they may therefore shirk their earthly responsibilities" (G.S. 43).

The second part of the document, "Some Problems of Special Urgency," introduces a twofold criteria for discerning what was needed to resolve those problems related to family life, the development of culture, the socio-economic life, the political community, and the issue of seeking peace in a world where nations have weapons capable of vast destruction. That dual criteria was the consideration of each of these issues "in the light of the gospel and of human experience" (G.S. 46). The first problem of special urgency treated in *Gaudium et Spes* is that of "Fostering the Nobility of Marriage and the Family." The criterion of "human experience" meant that the council would look at marriage and family in such a way as to take seriously what can be learned from the vast accumulation of human wisdom. Thus, the church leadership committed itself to utilizing both church teaching and the data of human experience (including science, psychology, sociology, and anthropology). The result of this process showed forth in a new and wholistic vision of married life as a "covenant of conjugal love" (G.S. 48), an understanding of sexual intercourse as the act through which "love is uniquely expressed and perfected" (G.S. 49), and a view of family as a "school of deeper humanity" (G.S. 52).

The fifth and final chapter of the second part, "The Fostering of Peace and the Promotion of a Community of Nations," treats the interrelatedness of the gospel message and the highest aspirations of the human family. "If peace is to be established, the primary requisite is to eradicate the causes of dissention.... Wars thrive on these, especially on injustice" (G.S. 83)

THE DEVELOPMENT OF LIBERATION THEOLOGY

Within two years of the promulgation of *Gaudium et Spes*, Paul VI wrote his encyclical, *Populorum Progressio* (On the Development of Peoples). Declaring that "development is the new name for peace," Pope Paul called for bold changes in the structures of the international economic system and sounded many of the themes that would soon be taken up by the advocates of "liberation theology."[10]

The church's identification of the griefs and hopes of the people of the world, "especially those who are poor or in any way afflicted" (G.S. 1), set the theme for the 1968 meeting of the Latin American bishops in Medellin, Colombia. The gathered bishops committed themselves and the church of Latin America to an "effective preference to the poorest and most needy sectors of society."[11] The Latin American hierarchy also took to heart the pastoral constitution's vision of a new international economic order that would enable the poor nations to have a more equitable share in the world's resources. At Medellin, the bishops advocated a process of "conscientization" of the poor, a process through which the poor could come to an awareness of the causes of their poverty and their powerlessness. The bishops also pledged themselves to give to their poor whatever help they could, so that the poor could organize themselves to overcome the injustice that weighed so heavily upon them. Asserting that seeking liberation from their miseries was their right both as human beings and as followers of Christ, the bishops declared: "God has sent his son so that in the flesh he may liberate all people from the slavery which holds them in thrall, from sin, ignorance, hunger, wretchedness, and oppression."[12]

In 1971, on the eightieth anniversary of *Rerum Novarum*, the first significant social justice encyclical, Pope Paul VI gave *Octogesima Adveniens* to the universal church. In his letter, he took up many of the themes addressed by the Latin American bishops three years earlier in Medellin. Pointing out that economic problems call for political solutions, Paul VI stressed the role of the people; their decisions shaped the society they lived in.

Also in 1971, Gustavo Gutierrez, a Peruvian priest, had collected the pastoral letters of the Latin American bishops, organized the themes in light of their position taken at Medellin, and published a book entitled *A Theology of Liberation*. Gutierrez contended that one's own place in the world and one's attempts to change it should be the starting point of theology. The positions taken by the bishops at Medellin, Pope Paul's *Octogesima Adveniens*, and Gutierrez's book converged in the theme that the poor should take action in helping themselves, instead of waiting for help from outside. The Latin American "base Christian communities" are a direct outcome of the stress on conscientization and the idea of the poor taking the initiative in their own situation. In these lay-administered base communities, men and women combine spiritual development with work for social change.

"Liberation theology," however, had its enemies. It threatened those who benefited from the status quo. At times, some advocates of liberation infused elements of Marxist revolutionary ideology into liberation themes. Pope Paul VI responded to the 1975 Synod on Evangelization in his encyclical *Evangelii Nuntiandi*, which included his continuing reflection on the theological meaning of liberation. The General Conference of Latin American Bishops was scheduled to meet in Puebla, Mexico, in 1978. Rome had been keeping a wary eye on liberation theology, fearing that it would get the church involved in political matters. The deaths of Popes Paul VI in August and John Paul I in September postponed the meeting until 1979, when Pope John Paul II was able to attend. Although many feared that Puebla would change the position taken at Medellin, the bishops affirmed their previous commitment, declaring: "We affirm the need for conversion on the part of the whole church to a preferential option for the poor, an option aimed at their integral liberation."[13]

Espousing the cause of the poor is dangerous. In March 1979, Archbishop Oscar Romero of El Salvador, protector of the poor and advocate of justice, was gunned down while offering the eucharist. In December of that same year, lay worker Jean Donovan, Sisters Ita Ford, Maura Clarke, and Dorothy Kazel, all from the United States, were murdered by death squads. Their deaths had a direct relationship with the increasing identification of the church with the poor and the desire to achieve social justice in El Salvador.

THE COUNCIL CONCLUDES, BUT CONTROVERSY CONTINUES

The council concluded with its masterpiece, *Gaudium et Spes*. It spoke with the world in terms of human experience rather than abstract, universal principles to which human experience was expected to conform. The church specifically recognized the dynamic aspect of world history and the practical unity of the interdependent human family. Instead of deploring the passing of monarchies, ancient philosophical systems, or a worldview that divided reality into the two planes of the natural and the supernatural, the bishops brought the light of the gospel to a living and developing world.

Even as the council ended, the pilgrim people of God began to debate what the sixteen conciliar documents meant. Each commission that had drafted a document for the council had members who represented the various portions of the theological spectrum. It was to be expected that the members of each committee would debate some points heatedly, and then work out compromises on the document's organization or content. Trade-offs were made, the progressives, for example, agreeing to include a conservative point in one section, if the conservatives would agree to include the progressives' position in another part of the draft. As a result, none of the documents submitted to the conciliar bishops contained a single, clear-cut orientation. Each document would be subject to different interpretations, depending upon what specific themes the interpreter would choose to emphasize. Subject to different interpretations, the documents of the Second Vatican Council became, in effect, a two-edged sword. They could cut in either a liberal or a conservative direction.

A certain polarization of the church resulted. In the 1960s and 1970s the fresh, biblical image of the church as the people of God was favored by those who wanted to play down the hierarchical elements that characterized the institutional model of the church. The traditionalists, like Archbishop Lefebvre, would have nothing to do with the populist, democratic perspective of the church. The progressives, on the other hand, promoted the new role of the laity in the decision-making processes of the church, and pushed for greater pluralism, more ecumenical openness, and greater autonomy for episcopal conferences. Throughout these post-conciliar years, Pope Paul VI skillfully moderated, mediated, and led the church. He admirably balanced tradition with innovation. Then, on August 6, 1978, the anniversary of the atomic bombing of Hiroshima, the pope, who had pleaded at the United Nations for an end to all war, died with the words of the *Our Father* on his lips. Yves Congar, one of the most influential theologians at the Second Vatican Council, described the way Giovanni Battista Montini was laid to rest:

Paul, who had such a wonderful sense of the meaningful gesture, planned his funeral with an eye to making it sum up his life. His coffin was on ground level. It was surmounted, not by the tiara that he had given away (and no future pope would use), not even by a mitre or a stole, but by the open book of the gospels, its pages riffled by the light breeze.[14]

POPE JOHN PAUL I, POPE JOHN PAUL II

The conclave of cardinals chose Alberto Luciani, the son of a poor Italian glassworker, to succeed Paul VI. Luciani's decision to take the names of his two predecessors indicated that the new pope, John Paul I, would continue to lead the church in the same direction it had been moving for the previous twenty years. This smiling, congenial man had endeared himself to many in a pontificate that lasted only thirty-four days.

At the next conclave, the assembled cardinals chose Karol Wojtyla (1920–), the first non-Italian pope since the Dutch Adrian VI four hundred and fifty years earlier. Not only was Wojtyla Polish, he had also experienced first-hand the Nazi reign of terror (1939–1945), and the Soviet-imposed communist government that rules Poland to this day. From the start, questions were raised: Would the new pope be able to overcome his cultural and social conditioning of living in a strongly traditional church under a state of siege from a hard-line, anti-church government? Would he be able to achieve the broadness of vision needed to lead a worldwide church through the post-conciliar period of continuing innovation? In his choice of name John Paul II indicated that he intended to continue in the direction of his predecessors, but his actions during the first ten years of his pontificate declared that he had his own agenda for the Catholic church.

BACK TO THE ROMAN CENTER

The balance between the two poles of the Catholic church, the local and the universal, had begun to be restored during Vatican II. The International Synod of Bishops and national episcopal councils were recognized as practical expressions of the doctrine of collegiality as stated in *Lumen Gentium*. Pope Paul VI asserted in *Octogesimo Adveniens* (1971) that the wide variety of the circumstances of believers throughout the world made it difficult for Rome "to put forward a solution which has universal validity" (O.A. 4). Paul realized that it was up to the particular Christian communities throughout the world, working with their bishops, "to analyze...the situation which is proper to their own country...and to draw principles of reflection, norms of judgment and directives for action from the social teaching of the church" (O.A. 4).

Pope John Paul II is of a different mind. He intends to speak for the whole church, and he wants the universal church to take its lead from Rome, hence the crackdown on world-class theologians, such as Hans Küng and Charles Curran, both of whom have been declared unfit to teach Catholic theology. Others, such as Edward Schillebeeckx, O.P., and Leonardo Boff, O.S.F., have been called to Rome, and even "silenced" by order of the Congregation of the Doctrine of the Faith.[15] Under Pope John Paul, dissent of any kind is not tolerated, and theological diversity is hardly acceptable. In light of the oath of fidelity of 1989, something reminiscent of the "Oath against Modernism" that was mandatory for priests and seminary teachers during the preconciliar period, many see a regression to the times of ecclesiastical censorship, blacklisting, and suppression of theological research.

Although John Paul has been hard on progressive theologians, he has been totally committed to proclaiming the dignity of the human person. His encyclicals, beginning with *Redemptor Hominis* (1979) through *Sollicitudo Rei Socialis* (1987), champion the rights of human beings and speak out unequivocally on the necessity of social justice. *Sollicitudo Rei Socialis* is the sharpest critique of the social justice shortcomings of both the capitalist and the communist systems that has ever been written by a pope. Nevertheless, John Paul II and his curia are strongly suspicious of certain aspects of liberation theology. The problem with liberation theology is that it is local, indigenous, and difficult to keep under Roman control. There is fear that the practitioners of liberation theology will involve priests in politics, as in Nicaragua. The concept that "Action on behalf of justice [is]...a constitutive dimension of the preaching of the gospel," a key statement of the 1971 synod, has never been repeated. Missionaries have been warned by Cardinal Jozef Tomko, head of the curial Congregation for the Evangelization of Peoples, to avoid reducing missionary work to social action.[16] Rome has investigated the seminaries in the United States, looking to see that they are ordaining men who see their liturgical and sacramental role as primary.

THE EXTRAORDINARY SYNOD OF 1985

Pope John Paul II announced that there would be an extraordinary synod in 1985 to examine the direction of the Catholic church twenty years after the Second Vatican Council. Over one hundred national and regional conferences of bishops were represented at the synod. While the agenda did not find fault with the Second Vatican Council, or with "the spirit of the council," there was a shift in perspective. That shift viewed the council not so much in terms of its breakthroughs or innovations, but in the context of the entire history of the church. Collegiality, for example, was not something new, but something that had been with the church since the beginning. In this way and others, the Second Vatican Council was portrayed in a more traditional perspective. Nevertheless, the renewal the council brought to the church was affirmed, and principles for the interpretation of the conciliar documents were worked out in light of the synod's discussions. Theologian Avery Dulles summarizes those principles as follows:

1. Each passage and document of the council must be interpreted in the context of all the others, so that the integral meaning of the council may be rightly grasped.
2. The four constitutions of the council...are the hermeneutical key to the decrees and declarations.
3. The pastoral import of the documents ought not to be separated from or set in opposition to their doctrinal content.
4. No opposition may be made between the spirit and the letter of Vatican II.
5. The council must be interpreted in continuity with the great tradition of the church, including earlier councils.
6. Vatican II must be accepted as illuminating the problems of our own day.[17]

THE 1990s: *RISORGIMENTO OR AGGIORNAMENTO?*

In 1988, John Paul II had been pope for ten years and had assembled a tough-minded curia along the way. In 1984, the year before the extraordinary synod, Cardinal Joseph Ratzinger had sounded the word that may well have expressed the pope's program: *risorgimento.* It is an Italian word that means "restoration," and it has a poignant resonance with another Italian word heard from the lips of John XXIII twenty-five years earlier—*aggiornamento*, "moving ahead."

There has been a Vatican strategy to downgrade national episcopal conferences since the extraordinary synod. It is clear that Rome would prefer to deal with the bishops one at a time. Whole conferences of bishops, particularly those of larger Catholic nations, such as Brazil and the United States, would be difficult for the Vatican to deal with in any matter of bureaucratic effectiveness. There is also a trend toward re-establishing a preconciliar monarchical style. This can be seen in the pope's preference for making unilateral decisions, and the curia's effort to have practical control over what happens anywhere in the church. Although the council called for local and regional churches to be more than communities called to carry out the directives of Rome, it appears that John Paul II has great difficulty in walking the line that separates Roman authoritarianism from legitimate diversity in the local churches of the world. The local churches of each nation were urged to develop "the ability to express Christ's message in their own way" (G.S. 44). Under Pope John Paul II, there has been a definite slowing down of the process of accommodating the preaching of God's word to specific peoples in their own unique cultures.

John Paul II has also gone back on the council's action in calling for a revised eucharistic liturgy. Although the Tridentine Latin Mass was suppressed, the pope pressed for its re-emergence. The pope also wants to make very clear what a Catholic must believe and practice. In particular, he has attempted to make the hard line of *Humanae Vitae*'s prohibition of artificial birth control the litmus test of episcopal loyalty and the criterion for being a faithful Catholic lay person. The pope does not want to admit shades of gray in his drive for a black and white statement of Catholic faith and morals. The universal Roman catechism scheduled for 1990 is expected to reinforce this papal agenda of order, organization, and orthodoxy.

The years after the council witnessed a style of episcopal appointments in which there was much consultation between the Vatican and the local church regarding the person who would be that church's next bishop. Under Pope John Paul II, consultation has been all but eliminated. The Vatican nuncio seems to be the key person involved as the Roman curia goes about a strategy of unilaterally appointing "safe" men to the vacant episcopal sees—a far cry from Nicaea I, which established that bishops should be elected by all the bishops of a province, with final confirmation by the metropolitan, and that no bishop can be transferred to another diocese. Controlled information and controlled access to those who make the decisions has become the norm. The beginning of certain democratic processes that started during the council has been replaced by more secretive procedures. With this increased secrecy, the Catholic church has lost its ecumenical verve; relations with other Christian churches can only grow in an atmosphere of diversity and the acceptance of pluralism. The Vatican reaction to the episcopal ordination of Barbara Harris in the Anglican church is typical of the Roman mentality. Rome chided the Anglican community for making the relationship between them take a turn for the worse because the Anglicans permitted a woman to be ordained as a bishop.

While one cannot say that the progressive openness of the Catholic church that began with the pontificate of Pope John XXIII is gone, it is obvious that Rome has embarked upon a double policy of reasserting its authority and recentralizing the Catholic church. Some would call this a policy of restoration. Others might say that perhaps Rome perceives that clear lines of authority and clear expressions of belief are essential to the preservation of unity in a global church that is moving into the twenty-first century.

The hope for the church's future lies in the traditional Catholic strength of the "both...and...." The hope is a balance between both the pope and individual conscience; both the universal church and the diocesan or national local church; both mystery and institution; both law and freedom; both Roman oversight and local initiative. There are also two areas where the church's hope for the future lies not so much in balance as it does in preference. One such preference is the preferential option for the poor. The other is the preference for the gospel of Jesus Christ above all else.

CHAPTER 24

The Church in the United States

SPANISH AND FRENCH BEGINNINGS

Much of the Catholic religious history of the United States has yet to be explored. In this chapter, we propose to give a brief resume of some of the activities, challenges, and attitudes of the Catholics who came to North America and of those who led them. The Spanish Catholics, who preceded the French and English by almost a century, were the first to come to the New World. In 1513, Ponce de Leon set foot in Florida and Balboa gazed at the Pacific Ocean. In 1541, de Soto explored the southwest. In 1562, de Ayllon saw his settlers celebrate the eucharist along the Chesapeake, forty-five years before the English Protestants settled at nearby Jamestown. Santa Fe (Holy Faith), the oldest capital city in the United States, was founded in 1605. All along the southern rim of the United States, from Florida to California, Spanish Catholicism was planted. The many Catholic names that exist today testify to their presence: St. Augustine, San Antonio, San Francisco, Los Angeles, and Corpus Christi. The distinctive Spanish architecture still graces the southwestern coastline. Since church and state were united in Spain, exploration was intimately bound up with the spread of the faith. Columbus himself remarked that one purpose of his voyage was that of seeking ways by which people could be converted to Christianity. Colonization and conversion were two sides of the same coin for the Spanish. In both the mother country and the colonies, there was the inevitable conflict between church and state regarding the spheres of influence and jurisdiction. This conflict was most pronounced in the treatment of the native Americans. The civil administration tended to exploit the natives, plying them with liquor, forcing them into slavery and taking over their land. The missionaries were squarely on the side of the native Americans. The Spanish theologian, Francisco de Vitoria, delivered lectures at the University of Salamanca in 1539 that helped to lay the foundation for a humane international law. He declared that the native populations of the Americas were not to be taken as slaves, that they should handle their own disputes according to their own customs, and that their property should not be taken from them except in fair trade. De Vitoria went so far as to suggest that neither the emperor nor the pope were masters of the universe and, even if they were, this would still not deny the rights of native Americans to hold property. We have already seen how Bartholomew de las Casas was a pioneer in attempting to get fair treatment for the "Indians." It was his influence, along with others, that led Pope Paul III to declare, in 1537, "The said Indians and all other people who may later be discovered by Christians, are by no means to be deprived of their liberty or the possession of their property, even though they be outside the faith of Jesus Christ."

The French followed the Spanish. These were mainly Jesuits and Franciscans, with men like Verrazano (an Italian in French service) exploring the North Atlantic seacoast, and Cartier sailing up the St. Lawrence River; and there are the famous names of Champlain, Joliet, Marquette, Duluth, LaSalle, and other French missionaries and lay explorers like them. They, too, were motivated by their faith. Many of them were persons of high culture, honored at their universities; yet they left such prestige and comfort to live, suffer, and die among the native Americans, sometimes experiencing horrifying and excruciating tortures, such as those endured by the famed Isaac Jogues and his companions.

The French attitude toward the natives was not to convert them forcibly, like the Spanish, or exterminate them, like the English, but to treat them as brothers. The historian Belton praises the French as "a force which made for the preservation of the Indians as opposed to their destruction, so characteristic of the Anglo-American frontier." The exploits and hardships of such as these make the most glorious pages in the history of the church's missionary activity. Many of their efforts proved in vain, but their blood nourished the faith; their efforts gave some benefit to the native Americans as they were taught how to weave, tan leather, and tend cattle. The efforts of these missionaries produced the early dictionaries and the first maps of the new world.

Eventually, as England was victorious in the colonial wars, the Spanish and French missionary and political enterprises receded in importance. Protestant England thus gained the ascendancy, and the Spanish and French disappeared as a political force, while their missions remained to survive as best they could. Later, in the seventeenth century, the suppression of the Jesuits would considerably cripple missionary activity. By 1763, Spain would cede Florida, and England, in turn, would gain all the territory east of the Mississippi from France. The area that would become the United States was on its way to becoming not a Catholic country with a Spanish or French culture, but a Protestant country with distinct Anglo-Saxon culture.[1]

PROTESTANT BEGINNINGS

It is important to note that the English came to the New World for a variety of purposes, bringing with them a variety of Protestant denominations. The Anglican English settlers of Virginia came for the purpose of economic gain, as did those who established New York (which was formerly the Dutch colony of New Amsterdam). Anglicans also established the colony of Georgia to provide relief for those in debtors' prisons in England. The English Puritans (better known to us as Pilgrims), fleeing persecution by the Anglicans, wanted religious freedom, and eventually settled in Massachusetts. (In time, they expanded to establish the colonies of New Hampshire and Connecticut.) Although they originally supported religious freedom, the Puritans established a theocracy requiring all others to follow their Congregational church. But their strict interpretation of Congregationalist doctrines soon forced some of their members to seek religious freedom in the establishment of Rhode Island, where religious toleration for all was the norm. Pennsylvania, founded by English Quaker William Penn, was also meant as a refuge for those fleeing religious persecution and became the haven for Lutherans fleeing the Thirty Years War, as well as for a variety of more radical European Protestants who were persecuted by Catholics, Lutherans, and Calvinists alike. Because of this overwhelming Protestant foundation, the United States soon became identified with Protestantism so that the two were practically interchangeable. One result of this identification was that non-Catholic historians tended to regard the nation as Protestant, and so United States history has largely been written, until modern times, from a Protestant bias.

The first Protestant settlers to these shores wanted to restore the old Carolingian ideal of church and state working as one, only the church this time was to be in the Protestant tradition, a Protestant theocracy. William Penn, whose colony of Pennsylvania had no established state religion, wrote in 1682, "Government seems to me a part of religion itself, a thing sacred in its institution and end...." Thus, many of the first settlers came to establish the millenarian's dream as seen in the very names they gave the new settlements: Salem (short for Jerusalem), New Haven, and New Hope. This ideal dream, however, was to be no more tolerant than any of the others, for the magistrates of these first settlements were bound to attack heresy, schism, and disobedience by the use of civil power. So, as in the early and medieval days of Christendom, the intention was clear: A person could not be a member of the state without being a member of the church.

It is important to note that this Protestant theocracy was established on a popularist model: that is, there was to be no determining hierarchical clerical structure, as in Europe. Rather, the model was a democratic one. This had expected results. One was that the United States started out and remained singularly lacking in anti-clericalism. There was no need to be anti-clerical, since the clergy was not a class set apart, was not aristocratic, and was definitely not in control. Another result was that logic, in due time, forced a complete separation of church and state as Christianity became a voluntary movement in the United States. Finally, doctrine mattered less and less in any Protestant consensus, because there was so much diversity among themselves in this area.

Another result of the Protestant dominance was that Catholics in the United States were always somehow seen as "foreign." After all, they were not democratic; they still operated under the old clerical, hierarchical structure. This smacked of the old European royalism. Then too, unlike the Protestants, doctrine mattered very much to the Catholics, for there seemed to be a strict canon of Catholic doctrinal positions on every question. It is no wonder that Protestants thought that Catholics could never adapt to "their" country. It is no wonder that so many Protestant historians in the past took little interest in Catholicism as a force in the United States. For them, Catholicism was still a foreign appendage (beholden to a foreign pope). As Jonathan Edwards said, America was "the principal kingdom of the Reformation"—Catholics were obviously out of place in it. Let us now see how the Catholics fared in this context.

Protestant dominance also led many Protestants to take it almost as an article of faith that the Catholic church, with its strong central control, could never adapt to American conditions. This explains why many American Catholic leaders thought that the way to get into the mainstream of America was to get into and to imitate the dominant Protestant culture. Let us now turn to the origins of this Protestant ascendancy.

THE ATLANTIC SEACOAST

The English brought to the Atlantic colonies a deeply ingrained hatred of anything Catholic. They had memories of their homeland's "Bloody Mary," the attempted Spanish invasion in 1588, and the inept Guy Fawkes Gunpowder Plot that tried to blow up the king and Parliament, supposedly to advance the Catholic cause. Catholics were hated not only for their "popish" religion, but for their attempts at political domination. The thirteen colonies were so vigorously anti-Catholic that it was a real challenge for the handful of Catholics to cling to their religion at all; some didn't. The rival denominations, the Anglicans in Virginia, and the Puritans in Massachusetts, agreed on one thing: their hatred for Catholics. They both passed similar laws against Catholics, and so did the other colonies, a serious case of overkill, since there were such a small number of Catholics around at that time. (In the English colonies, there were about 23,000 Catholics, with fewer than thirty priests.)

A small band of English Catholics came to North America for much the same reasons as their compatriot Protestants: economic gain and, perhaps, to be able to worship more freely, and to get out from under the English penal laws. English Catholic convert George

Calvert, who became the first Baron of Baltimore, was granted a charter to establish a colony in the New World. However, it was his son, Cecil Calvert, the second Lord Baltimore, who sent his brothers, Leonard and George, to lead the original colonists in Maryland. They included three Jesuit priests and sixteen Catholic gentlemen, and a larger contingent of Protestants. Although the colony was settled as a commercial enterprise, Calvert intended that it should remain neutral in regard to religion (this is often referred to as the "Maryland design"). He advised the Catholics to worship in private and to give no offense to the Protestants of the colony. The Maryland Assembly appeared to agree with these ideas of religious toleration when, in both 1639 and 1649, it issued Acts of Toleration, declaring that "no one was to be molested for his religion who professed to believe in Jesus Christ." (Their famous phrase "the free exercise thereof" was to be found a century and a half later in the Constitution.)

But the tensions in England between Anglican and Puritan spilled over into the colonies. Within a few years, a Puritan faction from Virginia, led by Richard Ingle, toppled the Calvert government and gained control of the Maryland colony. In 1654, they repealed the Acts of Toleration and outlawed Catholicism in Maryland. They condemned ten Catholics to death, executed only four, but plundered the houses of the Jesuits, forcing them to flee. The Calvert family regained control very briefly, but in 1691, Maryland became a royal colony. The Church of England was established by law in 1692, and Catholics were not permitted to participate in public life until 1781.

In New York in 1682, a Catholic governor had been appointed. The next year, he also issued a guarantee of religious freedom, thus joining George Calvert, William Penn, and Roger Williams as leaders in religious toleration. However, in 1689, a Calvinist overthrew his regime and began a reign of terror against Catholics. In 1693, the Church of England was established in New York with all of the usual anti-Catholic laws. So it was in every colony. It is worth mentioning, however, that in the two cases in the colonial period where Catholics were (briefly) in control, it was they who issued acts of religious toleration.

THE CARROLLS

Anti-Catholic prejudice slackened somewhat during the Revolutionary War (as it would during the Civil War). The loyal and noble conduct of Catholics went a long way to break down the barriers. In addition, Frenchmen from Catholic France (such as Lafayette) were assisting the colonies, and it would be without purpose to show an anti-Catholic bias in the presence of such allies. In contrast, the bias was quite active in the case of Canada. England had just granted the French Catholic Canadians religious freedom. The outcry in the American colonies was bitter and vocal. The Continental Congress itself denounced Catholicism to the king of England, and chastised him for giving freedom to a "religion that has deluged your island in blood and disbursed impiety, bigotry, persecution, murder, and rebellion through every part of the world." Later, when Congress turned to Canada, asking for help in the fight against England, Catholic Canada understandably refused to trust bigots who had persecuted their fellow Catholics in the colonies. The Canadians preferred to remain neutral toward England, which gave them religious freedom.

It was not only the Revolutionary War that brought relief to Catholics, but also the prominent family of the Carrolls. Charles Carroll, a member of the aristocratic colonial establishment, was a signer of the Declaration of Independence, and almost our first president. His patriotism was unimpeachable, even though he was a Roman Catholic. The Carrolls demonstrated that one could be a Roman Catholic and a good American at the same time. Charles's cousin, John Carroll, an able and talented man, became the first bishop of the United States in 1790.

EARLY COLLEGIALITY

If we recall that Catholics and their clergy were in North America from the 1500s, and that there was no bishop until 1790, we might be surprised to realize the consequences of this. It meant that for some one hundred and fifty years, there was no administration of the sacraments of confirmation and holy orders. It meant that all during this period, the church in the United States was led by what we could call a presbyterate. The local clergy were all members of religious orders. They and their superiors were the overseers of the Catholic population. Rome was far away and Rome considered the new country little more than barbaric. In 1757, Rome designated a bishop in London as Vicar Apostolic, overseer for the American church, but he was also far away, and his jurisdiction virtually ceased when England went to war with its colonies. It is not that the colonial clergy especially wanted a bishop. The Protestants were so hostile that Catholics did not want to risk further harassment by having a "foreign" bishop sent over to take control.

Finally, the matter was resolved. Rome, still thinking in European terms, asked the new government (through Benjamin Franklin) its opinion about the first United States bishop. Congress, to the perplexity of some, replied that it did not have competence in such matters. By this time, Congress was debating ten proposed amendments to the Constitution (known to us as the Bill of Rights); these were approved in 1791. The First Amendment forbade the establishment of any one religion as the official religion of the nation (which pleased the minority Catholics)—though some states did not abolish their "official" Protestant churches until 1835.

It was Benjamin Franklin who recommended to the Vatican his good friend, John Carroll, for the position of first bishop in the United States. Carroll had been for many years a leader among the American Catholic clergy, who had elected him as their choice for bishop in 1789. The American clergy were very concerned that this bishop be elected by the clergy and that he be dependent upon the pope only in spiritual matters, but neither was to be the case. Rome did the appointing without reference to their election, and in subsequent decades, the church in the United States would be Europeanized and assume more traditional positions. Still, the entire one hundred and fifty years' experience gave the bishops of the United States a tenuous independence from Rome from the start. It was this same innocent spirit that led the Third Provincial Council of Baltimore in 1837 to protest their loyalty to the pope, but only in spiritual matters. They boldly said, "We do not acknowledge any civil or political supremacy, or power over us, in any foreign potentate or power, though that potentate might be the chief pastor of our church." Even before Carroll's time, general chapters had been held, and the clergy decided all legal, liturgical, and disciplinary matters themselves. Carroll only continued that tradition, as did the half dozen Provincial Councils held over the next twenty years:

In each case, all the bishops of the country were present, and their legislation was binding on the Catholics of the entire nation. These were not merely meetings to discuss problems; they were legislative assemblies.... There is no other national

church within the Roman Catholic communion which met so
regularly and legislated so widely.[2]

THREE PRESSURES

No appreciation of Catholicism in the United States is possible without a profound recognition of the three basic pressures with which
the Catholic church had to contend. First of all, the Catholic church
was taking shape in prejudiced English colonies, where most people
were Protestants who regarded Catholics more as foreigners than as
citizens. This factor alone helps to explain the reaction of some
American bishops who unceasingly and vigorously protested that
Catholics were truly American. Second, the Catholic church in the
United States was a church of the immigrants. From the 1820s, but
more especially after the Civil War, a veritable deluge of foreigners
flowed into the country. Most of them were Catholic, and this posed
the enormous problem of demonstrating to the Protestant majority
that foreign-born Catholics could be loyal to the United States. Finally, there was the pressure brought about by the Vatican's reaction to revolutions taking place in Europe. It was the age of the fall
of the papal states, the Third Republic in France, and the papacy's
deep and abiding suspicion of democracy, freedom, and modern
civilization, as criticized in Pius IX's Syllabus of Errors. It was the
age which saw an increase of Roman centralization, a drive for uniformity in the church, and an inability to resolve the problems of
the church-state relationship. It was in the crush of pressures like
these—American Protestant hatred and fear of Catholics, the high
waves of immigration, and a suspicious and uncomprehending centralized Rome—that Catholicism in the United States came into its
own.

EARLY RIVALRIES

Before dealing with the rivalries among the various Catholic ethnic
groups in the United States, it is important to understand the rivalry
between the clergy and laity, which dates from colonial times. Although there were few Catholics in the colonies in the eighteenth
century, there were proportionally even fewer priests. Thus, it was
the laity who set up its own churches by establishing a committee of

trustees to purchase property, build the church, and pay the clerical salary. This practice of "hiring and firing" of the clergy was done without reference to a bishop, for there was no bishop until 1790.

This "lay-trustee" system continued into the nineteenth century and led to tensions not only between the clergy and laity but also, after 1790, between priests and the newly-ordained bishops. The issue was first addressed by John England, an Irish priest who was appointed as bishop of Charleston, South Carolina, in 1820. Bishop England, while upholding the basic notion of clerical authority and lay participation, proposed a constitution in 1823 to end the lay-trustee controversy. This constitution called for an annual meeting of the bishop with a congress-like body, composed of a house of clergy and a house of laity. This "congress" would watch over institutions in the diocese and make recommendations to the bishop, while the bishop alone would take action and be responsible for what happened in the diocese. Many, however, saw this as too innovative and, therefore, dangerous. In 1829, Pius VII admonished the bishops of the United States over the issues of trusteeship and authority and set down general rules about church property—henceforth all future property was put in the name of the bishop.

John England was an ardent ecumenist who accepted invitations to speak in non-Catholic pulpits. In 1826, he was the first Catholic priest to address Congress.[3] England also began the first "American" seminary, short-lived as it was. We put the word "American" in quotes to indicate a deep conflict and rivalry within the hierarchy. There already was a seminary, the one founded in Baltimore by the French Sulpicians at the invitation of John Carroll. The problem was that John England considered the French too foreign. The French bishops, on the contrary, considered John England and the immigrant Irish as latecomers, who threatened to make the church less American and more Irish. Having lived on this continent for more than one hundred years, the French felt that they represented the true American heritage. They and their French Sulpicians were more cultured, better educated, and in the tradition of the old Maryland Catholics. They felt that they should lead the young Catholic church and that they should protect the "American" way of life from the "foreign" tendencies of the Irish bishops. Therefore, they were not happy with John England and the growing Irish dominance of the hierarchy.[4] The Irish in turn, as they became more numerous through immigration, began to resent being led by the French clergy with their strange accents. Some Irish congregations went so far as to send for their own Irish clergy. Frequently, such clergy were troublemakers expelled from Ireland to seek their fortunes in the New World. The Irish and the French were not the only ones to experience such conflicts. Later, the immigrant Germans similarly resented the ministrations of English, or Irish, or French clergy.

PROTESTANT REACTIONS

The Catholic immigrants greatly alarmed the Protestants. Their fear of cheap labor and job layoffs agitated their traditional hatred and fear of Catholics. On January 2, 1830, a group of Protestant ministers launched the anti-Catholic weekly, *The Protestant*, which contained exaggerations, slanders, and horror stories about Catholics. The results of such inflammatory agitation were evident in the numerous incidents that took place. In Philadelphia, Bishop Kenrick submitted a respectful request to the city leaders, asking that Catholic children not be forced to use the King James version of the Bible. This request resulted in fearful rioting and destruction of church property. In Massachusetts, incited by the harangues of the Reverend Lyman Beecher (father of Harriet Beecher Stowe, author of *Uncle Tom's Cabin*), a mob burned down the Ursuline convent, even though most of the students were Protestant. Fictitious stories of ex-priests and escaped nuns (such as the widely believed fiction of Maria Monk) were circulated as if they were true.

Not all were as passive as Bishop Kenrick, however. Bishop Hughes of New York warned that if any Catholic churches were burned in his diocese, he would not prevent retaliation; he had a mob of willing Irishmen to back him up. His non-pacifist approach seemed to have prevented the burning of New York churches. It was this same Bishop Hughes who broke the monopoly of the Protestant groups in New York, by seeing that no state aid was given to the public schools that were inculcating Protestant religious principles. Inadvertently, however, he set up the precedent of no aid to any school teaching religion, and thus laid the foundation for the chronic school aid problems that plague parochial schools to this day.

The Protestants continued their attacks by organizing against Catholics. In 1854, a national organization known as the Know-Nothings, supported to a large measure by the Protestant ministers, appeared dedicated to issuing numerous anti-Catholic pamphlets, books, and newspaper articles. They also organized politically as the American Party to get their members elected to Congress and "save the republic from the pope." Although seventy-five members were eventually elected to Congress, the American Party was powerless by 1860.

It was the loyalty and dedication of Catholics during the Civil War that disproved such open bias. Catholics fought on both sides and conducted themselves loyally. The conduct of the Catholic chaplains and sisters again merited high praise. President Lincoln himself remarked, "Of all the forms of charity and benevolence seen in the crowded wards of the hospitals, those of some Catholic sisters were among the most efficient." We should note here that the issue for Lincoln and many Northerners was not abolition, but preserving the Union. As regards slavery itself, the church did not oppose the owning of slaves, which is described as one of the consequences of sin, but rather only condemned the slave trade—the buying and selling of human beings. (Gregory XVI had condemned the slave trade in 1838.)

After the war, prejudice again came to the forefront. In 1887, a new organization was founded by some ninety-four Protestant ministers. It was called the American Protective Association (A.P.A.), and it proposed to keep the nation both American and Protestant.

THE CHURCH OF THE IMMIGRANTS

Perhaps the best way to see the growth of Catholicism in the United States during the nineteenth century is to look at the statistics about Catholic immigrants and population. At the time of the establishment of our country, Catholics numbered about forty thousand in a general population of four million.[5] This number had grown to about half a million in a population of twelve million by 1820, just prior to the waves of immigrants from Europe and Asia.

In the two decades between 1830 and 1850, more than two million people, mostly Catholics, arrived in the United States. The Irish generally settled in the cities of the east coast, while the French and German immigrants tended to move further west. By 1860, the estimated three million Catholics in the United States were being served by forty-five bishops and two thousand priests: Catholics represented the largest single denomination in the United States.

But the greatest period of growth was just beginning. The American Catholic population grew to nine million by 1890, and to fifteen million (served by twenty thousand priests) by 1920, when new immigration laws set quotas by country on the number of immigrants.

Life for these Catholic immigrants was indeed difficult. Harassed because of the chronic Protestant bias against Catholics, they were often faced with the practical choice of renouncing their religion in order to advance socially and economically, or retaining it and thereby accepting a permanent status of inferiority. The immigrants tended to move into the cities, which in time gave Catholicism in the United States its distinctive urban character. But even more important, the immigrants settled in specific neighborhoods or "ghettos" as a means of preserving their ethnic heritages. They also established ethnic parishes, sending to the "old country," if necessary, for a priest who spoke their language. At the same time, the parish or parochial school was established, both as an escape from the predominantly Protestant public schools, and to preserve "the faith"; usually as celebrated in their homelands. (In 1884, at the Third Plenary Council of Baltimore, the bishops required all parishes to have a parochial school, so that there were more than four thousand parochial schools in the United States by 1900.)

The parish soon became the center of life for the immigrants—it was the place for social life, education, and political dialogue—and it was the parish priest who was the leading figure. He spoke their language and understood their customs; he was the most educated person in the parish; he had learned how to deal with the political and economic systems outside the parish, and advised his flock on most issues. There was little anti-clericalism among these Catholics. And so it continued for many parish priests until the middle of the twentieth century, when the laity, mostly through the G.I. Bill, and women's religious orders, through the need for more and more teachers for the parochial schools, had the opportunity to become better educated. By the 1960s, many parishioners were better educated than their clergy. This, added to the changes following Vatican II, would soon produce a real identity crisis for clergy in the United States.

AMERICANISTS VERSUS THE CONSERVATIVES

As the Catholic church moved toward the end of the nineteenth century and into the twentieth, divisions arose in the American hierarchy, not so much along lines of nationality, but along the lines of how best to live the faith in the United States. The bishops were divided into two factions. One faction felt that the church should not assimilate itself into the mainstream (for heaven was the true home of the church); that it could make no headway against the Protestants, who saw to it that the public schools were in reality Protestant schools, and that hedged in Catholics at every turn. To be pious, quiet, isolated citizens preparing for another world was the chief role of Catholics. The bishops who espoused these conservative positions were represented by Ryan of Philadelphia, Elder of Cincinnati, Gilmour of Cleveland, and especially Corrigan of New York, and McQuaid of Rochester.

The other faction, more liberal in their thought, called themselves the Americanists. As the name implied, they totally supported the American culture, supported the public schools, reached out to Protestants, and firmly believed in the nation's posture of complete separation of church and state. Such were Bishops Keane, Spalding, Ireland, and Gibbons. Gibbons was especially important, for he became a cardinal in 1886, and was *the* churchman in the United States. He had worked in North Carolina, where he became acquainted with the Protestants, preached in their churches, and made many converts. As a leader of the Catholic church for some forty years, he did more than anyone else to mediate between the church and the country. He was in demand as a speaker, was consulted by presidents, and did much for church-state relations. At his jubilee in 1911, people of all faiths gathered to honor him, including President Taft and ex-President Theodore Roosevelt. He was a good balance to his more outspoken Americanists, Ireland and Keane, and a hard-pressed diplomat in trying to appease both factions of the Catholic church in the United States.

KNIGHTS OF LABOR

For good reasons, Rome had always been suspicious of secret societies. In Europe, they had frequently been revolutionary and anticlerical. In the United States, however, many of these societies, such as the Knights of Pythias, the Sons of Temperance, and the Ancient Order of Hibernians, were harmless. The exceptions were those few anti-Catholic masonic lodges. Since they posed no threat, the Americanist bishops felt that condemning them would only invite new hostilities. The conservative bishops, however, wanted the secret societies condemned, and prodded Rome to do so. But when Rome did condemn a few of the secret societies (such as the Knights of Pythias and the Odd Fellows), Gibbons would not publish the decree until forced to do so.

The real issue in which Gibbons triumphed, however, concerned the Knights of Labor, a workingman's organization, and forerunner of the American Federation of Labor (A.F.L.). The conservatives also wanted this organization condemned, but, in 1887, Gibbons spoke strongly on behalf of the A.F.L. to Rome, and became the hero of the working man. Four years later, when Leo XIII issued his encyclical, *Rerum Novarum*, which defended the rights of workers to organize, Gibbons was vindicated.

CONTROVERSY AND THE CATHOLIC UNIVERSITY

The conservatives and Americanists also clashed over the establishment of a Catholic university. The problem centered on its location and curriculum. Some wanted the university in their own dioceses, but others, like Cardinal Gibbons, did not. (His choice was Philadelphia.) Finally, the issue was settled, and the university was erected in Washington, D.C., with Bishop Keane as its first rector.

Some Americanists also opposed the appointment of an apostolic delegate for many reasons. First, it was the heyday of anti-Catholic organizations, which would make much of a foreign bishop coming to oversee Catholics in the United States. The previous visit of an apostolic delegate (Bishop Bedini in 1853) was the occasion of rioting wherever he went. Besides, the bishops felt they could handle things by themselves. Rome, however, had its way, and Archbishop Satolli came as apostolic delegate. At first, he sided with the Americanists. A few years later, however, when he returned to Rome, he was instrumental in having Keane removed as rector of Catholic University, and influential in Leo XIII's condemnation of "Americanism."

APPROACHES TO PROTESTANTISM

These two major Catholic factions, as might be expected, had extremely different views about Protestantism. The conservatives, distressed at the treatment of Catholics by the Know-Nothings and the A.P.A., were deeply suspicious of the Protestants, and felt that keeping a distance between Catholics and Protestants was the best policy. The Americanists, on the other hand, were always ready to reach out and recognize the virtues and truths possessed by Protestants. Conservative Catholic leaders wanted a rigid interpretation that "outside the church there is no salvation" (they understood "church" to mean the Catholic church). In those days of high bigotry, these Catholics found consolation in their conviction that no Protestant would be in heaven.

The liberal Americanists and the Paulists (newly founded by convert Isaac Hecker) held the opposite position, and interpreted the word "church" in the most inclusive sense possible. It was the Paulists who, in 1904, established the first house at Catholic University to train priests for the special mission of converting Protestants to Catholicism. The liberal bishops accepted all invitations to speak in "Protestant" territory. Because of this, Bishop Keane, who spoke at Harvard in 1879, was refused permission by Bishop McQuaid to speak in his diocese at Cornell University. In 1893, the Americanist bishops attended the great Ecumenical Parliament in Chicago, another action which proved to be too radical for the conservative church leaders.

THE SEPARATION OF CHURCH AND STATE

Conservative Catholics in the United States were wary of church-state separation. They saw that the Protestants often dominated all issues, that the public schools were, in effect, Protestant, and that Catholics were discriminated against most of the time. They saw this kind of separation as an aberration, a departure from centuries of European Catholic tradition, and boding no good for the church as a whole. The Americanists, on the other hand, felt that the medieval union of church and state was merely an historical "accident," not something essential to the faith. They therefore lost no opportunity to tell their Protestant neighbors that the Catholic church had no intention of uniting church and state. They could point to Catholics in Maryland and New York who had issued the first acts of religious toleration (which were later repealed by the Protestants). Americanists were content with the freedom of the Catholic church to do what it wanted in the United States, in contrast to the European situation where concordats and traditional customs hindered the Catholic church at every turn. The Protestants themselves were not quite convinced of this, believing that Catholics took their political orders from the clergy and ultimately from the pope.

One of the ticklish situations came for the Americanists when Pope Pius IX demanded worldwide Catholic support for Vatican efforts to regain the papal states lost to Italian unification. His successor, Leo XIII, also argued that the church's possession of the papal states was the best safeguard to the church's independence. The Americanist bishops disagreed with the pope on this issue, but American conservative bishops could not have agreed more. They and their followers, like the Jesuits, seemed to make the right of the papacy to the papal states an article of faith. The Americanist bishops, under Gibbons, side-stepped the issue by wrapping up the pope's wishes in harmless rhetoric and outright disagreement.

THE SOCIAL ATTITUDES

The early approach to the social problems of the country has been summarized by historian Robert D. Cross:

> The transition was particularly difficult for a Catholic priest. The clerical education of a traditional church prepared the young man to deal with social problems as they had been known to the church for centuries. The discipline of an authoritative church was better designed to preserve unity by continuing traditional actions than to promote innovation. Where prelates of liberal conviction were installed, it is true, liberal priests enjoyed greater sanctuary from outside coercions than did Protestant ministers mortgaged to the approval of their middle-class congregations. But since it was logical for the church to place conservatives like Archbishop Corrigan where immigrants were most numerous, those priests who found conditions in the eastern cities an incentive to reform activities usually had to fight a running battle with tradition-minded superiors. Moreover, in most areas, unless a priest chose to conduct a one-man campaign, he had to join nondenominational reform movements, which too often in the past had been hostile to the church. The greatest incubus to Catholic reform,

however, was not organizational, but the widespread religious belief that human enterprise was presumptuous.

To the Catholic conservatives, the most proper response to social difficulties was devout passivity....[6]

It was the Americanist bishops who moved the church from this "devout passivity" to an embracing of social reform. They led the way by cooperating with non-Catholics, and moving people toward active charity and the rights of workers.

HERESY OF AMERICANISM

Perhaps nowhere did the Americanists and the conservatives disagree more basically than on the issue of accommodation to American ideals. The Americanists were wary of the contemplative life, and were for the more active and enterprising, that is, "American" virtues. They looked with suspicion on too much devotionalism as taking away energies better spent on action on behalf of the church. They firmly believed in individual freedom and liberty. They thought that laymen should have more of a part in the church and more participation in the liturgy. They much preferred Isaac Hecker's new American order of active and liberal Paulists to the ultra-conservative Jesuits, whom Bishop Ireland attacked. In their super-patriotism, the Americanists imprudently lectured their European brethren on the merits of the American model. This caused renewed attention and suspicions. European conservatives, abetted by Corrigan and McQuaid, listed problems such as the attacks on the religious orders, the Germans' unhappiness with Irish domination, and the biography of Father Hecker, with Abbe Klein's disastrous preface, seemingly extolling the active virtues and the inner spirit at the expense of the contemplative virtues and the traditional church structures. In brief, to some Europeans, the Catholic church in the United States seemed little more than liberal Protestantism. A catch-all term was invented. It was called the heresy of "Americanism."

Before long, liberal Denis O'Connell was relieved of the rectorship of the American College in Rome. Bishop Keane was removed from a similar position at Catholic University in Washington, D.C. Finally, in 1899, Leo XIII promulgated his letter, *Testem Benevolentiae*, on "Americanism." Mild, cautious, and without mentioning names, the encyclical was directed at Baltimore, and the slap at the

Americanists was unmistakable. The conservatives and the Jesuits rejoiced. Gibbons protested that no such heresy existed, but the cloud of suspicion could not be removed. In time, we might add, the Americanists did recover. In 1900, Keane was made bishop of Dubuque, and Denis O'Connell became the rector of Catholic University. Rome, however, would not bestow the cardinal's hat on any of the Americanists. Instead, Rome made cardinals of the moderate Archbishop Farley of New York and the reactionary conservative, William O'Connell of Boston.

CONTRIBUTIONS OF THE AMERICANISTS

We must recognize the stature of leaders like Gibbons, Keane, Ireland, and Spalding. They were men of strong personalities, and by their actions and insights, they helped to forge a forward-looking church in the United States. Probably many of the clergy and laity were of a more traditional mindset, but these Americanists led them well in coming to terms with the American way of life. It must be admitted, however, that the Americanists had one thing going for them: They usually had the backing of the pope. While Leo XIII was no flaming liberal, he was more open to democracy than his predecessor, Pius IX. This was true, despite the fact that he almost condemned the Knights of Labor. Leo's rebuke of "Americanism" was mild and courteous. He was open to the Americanists, and received their letters and personal visits. Even when he did not agree with them, they credited him with being misinformed, rather than being in basic disagreement.

Yet, it must be noticed that the victories of the Americanists were not as long lasting as might be hoped in many cases:

The decade 1900–1910 which succeeded the final failure of the Americanist attempt to harmonize Catholicism with American life appears to have been one of retrenchment significant of the spirit of conservatism which had emerged from the struggle victorious.

True enough, John Keane had been elevated to the rank of archbishop, and Denis O'Connell was made the rector of Catholic University, but John Ireland was never to wear the cardinal's red hat which he desired with such unbecoming ardor, and in American public life Catholics were to hold positions of influence or authority which, in proportion to their numbers, could hardly have been fewer and farther between. Intellectually, Catholics also were remiss, compelling the British observer D.W. Brogran to remark: "In no Western society is the intellectual prestige of Catholicism lower than in the country where in such respects as wealth, numbers, and strength of organization it is so powerful."

The Catholic laity was an anonymous, amorphous mass. Ireland and Gibbons might sing the praises of the American way of life from sunup to sundown, but the fact is that it was the conservative prelates who had the layman's ear. They had convinced them of the "contaminations" of "pagan" America, and had virtually herded them into a mental ghetto.... Catholics...seldom entered the national arena. In the field of social justice they were a cipher. And this, again, is because the layman had almost no standing. Having been indoctrinated with the siege mentality characteristic of the Council of Trent, they regarded themselves, to extend the military metaphor, as the ordinary soldiery, while the priests were the captains, the bishops were the colonels and the archbishops were generals. Generally speaking, for a layman actually to do anything without orders was not only unthinkable but perhaps even insubordinate. And this habit of mind, it seems, is directly attributable to the fact that the bishops actually did not trust the laymen.[7]

Yet, it must be noted that by the 1960s, the church in the United States had come full circle, back to the positions held by the Americanists. At the Second Vatican Council, John Courtney Murray, S.J., an "Americanist," worked with the bishops, who used his insights as the basis for The Declaration on Religious Freedom. Likewise, the role of the laity in the church has also been expanded to include both administrative and ministerial duties.

SCHOOLS

In 1908, the United States Catholic church was removed from the list of mission territories under the care of the Congregation for the Propagation of the Faith, and given status as a national church. The fifty-year period which followed has been described by many as "the heyday of the brick and mortar bishops." This denoted a time of tremendous expansion, stability, and optimism. The holdings of most dioceses increased through the construction of parishes, parochial schools, hospitals, orphanages, and homes for the aged. The hierarchy began to use newly-developed organizational skills and became, in effect, powerful diocesan "corporations." Catholics at this time were concentrated in the east. Catholics who lived in the south, southwest, and rural midwest were fewer in number, and often more impoverished. Thus, the parish churches and such schools as they had in these areas were more moderate in style and development.

One of the major areas of development in the late nineteenth and early twentieth centuries was parochial school systems. As noted earlier, many of the ethnic parishes built schools so that their children could avoid the blatant Protestantism of the public schools. This idea was encouraged by the conservative, isolationist bishops. In 1864, the archbishop of Cincinnati required all Catholic parents to send their children to Catholic schools under pain of mortal sin. This was followed in 1884 by the mandate from the Third Plenary Council of Baltimore (at the behest of Rome) that all parishes must have parochial schools (they were given two years to comply). The rationale given was that "...the only practical way to secure a Christian people is to give the youth a Christian education...." At about the same time, distinct parish school systems were combined into a system administered and supervised at the diocesan level. Many religious communities were created or expanded to supply the teachers for this growing system. By the 1920s, the concept of "Catholic education" had taken hold to the extent that the parochial school system was seen as necessary in the Catholic view of life. Indeed, it was these schools that helped to create a Catholic identity, even among those who had never attended them.

A parallel system of non-school religious education, called the Confraternity of Christian Doctrine (C.C.D.), grew out of a more ambitious program in the 1930s, which suggested a variety of religious education roles for various members of the parish. After some time, this larger program was scaled down to weekly religion classes for children, to be held after school or on Saturdays. This C.C.D. movement received a powerful boost with the publication of Mary Perkins Ryan's controversial book, *Are Catholic Schools the Answer?*, to which she responded with a resounding "no." The bishops denounced her answer, but in fact acquiesced to it. They stopped building Catholic schools and lost their taste for them, especially as inflation hit, coupled with the drastic drop in teaching sisters after Vatican II. Lower birth rates, inner city problems, all conspired to hasten the decline of the parochial school.

Today, with limitations of funds and personnel in most parishes and dioceses, some tensions exist between the advocates of parish schools on the one hand and parish religious education programs on the other. Ironically, recent research has confirmed the considerable value of the parochial school:

> Catholic schools had a religious impact over and above that of the Catholic family, whereas C.C.D. had no measurable religious impact. The schools were more important in the transition after the Second Vatican Council than they were before the council.... They provided better education than most public schools and as good as the best public schools...Their students were less prejudiced and more enlightened than Catholics who went to public schools. They were especially successful in educating the disadvantaged.... the Catholic schools have produced substantial impact on the educational, political, moral, religious, sexual and financial behavior of those adults who attend them during their school years, the kind of impact that no other institution can claim...Those who went to Catholic schools scored systematically higher on measures of support for the equality of women.... The Catholic school group also consistently scored higher on measures of morale....[8]

Furthermore, research has shown that American Catholics have so entered the mainstream that, after the Jews, they are in the highest income bracket in the country. Therefore, they could pay for education. Research like this is generating a second look at the value and importance of the Catholic parochial school system.

THE WORLD WAR I ERA

World War I served to unite Catholics previously divided by custom, prejudice, and language. Though many had originally come from countries which were then at war with one another, Catholics pulled together "for God and Country," and vigorously supported the war effort. Since most dioceses could not provide adequately for the spiritual needs of Catholic soldiers, the Knights of Columbus, a national lay group, came to the rescue by providing financial support for additional clergy from religious orders to help the "official" military chaplains. They also set up many USO-like facilities which were opened to all faiths, thus providing an additional setting for Catholics to interact with people of other religious denominations.

About the same time, and for the same reasons, Paulist Father John J. Burke organized leaders among the clergy and the laity into the National Catholic War Council. This group eventually gained the support of the United States bishops and acted in their name to recruit chaplains and raise money to meet the religious needs of Catholic service men and women. Following the war, the NCWC was reorganized as a service organization, the National Catholic Welfare Council, which became the quasi-official voice of the United States bishops.

Perhaps the most noteworthy of the NCWC's efforts was *Social Reconstruction: A General Review of the Problems and Survey of the Remedies*. This "Bishops' Program," as it was known, was drawn up by Father John A. Ryan in 1919. This statement proposed a minimum wage for all workers, the right of workers to organize trade unions, equal pay for equal work for women, the abolition of child labor practices, and free medical care and welfare benefits for the poor. This last was to be paid for by the establishment of a graduated income tax and higher inheritance taxes. Thus, while maintaining separation of church and state, the document did advocate government participation in searching for justice and providing for the welfare of all citizens. In general, these ideas had been accepted by the bishops as a contemporary application of *Rerum Novarum* (1891). Most people, however, Catholics included, considered such proposals as too progressive, although many were later to become part of Franklin Roosevelt's New Deal.

After Vatican II in 1966, when the American bishops organized themselves into the National Conference of Catholic Bishops (NCCB), the NCWC was reorganized, this time into the United States Catholic Conference (USCC), which is the official voice of the bishops of the United States.

WOMEN AND THE CHURCH

A word of caution is in order here regarding women and the church. Despite the inclusion of "equal pay for equal work" in the Bishops'

Program (1919), the main thrust of the document focused on strengthening the family by urging women to stay at home and tend to their families. This was particularly directed to those women who had earlier taken jobs to help with the war effort. This directive was, after all, in keeping with the Victorian attitudes about women that still prevailed among most of the population, women included. The bishops' proposal only went so far as to say that if women had to work, or did in fact work, they deserved equal pay for equal work. As for women's suffrage, the Catholic hierarchy provided little help and were more often part of the opposition. Despite this, the Nineteenth Amendment went into effect in 1920, thanks in part to the Catholic lay women who led suffrage rallies in Massachusetts and other key states.

ANTI-CATHOLICISM CONTINUED

The years following World War I saw the revival of the Ku Klux Klan, a secret society founded in the south after the Civil War. The Klan was dedicated to the ascendancy of white Protestant America and, therefore, was anti-Negro, anti-Semitic, and anti-Catholic. In 1922, the Klan allied itself with the Scottish rite of Masons. Together, they were the primary advocates of an Oregon law that obliged all parents to send their children to public schools. It was a blatant effort to close parochial schools. The United States Supreme Court struck down the law as unconstitutional. After this effort and a similar case in Michigan that was also unsuccessful, the Klan went into decline until the 1960s. At that time, it again reorganized in an attempt to prevent the desegregation advocated by the new civil rights movement.

During the 1920s, most U.S. Catholics (now one out of every six people) did not concern themselves with social justice issues or with papal encyclicals. Middle-class America appeared satisfied with the status quo. In 1926, the United States for the first time hosted the International Eucharistic Congress, in Chicago. This twenty-eighth such annual meeting, being a most solemn religious event, gave American Catholics an opportunity to take great pride in their religious heritage. This decade also saw the nomination of the first Catholic for president of the United States. Although Alfred Smith, a former New York legislator, and its governor then, was opposed for his lack of formal education and his stance in favor of the repeal of Prohibition, the major issue from the beginning was his religion.

Thus began another anti-Catholic campaign, led this time primarily by the Klan. They claimed that Smith's candidacy was a Vatican plot to take over the country, and they circulated old stories about immorality in religious communities. Smith was soundly defeated, much to the embarrassment of his Quaker opponent, Herbert Hoover. As a result, disillusioned Catholics retreated into their ghettos.

SOCIAL CATHOLICISM

During the 1930s, Catholicism in the United States developed social movements on both the left and the right. This was in response to the worldwide economic depression and to the clashes of political ideologies (facism and communism) that were occurring in Europe. The promulgation of *Quadragesimo Anno* (1931), on the fortieth anniversary of *Rerum Novarum*, also contributed to the emerging debate. This new social encyclical, extensively preached by the clergy, was studied in many parishes. Many Catholics responded by calling for slum renewal and an end to segregation.

At one end of the Catholic political spectrum was Father Charles E. Coughlin, a conservative and socially concerned parish priest from Royal Oak, Michigan, who spoke to a record number of Catholics, and a smattering of Protestants, through his Sunday afternoon radio broadcasts. He supported papal teachings and applied them to domestic politics. Seen as a hero by the Catholic masses, he soon became a force to be reckoned with in Washington. Initially, he supported Franklin Roosevelt and his New Deal policies. Coughlin then began advocating his own economic theories, in order to aid in defeating Roosevelt's bid for a second term. At about the same time, Coughlin began to distort many Jewish teachings, and eventually to espouse anti-Semitic ideas. When the war began in Europe, he expressed sympathy for Hitler and his Nazi ideals. This resulted in Coughlin's losing most of his Catholic audience. He was soon silenced by his archbishop in accordance with canon law. After Pearl Harbor, he returned to parish work until his death in 1966.

At the other end of the Catholic political spectrum were the founders of the Catholic Worker Movement (1933), Dorothy Day and Peter Maurin. Dorothy Day was a former socialist whose religious conversion only strengthened her social commitment to the poor. As a journalist, she created *The Catholic Worker*, a monthly newspaper (which still sells for a penny a copy), to refute the charge that Catholicism was indifferent to the conditions of the workers. *The Catholic Worker* used the papal social encyclicals, interpreting them most liberally, to show that the Catholic church did advocate justice, the rights of the worker, and efforts on behalf of the poor and oppressed.

Day's mentor, Peter Maurin, was a self-taught working man, a French immigrant who lived a life of voluntary poverty and preached a gospel of personal responsibility for the poor. He has been called a "modern-day St. Francis" by many. The Catholic Worker Movement also involved itself directly with the poor by the establishment of Houses of Hospitality for the homeless and communal farms where young families could look after the elderly. Although this movement never involved large numbers of people, it did serve to radicalize the religious thinking of many and continues to attract youthful idealists to the present time.

In addition to such social movements, there were two other loosely related movements that slowly spread across the United States, but which had their origins in Europe a decade earlier. The first of these was a liturgical movement that pointed to the relationship between communal worship and social action—we cannot properly worship God as the "Body of Christ" unless we tend to the needs of all members of that body. This movement was led by the Benedictine monks of St. John's Abbey in Collegeville, Minnesota. The monks sought to promote a better understanding of the liturgy and to encourage more lay participation. In particular, the proponents of this movement wanted the priest facing the people while celebrating Mass, called for the use of the vernacular at Mass and at the celebration of other sacraments, advocated the concelebration of Mass by several priests, and sought to provide a eucharistic bread that needed to be chewed as a means of affirming the "meal" aspect of eucharist—all of which were scorned as "non-traditional" at that time, but were eventually granted as a result of Vatican II.

The second movement was an effort begun by some of the other churches (in particular, the Episcopal church in the United States and the Anglican church in England), to work ecumenically, that is, to search for the unity of all Christian denominations. Initial efforts concentrated on forming interfaith groups for the purpose of discussion, shared prayer, and efforts toward common goals, which often meant goals of social justice. This movement eventually led, at the international level, to the formation of the World Council of Churches in 1948. Although the Catholic church has never officially joined this confederation of churches, it did begin to participate in the work of some of the WCC committees after Vatican II. In addition, the Catholic church entered into bilateral discussions with major denominations about the possibility of some form of ecumenical union.

AFTERMATH OF WORLD WAR II

Just as World War I served to bring Catholics out of their ghettos to meet with people of other churches in defense of their new homeland, World War II brought about the breakdown of those ghettos. Catholics in record numbers enlisted in the military to "defend America and save the free world." Having seen other cultures, lived closely with people of other religions, and experienced death at close hand, those who returned could not settle down to life as usual. Following the war, attendance at eucharist liturgies increased and there was renewed interest in the contemplative orders. A grateful nation, through the G.I. Bill, provided educational opportunities for the veterans, who then found their way to college and university campuses. As these men and women worked to better their chances for higher paying jobs by getting college degrees, they were required, in Catholic colleges and universities, to study theology and philosophy. Thus, there was soon to be a new kind of laity—a theologically sophisticated laity—some of whom were better educated than their clergy.

But perhaps the most significant change for the Catholic church came with the postwar move to the suburbs. Thousands of young, well-educated Catholics wanted more for their children than they had had in the ghettos of the big cities. They established new parishes, built new parochial schools, and found a new sense of community. Instead of social movements, they gathered together around the issues and problems of their own lives, giving rise to such groups as the Cana Conference, the Christian Family Movement, Serra Clubs, and the Cursillo Movement (imported from Spain). By 1959, the United States was the largest Roman Catholic country in the world (and also the wealthiest), and Catholicism was the largest single denomination in the United States.

A NEW OPTIMISM

Things were looking up for American Catholics as the 1960s began. In 1958, when Pius XII died and Angelo Roncalli was elected, Catholics expected nothing much to change. John XXIII, as he chose to be called, was to be an interim pope, someone to take charge until a clear leader among the Italian archbishops and cardinals emerged. Yet, he proved to be quite a change from the authoritarian figures of the last seven popes. John appeared friendly to non-Christians and communists alike, and cordially received leaders of the Protestant churches: he seemed to minimize theological differences. But most important, he called for an ecumenical council for the purpose of updating the Catholic church. Those Catholics who had been involved in the social and ecumenical movements of the previous thirty years looked forward to the new possibilities then on the horizon.

At the same time, another Catholic was nominated for president of the United States. His name was John Fitzgerald Kennedy; he was an Irish-American Catholic from Massachusetts. There was an initial resurgence of anti-Catholicism as more than three hundred different anti-Catholic tracts were distributed nationwide. But Kennedy, in a speech to Protestant ministers in Houston, convinced many in the nation that his religion and his patriotism were not in conflict. He assured Americans that he alone would be responsible for his political decisions. As a result, his religion became a minor issue. (A few years later, religion was a non-issue for Eugene McCarthy, Robert Kennedy, and several others in their bids for national office.) Where Smith's defeat in 1928 resulted in the disillusioned retreat of Catholics back into their ghettos, Kennedy's victory in 1960 was symbolic of America's acceptance of its Catholic citizens.

AMERICAN INFLUENCE AT THE COUNCIL

Vatican II was not the first council for the bishops of the United States. They had attended the First Vatican Council in 1869–70, where one of their number, Bishop Fitzgerald of Little Rock, Arkansas, had been one of only two bishops who voted "no" on the issue of papal infallibility prior to the final vote. (Both dissenting bishops asked for another vote in view of the overwhelming numbers against them, so that the final vote would be unanimous.)

It should also be noted that the United States delegation to the Second Vatican Council, both the bishops and their theological advisors, were for the most part fairly traditional in their approach to doctrine. Most of the new ideas that would be considered at Vatican II came from Germany, Belgium, Holland, and France. Some of these ideas were, however, known to some in the United States through their studies of theology, or by means of the various movements in the thirty years prior to the Council.

There were two areas at the council, however, where the influence of the bishops and theologians of the United States was felt. These involved the Catholic attitude toward the Jewish people, and the relationship of church and state. Often, the Jews were thought of as "Christ-killers," and charged with deicide. The American bishops found this mindset both repugnant and theologically unsound. Despite opposition, they helped to fashion the conciliar teaching that refuted these false ideas. As for the relationship of church and state, the official Catholic position for centuries had been that the will of God called for the union of the state (preferably a monarchy) with the Catholic church. Just ten years prior to the council, John Courtney Murray, the American Jesuit, had been silenced by the Vatican and forbidden to publish his ideas about religious liberty. But, it was Murray himself who was called to Rome by Cardinal Spellman to become the chief architect of the Declaration on Religious Freedom.

On the other issues discussed at the council, the bishops of the United States were divided along conservative and liberal lines. The documents themselves were created through compromises made on both sides. Thus, each side could claim that its position was represented in the conciliar teaching, but neither side was totally happy with the final results.

EFFECTS OF THE COUNCIL

As news of the discussions in Rome filtered back to the United States through the news media, Catholics saw some of their most cherished ideas and securities challenged. Since Catholics were treated (and often thought of themselves) as strangers in a Protestant country, they had heretofore concentrated their efforts on those features of their religion that most distinguished them from Protestants. A framework of strong Catholic identity came from Friday abstinence, compulsory worship on Sundays and the six holy days of obligation, a fixed moral code giving clear and unambiguous rules on sexual and marital questions, and so on. But these external signs of Catholic conformity and identity became secondary matters, because the Second Vatican Council stressed continuing conversion, inner freedom over external constraints, and social responsibility toward other persons and groups.

The United States bishops returned from the council in good spirits, many moving quickly to implement the documents of Vatican II. But, despite all these good intentions, they often moved too quickly, imposing the new ideas on the people without educating them as to why this new way was better. For other Catholics, the bishops did not do enough. They had expected more sweeping changes, which did not materialize.[9]

There was, however, a "honeymoon" of sorts in the United States following Vatican II. The laity became more involved with what was happening in the parish through participation in parish councils. A newer theology of church replaced the static, legal definition of "church" with the more democratic sounding "people of God." Liturgical experimentation abounded as various groups tried to make the celebration "relevant" to their own situations. The promotion of ecumenism made contacts with Protestants respectable. Religious communities, following directives from Rome, sought to renew the charisms of their founders, and attempted to adapt these to the modern world.

Such changes, however, were to prove disappointing to many. For instance, liturgical reforms, aimed at revitalizing parish life, often brought about division between those parishioners who wanted change and those who were satisfied with the old familiar rituals. Nor did the prosaic English translation of the eucharistic canons bring forth any great spiritual or social awakening. The stress put on the laity's role in church matters and liturgy blurred the priest's role and produced, for some, an identity crisis. When the Decree on Religious Freedom recognized that all believers of any faith had the right to follow their consciences in matters of faith, Catholics felt justified to apply the same right to themselves. Some Catholics, unprepared to distinguish between non-essential religious practices and authentic church teaching, began to make up their own minds about what they would accept or disregard. (This self-styled choosing of church teaching has sometimes been called "supermarket" or "cafeteria" Catholicism.) Other Catholics, realizing that they were no longer bound to certain practices "under pain of mortal sin," simply ceased doing them. Whereas over 80 percent of all Catholics attended weekly Sunday Mass before the council, by the late 1980s, less than 50 percent of Catholics were doing so each Sunday. Confessions fell off drastically. Popular devotions were lost in the liturgical renewal of the Mass.

Still, for all of this, there remained a persistent interest in local parish life. Parishes struggled to implement the concepts of shared and collaborative ministries. The people tried to come to terms with their new roles, responsibilities, and ownership. The clergy sought to restyle its leadership. The theoretical underpinnings stressed baptism rather than ordination as the primary commitment and basis for discipleship. But none of this was done, is being done, without considerable tension. Part of the tension, of course, was the phenomenal loss of priests and seminarians after the council. In 1970, there were some 37,000 diocesan priests for about 53 million Catholics in the United States. By the year 2000, there will be an estimated 13,000 to 15,000 diocesan priests for about 65 to 75 million Catholics. Of the 368,000 parishes in the world, 157,000 have no resident priests. In 1966–67, there were some 42,900 seminarians in the United States. In 1988–89, there were 9,900 (a drop of four-fifths). All this has put pressure on the hierarchy and the Vatican to allow married priests and the ordination of married men and women. These facts have added to the inevitable tensions that followed Vatican II.

In short, the new sense of direction with its stress on freedom and responsibility in the church did not, as hoped, move Catholicism to a new unity of action and moral posture. Rather, it occasioned deep and serious divisions within the church, divisions which were bound to increase. Frightened Catholics, both clerical and lay, retreated into the old securities, while disillusioned liberals faced crises of faith and conscience.[10]

SOCIAL JUSTICE MOVEMENTS

Amid this confusion over changing practices and hierarchical authority, there continued to be movements rooted in the church's tradition of social justice. In the spirit of *Rerum Novarum*, Cesar Chavez urged all Americans to boycott certain farm products because of the injustice accorded to migrant workers, who are predominantly Hispanic. In a similar vein, clergy, such as the Jesuit Daniel Berrigan and his brother Philip, as well as members of various religious communities and the laity, actively opposed the participation of the United States in the Vietnam War. In the late 1970s and 1980s, they opposed the production of nuclear weapons and worked on behalf of an international effort to bring about world peace.

In all these cases, the activists used civil disobedience to attract attention to their causes, and Catholic social teachings for their justification. It is ironic that Catholics, who for so long wanted only to blend into the American scene and worked hard to convince everyone of their patriotism, would now use disobedience to civil law in an effort to influence the economic and political policies in the United States. But they did so alongside people of various denominations, and they continue to do so.

HUMANAE VITAE

The watershed for many Catholics in the United States came with the promulgation of *Humanae Vitae* in 1968. The issues of clerical celibacy and artificial birth control had been removed from discussion at the council and were reserved to papal commissions for later action. In each case, the final outcome was a continuance of the traditional stance: no voluntary celibacy for the clergy, and no artificial birth control for the laity. Perhaps this would not have been so startling except for the fact that the commission appointed by Paul VI to study the issue of birth control had overwhelmingly voted in favor of some change in the church's position. For many Catholics, the church leadership had lost credibility, while for others, the issue was one of taking responsibility for one's own decisions.

...The encyclical *Humanae Vitae* encouraged more adult discussion, theological research and serious examination of conscience than almost any document issued from any source during the sixties. It engendered not indifference but thought. That it prompted people to look within themselves to make moral decisions on intimate matters represents a step forward, away from priest-ridden sexual mores, away from dependence on authority for choices that men and women ultimately must conscientiously make for themselves.[11]

This was a difficult time for clergy and laity alike. The church seemed to be moving toward the twenty-first century, having finally reconciled itself with the modern world. Yet there were elements within the church, hierarchy and laity alike, who were holding on tight to the Tridentine church of the past. As a result, both sides dug their heels in deeper, while some walked away from their commitment to religious life, clerical life, and/or to the Catholic church.

THE IMPACT OF JOHN PAUL II

The tide of the post-Vatican II tensions seemed to be flowing toward the side of the liberals when John Paul II was elected pope—the first non-Italian pope in four hundred and fifty years. It seemed that the decrees of Vatican II would be implemented from a liberal perspective. In his first encyclical, *Redemptor Hominis*, John Paul himself said that he would continue the work of his namesakes: "John XXIII and Paul VI are a stage to which I wish to refer directly and a threshold from which I intend to continue." He praised them for their "charism of transformation," yet he was different from both his predecessors. John Paul was trained as a philosopher, while the perspective of John XXIII was that "history is the teacher of life." John looked to the living community and "the signs of the times" in order to guide the church. John Paul, on the other hand, looks for church guidance in the continuity of the institutions and traditions which have developed over the centuries. He comforted those who were concerned about all the changes by saying: "We are what we have always been—and by that I mean we must remain as Christ the Lord wanted." He would characterize his pontificate by order, organization, and orthodoxy.

Such an occurrence was probably to be expected; much the same had happened after Trent and other ecumenical councils. The confusion and polarity that followed the council called for a slowing down of the processes of change which had occurred too quickly for many. Also to be expected was the backlash of complaints by conservatives trying to hold liberals to the letter of the law. Perhaps the most prominent example of this involves Archbishop Raymond Hunthausen of Seattle. One of the charges brought against Hunthausen was his permitting homosexual persons to use archdiocesan buildings for meetings and liturgies. Following complaints from conservatives, the Vatican put another bishop in charge of worship and other archdiocesan offices, thus relieving Hunthausen of his authority while he was under investigation. However, with his fellow bishops interceding with Rome on his behalf, Hunthausen's authority was restored.

In another case, this time with Rome taking the initiative, Father Charles E. Curran, Ph.D., was removed from his teaching post at Catholic University because of his disagreement with certain church teachings (in particular, *Humanae Vitae* in 1968 and the *Decree on Sexual Ethics* in 1975, neither of which are considered to be infallible teachings). At the time of his dismissal in 1987 (Rome charged that he was "unfit to teach Catholic theology"), he was no longer teaching moral theology, but did have tenure with the university. Curran took his case to court, but the decision of the Board of Trustees was upheld by the court, in light of the fact that Catholic University is a pontifical institution that did not want Dr. Curran on its faculty. So, it would appear that while one issue is resolved, the greater issue of "academic freedom" is still to be decided.

In 1989, the Vatican Congregation for the Doctrine of the Faith issued an "oath of fidelity" which would be required of all new pastors, deacons, seminary rectors, professors of theology in seminaries, and "teachers in any universities whatsoever who teach disciplines which deal with faith or morals" (Canon 833). The call for such an oath threatens the existence of "academic freedom" at Catholic institutions of higher learning, and limits severely the intellectual and theological speculation necessary for the development of theology. It will likely be a matter of contention for years to come. This oath, along with the papal appointment of conservative bishops and the crackdowns of the Vatican offices, has caused rejoicing among some, unease among others. All concur in the critical need for the papal office that Pope John Paul II represents, but some would wish for different collaborators:

The authentic Catholic senses that the Petrine ministry as claimed by the Roman bishop is part of the whole and that the Catholic church is somehow not "whole" without it; that without its captain the ship will eventually founder.... But...it may be time for the ship's captain to admit that he needs the crew in a sense far different than he so far seems to have realized.[12]

PASTORAL LETTERS

One of the most significant post-Vatican II developments for the Catholic church in the United States has been the process and promulgation of pastoral letters by the National Conference of Catholic Bishops (NCCB), the collegial body made up of all the bishops of the United States. In the 1980s, these bishops worked out a revolutionary process of consultation leading to the publication of pastoral letters on peace and economic justice. A third pastoral letter, on the subject of women's concerns, is going through a similar process in the late 1980s. One major change after the first draft was the retitling of the document as *Partners in the Mystery of Redemption*, to acknowledge that the concerns discussed come from all the people and that women are involved in the mission of the whole church.

The first pastoral, *The Challenge of Peace*, completed in 1983, began sometime earlier, with the bishops' recognition that the United States was one of two nuclear superpowers of the world. It seemed therefore fitting that they address the issues of nuclear deterrence, the development of a policy of "no first use" of nuclear weapons, the relevance of the "just war theory" with regard to nuclear war, and the de-escalation of the arms race.

After an unprecedented and widespread consultation with experts in the military, industrial, and diplomatic fields, and with futurists, scientists, and theologians, the bishops put forward a document that had three levels of authority. At the first level were the non-negotiable biblical teachings and principles of moral law; the second level included papal and conciliar social teachings; the third level consisted of those particular applications of these biblical perspectives, moral principles, and church teachings to the particulars of the national and world situations. Especially significant is the fact that the bishops did not impose their conclusions on the consciences of Catholics in the United States. The bishops recognized that their prudential judgments were "based on specific circumstances which can change or which can be interpreted differently by people of good will" (*Chall. Peace* 10).

The second pastoral, *Economic Justice for All*, went through a similar development. There were hearings held throughout the nation, compilation of different viewpoints, initial drafts that were presented to the public for comment and criticism, and revision of those drafts in light of the responses made by the people. When the final document was officially released by the NCCB in 1986, the bishops, as they had done in their first pastoral, acknowledged that their recommendations and judgments "on specific economic issues...do not carry the same moral authority as our statements of universal moral principles and formal church teachings; the former are related to circumstances which can change or which can be interpreted differently by people of good will" (*Econ. Just.* 135).

But the bishops were not offering these pastorals on a simplistic "take-it-or-leave-it" basis. They expected that their conclusions on disarmament or on the preferential option for the poor or on other issues be "given serious consideration by Catholics as they determine whether their own moral judgments are consistent with the gospel and with Catholic social teaching." Believing "that differences on complex economic questions should be expressed in a spirit of mutual respect and open dialogue," the American bishops left the final decisions to be made by the Catholic people. Thus, these pastoral letters signal a new and more respectful attitude toward Catholic believers. There were no authoritative pronouncements with the accompanying expectation of obedient compliance by the faithful. Instead, the bishops of the United States placed before the adult members of the church those moral principles and church teachings which have a bearing on a particular topic, and asked the faithful, after their examination of the issues, to make their own informed and conscientious decisions.[13]

As matters now stand, Catholics in the United States, like the rest of the Catholic world, must struggle with that most basic of all questions: "What does it mean to be church?" They can only live in hope while they learn to accommodate themselves to a plurality of structures. Catholics must engage in the continuing process of being church, a church once preserved in medieval power and influence, and enshrined in authority and monarchical structure, but now rediscovering its dynamism as servant, messianic sign, and prophet to the world. Catholics in the United States now have a different mandate; they are called, not to be a reflection of American values and culture, but to be witnesses of gospel values to the very nation they have ever sought to emulate and have never ceased to love.

CHAPTER 25

Final Reflections

THE PAST

Now that we have reached the end, we must pause, as we did half-way through the book, and reflect on what we have seen. We will do this by taking a brief look at the past, the present, and the future of Catholics and their church.

Concerning the past, there are a few conclusions that can be comfortably drawn. For one thing, there is no educated Catholic who can say about some favorite devotion, ritual, or concept, "That's the way it always was!" On the contrary, today's Catholics know that variety (pluralism), more than uniformity, has been the rule. They now know that there have been great variations regarding the role of the pope, the eucharistic liturgy, clerical lifestyles, and popular devotions. We know, for example, that the small, round, white host we use today goes back only to the eighth century, that the Nicene Creed was included universally in the Mass only in the eleventh century, that eucharistic devotions such as benediction go back only to the fourteenth century, that the rosary is a fifteenth-century contribution, and that first eucharist at age seven is a twentieth-century novelty. Today's Catholics know now that there were many schools of theological thought, a variety of ministries, and variations in the sacraments. We have seen in these pages the progress of political and ecclesiastical centralization, and are witnessing today the painful struggle between those who would again recentralize the church, and those who want the church to be locally rooted while always in communion with the bishop of Rome. In summary, the average educated Catholic cannot claim "That's the way it always was!" about very much in the Catholic church except that "Jesus is Lord!"

Concerning the past, there is also this conclusion: Catholics must learn to feel a great deal of pride regarding their heritage, both cultural and spiritual. During recent times, when we have heard so much criticism, we must renew our perspective. Catholics must come to feel at home with Ignatius, Irenaeus, Augustine or Anselm, Pope Gregory or Catherine of Siena, Francis of Assisi or Thomas Aquinas, Teresa of Avila or Therese of the Little Flower. We must see in the bishops, leaders of the local churches, the result of a long process that stretches back to apostolic times. We must recognize in the monasteries the legacy of our ability to speak and read and write. We should recite with pride the ancient creeds and celebrate the various liturgies and devotions which have nourished millions of believers before us. We should feel a part of the whole world where Catholic missionaries have gone to proclaim the word of God, sometimes watering the seeds of faith with their blood. We should feel a part of the countless unknown reconciliations, the works of charity, the numerous schools, hospitals, and orphanages that have been (and still are) a part of our Catholic heritage. There is a past that lives—a Catholic past that has touched every corner of the globe. The past of the Catholic church is the past of a community of human beings and, in spite of our sins, great moments have been reached and many have seen and praised "the wonderful works of God" (Acts 2:11).

THE PRESENT: CONFUSION

Concerning the present, it would almost be superfluous to say that the Catholic church is going through a time of confusion, crisis, and turmoil. But this is not superfluous, because our church has been going through confusion, crises, and turmoil from the beginning;

we will continue to do so, because we are a multicultural, multifaceted communion of churches, united in one Lord, one faith, one baptism, and joined with each other through our union with the bishop of Rome.

But if there is anything we have learned in reading this book, it is this: Yes, the church of Vatican II is different from the church of Vatican I, but the church of Constantine was different from the church of the fathers. So also was the church of the barbarians different from the church of Constantine. And the church of Charlemagne was different from the church of the barbarians. The church of the popes was different from the church of Charlemagne, and the church of Trent was different from the church of the popes.

Nor were the transitions from one "style" of church to the other made without considerable pain and hardship. The aspirations, the greatness, the pretensions, and the mistakes of each type of church could not stand forever. This accounts for the styling of the present church by the bishops of Vatican II as a "pilgrim church." The concept is that of movement, journeying, change. Ours is a "process" church, and it has always been such.

As in every age, people today are asking where all the changes will end; they are weary of all the "instant" cures that have been offered, tried, and failed. They are distrustful of the latest panacea, whether it be small group meetings, charismatic movements, cursillos, parish councils, nuns' and priests' federations, renewal programs, video cassette studies, and so forth. People may be suspicious of the "expert" theologians and the latest liturgist, and wish these would all go away. People may be hostile to those who offer answers that try to solve problems that took centuries to arise and which will not give way to six months' solutions. For many, there is a failure of nerve about the whole concept of renewal and reform.

THE PRESENT: CHALLENGE

For the present, there are two challenges. One is for the individual Catholic. Each of us must regain a sense of appreciation of our heritage, our past. But this appreciation is not the appreciation of looking at familiar artifacts in a museum; it is the appreciation of learning from and building organically on the past. To be a Catholic is to have a large and long "context" in which to assess the world as it is today. To be a Catholic is to evaluate the present in the light of the past, to be sensitive to what moved the people then—what were their inspirations, their motivations, and their spirit—so that we might recapture such for ourselves. Michael Novak catches the meaning of all of this (and the point of this book):

> To be a Catholic is, for many conservative persons, to belong to an institution whose concepts, rules, dogmas and offices have already been defined and remain only to be accepted whole. In my view, it is rather to belong to an historical people, to whom that institutional structure belongs and who must seriously reform it. A serious Catholic, I would argue, takes every historical dogma or practice of his people seriously, hoping to learn why it was that persons in earlier times (or yet today) found them illuminating and helpful. Such historical materials are not absolutes, but data, data to be understood, to be sifted and weighed and compared with other data. A serious Catholic wishes to ignore none of them and, on the other hand, to account for each....[1]

The second challenge is for the whole church. It is the ever-present challenge that the church must be relevant to the modern world, and yet at the same time not be absorbed by it. Much of the liberalism of the present has failed because it was willing to sacrifice the church's identity for the sake of the church's growing "relevance" to the modern world.

As Philip Gleason stated so well, the main problem is to grasp "the dialectical relationship of the demands and dangers of a situation in which the church must maintain identity without isolation and achieve relevance without absorption."[2] As Catholics adjust to entering more solidly into a real concern for social justice, into the world as it is, and into the mainstream of society, they must keep the balance of identity and affirmation regarding what the church stands for. If the church is to truly be a sacrament, an effective sign of what God has done and is doing through Jesus the Christ, then the church must fight for the earthly implications of the spiritual values it affirms; the church can never again divorce God from any race of people, or the poor, or those dying in war, or those of other religious beliefs.

It is only by a sense of history, by a sense of our own heritage, that we will escape—in spite of a highly sophisticated mass media—the assimilation into a materialistic society, and will remain to bear witness in our world.

THE PRESENT: WITNESS

Secularism is the outlook on life that reduces all value and meaning to the confines of this world. Therefore, Christians cannot be secularistic, for we pray that God's kingdom will come. However, Christianity is secular in the sense that we can only live and have faith in this world. We must have our feet planted firmly on this planet earth, this tiny portion of God's creation we call our world. While a secularistic society would replace internal spiritual motivation with psychological jargon and behavioristic manipulations, faith addresses authentic human persons in their true environment. That is why it can be said that religion has a relevance, if for no other reason than to challenge the manipulators of humanity and the all-embracing commercial spirit that has marketed sex, polluted the water, uglified the landscape, and filled the atmosphere with smoke and emissions solely in the interest of the almighty Gross National Product. We, the church, as the bearer of a sacred tradition, the guardian of all the richness of the inner life, the home of mystics and visionaries, must be there to challenge the crass commercialism of the so-called "free world," the reduction of the person to a servant of the state in the Marxist world, and to hold out hope to the suffering people of the Third World.

To incarnate new embodiments of the one gospel—this is the present challenge of the church today as it was in the past, and, we might add, the key to its endurance. For although we have necessarily focused on the major figures who occupied center stage in the pageantry of Christianity (some villains, some saints), history is always made up of more than popular movements and charismatic leaders. Beneath the political intrigues and social upheavals, the faith has managed to survive. More than that, the Catholic faith has literally nourished millions and millions of people in the past two thousand years. Whatever the leadership did, or did not do, it seems that the persistence of faith, the endurance of hope, and the applications of charity remain steadfast.

Not only that, but what also amazingly emerges in all of the machinations of history's principal actors is the persistence of Jesus himself. Somehow, through all of the problems of the early church, the church of Charlemagne, the medieval times, the Modernist crisis, and the present-day secularism, Jesus himself has remained the firm and constant center. He is the magnetic figure who compels the allegiance of many, and causes many more to be "born again." As we near the twenty-first century, it is Jesus who gives the rationale for the renewal movements, the charismatic responses, the advances in adult education, the prayer groups, and the Scripture study meetings that exist only because Jesus the Christ exists. "Jesus is Lord," and that is still being proclaimed today as it was in Paul's time. It is that amazing persistence of Jesus, beneath the ebb and flow of history, that makes Christianity so distinctive. He also seems to guarantee that, whatever form Christianity may take, it has a future. That future is with and in the church, which the Second Vatican Council has called "the initial budding forth of the kingdom" (L.G. 5).

THE FUTURE

While no one knows what the future will bring, a knowledge of history should enable us to reflect on the present and make some projections about the future. In our study of the history of the church, we have seen some aspects come full circle. What was treated with suspicion in one era has often been accepted as appropriate in another era. What might have been the solution to a problem in one era became the source of problems in another era. Yet, the church never duplicates exactly what has happened before. The church does not stay on the same plane. We appear to be spiraling upward, as suggested by Teilhard de Chardin, toward the kingdom of God, the Omega point.

We can say with some certainty that the center will hold together, that the pope, the bishop of Rome, will continue to be the principle of unity uniting all the local Catholic churches of the world with Rome and with one another. Inasmuch as we have seen the development of this Petrine office from the pre-eminent bishops of Rome to the papal monarchs, we can expect the possibility, at least, of further development, especially now that more cardinals from around the world are involved in the process of electing the pope. Certainly we can expect the continuing variety of leadership styles, as each new successor of Peter brings his own cultural experience and agenda to the chair of Peter.

It also seems likely that the future belongs to those who are rooted historically in the faith and traditions of the church. Growth is always organic and it is the "organic" person who will shape the church of the future. As Karl Rahner reminds us in his work *Chris-*

tian Commitment, the church of the future will likely be a smaller "diaspora church," a more voluntary grouping that places greater demands on its members. The church of the future even may be something like the church of the past, like the early church: a minority in a hostile society, yet a community full of fervor centered around its perennial eucharistic liturgy and the affirmation that "Jesus is Lord!"

Since prediction is such a nebulous process, perhaps it would be helpful to remember the insightful words of John C. Meagher:

> The church is forever engaged in the process of understanding the Christ of history through its life of Christ in history, going about his father's business. Precisely how the church's encounter with the new world of reforming movements will affect its understanding of itself and the Christ of history remains to be seen. We can only know that such heady new wine is bound to stretch and reform the old skins. This is the way it has always worked. We cannot yet predict what more of the church's belief will eventually go the way of the apostolic expectation of a first-generation Parousia, nor what may be added through new spirits, as the church once learned to repent of the toleration of slavery. Our task is simply to go about this business faithfully, with as much mutual trust as we can summon.
>
> Such faithfulness does not require us to repudiate the past in order to participate in the formation of the future....To be faithful must mean both to preserve and to create....There will be time for new harmonies to arise out of new discords as long as we remember that nothing less than the reverent appropriation of Christianity's whole experience can provide a sufficient basis for the discernment of spirits.[3]

History has shown us that the Catholic church is always in need of reform. However, when reformers came forward, the church leadership often would not tolerate hearing about the reform it needed. Sometimes, the reformers were martyred, but more often they were silenced. In one way or another, however, the church did reform, and, in the process, experienced in its life the paschal mystery of the dying and rising of Jesus the Christ.

Notes

CHAPTER 1

1. Christopher Dawson, *Religion and the Rise of Western Culture* (New York: Doubleday, 1958), p. 12.
2. This commentary was called the Midrash (sermon) and came into vogue about 200 B.C.E. Soon oral customs and traditions were added as supplements to the Torah. During the first and second centuries of the Christian era this combination of Torah and supplements was in turn commented on and thus was born the Talmud.
3. *Encyclopedia Britannica*, 1971, vol. 12, p. 1063.
4. The present Wailing Wall in Jerusalem is said to contain some original stones from the Temple of Solomon, stones no doubt included in the foundations left by Titus.
5. For a fascinating account of this uprising and its hero, Bar-Kokhba, read the book, *Bar-Kokhba: The Rediscovery of the Legendary Hero of the Second Jewish Revolt* by Yigael Yadin (New York: Random House, 1971). See also Paul Johnson's acclaimed *A History of the Jews* (New York: Harper & Row).
6. It should be noted that the U.N. Partition Resolution of 1947 talked about *two* states in Palestine, a Jewish state and an Arab state, a division accepted by world Jewry at the time, but significantly not mentioned by Ben-Gurion in 1948 when the state of Israel was established or rather the Jewish state. (See "The Morning After" by Anton Shammas in the *New York Review*, September 29, 1988). This deletion led to the fierce uprising in 1987 by the Arabs and its brutal suppression by the Jews—provoking United Nations and United States rebuke for human rights violations—who for the first time in two millennium had an army and the use of force. See *Through Different Eyes* by Hyman Bookbinder and James G. Abourezk (Bethesda, MD: Adler & Adler, 1988), *Blaming the Victims*, edited by Edward Said and Christopher Hitchens (Verso, 198), *The Yellow Wind* by David Grossman (New York: Farrar, Straus & Giroux, 1988), and *Israel's Fateful Hour* by Yehoshafat Harkabi (New York: Harper & Row, 1988).
7. A.H.M. Jones, *Constantine and the Conversion of Europe*, rev. ed. (New York: Collier Books, 1962), p.41.
8. J. Danielou and Marrou, *The Christian Centuries* (New York: McGraw-Hill, 1964), I, 5. See Also W.H.C. Frend's book *The Rise of Christianity* (Philadelphia: Fortress Press, 1984).
9. Rudolf Bultmann, *Primitive Christianity in Its Contemporary Setting,*

quoted in *A Short History of Christianity* by Martin E. Marty (New York: The World Publishing Company, 1959), p. 26.

10. *The New York Times,* February 13, 1972.
11. Jaroslav Pelikan, *The Emergence of the Catholic Tradition* (Chicago: University of Chicago Press, 1971), p. 14.
12. *Ibid.*
13. *U.S. Catholic,* September 1971, p. 29.
14. *Sacramentum Mundi,* Karl Rahner, Cornelius Ernst, and Kevin Smyth, eds., Sacramentum Mundi (New York: Herder and Herder, 1969) III, 228.

CHAPTER 2

1. J. Danielou and Marrou, *op. cit.,* p. 128. See *Antioch and Rome* by Raymond E. Brown and John Meier (New York: Paulist Press, 1983).
2. E.R. Dodds, *Pagan and Christian in An Age of Anxiety* (New York: Cambridge University Press, 1965), pp. 136-138.
3. Ben F. Meyer, *The Church in Three Tenses* (New York: Doubleday, 1971), p. 84.
4. Quoted in Philip Hughes, *The Church in Crisis: A History of the General Councils, 325-1870* (Garden City, NY: Hanover House, 1961), p. 20.
5. There is a ten-volume publication in process from Claremont Graduate School in California on Gnosticism. It will be a translation of the original Coptic documents discovered in 1945 and should throw much light on the origins of early Christianity.
6. Quoted in Pelikan, *op. cit.,* p. 41.
7. *Ibid.,* p. 55.
8. Ben F. Meyer, *op. cit.,* p. 111.
9. William J. Bausch, *Ministry Traditions, Tensions, Transitions* (Mystic, CT: Twenty-Third Publications, 1982), Chapter 4.

CHAPTER 3

1. Raymond E. Brown, S.S. *Priest and Bishop: Biblical Reflections* (Paramus, NJ: Paulist Press, 1970), p. 19. See also Frederick J. Cwiekowski, *The Beginnings of the Church* (Mahwah, NJ: Paulist Press, 1988). For a good survey see the essay, "The New Testament Background for the Emerging Doctrine of 'Local Church'" by Raymond E. Brown, *Biblical Exegesis and Church Doctrine* (New York: Paulist Press, 1985), Chapter 7. We must remember, of course, that for Catholics "the ordained ministry is not simply a function with the church but an essential as pect of the ecclesiastical mystery itself." Richard McBrien, *Who Is a Catholic?,* p. 111.
2. Michael Rogness, *The Church Nobody Knows* (Minneapolis, MN:Augs-

burg Publishing House, 1971), pp. 84, 85. See also *Priesthood: A History of the Ordained Ministry in the Roman Catholic Church* by Kenan B. Osborne, O.F.M. (Mahwah, NJ: Paulist Press, 1988).

3. See Raymond Brown, *The Church the Apostles Left Behind* (New York: Paulist Press,1984).

4. John Macquarrie, *Principles of Christian Theology* (New York: Charles Scribner's Sons, 1966), pp. 368, 369.

5. *National Catholic Reporter*, October 8, 1971. Documentation Report.

6. Hans Küng, *Why Priests?* (New York: Doubleday, 1972), p. 44. Thomas Rausch, S.J. makes the point in his book, *The Roots of the Catholic Tradition* (Wilmington, DE: Michael Glazier, 1986), p. 139: "Certainly there seems to be more than one form of church order visible within the New Testament, as well as different stories of development....Yet some of the Johannine communities and probably others with less developed ministries of leadership ultimately accepted the office of presbyter-bishop which by the end of the century was becoming commonplace. Thus these communities and their ministries were integrated into a ministry of leadership which claimed—not without reason—apostolic succession; similarly whatever Koinonia existed between these communities and the other churches took on a visible, institutionalized expression. The real meaning of apostolic succession of the ordained ministry is to be found here. It is not a guarantee of the church's fidelity nor an unbroken chain which, like an electric current, transmits sacramental power, but rather a sign which makes visible the link between the church and its ordained ministry today and the original apostolic church."

7. *Sacramentum Mundi* (New York: Herder and Herder, 1968),Volume I, p. 89.

8. Thomas Rausch, S.J. *The Roots of the Catholic Tradition* (Wilmington, DE: Michael Glazier, 1986), p. 169. See also *Peter in the New Testament* by Raymond Brown, Karl Donfried, and John Reumann, (Minneapolis and New York: Augsburg and Paulist Press, 1973).

9. *Concilium* (New York: Herder and Herder, 1972), Volume 74, p. 21.

10. The term "pope" or papa (from the Greek) was originally a title of respect given to all bishops. It was used frequently from the fifth century to apply to the bishops of Rome, but was not exclusive to the Bishop of Rome until the eleventh century. Our word "papacy" comes from the medieval period during which there was a struggle between the state and the church (imperium et papatum). The modern term often used for the successor of Peter is the Petrine Officer.

11. William J. Bausch, *Ministry: Traditions, Tensions and Transitions* (Mystic, CT: Twenty-Third Publications, 1982), p. 16.

12. Andrew Greeley, *The Hesitant Pilgrim* (New York: Sheed and Ward,

1966), pp. xiv, xv. Note also Richard McBrien's words in his book *Who Is a Catholic?*, p. 112. "There is a tendency, too, among some Catholics to minimize or even reject the place of ministry in the church. Occasionally the rhetoric of the so-called 'underground church' reflects this spirit. The charismatic is exalted at the expense of the structural; the tyranny of the old legalism is supplanted by a new tyranny of the spirit (with a small 's')."

13. *Concilium, op. cit.*, pp. 29, 30.
14. *Op. cit.*, p. 84.
15. As a matter of fact, the Roman Catholic and the Lutheran theologians have met to discuss the eucharist and the ministry and both have concluded that each church is able to recognize the clergy of the others as valid and that their eucharist is valid. See the very interesting series called *Lutherans and Catholics in Dialogue* (volume IV) published jointly by the U.S.A. National Committee of the Lutheran World Federation and the Bishops' Committee for Ecumenical and Interreligious Affairs, 1970. Copies can be obtained from the United States Catholic Conference, 3211 4th Street, N.E., Washington, D.C. 20017.

CHAPTER 4

1. Edward P. Echlin, S.J. *The Deacon in the Church* (Staten Island, NY: Alba House, 1971), p. 16. I am indebted for most of this section to this small but excellent book.
2. *Ibid.*, p. 131.
3. Roger Gryson, *The Ministry of Women in the Early Church* (Collegeville, MN: The Liturgical Press, 1976), p. 20. This excellent reference book covers the sources about the ministry of women through the sixth century.
4. See *The Lady Was a Bishop* by Joan Morris for the complete details on this little discussed phenomenon in church history.
5. The ordination of women didn't become a major issue again until the nineteenth and twentieth centuries, when Antoinette Brown was ordained in 1853 to minister in the Congregationalist Church. Yet it was not until well into the twentieth century that mainline Protestant churches, such as the Lutheran, Episcopalian, and Presbyterian churches, admitted women to the ordained ministry. In the U.S.A. in the late 1980s, more than 50 percent of the students at Harvard Divinity School are women; there are approximately 950 women Episcopal priests, of whom 127 are also rectors (meaning pastors); and there are 134 women rabbis serving Reform Judaism.

It was in 1988 that the Lambeth Conference of the Anglican/Episcopal Church agreed that "each province respect the decision of those of other provinces in the ordination and consecration of women to the episcopate, without such respect necessarily indicating acceptance of this principle and while maintaining the highest possible degree of communication with those provinces that differ." That same year the Reverend Barbara Harris was elected suffragan *bishop* of an Episcopal diocese in eastern Massachusetts.

6. "Biblical Commission Report. Can Women Be Priests?" *Origins,* Vol. VI, No. 6, (July 1, 1976), pp. 92-96.

7. Notice that the process of selecting the deacons was democratic, the work of the entire community. Yet, after the election of the deacons, they were "appointed" and consecrated into their office by the disciples. Thus, there is evidence "of an apostolic office (or bishop) who somehow confirms or ratifies the action of the people. The whole episode indicates how impossible it is to categorize the early church into any single pattern or structure." Rogness, *op. cit.* p. 83.

8. We might mention here, perhaps to the surprise of some Catholics, that government in the church need not necessarily be centered in the bishops. They were given the spiritual mission to teach and sanctify (Mt 28:18), not to govern. Many early bishops, like Augustine and Cyprian, did not govern. That was done by some other body. It could be today—or could come about—that decisions about schools, parish boundaries, finances, etc., be made by people other than bishops (as in some places parish councils or pastoral councils do). The centralization of church government in the hands of the episcopacy is neither scriptural nor necessary. It just turned out that way.

9. Thomas F. O'Meara, "Emergence and Decline of Popular Voice in the Selection of Bishops," in *The Choosing of Bishops,* edited by William W. Bassett (Washington, D.C.: The Canon Law Society of America, 1971), p. 27.

10. However, by the beginning of the third century, a milestone was reached: Buildings were specifically set aside for Christian worship. One such church (built during a relatively peaceful time between persecutions) has been found. It is called the Dura Europos and was built before 256. It is an ordinary house transformed into a church.

11. Joseph A. Jungmann, S.J. *The Early Liturgy* (Notre Dame, IN: University of Notre Dame Press, 1959), p. 37.

12. See William J. Bausch, *A New Look at the Sacraments* (Mystic, CT: Twenty-Third Publications, 1983), Chapters 11-13.

13. E. Schillebeeckx, *Celibacy* (New York: Sheed and Ward, 1968), pp. 24, 25.

14. 7:12, in ANF, 2:543.

CHAPTER 5

1. At this time it was not unusual to defer baptism. On the other hand, Constantine had other reasons to defer his official commitment. His

crimes included putting to death his father-in-law, three brothers-in-law, his eldest son, and his wife.

2. We mentioned in the last chapter that the "Believers Church" or Free Church people would proclaim that a "fall of the church" occurred when Theodosius established Christianity as the religion of the Roman Empire. These Free Church people believe that their movement represents a return to the pristine, apostolic, pre-Theodosian church of Christ.

3. A.M.M. Jones, *op. cit.*, p. 206, 207. For a brief overview of this period, see *The Excellent Empire*, by Jaroslav Pelikan (Harper & Row, NY, 1987).

4. John L. McKenzie, S.J., *The Roman Catholic Church*, pp. 201, 202. Holt, Rinehart, Winston, NY, 1969. See also Leo Donald Davis, S.J., *The First Seven Ecumenical Councils: Their History and Theology*, Michael Glazier, Inc., Wilmington, DE, 1987.

5. We point out here that Leo did not have the exclusive title of pope (papa, father), for it was a title applied to other bishops, and even to priests. It took many centuries for it to be reserved only for the bishop of Rome. Nevertheless, it was through Leo that the basis of papal supremacy became explicit, and succeeding popes would look to Leo to bolster their claims.

6. Knowles and Obolensky, *The Christian Centuries: The Middle Ages*, Vol. II, p. 106.

7. This great church remains the high point of the Byzantine style. It took ten thousand men five years to build it and it cost, in modern terms, some 134 million dollars to erect.

CHAPTER 6

1. For an excellent overview, see Luke T. Johnson, *The Writings of the New Testament*, Fortress Press, Philadelphia, 1986, and the more popular *Why Is There a New Testament?* by Joseph F. Kelly, Michael Glazier, Wilmington, DE, 1986.

2. Raymond E. Brown, "Canonicity," *The Jerome Biblical Commentary*, p. 533. Prentice-Hall, Englewood Cliffs, NJ, 1968.

3. For a good overview, consult Eric G. Jay, *The Church: Its Changing Image Through Twenty Centuries*, John Knox Press, Atlanta, 1977.

CHAPTER 7

1. Pope Gregory VII would almost resort to the Donatist heresy in trying to reform the clergy in the eleventh century.

2. Gerald Simons and the Editors of Time-Life Books, *Barbarian Europe, Great Ages of Man Series*, p.14, NY, 1968.

3. Denys Hay, *The Medieval Centuries*, (New York: Harper & Row, Harper

Torchbooks, 1964) p. 2.

4. *Barbarian Europe, op. cit.,* p. 57.

5. Christopher Dawson, *Religion and the Rise of Western Culture,* (New York: Image Books, 1958) pp. 31-32.

6. Henri Pirenne, *A History of Europe,* (New Hyde Park, NY: University Books, 1936) p. 59. See Peter Brown's masterful little book, *The Making of Late Antiquity,* (Cambridge, MA: Harvard University Press, 1978), and Robin Lane Fox's insightful *Pagans and Christians,* (New York: Alfred A. Knopf, 1987).

7. Michael Walsh, *An Illustrated History of the Popes,* (New York: Bonanza Books, 1980) p. 8.

8. Dawson, *op. cit.,* pp. 61, 62.

CHAPTER 8

1. R.W. Southern, *Western Society and the Church in the Middle Ages,* (Baltimore: Penguin Books, 1970) p. 99.

2. Hobbes said this disparagingly of the church, but his remark was more accurate than he thought.

3. Denys Hay, *op. cit.,* p. 68.

CHAPTER 9

1. Dawson, *op. cit.,* p. 91, 92.

2. Dolan, *Catholicism* (Woodbury, NY: Barron's Educational Series, Inc., 1968) pp. 165, 166.

3. Henri Piereen, *op. cit.,* p. 184.

4. "Archaeological discoveries provide additional information about the Roman church at this period. The excavations carried out under St. Peter's on the Vatican Hill show that in about the year 120 the memory of the apostle Peter was already venerated there. It is even possible that it may be Peter's tomb which has been discovered, but in any case it is certain that his memory is preserved there by a monument. The priest Gaius, at the end of the century, says he saw the trophies of the apostles Peter and Paul on the Vatican Hill and on the road to Ostia. The fact that this monument is in a cemetery seems to confirm that it is indeed a memorial of Peter at Rome. The *graffitti* on the wall around the monument are also evidence that he was venerated there." Danielou and Marrou, *op. cit.,* p. 53. For more information on the excavations see *The Bones of St. Peter* by John Evangelist Walsh, (New York: Doubleday, 1985).

5. R.W. Southern, *op. cit.,* p. 96. The following pages in this chapter rely on ideas from this book.

6. Marshall W. Baldwin, *Christianity Through the Thirteenth Century*

(New York: Walker and Company, 1970), p. 165.
7. For an interesting essay on medieval forgeries, see "Approaches to Medieval Forgery" in the book *Medieval Church and Society* by Christopher Brooke (New York: New York University Press, 1971), p. 100.
8. If you are interested in the development of the election process for a pope, see Andrew Greeley's *The Making of the Popes 1978* (Kansas City: Andrews and McMeel, Inc., 1979).
9. Dolan, *op. cit.*, p. 74. One of the best books on the popes is J.N.D. Kelly's *The Oxford Dictionary of Popes* (New York: Oxford University Press, 1986).

CHAPTER 10

1. Schweitzer, *op. cit.*, p. 87.
2. There are reputable scholars, however, who maintain that the whole story of Abelard and Heloise is a hoax.
3. Other attempts to explain redemption include: the ransom theory, in which Jesus offered himself as a ransom for sinful humanity; the penal substitution theory, in which God's *justice* can be satisfied only by a sinless substitute; and the moral influence theory, in which Jesus' life and death serve as a moral example for all humanity. Each of these theories finds support from some within the various Christian denominations today.
4. Kenneth Clark, *Civilisation* (New York: Harper & Row, 1969), p. 64.
5. *Ibid.*, pp. 56 and 60.
6. For this reason, the time between Benedict (sixth century) and Bernard (twelfth century) is known as the "monastic age" or the "Benedictine centuries."
7. Henri Pirenne, *op. cit.*, p. 240.
8. Kenneth Clark, *op. cit.*, pp. 77, 78.
9. Roland H. Bainton, *The Horizon History of Christianity* (New York: Avon Books, 1966), p. 211.
10. Knowles and Obolensky, *op. cit.*, pp. 290, 291.
11. Marshall W. Baldwin, *op. cit.*, p. 281.

CHAPTER 11

1. Quoted in Knowles and Obolensky, *op. cit.*, p. 101.
2. *Ibid.*, pp. 114-115.

CHAPTER 12

1. We must remember that what really started out as ecclesiastical reform ended up as political power, but it was not originally meant to

be that way.

2. *Concilium,* volume 64, p. 90, 1971.
3. Richard P. McBrien, *Who Is a Catholic?* (Denville, NJ: Dimension Books, 1971), p. 162. For a balanced view, see Patrick Granfield, *The Limits of the Papacy.*
4. Martin Marty, *op. cit.,* p. 137.
5. Christopher Dawson, *Christian Culture and the Western World,* p. 42.

CHAPTER 13

1. Looking ahead a bit, full-blown nationalism and its child, the Enlightenment, were to replace religion and usher in an era of tolerance, reason, and an end of wars. No such thing happened, of course. One acerbic commentary reads: "For many centuries, the grand legitimizer of hatred in our culture was called Religion. Then, after the great surfeits of the Wars of Religion, the power of religion to legitimize war and persecution began to fade. The more optimistic...were inclined to believe that war, persecution, and the spirit of intolerance would [now also] fade....What went wrong?...The older supernatural God had faded into the distance, indeed, but it was not Reason, mostly, that took His place. It was new terrestrial creeds...the most enduring, the most seductive, and the bloodiest by far of all the new terrestrial creeds is Nationalism. The cult of the Nation proved to be the most effective engine for the mobilization of hatred and destruction that the world has ever known" (Conor Cruise O'Brien, "A Last Chance to Save the Jews?" *New York Review of Books,* April 27, 1989, p. 27).
2. These Vikings absorbed Christianity and transferred it to the north countries.
3. Boniface was the product of a century-long stream of canonical thought that ran in the direction of universal papal dominion. What was learned at Bologna (specializing in canon law) was practiced at Rome. At the same time, there was a tradition of canonical thought that was more conciliar and corporate, and which was defended even in Boniface's time by a series of canonists.
4. Henri Pirenne, *op. cit.,* p. 292.

CHAPTER 14

1. Philip Hughes, *A Popular History of the Catholic Church* (New York: Macmillan, 1962), p. 161.
2. *Concilium,* volume 64, p. 150, 1971.
3. Leonardo Boff's book, *Church: Charism and Power* (New York: Cross-

road, 1985), is one of the recent critiques of the use of a certain kind of organizational pomp and power practiced in the church of our day.

4. Cf. F.J. Sheed, *What Difference Does Jesus Make?* (New York: Sheed and Ward, 1971), pp. 77-79. For a view of the modern church's wealth see James Gollin, *Worldly Goods* (New York: Random House, 1971), especially chapter 17.

5. Ingmar Bergman's *The Seventh Seal*, a classic Swedish film produced in 1956, provides a cinemagraphic glimpse of a plague-ravaged and nearly hysterical population.

6. R. W. Southern, *op. cit.*, p. 342.

7. J. Huizinga, *The Waning of the Middle Ages* (New York: Doubleday Anchor Books, 1954), p. 167. See also *The Oxford Illustrated History of Medieval Europe*, edited by George Holmes (New York: Oxford University Press, 1988).

8. Frederick M. Schweitzer, *op. cit.*, p. 119.

9. We should also note that the Renaissance was indifferent to women's position—an attitude picked up from the classical age of Aristotle and Pericles. Slowly but surely, women were relieved of their positions in the Catholic hierarchy. Two interesting books on the subject of women in the ministry are Joan Morris, *The Lady Was a Bishop* (New York: Macmillan, 1973) and Emily C. Hewitt and Suzanne R. Hiatt, *Women Priests: Yes or No* (New York: Seabury Press, 1973).

CHAPTER 15

1. Hans J. Hillerbrand, *Christendom Divided* (New York: Corpus, Philadelphia: Westminster, London: Hutchinson, 1971), p. 288.

2. Owen Chadwick, *The Reformation* (Baltimore: Penguin Books, 1964), p. 25.

3. Historian Norman Cantor gives five reasons why the Reformation did not occur earlier: (1) the absence of the printing press; (2) the long depression that sapped society's energies from active reform; (3) the weakness of the papacy; (4) a fear of the social reactions that might result from widespread heresy; (5) royal governments previously were too distracted with other matters. Cf. Cantor's *Medieval History, The Life and Death of Civilization* (New York: Macmillan, 1968.

4. Martin Marty, *op. cit.*, p. 208. See also Peter Manns, *Martin Luther* (New York: Crossroad, 1983).

5. Hans Hillerbrand, *op., cit.*, p. 42.

6. *Ibid.*, p. 127.

7. Owen Chadwick, *op. cit.*, p. 76.

8. Martin Marty, *op. cit.*, p. 246.

9. Hans Hillerbrand, *op. cit.*, p. 265.

CHAPTER 16

1. Donald F. Durnbaugh, *The Believers' Church: The History and Character of Radical Protestantism* (London: Macmillan, 1968), p. 4.
2. In May of 1972, the Amish in the United States won the right from the Supreme Court to keep their children from the "ungodly" compulsory high school education.
3. R.S. Knox, *Enthusiasm* (Oxford: Clarendon Press, 1950), p. 591.
4. Roland Bainton, *op. cit.*, p. 288.
5. Owen Chadwick, *op. cit.*, p. 109.
6. Roland Bainton, *op. cit.*, p. 290.
7. Hans Hillerbrand, *op. cit.*, p. 202.
8. *Ibid.*, p. 223.
9. William and Mary of Orange sought to regain control of England by first establishing control over Ireland. Meanwhile, Protestant Ulstermen at Londonderry successfully fought the deposed King James who had arrived in Ireland. The following year William came and defeated James at the Battle of the Boyne, rejoicing Ulster's "Orangemen."
10. Carlton J. H. Hayes, *A Political and Cultural History of Europe*, Vol. I (New York: Macmillan, 1932), p. 274.
11. Bainton, *op. cit.*, p. 272.
12. Catholics should not take their impressions of Protestantism from the insincere or ignorant Protestant any more than Protestants should take their impressions of Catholicism from the insincere or ignorant Catholic.
13. Hans Hillerbrand, *op. cit.*, p. 287.
14. *Concilium*, p. 72, volume 64, 1971.
15. Martin Marty, *op. cit.*, pp. 225 and 228.
16. Hans Hillerbrand, *op. cit.*, p. 290.
17. Roland Bainton, *op. cit.*, p. 270.
18. Martin Marty, *op. cit.*, p. 244.
19. *Ibid*, p. 350. We have mentioned some of the positive contributions of Protestantism. It would go beyond the scope of this book to mention its negative aspects. Suffice it to say that, by the late 1980s, mainline Protestant churches were in serious decline. Secular humanist Sidney Hook considered Protestants to be pantheists who are afraid to admit it, and Marx declared that the last stage of Protestantism is atheism. But perhaps the biggest loss to Protestantism was the Catholic religious imagination. In its reaction to Catholic superstition, Protestantism jettisoned the practical incarnation. For them God is totally Other: no intermediaries of sacrament, pope, ritual or sign were necessary and perhaps here it stands in sharpest practical contrast to Catholicism: "The Catholic religious imagina-

tion, and the theological systems emerging from it tend to emphasize the similarity between God and objects, events, experiences, and persons in the natural world, while the Protestant (and Islamic and Jewish) religious imaginations and the theologies emerging from them tend to emphasize the difference between God and objects, events, experiences, and persons in the natural world. The tendency of the Catholic imagination is to say 'similar' first and the Protestant imagination to say 'different' first. The Protestant imagination stresses opposition between God and the World: God is totally other, radically, drastically, and absolutely different from his creation. The Catholic imagination responds by saying that God is similar to the world and has revealed himself/herself in the world, especially through the human dimension of Jesus" (Andrew Greeley).

In addition to this is the celebrated thesis of Max Weber that Protestantism is the basic ethic behind the growth of capitalism and ruthless industrialism. The Catholic writer, Michael Novak, adds his critique: "Perhaps no belief about man is more deeply Catholic than that: a fundamental and radical trust in the goodness of creation, however wounded, bloodied, flawed. It is (in Catholic eyes) the Protestant who quintessentially announces the depravity and corruption of nature, culture, and man himself—and then, paradoxically, announces with the utmost cool extravagant plans for organizing the world reasonably, sinlessly, and spotlessly. The Protestant is forever confessing his contriteness, and then exalting his own acceptance of his 'responsibilities' for changing history.... To the Protestant, creation is apparently 'redeemed' only through being mastered. Protestant countries tend to be avid for modernization; Catholic countries are 'backward'" (*The Rise of the Unmeltable Ethnics* [New York: Macmillan, 1972], p. 290).

With such criticism from many quarters, no wonder the Lutheran historian Martin Marty says, "The Protestant era may, indeed, be coming or have come to its end."

20. Unfortunately, division would always plague the Protestants because they tended to become rigid and could not themselves tolerate diversity. The only way to have a tolerable alternate interpretation of the Bible was to start a new sect. Catholicism, on the other hand, could subsume many diversities within itself. It even had the escape valve of monasticism, "which allowed those dissatisfied with the standard of ecclesiastical practices to go their own way and yet remain within the church. Such possibilities did not exist in any of the Protestant churches, where a break was necessary to assert a different religious or theological position" (Hans Hillerbrand, *op. cit.*, p. 291).

21. For a sensitive and sensible commentary on the whole question of transubstantiation, see John Macquarrie's fine book, *Paths in Spirituality*, p. (New York: Harper and Row, 1972), p. 88f.
22. Michael Rogness, *op cit.*, p. 58.
23. Hans Kung, *Justification*, (New York: Thomas Nelson and Sons, 1964).

CHAPTER 17

1. In spite of the fact that the Catholic world was stunned when its vicar general became a Protestant in 1541.
2. This was the same pope who approved the Ursulines, Barnabites, and the Jesuits. He took an interest in the overseas missions, enriched the Vatican library, and appointed Michelangelo as the chief architect of St. Peter's.
3. The Council of Chalcedon in 451 had some 630 participants, Vatican I in 1869-70 over 700, and Vatican II in 1962-1965 over 2,000.
4. The decrees, the soul of brevity and completeness, were largely the work of the Augustinian (fittingly, the same order as Luther's) Seripando.
5. Owen Chadwick, *op. cit.*, p. 276.
6. A.G. Dickens, *The Counter Reformation*, (New York: Harcourt, Brace & World, 1969) pp. 132, 133.
7. Owen Chadwick, *op. cit.*, p. 300.
8. For a superior insight into the influence of moral concerns at this time see John Mahoney, *The Making of Moral Theology*, (Oxford: Clarendon Press, 1987).
9. Kenneth Clark, *op. cit.*, pp. 174, 175.
10. Owen Chadwick, *op. cit.*, p. 328.
11. H. Daniel-Rops, *The Catholic Reformation*, (New York: Dutton, 1962), pp. 292, 293.

CHAPTER 18

1. Enlightened as he was, however, Voltaire was anti-Semitic. In his book, *The French Enlightenment and the Jews*, Rabbi Arthur Hertzberg says, "An analysis of everything Voltaire wrote about the Jews throughout his life establishes the proposition that he is the major link in Western intellectual history between the anti-semitism of classic paganism and the modern age."
2. Philip Hughes, *op. cit.*, p. 222.
3. Karl Otmar von Aretin, *The Papacy and the Modern World*, World University Library, (New York: McGraw-Hill, 1970) p. 20.
4. Philip Hughes, *op. cit.*, p. 222.

5. Roland Bainton, *op. cit.*, p. 354.

6. *Age of Enlightenment* (New York: Time-Life Books, 1966), p. 32.

7. Christopher Dawson, *The Gods of Revolution* (New York: New York University Press, 1972), p. 13.

8. Indeed, there are those who maintain that it was the Enlightenment that set the world on its rise to dehumanizing power control. By downgrading true medieval culture, the Enlightenment turned aside forces that might have prevented modern day economic and cultural alienation. Thus, Lewis Mumford in his book, *The Myth of the Machine*, writes: "Our current views of both the terrestrial and the mechanical New Worlds have been falsely colored by the opaque religious prejudices of the eighteenth-century Enlightenment. Thinkers like Voltaire and Diderot, judging medieval institutions by the decayed survivals of their own day, took for granted that the Middle Ages were a period of besotted ignorance and superstition; and in their desire to throw off the influence of the established church, they converted the High Middle Ages, one of the great moments in European culture, into a neo-Gothic horror story, assuming that no serious progress had been made in any department until their own period. This anti-Gothic obsession resulted not only in the devaluation of medieval achievement but also in the wholesale destruction of buildings and institutions that, if preserved and renewed, might have helped to humanize the rising power system" (p. 6). For an eloquent critique of the Enlightenment's fallout, see Don S. Browning, *Religious Thought and the Modern Psychologies* (Philadelphia: Fortress Press, 1967).

9. Christopher Dawson, *op. cit.*, p. 34.

CHAPTER 19

1. Actually the American Revolution was inspired not by constitutional questions, but by commercial and capitalist considerations. The original quarrel began over taxation, over the fear of losing the frontiers gained by the Yankees and others, to the British crown. There was not an especial fervor for the "Rights of Man." Witness the tarring and featherings, the rank discrimination against minority groups, the mob rule. We forget that the liberal and cultured life of Jefferson at Monticello and of Washington at Mount Vernon was made possible by the existence of slavery. It was only later that the myth of humanity and the rights of all people got intertwined into the American Revolution and became a source of admiration to the French. Its real origins rest in the commercial and capitalistic desires of the average person.

2. One of the things that makes the French Revolution so difficult to un-

ravel is the great number of names that flit on and off the stage, as it were, and disappear without a trace. The reason is that for about ten years there were no great leaders, except perhaps Robespierre. Then in 1798, we shall see, they got a leader with a vengeance: Napoleon. See the essay, "What Was Revolutionary about the French Revolution?" by Robert Darnton *(The New York Review,* January 19, 1989).

3. Christopher Dawson, *The Gods of Revolution,* p. 63.

4. Carlton J.H. Hayes, *op. cit.,* p. 612.

5. E.E.Y. Hales, *The Catholic Church in the Modern World* (Garden City, NY: Hanover House, 1958), p. 50.

6. It deserves more than a footnote, but Napoleon terminated the Holy Roman Empire. In July 1806, he cleaned up the feudal remains of more than 303 independent sections of Germany. He consolidated them into 38 sections, into the federation of the Rhine. From the church's point of view this left only five bishops and there was the imminent danger of a national German church forming. This never materialized because of the efforts of people like the Redemptorist priest, Clement Hofbauer.

7. In France itself, Napoleon reformed the legal system, patronized the arts and improved education. But his colonial enterprises were not successful. He unloaded Louisiana on the United States in 1803 because of his imminent war with England. He repressed his critics and royalists, and killed the young Bourbon prince.

8. E.E.Y. Hales, *op. cit.,* p. 62.

9. This new apologetic, of seeing in Catholicism the preserver of civilization and being capable of assuming the new liberal ideals was taken up by the famous writers Chesterton and Belloc.

10. Introduction to Dawson, *op. cit.,* p. xx.

CHAPTER 20

1. Pius IX was commonly called "Pio Nono" (*nono* means "ninth" in Italian). The term could be one of endearment. It could also be one of disdain, for *nonno* means "grandfather," referring to the pope as being old and doughty. That is the way his enemies used the term. Modern liberals who enjoy taking pot shots at Pius IX insert a hyphen to indicate his intransigency: "Pio No-No."

2. Alec R. Vidler, *The Church in an Age of Revolution* (Baltimore: Penguin Books, 1961), p. 148. See also Owen Chadwick, *The Popes and European Revolution* (Oxford: Clarendon Press, 1981).

3. About 750 bishops came to Rome at one time or another in the seven months of the council's existence. They included 46 bishops from the United States.

4. Quoted in Meriol Trevor, *Prophets and Guardians* (New York: Dou-

bleday, 1969), p. 117.

5. *Ibid.*, p. 118.

6. It is interesting to note that the hundredth anniversary of the proclamation of the dogma of infallibility was passed over in silence by Rome; surely a symptom of the unfinished questions raised by Vatican II and the post-council upheavals.

7. Robert D. Cross, *The Emergence of Liberal Catholicism in America* (Chicago: Quadrangle Paperbacks, 1958), pp. 2-5.

8. Meriol Trevor, *op. cit.*, p. 110.

9. Karl von Aretin, *op. cit.*, p. 120.

10. R.R. Palmer, *A History of the Modern World*, 2nd edition, (New York: Alfred A. Knopf, 1960), p. 603.

11. David J. O'Brien, *The Renewal of American Catholicism* (New York: Oxford University Press, 1972), p. 80.

CHAPTER 21

1. Carlton J.H. Hayes, *op. cit.*, p. 566.

2. In 1905 the appeals court acquitted Dreyfus of all charges and reinstated him in the army. He was promoted to major, decorated with the Legion of Honor, and died in 1935.

3. William L. Shirer, *The Collapse of the Third Republic* (New York: Simon and Schuster, 1969), p. 70. For a good summary of the whole sordid Dreyfus affair, see the first chapter of this book.

4. Actually, at the time Cardinal Rampolla was the favorite to be chosen pope, but the Austrian emperor had the Polish cardinal exercise an old veto over this choice. Thus the vote shifted to Cardinal Sarto, Pius X. One of his first acts as pope was to abolish the privilege of veto.

5. Pope John XXIII expanded Leo XIII's notions concerning church-state relationships in his encyclical *Pacem in Terris* and repeated much of Leo's basic teaching of *Rerum Novarum* in his *Mater et Magistra*.

6. Alec R. Vidler, *op. cit.*, p. 180.

7. *Sacramentum Mundi* (New York: Herder and Herder, 1968), s.v. "Modernism" by Roger Aubert.

8. Meriol Trevor, *op. cit.*, p. 80.

9. Actually, the references were to the French writers of the times: Henri de Lubac, Jean Danielou, Yves Congar—all names held in high esteem today (Danielou became a cardinal).

10. See "Who Are the Catholic 'Fundamentalists'?" by John A. Coleman, S.J. in *Commonweal* (January 27, 1989). Also Philip Kaufman's "Autocracy Isn't the Catholic Style," the January 24, 1989 issue.

11. E.E.Y. Hales, *op cit.*, p. 249.

CHAPTER 22

1. Karl Otmar von Aretin, *op. cit.*, p. 214.
2. See *Pius XII and the Holocaust* (Milwaukee: Catholic League for Religious and Civil Rights, 1988).
3. Paul I. Murphy in his book, *La Popessa* (New York: Warner Books, 1983), suggests that Sr. Pascalina, who had charge of the papal household, was Pius XII's confidante and shared her opinions with him on many issues.
4. However, books like Malachi Martin's *Three Popes and the Cardinal* (New York: Farrar, Straus & Giroux, 1972) are of little help, being so one-sided. Better are the books of Carlo Falconi.
5. Xavier Rynne, *Vatican Council II* (one volume) (New York: Farrar, Straus & Giroux, 1968), p. 18. An entertaining if slightly prejudiced account of the speeches at Vatican II. The best one-volume study around.

CHAPTER 23

1. George Gallup, Jr., and Jim Castelli, *The American Catholic People: Their Beliefs, Practices, and Values* (New York: Doubleday, 1987), p. 50.
2. Walbert Buhlmann, *The Coming of the Third Church* (Maryknoll, N.Y.: Orbis Books, 1977), p. 271.
3. Karl Rahner, "Chapter III, Articles 18–27," in *Commentary on the Documents of Vatican II*, Volume I (New York: Herder and Herder, 1969), p. 216.
4. Thomas Bokenkotter, *A Concise History of the Catholic Church* (New York: Doubleday, 1979), pp. 427 ff.
5. Avery Dulles, *The Reshaping of Catholicism* (San Francisco: Harper & Row, 1988), pp. 166 ff.
6. G.K.A. Bell (editor), *Documents on Christian Unity: A Selection from the First and Second Series, 1920–1930* (London: Oxford University Press, 1955), p. 190.
7. *Ibid.*, p. 194.
8. "23 Bishops in Caribbean Confess Guilt," *National Catholic Reporter*, January 30, 1976, p. 15.
9. See Raymond Brown, *The Birth of the Messiah* (New York: Doubleday, 1977), pp. 299 ff.
10. For more information on particular theologians and their expressions of liberation theology, refer to these two books by Deane William Ferm, *Third World Liberation Theologies: An Introductory Survey* (Maryknoll, N.Y.: Orbis Books, 1985), and *Profiles in Liberation* (Mystic, CT: Twenty-Third Publications, 1988).

11. Donal Dorr, *Option for the Poor* (Maryknoll, N.Y.: Orbis Books, 1983), p. 257.
12. Peter Hebblethwaite, *In the Vatican* (Bethesda, MD: Adler & Adler, 1986), pp. 81–82.
13. Dorr, *op. cit.*, p. 210.
14. Cited by Peter Hebblethwaite, *op. cit.*, p. 38.
15. For an insight into the Vatican's approach to those suspected of being too progressive, read Harvey Cox's *The Silencing of Leonardo Boff* (Oak Park, IL: Meyer-Stone Books, 1988).
16. "Cardinal says mission role weakened," *Catholic Telegraph*, October 1, 1988, p. 28.
17. Dulles, *op. cit.*, p., 187.

CHAPTER 24

1. In our day, according to some, this Anglo-Saxon dominance is on its way out. See books like Michael Novak's *The Rise of the Unmeltable Ethnics* (New York: Macmillan, 1972). The classic work on Protestant dominance is Ray Allen Billington's *The Protestant Crusade*, first published in 1938, and reprinted several times since.
2. *Catholicism in America*, edited by Philip Gleason. Chapter, "The Distinctive Tradition of American Catholicism" by James J. Hennesey, S.J. (New York: Harper & Row, 1970), p. 38.
3. Father Gabriel Richard was a congressman and functioned in that capacity. His speeches were those of a congressman.
4. The positions of the French and the Irish are still disputed. The Notre Dame school of American history, represented by Thomas T. McAvoy, holds the French view as given in the text. The Catholic University school, headed by John Tracy Ellis, contends that it was the Irish who were the true purveyors of the American tradition.
5. All of these statistics can be found in John Cogley's *Catholic America* (New York: Image Books, 1973).
6. Robert D. Cross, *op. cit.*, pp. 106–107.
7. Robert Leckie, *American and Catholic* (New York: Doubleday, 1970), pp. 262–263.
8. Andrew M. Greeley, "Catholic Schools: A Golden Twilight?" *America*, February 11, 1989, p. 106. Studies of student attendance show that parochial schools reached their peak in 1967 with only 50% of the Catholic student population enrolled. Of the remaining 50%, only 25% were attending other parish religious education programs.
9. According to the Gallup Study of the Unchurched American, two and a half times more Catholics left the church because the liturgical changes were too little than because the liturgical changes were too many.

10. This can be documented from the first-hand stories contained in the book, *Once a Catholic* by Peter Occhiogrosso (Boston: Houghton Mifflin, 1987).
11. Eugene Kennedy, *The Now and Future Church* (New York: Doubleday, 1984), p. 167.
12. J. Robert Dionne, *The Papacy and the Church: A Study of Praxis and Reception in Ecumenical Perspective* (Philosophical Library, 1986).
13. Research done by Andrew Greeley showed that 20% of Catholics in the United States changed their minds to agree with the bishops on the issues dealt with in *The Challenge of Peace* within two years after the pastoral was completed. Furthermore, the bishops' teachings in these two pastoral letters have been incorporated into the religion textbooks used in both Catholic schools and parish religious education programs, thus insuring some significant long-range results in the United States Catholic church of the future.

CHAPTER 25

1. Michael Novak, *All the Catholic People* (New York: Herder and Herder, 1971).
2. Philip Gleason, editor, *Catholicism in America* (New York: Harper & Row, 1970), p. 150.
3. John C. Meagher, "Creating a Christian Identity," *Commonweal*, February 11, 1972, p. 439.

Bibliography

In addition to the books listed in the footnotes of each chapter, the books listed below are especially helpful in the study of Catholic Christianity.

The Pelican History of the Church, chief editor, Owen Chadwick, a six-volume series by Penguin Books.
  Henry Chadwick, *The Early Church*
  R.W. Southern, *Western Society and the Church in the Middle Ages*
  Owen Chadwick, *The Reformation*
  Gerald R. Cragg, *The Church in the Age of Reason 1648–1789*
  Alex R. Vidler, *The Church in the Age of Revolution*
  Stephen Neill, *A History of Christian Missions*

Walter M. Abbott, editor. *The Documents of Vatican II.* New York: Guild Press, 1966.

Sydney E. Ahlstrom. *A Religious History of the American People.* Garden City, N.Y.: Image Books, 1975 (2 volumes).

Thomas Bokenkotter. *A Concise History of the Catholic Church.* Garden City, N.Y.: Image Books, 1979.

Jay P. Dolan. *The American Catholic Experience.* Garden City, N.Y.: Doubleday & Company, Inc., 1984.

Eerdman's Handbook to the History of Christianity. Grand Rapids, Mich.: William B. Eerdman Publishing Co., 1977.

George Gallup, Jr. and Jim Castelli. *The American Catholic People, Their Belief, Practices and Values.* Garden City, N.Y.: Doubleday & Company, Inc., 1987.

James Hennesey, S.J. *American Catholics.* New York: Oxford University Press, 1981.

J. Derek Holmes and Bernard W. Bickers. *A Short History of the Catholic Church.* New York: Paulist Press, 1983.

456

Eugene Kennedy. *The Now & Future Church: The Psychology of Being an American Catholic.* Garden City, N.Y.: Doubleday & Company, Inc., 1984.

Richard McBrien. *Catholicism.* Minneapolis: Winston Press, 1980.

William A. Scott and Frances M. Scott. *The Church Then and Now: Cultivating a Sense of Tradition.* Kansas City: Leaven Press, 1985.

Peter M.J. Stravinskas and Robert A. McBain. *The Church After the Council.* New York: Alba House, 1975.

Martin E. Marty. *Invitation to American Catholic History.* Chicago: The Thomas More Press, 1986.

The National Conference of Catholic Bishops has authorized the publication of six volumes on the history of the church in the United States under the editorship of Christopher J. Kauffman. All are published by Macmillan and are now in print.

Index

Other books by Fr. Bausch...

The Hands-On Parish
Reflections and Suggestions for Fostering Community
Father Bausch shares more than 100 tried and workable ideas to
build a strong parish community as well as great ideas for clergy
and laity to work together in the future Church.
ISBN: 0-89622-401-5, 228 pp, $9.95 (order C-08)

A New Look at the Sacraments
In this book, Father Bausch explores the difference between "going to
church" and "being church." He traces the history and development
of the sacraments with the intention of transforming sacraments from
things to ongoing actions. He brings the sacraments into the realm
of the life of the everyday person and views them with a new vitality.
ISBN: 0-89622-174-1, 306 pp, $9.95 (order B-48)

The Parish of the Next Millennium
This book does not make predictions as one might surmise from the
title. Rather, it summarizes the social and cultural forces that shape
our lives and our church by pulling together current research and
issues that indicate where we are and where we might be going. Here
is a great resource to help individuals and groups discern the current
movements in their parish and to begin planning the kind of spiritual
and operational posture their parish should take on in the future.
ISBN: 0-89622-719-7, 160 pp, $9.95 (order M-93)

While You Were Gone
A Handbook for Returning Catholics And Those Thinking About It
Father Bausch presents in a welcoming manner an overview of the
changes that have taken place in the church since Vatican II. His
program is divided into three parts: *The Context*, surveys the
changes in the Church. *The Changes*, presents a practical perspective
of what is different in the Church today, as well as how and why
these changes came about. *The Challenge*, gives an honest overview
of the unfinished business facing the contemporary Church.
ISBN: 0-89622-575-5, 112 pp, $5.95 (order B-91)

Available at religious bookstores or from:

 TWENTY-THIRD PUBLICATIONS
P.O. Box 180 • Mystic, CT 06355

For a complete list of quality books and videos call:
1 - 8 0 0 - 3 2 1 - 0 4 1 1